Alternatives to Deforestation: Steps Toward Sustainable Use of the Amazon Rain Forest

ALTERNATIVES TO DEFORESTATION: STEPS TOWARD SUSTAINABLE USE OF THE AMAZON RAIN FOREST

ANTHONY B. ANDERSON, *Editor*

COLUMBIA UNIVERSITY PRESS   NEW YORK

COLUMBIA UNIVERSITY PRESS
New York   Chichester, West Sussex
Copyright © 1990 Columbia University Press

Library of Congress Cataloging-in-Publication Data

Alternatives to deforestation: steps toward sustainable use of the
Amazon rain forest
Anthony B. Anderson, editor.
p.   cm.
Papers presented at an international conference held in Belem,
Brazil, January 27–30, 1988.
Includes bibliographical references.
ISBN 0-231-06892-1
ISBN 0-231-06893-x (pbk.)
1. Deforestation—Control—Amazon River Region—Congresses.
2. Sustainable forestry—Amazon River Region—Congresses.
3. Rain forest ecology—Amazon River Region—Congresses.
4. Forest management—Amazon River Region—Congresses.
5. Rural development—Amazon River Region—Congresses.
I. Anderson, Anthony, B. (Anthony Bennett).
SD418.3.A53A526   1990
333.75'16'09811—dc20
89-24034
CIP

Casebound editions of Columbia University Press books are
printed on permanent and durable acid-free paper

Book design by Jennifer Dossin

Printed in the United States of America
c 10 9 8 7 6 5 4 3 2 1
p 10 9 8 7 6 5 4 3 2

To Francisco ("Chico") Mendes (1944–1988)

CONTENTS

PREFACE

Since 1987, deforestation in the Amazon Basin has become an issue of worldwide concern. Yet the destruction of the Amazon rain forest has been occurring on a large scale since the mid-1970s. During the dry season each year, extensive areas of the region's rain forests are cleared and burned for establishment of agricultural plantations and cattle pastures. In 1987, however, the dry season was unusually long and, as a result, the forest fires in Amazonia were exceptionally intensive and widespread. And, for the first time, satellite images brought home the immense scale of these fires, raising concern both within Amazonian countries and abroad about the future of the region's rain forests.

In 1988, the annual burning of Amazonia coincided with the worst U.S. drought in fifty years. The Amazon suddenly loomed large in the lives of temperate zone residents worried about global warming, and tropical deforestation, once perceived as a remote problem of marginal significance, was transformed into a major environmental issue. The assassination of Chico Mendes, a leader in the rubber tapper's movement for sustained use of the Amazon rain forest, galvanized this concern by giving a human dimension to tropical deforestation.

Although the 1988 U.S. drought was not provoked by forest fires in Amazonia, the ongoing destruction of the world's largest tropical rain forest is producing deleterious effects that are or soon will be felt by us all. The two most widespread and long-term effects include climatic change and loss of genetic diversity. On a regional level, the effects are already manifest in the form of erosion, flooding, destruction of forest resources, spread of diseases, and increasing poverty.

The tragedy of deforestation in Amazonia as well as elsewhere in the tropics is that its costs, in both economic, social, cultural, and aesthetic terms, far outweigh its benefits. In many cases, destruction of the region's rain forests is motivated by short-term gains rather than the long-term productive capacity of the land. And, as a result, deforestation usually leaves behind landscapes that are economically as well as ecologically impoverished.

This volume explores a number of alternatives to the above scenario, many of which are already practiced by people who live in Amazonia. People, in fact, are a constant theme here, because without them, conservation of the Amazon rain forest doesn't have a chance.

This volume and the symposium on which it was based are the result of many people's efforts. Jean Dubois, Virgílio Viana, Phil Fearnside, and Bob Buschbacher gave many helpful suggestions in the organization of the symposium, which, in turn, had a powerful influence on the design of this volume. Through the good offices of Guilherme de La Penha and Pedro Lisbôa, I could count on the full support of the Museu Goeldi, without which the symposium and this volume would not have been possible. I am grateful to the many reviewers of the essays contained herein, including Janis Alcorn, John Browder, Foster Brown, N. R. de Graaf, Gary Hartshorn, Susanna Hecht, Peter May, Chuck Peters, Kent Redford, Marianne Schmink, and Chris Uhl. Finally, special thanks go to Steve Sanderson and Peter May, who provided financial as well as moral support from the Ford Foundation.

Belém, Brazil   *Anthony B. Anderson*

CONTRIBUTORS

Janis B. Alcorn
Biology Department
Tulane University
New Orleans, LA 70118
USA

Mary Helena Allegretti
Instituto de Estudos Amazônicos
Rua Itupava, 1220
80.040—Curitiba—PR
Brasil

Anthony Anderson
The Ford Foundation
Praia do Flamengo, 100
22.210 Rio de Janeiro—RJ
Brasil

Robert Buschbacher
The Conservation Foundation/World
  Wildlife Fund—U.S.
1250 24th St., N.W.
Washington, DC 20037
USA

Kathleen Clark
c/o Dr. Howard Clark
Agency for International Development
US AID Ecuador
Washington, DC 20523
USA

Jean C. L. Dubois
Rua Redentor, 275 (401)—Ipanema
22.421—Rio de Janeiro—RJ
Brasil

Philip M. Fearnside
Departmento de Ecologia
Instituto Nacional de Pesquisas da
  Amazônia—INPA
C.P. 478
69.011—Manaus—AM
Brasil

Arturo Gómez-Pompa
University of California
Botany and Plant Sciences
Batchelor Hall, Room 4151
Riverside, California 92521
USA

N. R. de Graaf
Department of Silviculture
Agricultural University
P. O. Box 342
6700 AH—Wageningen
The Netherlands

Gary S. Hartshorn
World Wildlife Fund—U.S.
WWF—US
1250 24th Street, NW
Washington, DC 20037
USA

Boone Kauffman
Department of Rangeland Resources
Oregon State University
Corvallis, OR 97331
USA

Andrea Kaus
University of California
Botany and Plant Sciences
Batchelor Hall, Room 4151
Riverside, California 92521
USA

Daniel Nepstad
National Wildlife Federation
1400 Sixteenth Street, N.W.
Washington, DC 20036
USA

Robert B. Peck
Avenida Guadalupe, 1-A-10
Cali—Colombia

Charles M. Peters
Institute of Economic Botany
The New York Botanical Garden
Bronx, NY 10458
USA

R. L. Poels
Department of Silviculture
Agricultural University
P. O. Box 342
6700 AH—Wageningen
The Netherlands

Donald Sawyer
Universidade Federal de Minas Gerais
Centro de Desenvolvimento e
  Planejamento Regional—
  CEDEPLAR
Rua Curitiba, 832
30.170—Belo Horizonte—MG
Brasil

Emanuel Adilson Serrão
Empresa Brasileira de Pesquisas
  Agropecuárias—EMBRAPA
CP 48
66.050—Belém—PA
Brasil

Scott Subler
208 Müeller Lab
The Pennsylvania State University
University Park, PA 16802
USA

José M. Toledo
Centro Internacional de Agricultura
  Tropical—CIAT
Apartado Aereo 6713
Cali—Colombia

Christopher Uhl
Empresa Brasileira de Pesquisas
  Agropecuárias—EMBRAPA
Centro de Pesquisa Agropecuária dos
  Trópicos Umidos—CPATU
C.P. 48
66.050—Belém—PA
Brasil

Virgílio M. Viana
Depto. de Ciências Florestais
ESALQ/USP
13.400—Piracicaba—SP
Brasil

Alternatives to Deforestation: Steps Toward
Sustainable Use of the Amazon Rain Forest

1
BACKGROUND

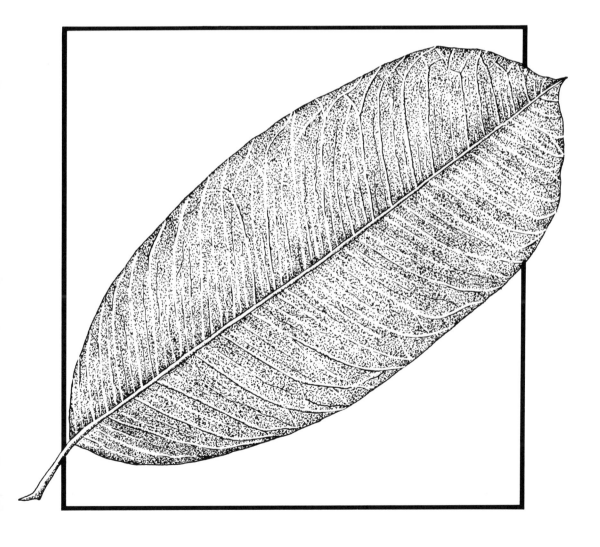

1. Background.–The Brazil nut tree (*Bertholletia excelsa* H. B.) is a characteristic element of the Amazon landscape, occurring in both intact forests and as a relic on deforested sites. Gathered primarily from wild trees, its edible nuts represent one of the Amazon's major extractive products. Newly developed cultivation techniques have also brightened Brazil nut's potential for agroforestry.

1

Deforestation in Amazonia: Dynamics, Causes, and Alternatives

∎

ANTHONY B. ANDERSON

Tropical deforestation is one of the major environmental crises of our time (Gomez-Pompa et al. 1972; Myers 1979, 1980; WRI 1985). In drier tropical zones, where human population densities are frequently high, deforestation has often led to irreversible changes in vegetation, soil, and possibly even climate, undermining the carrying capacity of ecosystems as well as their capacity to recover. The results are erosion, devastating floods, chronic fuelwood shortages, and desertification. In moister tropical zones,[1] where human populations are generally low, large-scale deforestation is a recent phenomenon, and its environmental effects are currently far less apparent than in drier zones. But an increasing array of evidence suggests that the long-term effects could be equally severe.

The dangers of deforestation in the moist tropics are largely due to the nature of ecosystems that predominate in this zone. Despite their luxuriant growth, moist tropical forests generally occur on soils of low fertility. Most of the nutrients are stored in the biomass, and cycling of nutrients takes place via litter fall and root uptake. Prolonged removal of this biomass—as is currently occurring over increasing areas of the moist tropics—effectively depletes essential nutrients from the ecosystem while promoting erosion, soil compaction, and weed infestation. Although the possibility of converting moist tropical forests into a "red desert" (Goodland and Irwin 1975) may be nil, overintensive use of deforested sites in this zone could lead to permanent degradation of regional ecosystems (Uhl 1983; Uhl, Buschbacher, and Serrão 1988). Furthermore, destruction of moist tropical forests leads to the demise of indigenous cultures that are best adapted to these ecosystems (Davis 1977; Hemming 1978; Posey 1983), and to the increased marginalization of newly arrived settlers as well (Wood and Schmink 1978; Barbira-Scazzocchio 1980; Hecht, Anderson, and May 1988).

In moist as well as dry zones, tropical deforestation can have a potentially disruptive effect on global geochemical cycles and, ultimately, climate. The popular conception of the Amazon forest as the world's "lungs" that generate the oxygen we breathe has been debunked (Fearnside 1985). But at least half of the rainfall in the Amazon Basin comes from water evapotranspired from the forest itself (Salati 1985), and widespread deforestation is likely to result in a pronounced reduction in regional rainfall. Moreover, moist tropical forests contain approximately 35 percent of the world's living terrestrial carbon pool (Brown and Lugo 1982); release of this pool into the atmosphere through felling and burning could contribute substantially to global warming.

Perhaps the greatest danger of tropical deforestation in the loss of genetic diversity (Buschbacher 1986). Widespread destruction of tropical moist forests, which contain 40–50 percent of the earth's species, will inevitably result in large-scale extinctions. If allowed to occur on this scale, such extinctions will eliminate a genetic heritage not only of inestimable aesthetic value, but of current use in essential ecological services (i.e., pollination, seed dispersal, etc.), and of future use in development of agricultural crops, pharmaceutical products, and industrial materials (Myers 1979, 1984).

The scale of deforestation in the moist tropics has only recently been quantified on a worldwide basis. Data compiled by FAO show that during 1980–1985, loss of tropical closed forests[2] averaged 75,000 km^2 per year,[3] or an area roughly equivalent to the country of Panama (WRI 1986). Rates of deforestation during this period varied considerably from country to country, ranging from 0.1 percent in Papua New Guinea to 5.9 percent in the Ivory Coast. On a regional basis, deforestation rates during 1981–1985 were highest in Latin America, both in absolute area (43,000 km^2 per year) and in percentage of total forest area (0.64 percent per year).[4]

Deforestation in Amazonia

Dynamics

The Amazon Basin, drained by the largest river system on earth, covers a total land area of 7.05 million km^2, of which approximately five million km^2 are covered by rain forest (Sioli 1984). This forest varies considerably in structure and composition (Ducke and Black 1954; Pires and Prance 1985); on a regional basis, its richness of bird, fish, and insect species is unmatched (e.g., Haffer 1969; Goulding 1980; Brown 1982). This extraordinary diversity may in large part be due to repeated contractions and expansions of the Amazon rain forest during the Pleistocene (Prance 1985).

More recently, the rain forest has been subjected to human-caused disturbances following the arrival of indigenous groups approximately 12,000 years ago (Meggers 1985). Evidence suggests that population densities along the major rivers may actually have been higher prior to European contact, when the indigenous population of Amazonia was perhaps six million people (Denevan 1976). Even today, most of the rural population continues to live in close proximity to rivers and subsist by shifting cultivation and extraction of forest products.

Until recently, deforestation seemed to be a remote problem in this region.[5] Available data indicated that both the absolute area and rate of deforestation were exceptionally low in Amazonia. For example, in 1980 Brazil's Institute of Space Research (INPE) published results obtained from satellite imagery of the Brazilian Amazon through 1978 (Tardin et al. 1980). The study concluded that only 1.55 percent of the region's forest cover had been removed, and that the rate of deforestation was a mere 0.33 percent per year (Table 1.1). Although the extent and rate may have been underestimated (Fearnside 1982), this study reflected the fact that the impact of deforestation was, at that time, practically insignificant given the immensity of the region's rain forest.

Since 1980, however, the situation has changed dramatically. The 1980s have been a decade of ambitious, government-supported development projects in the Amazon. A network of highways begun in the 1960s now crisscrosses the region, hydroelectric dams are being planned or constructed in many of the principal river systems, and large-scale extraction of minerals and fossil fuels is now underway.

In recent years the development of Amazonia has moved increasingly beyond the control of the public sector. Whereas in the past government incentives and infrastructure were a *sine qua non* for private sector involvement in regional development, today groups such as ranchers, farmers, miners, loggers, and charcoal producers operate independently. Up until a decade ago, conversion of rain forest to cattle pastures in the Brazilian Amazon required massive government incentives and costly infrastructure such as highway construction and maintenance. But today, ranchers near the town of Paragominas in the state of Pará are currently constructing their own highways to the neighboring state of Maranhão, for extraction of timber and establishment of new ranches—largely on public lands (Oren 1988). In the vicinity of the government-controlled Carajás mining project in southern Pará, private processing plants have begun producing pig-iron using minerals from the mine and fuel from the native forest. By the 1990s, the area of forest that will have to be cleared to support this activity is estimated at between 900 and 2,000 km^2 per year (CODEBAR/SUDAM 1986; Mahar 1988). Privately held gold mines are springing up throughout the region and polluting major river systems. An estimated 250 tons of mercury from gold mines have entered the Tapajós River basin in Pará, and government attempts at regulation have thus far failed.

Whether spontaneous or planned, colonization in the Amazon Basin is now largely under private initiative, and settlements are spreading along the southern flank of the region and wherever new roads are built. The influx of new settlers often overwhelms the capacity of frontier communities to absorb them.

The convergence of these factors is producing a marked increase in the rate and scale of deforestation in the Amazon. Recent estimates based on LANDSAT data indicate that deforestation has accelerated sharply in the 1980s.[6] As shown in table 1.1, the total area deforested increased to almost 600,000 km^2 by the end of 1987. This area represents 12 percent of Legal Amazonia[7] and is larger than France. Most deforestation is occurring in an arc along the western, southern, and

TABLE 1.1. LANDSAT Surveys of Forest Clearings in the Brazilian Amazon (after Mahar 1988).

State or Territory	Area in Legal Amazonia (km²)	AREA CLEARED (km²)				PERCENT OF STATE OR TERRITORY CLASSIFIED AS CLEARED			
		Through 1975	Through 1978	Through 1980	Through 1988	Through 1975	Through 1978	Through 1980	Through 1988
Amapá	140,276	152.5	170.5	183.7	571.5	0.1	0.1	0.1	0.4
Pará	1,248,042	8,654.0	22,445.3	33,913.8	120,000.0	0.7	0.8	2.7	9.6
Roraima	230,104	55.0	143.8	273.1	3,270.0	0.0	0.1	0.1	1.4
Maranhão	257,451	2,940.8	7,334.0	10,671.1	50,670.0	1.1	2.8	4.1	19.7
Tocantins (Goiás)	285,793	3,507.3	10,288.5	11,458.5	33,120.0	1.2	3.6	4.0	11.6
Acre	152,589	1,165.5	2,464.5	4,626.8	19,500.0	0.8	1.6	3.0	12.8
Rondônia	243,044	1,216.5	4,184.5	7,579.3	58,000.0	0.3	1.7	3.1	23.7
Mato Grosso	881,001	10,124.3	28,355.0	53,299.3	208,000.0	1.1	3.2	6.1	23.6
Amazonas	1,567,125	779.5	1,785.8	3,102.2	105,790.0	0.1	0.1	0.2	6.8
Legal Amazonia (total)	5,005,425	28,595.3	77,171.8	125,107.8	598,921.5	0.6	1.5	2.5	12.0

eastern edges of the region, which coincides with current zones of frontier expansion (figure 1.1). On a percentage basis, deforestation has been highest in the states of Rondônia and Mato Grosso, followed by western Maranhão, Acre, and northern Goiás.[8] On this basis, deforestation has been less in the more centrally located and larger states of Pará and Amazonas. But in absolute terms, the impact has been immense: in both states, over 100,000 km^2 have been cleared, mostly in their southerly portions (the Tocantins basin in Pará and the Madeira basin in Amazonas). The northern states of Roraima and Amapá,[9] as well as the northerly portions of Pará and Amazonas, have thus far suffered little deforestation in both relative and absolute terms.

The data in table 1.1 indicate that not only the scale but the rate of defores-

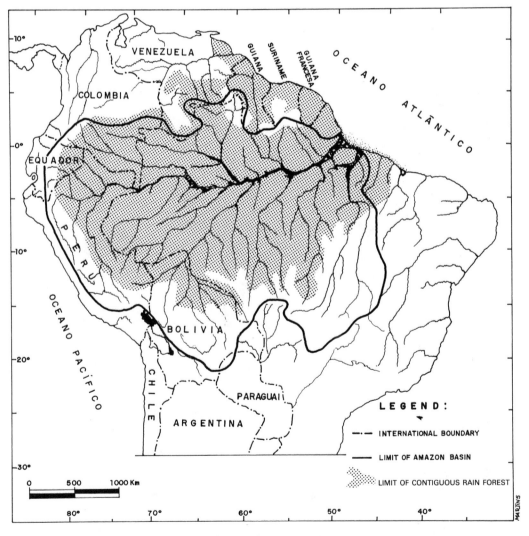

FIGURE 1.1. The Amazon Basin.

tation is rapidly increasing. From 1976 through 1978, the average annual rate was 0.3 percent of Legal Amazonia. From 1979 through 1980, the rate had increased to 0.5 percent, and from 1981 through 1988, to nearly 1.2 percent.[10] This trend suggests that the rate of deforestation in Amazonia is increasing exponentially, which could have ominous implications for the future of the region's remaining forests (cf. Fearnside 1982).

Recent evidence suggests that deforestation in Amazonia occurred on an unprecedented scale during the particularly dry year of 1987. On August 24 of that year, INPE detected 6800 fires just in the states of Mato Grosso and a small portion of southern Pará and eastern Rondônia (figure 1.2; Silveira and Nestlehner 1987): it was the largest-scale burn recorded in the history of the region. Smoke from Amazon fires lasted until December and resulted in the closure of most regional airports.

Once essentially local in scale, the destruction of the Amazon rain forest has become, for the first time, a regionwide phenomenon. And given the immensity

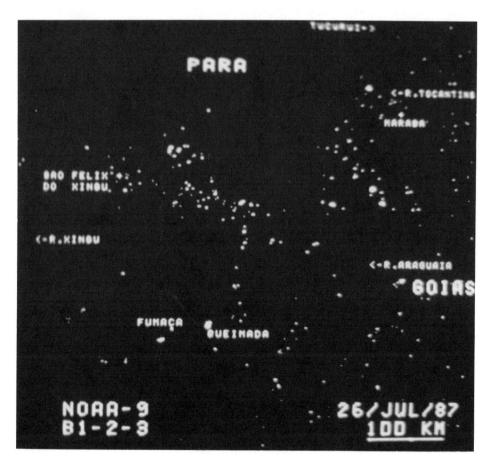

FIGURE 1.2. LANDSAT image taken on July 26, 1987, showing forest fires in a section of eastern Amazonia. (Source: Setzer et al. 1988).

of the region and its recent propensity for growth, deforestation in Amazonia is soon likely to occur on a scale unprecedented in human history and exert impacts on a global level.

Causes

The underlying causes of deforestation are extremely complex and often defy rational analysis. One persistent myth is that tropical deforestation is caused by overpopulation. Excessive population densities may indeed contribute to deforestation in certain areas of Asia and Africa, but even here the ultimate cause often boils down to unequal land distribution. Excluding the Amazon forest, Brazil has a population density of approximately 23 people per km^2, roughly equal to the United States, the world's greatest exporter of food. If all potential farmland outside of Amazonia were equally distributed, each person in Brazil could have four hectares. Instead, 4.5 percent of Brazil's landowners hold 81 percent of the country's farmland, and 70 percent of rural households are landless (Caufield 1984). With insufficient land, rural poor are constantly compelled to seek new frontiers where they can clear the rain forest for shifting cultivation. Often maligned as a cause of deforestation, shifting cultivators are more frequently victims of an unequal distribution of resources (Wood and Schmink 1978).

Government incentives, often for establishment of land uses that would otherwise be economically as well as ecologically inviable, have played an enormous role in promoting deforestation in the region (Mahar 1988). For example, during the past three decades over 10 million hectares of Amazon rain forest were converted to cattle pastures, largely through government policies (paper 13). A recent calculation by Uhl and Parker (1986) reveals just how unproductive Amazon pastures are: one-half ton of rain forest is required to produce a single quarter-pound hamburger.[11] Moreover, on government-subsidized ranches, for every quarter-pound hamburger that cost an average of $0.26 to produce, Brazil expended $0.22 in the form of subsidies (Browder 1988).

Even given current reductions of government incentives in debt-strapped Amazonian countries, combined with the economic inviability of this form of land use, cattle pastures continue to spread in frontier areas throughout the region. This apparently irrational activity seems to be motivated by 1) the value of land as a speculative investment in inflationary economies (such as those of Brazil, Peru, and, until recently, Bolivia), which often outweighs returns from the actual *use* of the land (Hecht 1985; Hecht, Norgaard, and Possio 1988); and 2) the facility of establishing claim to large areas of land once they have been converted to pasture, which is especially important in a region of chronic land conflicts (Branford and Glock 1985). The long-term investment required by most potentially sustainable forms of land use is unattractive when inflation is high and tenure insecure. As a result, most regional investment is geared toward shorter-term profits that can be generated either by simply clearing the forest or selectively extracting its components. In the current social and economic environment, the Amazon rain forest is usually treated as an obstacle to development rather than as a foundation for sustainable forms of land use.

The irrationality of Amazon development is not only socioeconomic but political in nature. Development policies in the region are frequently incoherent because they are determined by a plethora of conflicting government agencies (Mahar 1979). Long-range planning is rarely a component of development projects in Amazonia. A classic example is the implantation of the Transamazon Highway and its associated colonization project in the Brazilian Amazon during the 1970s. This project was initially conceived to settle 70,000 families between 1972 and 1974, but largely due to lack of planning and inadequate infrastructure, a mere 5700 families were effectively settled by the end of 1974 (Mahar 1979; Moran 1981; Smith 1982). The opposite occurred during the more recent colonization of the Brazilian state of Rondônia during the late 1970s and 1980s. Here plans were carefully made to integrate construction of a new highway with a World Bank–supported settlement program designed to receive small-scale producers from other regions of Brazil. But massive displacement of small producers due to lack of land reform in other parts of the country, relatively fertile soils along extensive portions of the highway in Rondônia, and an enormously effective government campaign to attract settlers resulted in explosive demographic growth: At an annual rate of 28 percent during most of the 1980s, Rondônia's growth has been over ten times the national average and well beyond the capacity of the state's meager infrastructure.

In short, deforestation in Amazonia results, to a large degree, from socioeconomic and political processes that originate outside of the region. These processes are frequently complex and elude simple analysis—as well as simple solutions.

Alternatives to Deforestation in Amazonia

Given the complex situation described, it would appear that the complete destruction of the Amazon rain forest is only a matter of time. Yet this text is based on the firm conviction that the current scenario *is* reversible, and that viable alternatives to deforestation—both within Amazonia and elsewhere in the moist tropics—*do* exist.

The idea for this book grew out of a perception that the myriad problems associated with tropical deforestation have been widely trumpeted in the popular and scientific media, while potential solutions have gone relatively unnoticed. One reason for this discrepancy is that the problems are far more dramatic—and, hence, more newsworthy—than the solutions, many of which have been quietly occurring in rural communities or in the minds of a small contingent of researchers. Another reason is that the people involved in the search for or implementation of alternatives to tropical deforestation represent a heterogeneous group comprised of ecologists, foresters, agronomists, anthropologists, geographers, extension agents, policymakers, and—most significantly—the actual inhabitants of tropical landscapes. Such people rarely have an opportunity to communicate among themselves, much less in concert to a wider audience. The few attempts to promote such communication to date (e.g., Gradwohl and Greenberg 1988), although important for promoting public awareness, have invariably occurred in temperate countries, far removed from the landscapes and inhabitants that have the ultimate stake in tropical deforestation and its alternatives.

This book presents a selection of papers presented at an international conference held in Belém, Brazil, during January 27–30, 1988. The location of this conference in the Amazon region of Brazil was appropriate for three reasons. First, the region contains the world's largest expanse of intact tropical forests. Second, current development policies and programs in Brazil are aimed at removing these forests on an unprecedented scale. And third, the destruction of the Amazon rain forest has recently aroused the concern of the general public and policymakers, not only within Brazil but worldwide. For the first time, public officials at the highest levels have expressed resolve to change the destructive policies of the past and seek more sustainable alternatives. This book is about such alternatives.

Conservation is frequently cited as one alternative to tropical deforestation. But this is not a book about conservation as most people in developed countries understand the term, that is, protection of natural ecosystems from human intervention. Rather, this book is about how tropical forests can be used sustainably—which, in the final analysis, must be a part of any long-term effort to promote conservation. In Amazonia, sustainable forms of land use are currently limited to a small minority of the rural population under highly specific conditions. Developing such practices for the population as a whole—including small farmers and ranchers, as well as private and public companies—has only just begun.

The subtitle of this volume expresses its underlying theme: "steps toward sustainable use of the Amazon rain forest." These steps consist of innovative technologies or approaches that permit simultaneous use and conservation of the rain forest, and that have the potential to provide a better way of life for people than do the land uses that currently predominate in the region. Although some of these steps may be promising, many are merely tentative and most seem insignificant when compared with the scale and velocity of deforestation in the region. Thus, although this text offers hopeful alternatives to the specter of tropical deforestation, one should not forget that these alternatives are currently remote.

Natural and Human Disturbances

Developing viable land-use alternatives to deforestation in Amazonia requires an understanding of how the Amazon rain forest responds to disturbances. A popular misconception is that, prior to recent deforestation, Amazonia was undisturbed. Yet an increasing array of evidence suggests that rain forests in Amazonia and elsewhere in the tropics have suffered repeated contractions and expansions in the geologic past (Prance 1985). In addition, natural disturbances on both a small and large scale have been common components of the Amazon rain forest throughout its history. Clearing of small patches of forest for agriculture has been a widespread practice since the arrival of humans approximately 12,000 years before present, and it continues to be widely practiced today. It is only in the past three decades that large-scale, prolonged deforestation has assumed major importance in Amazonia (figure 1.3). Yet, albeit vastly greater in scale and duration, today's deforestation is part of a continuum of disturbance that has long been a part of the Amazonian landscape.

Studying how the rain forest responds to different kinds of disturbances offers insights for the design of more sustainable forms of land use. In this volume, ecologist Chris Uhl and co-authors examine a spectrum of disturbance types (ranging from small-scale, natural disturbances to large-scale, anthropogenic disturbances), and use their findings to suggest ecologically sound land-use alternatives. For example, their studies of small-scale disturbances indicate that land-use systems such as agroforestry, which incorporate many of the structural and functional aspects of natural forest ecosystems, can protect fragile soils and provide steady yields. Likewise, their research on abandoned, degraded cattle pastures is helping to develop appropriate technologies for restoring the native forest cover on these derelict lands. Overall, they have found that management practices that mimic natural disturbances in size, duration, and frequency can protect the functional integrity of forest ecosystems while providing modest economic returns. Their paper provides a theoretical foundation for many of the land-use alternatives discussed in subsequent essays.

Natural Forest Management

Natural forest management has been maligned due to its low yields, slow economic returns, difficulty of implementation, and vulnerability to disruptive land

FIGURE 1.3. Large-scale clearing for cattle pastures in the Brazilian state of Maranhão. As deforestation increases in scale, forest resources become increasingly scarce.

uses such as shifting cultivation (Spears 1984). From this perspective, silvicultural plantations are seen as the only viable source of wood products in the tropics. Yet factors such as changing market demands and pest outbreaks make plantations a risky alternative, and they cannot replace all the ecological functions of natural forest. In short, plantations and natural forest management are not competitive but complementary forms of land use that provide different types of products and are suited to different terrains (Schmidt 1987).

The search for successful forms of tropical forest management should begin in traditional communities where such land uses have been carried out for centuries or even millennia. Indigenous peoples throughout the tropics frequently manage natural forests for a wide variety of so-called "minor" forest products, including fibers, fuelwood, fruits, latex, resins, gums, medicines, game, etc. Some of the best research on tropical forest management by indigenous peoples is being conducted in Mexico. Ecologist Arturo Gomez-Pompa and anthropologist Andrea Kaus describe the major indigenous forms of forest management in this country. They show that many so-called "natural" forests have in fact been managed by aboriginal groups in the past, and that this past management accounts, at least in part, for the current distribution of many economic tree species. Among present-day traditional farmers, agriculture and forest management are part of a spatial and temporal continuum, as evident in such practices as the maintenance of kitchen gardens and the enrichment of forest fallows. In contrast to the patterns of land occupation and degradation predominant today, these practices have supported high population densities over long periods of time. They thus provide important clues in the search for sustainable land uses in the humid tropics.

The forms of land use utilized by indigenous peoples often require a profound knowledge of highly complex ecosystems. Yet many forested ecosystems in Amazonia and elsewhere in the moist tropics are dominated by one or a few economic species (Anderson 1987); such ecosystems can be managed with relative ease. In paper 4, I describe one such management system utilized by nonindigenous river dwellers in floodplain forests of the Amazon estuary. The simplicity of this management, its low input requirements, significant economic returns, and general acceptance by the rural population make it an attractive land-use model in floodplain forests of the Amazon.

In the following paper, ecologist Chuck Peters examines the viability of harvesting native fruits in a similar ecosystem in the Peruvian Amazon. Peters demonstrates that natural populations can produce astonishingly high fruit yields that can be harvested without undermining the regenerative capacity of these populations. His paper provides a scientific basis for sustainable (as well as potentially profitable) utilization of Amazonian forests.

The technical success of natural forest management ultimately depends on the regeneration of desirable species. In paper 6, forester Virgilio Viana examines the ecological factors that govern the availability of seeds and seedlings, using a case study of a promising timber species in Central Amazonia. Viana illustrates how theoretical principles derived from ecology can have practical application for the management of tropical forests.

Although its potential is high, implementing forest management on a commercial scale has been an elusive goal in the Amazon Basin (Rankin 1985). Part of the reason for this is the lack of long-term research efforts aimed at testing management alternatives. The longest continuous research on sustained timber production in Amazonian forests has been carried out by Dutch foresters in Suriname. N. R. de Graaf and R. L. H. Poels describe a management system based on selective harvesting of high-quality timbers and periodic, low-level silvicultural treatments over a twenty-year cycle. Its minimal ecological impacts and relatively high economic returns make this system especially attractive as an extensive land-use alternative in Amazonia.

Implementation of natural forest management in the moist tropics is often undermined due to a lack of support and involvement of local residents. Ecologist Gary Hartshorn closes the section on natural forest management by returning to a rural community in the Peruvian Amazon, where Yanesha Indians have established a forestry cooperative. He describes the cooperative's forest management system, which appears to be ecologically sustainable as well as economically profitable. This paper demonstrates how programs for managing tropical forests can be designed so that local inhabitants can make a living from renewable natural resources, which gives them a stake in making these programs work.

Agroforestry

Agroforestry has recently gained considerable attention as a promising alternative to tropical deforestation that is both potentially sustainable and highly adaptable to the needs of smallholders (e.g., Weaver 1979; Hecht 1982). Yet this form of land use often eludes precise definition. At one extreme, which can be referred to as "extensive" agroforestry systems, the degree of management intervention is low, and the conservation of native forest structure and function is high. Agroforestry systems of this type are extremely common in the Amazon Basin and throughout the American tropics. In paper 9, ethnobotanist Janis Alcorn compares such systems between indigenous groups in Mexico and the Peruvian Amazon. The land uses of both groups are characterized by the inclusion of native trees and natural successional processes, the multiple use of a given species, and the spreading of risk through maintenance of high biotic diversity.

Extensive forms of agroforestry such as those I have described generally occur in regions characterized by low land-use pressures and loosely defined tenure relationships. In contrast, "intensive" agroforestry systems, which substitute native forest vegetation with plantations that must be maintained against weed and pest invasions, are associated with relatively high land-use pressures and more rigidly defined tenure relationships. Although intensive forms of agroforestry are exceptionally common in Asia and Africa, they are relatively rare in tropical America (Nair 1985) and extremely so in traditional communities of Amazonia.

It is probably no accident that the classic example of intensive agroforestry systems in Amazonia is practiced by immigrants to the region. In paper 10, ecologists Scott Subler and Chris Uhl describe the Japanese agroforestry systems in Tomé-Açu, a small farming community in eastern Amazonia. These systems are characterized by intensive cultivation of relatively small areas and require high inputs of capital, labor, and materials. The emphasis is on high-value cash crops, and these systems are both profitable and apparently sustainable. The intensity of land use characteristic of Japanese farms is part of a complex legacy that will be difficult for local farmers to adopt. In fact, the few cases in which Japanese farming techniques have been adopted involve relatively wealthy Brazilians from other regions who are, in a sense, immigrants themselves.

Although agroforestry systems are an integral part of indigenous and Japanese land-use strategies, they are surprisingly rare among newly arrived settlers in frontier zones of Amazonia. This rarity is largely due to the nature of frontier expansion in the region, where large-scale land uses such as cattle pastures frequently encroach on small-scale production systems. Faced with uncertain land tenure, distant markets, and lack of technical support, the small holder is frequently compelled to practice degenerate forms of shifting cultivation for subsistence.

Promoting sustainable land uses such as agroforestry in frontier zones requires effective extension services aimed at small-scale producers. Agronomist Robert Peck describes a project in Amazonian Ecuador that addresses many of the problems characteristic of extension through the use of on-farm demonstrations. These demonstrations effectively promote agroforestry practices in isolated areas, encourage participation and experimentation by resident farmers, and can be periodically modified to suit local needs. As a result, agroforestry systems have become an integral part of the local landscape. Through practical extension efforts such as these, settlers in frontier zones of Amazonia can be induced to adopt more sustainable forms of land use.

Landscape Recovery

Despite efforts to promote agroforestry, degraded landscapes are an increasingly familiar sight in frontier zones throughout Amazonia. Degradation here refers to long-term modifications of natural ecosystems that undermine their capacity to recover through natural successional processes. Nature, especially in the moist tropics, abhors a vacuum, and natural forest ecosystems in this zone exhibit an extraordinary (and frequently underestimated) capacity to recover from human-induced disturbances. Yet this capacity can be seriously or even permanently undermined in areas where such disturbances are excessively widespread, prolonged, or intensive. And it is precisely in such areas that settlement in Amazonia tends to be concentrated.

In paper 12, agronomist Jean Dubois reviews case studies showing how rural inhabitants in the South American tropics are actively engaged in restoring forest cover on sites previously cleared for agriculture or other activities. Although secondary forests are frequently indicators of land abandonment following shifting cultivation, Dubois shows that they are in fact frequently utilized and managed. Management techniques include selective weeding and enrichment planting, which result in high-density stands of economically important forest resources on sites that were previously marginal. Dubois illustrates the significant role of rural inhabitants in the process of landscape recovery and suggests that intensified use of secondary forests in already settled areas can reduce land-use pressures at the frontier.

Peck demonstrates that, even in highly altered ecosystems, people can continue to utilize forest resources and manipulate natural processes on a sustainable basis. On sites where these processes have been seriously impaired, however, land restoration requires other approaches.

With a current coverage of over 100,000 km^2, abandoned pastures constitute the most extensive form of land degradation in Amazonia. Two alternatives exist for recovering these lands: restoration of the pasture or regeneration of the natural forest. In paper 13, agronomists Adilson Serrão and José Toledo evaluate prospects for the first alternative. Restoring the productivity of pastures that are already severely degraded requires energy- and capital-intensive measures such as mechanized soil turnover and application of fertilizers and pesticides. They conclude that the most rational strategy is to reduce degradation and extend the useful life of still-productive pastures through introduction of better-adapted forage germplasm, together with appropriate techniques for pasture establishment and grazing management.

If the land-use goal on highly degraded pastures is to reestablish the natural forest cover, ecologist Dan Nepstad and co-authors recommend a high-information, low energy approach in paper 14. Their research indicates that an economic way to accelerate natural forest regeneration is through dissemination of seeds from selected, large-seeded, drought-tolerant tree species. Rather than blanketing the landscape, reforestation should focus on "high resource" tree islands, from which regeneration can naturally spread. By investigating the barriers to forest regeneration on highly degraded sites, this last paper illustrates how Amazonian ecosystems recover following severe disturbance. Comparison with similar research on landscape restoration in Costa Rica (Janzen 1986) provides interesting insights concerning forest regeneration processes in moist and dry tropical zones (see also Ewel 1977). A key underlying difference involves the microclimatic gradient between forested and nonforested sites. In the moist tropics, natural forests are relatively closed, which means that their microclimate is considerably less harsh than on nonforested sites; in contrast, the relative openness of natural forests in the dry tropics makes this difference less pronounced. As a result, plants that grow in dry tropical forests can often grow on nonforested sites as well. The propagules of many tree species are dispersed by wind, which is typically high in the dry tropics and continues to blow even when other dispersal agents, such as mammals and birds, have been reduced by hunting or habitat destruction. In contrast, the steep environmental gradient between forested and nonforested sites may be beyond the physiological tolerance of many forest trees in the moist tropics. As Nepstad and colleagues show, forest species that do exhibit such tolerance generally possess large propagules, which contain sufficient metabolic reserves to permit rapid development of deep root systems; the latter, in turn, permits tapping of deep soil moisture reserves. Such species, however, rarely arrive on nonforested sites, as dispersal of large propagules from forested sites appears to be minimal. Wind is generally less pronounced in the moist tropics, and few of the dispersal agents that remain surmount the steep environmental gradient surrounding forest remnants.

As a result, reforestation of highly degraded sites is a far more difficult task in the moist tropics than in the dry tropics. Technical research in this field must focus on species that can tolerate the harsh conditions of deforested sites. Establishment of such species can help restore essential ecological functions and may eventually serve to promote subsequent establishment of a wider range of native species.

Although complex, the technical issues involved in landscape recovery in the moist tropics are probably resolvable. The success or failure of landscape recovery, as well as of other alternatives to deforestation described in this text, ultimately requires the participation of the people who inhabit Amazonia. And in a region of constantly beckoning frontiers, a key challenge is to engage rural inhabitants in restoring the land in areas where the frontier has already passed.

Implications for Regional Development

The papers summarized in the preceding pages indicate that a wide variety of alternatives to tropical deforestation exist and are currently practiced by rural inhabitants. In Amazonia, these alternatives are generally at an early stage of development. All of the alternatives described—natural forest management, agroforestry systems, and landscape recovery—appear to be technically feasible, but data are generally lacking on their ecological and economic sustainability. Because these alternatives promote maintenance or restoration of a diversified forest cover, one can safely assume that they are more ecologically sustainable than land uses currently in vogue; the long-term practice of many such alternatives by rural inhabitants in Amazonia and elsewhere in the tropics lends credence to this assumption. A more crucial gap in our knowledge is the current lack of data on the economic costs and benefits of these alternatives. The few economic data that are presented (e.g., papers 3, 4, 7, and 8) suggest, however, that they are highly competitive.

Although the alternatives presented in this volume would thus appear to be promising, one must not forget that they comprise only a small fraction of the land uses that currently predominate in Amazonia. Ecologist Phil Fearnside puts these alternatives in perspective by analyzing land uses practiced on a large scale, such as logging, shifting cultivation, and cattle ranching. In frontier zones of Amazonia, none of these land uses utilize native forest ecosystems in a sustainable way. Even when carried out selectively, logging causes severe damage and leaves forests highly susceptible to subsequent destruction by fire (Uhl and Buschbacher 1985). Other major land uses require wholesale removal of the rain forest. Although shifting cultivation incorporates forest regeneration during the fallow period, this period is often truncated as populations increase and/or available land decreases (Sioli 1973; Hecht, Anderson, and May 1988). With a useful life that typically ranges from four to ten years before abandonment, Amazonian pastures have been aptly characterized as a prolonged form of shifting cultivation (Buschbacher 1986). But when pastures are abandoned after intensive use, a scrubby, fire-resistant vegetation often takes over, and forest regeneration is brought to a standstill (Uhl, Buschbacher, and Serrão 1988). The ecological and economic un-

FIGURE 1.4. Rubber tapper in the São Luis de Remanso extractive reserve in the Brazilian state of Acre.

sustainability of these land uses may ultimately lead to increased acceptance of more rational alternatives, provided that current policies that promote landscape degradation are changed.

As emphasized earlier in this essay, development policies in Amazonia have largely been determined outside of the region and, until recently, were rarely questioned by the people who stood most to lose by their implementation. But whereas development was frequently viewed as a panacea in the past, today it is increasingly being questioned by the regional press, politicians, and popular groups in both urban and rural areas of Amazonia. One of the most significant results of such questioning has been the birth of a social movement comprised of rubber tappers engaged in nonviolent resistance of deforestation in the Brazilian state of Acre. This movement, described by anthropologist Mary Allegretti, is now supported by a broad coalition of indigenous and environmental groups, as well as by policymakers and government officials in and out of Brazil. The rubber tappers have called for the establishment of so-called "extractive reserves," comprised of public lands designated for the specific purpose of exploiting forest products such as rubber and Brazil nut on a sustainable basis. By late 1988, three such reserves had been established in Acre (figure 1.4), and others were being planned elsewhere in the Brazilian Amazon. In effect, establishment of extractive reserves represents an important step toward implementing simultaneous use and conservation of the Amazon rain forest.

As the rubber tappers' movement clearly illustrates, development of the Amazon need not imply its destruction. In the final paper of this volume, sociologist Donald Sawyer argues that the current environmental destruction taking place in the region is not an inevitable consequence of development, but rather the result of highly artificial—as well as socially and economically questionable—policies that can be reversed. Sawyer examines policy initiatives that could radically change current scenarios of land use in Amazonia, such as 1) cutting economic incentives to deforestation within the region; 2) relieving pressures for settlement by strengthening land, health, and welfare reform programs outside of Amazonia; 3) consolidating existing settlement by improving infrastructure in already occupied areas of Amazonia; and 4) promoting ecologically and economically sustainable forms of land use. If adopted in concert, such policies could contribute substantially toward reversing current deforestation trends in Amazonia.

Implementing alternatives to tropical deforestation is a process that has just begun. This book illustrates how—with technical knowledge, political will, and sensitivity to the needs of local inhabitants—the Amazon region can be developed in ways that assure its preservation.

ACKNOWLEDGMENTS

Many of the ideas in this paper were conceived while preparing a report for the Ford Foundation on forest management issues in the Brazilian Amazon. I thank Steve Sanderson and Peter May of the Ford Foundation for their encouragement, and Chris Uhl and Marianne Schmink for their critical review of the manuscript.

ENDNOTES

1. "Dry" and "moist" are used here to refer to different climatic zones and their associated forest vegetation in the tropics. The "dry" tropics refer to regions with a pronounced dry season (i.e., monthly precipitation under 100 mm for at least four months); the native forests in these regions are distinctly deciduous. In contrast, rainfall in the "moist" tropics is less seasonal and native forests are generally evergreen. Of the world's currently existing 9 million km^2 of tropical forests, approximately one third are of the former type and two thirds of the latter (Postel and Heise 1988).

2. Closed forest has a cover of trees sufficiently dense to prevent the development of a grass understory. By contrast, open forest has at least 10% tree cover but enough light penetration to permit the growth of grass under the trees (WRI 1986).

3. The overall rate of deforestation in both the moist and dry tropics has been estimated at approximately 110,000 km^2 per year (cf. WRI 1986). According to Myers (1986), the total rate of tropical forest destruction is closer to 200,000 km^2 per year, if one includes forest "depletion" through selective harvesting of wood by commercial loggers and fuelwood gatherers.

4. This rate is expressed as percentage of total forest area in existence in 1980.

5. The following discussion on deforestation in Amazonia focuses on Brazil, which encompasses 80% of the region and where deforestation rates appear to be highest.

6. As this volume was in press, Brazil's Institute of Space Research (INPE) published an updated report on forest clearing in Amazonia (INPE 1989) that differs considerably from the World Bank estimates (Mahar 1988) reproduced in Table 1.1. According to the INPE report, total forest clearing for the region through 1988 was approximately 250,000 km^2, or a mere 5.1% of the total area of Legal Amazonia. This report, however, has been received with considerable skepticism within Brazil (Antônio 1989). For example, prominent members of the national scientific community charge that the figures were underestimated to still international criticism of Brazil's environmental policies in the Amazon. Likewise, technicians at INPE complain that the report was prepared too hastily (less than one month), and that the scientific staff was excluded from the final data analysis and synthesis. Finally, "old" clearings made before 1970 were excluded from the estimates, including approximately 87,000 km^2 in the states of Pará and Maranhão alone (INPE 1989; Marcos Pereira, personal communication). Due to the questionable manner in which this report was carried out, I have decided to exclude it from current analysis of the scale of forest clearing in Amazonia, which is based exclusively on the World Bank figures.

7. "Legal Amazonia" is a concept used in Brazil to define seven states (Amazonas, Pará, Mato Grosso, Rondônia, Roraima, Acre, and Amapá) and parts of two others (Goiás and Maranhão). This definition, which is used for regional planning and political purposes, includes extensive areas outside of the Amazon Basin as well as over one million km^2 of nonforest savanna and scrub vegetation.

8. In 1988, northern Goiás was transformed into the state of Tocantins.

9. In 1988, the territories of Roraima and Amapá became states.

10. An annual deforestation rate of 1.2% for Amazonia translates into an area of almost 60,000 km^2 per year, or nearly 80% of the recent estimate of 75,000 km^2 annual rain forest removal for the whole world during 1981–1985 (cf. WRI 1986). The latest data from Amazonia suggest that this worldwide estimate should be substantially increased.

11. Although striking, the hamburger analogy is not especially appropriate in this case, since Brazil does not export beef to the United States (Browder 1988).

REFERENCES

Anderson, A. B. 1987. Management of native palm forests: A comparison of case studies from Indonesia and Brazil. In H. L. Gholz, ed., *Agroforestry: Realities, Possibilities and Potentials*, pp. 155–167. Dordrecht, The Netherlands: Martinus Nijhoff.

Antônio, L. 1989. Sarney defende os dados maquiados sobre Amazônia. *Folha de São Paulo*, p. C-3, 8 May 1989.

Barbira-Scazzocchio, F. 1980. From native forest to proviate property: The development of Amazonia for whom? In F. Barbira-Scazzocchio, ed., *Land, People, and Planning in Contemporary Amazonia*, pp. iii–xvi. Cambridge, England: Centre of Latin American Studies Occasional Publication No. 3.

Branford, S. and O. Glock. 1985. *The Last Frontier: Fighting Over Land in the Amazon*. London: Zed Books.

Browder, J. O. 1988. The social costs of rain forest destruction: A critique and economic analysis of the "hamburger debate." *Interciencia* 13(3):115–120.

Brown, Jr., K. S. 1982. Paleoecology and regional patterns of evolution in Neotropical forest butterflies. In G. T. Prance, ed., *Biological Diversification in the Tropics*, pp. 255–308. New York: Columbia University Press.

Brown, S. and A. E. Lugo. 1982. The storage and production of organic matter in tropical forests and their role in the global carbon cycle. *Biotropica* 14(3):161–187.

Buschbacher, R. J. 1986. Tropical deforestation and pasture development. *Bioscience* 36(1): 22–28.

Caufield, C. 1984. *In the Rainforest: Report from a Strange, Beautiful, Imperiled World*. Chicago: University of Chicago Press.

CODEBAR/SUDAM. 1986. *Problemática do Carvão Vegetal na Area do Programa Grande Carajás*. Belém, Brazil: Companhia de Desenvolvimento de Barcarena (CODEBAR) and Superintendência do Desenvolvimento da Amazônia (SUDAM).

Davis, S. 1977. *Victims of the Miracle*. Cambridge, England: Cambridge University Press.

Denevan, W. M. 1976. The aboriginal population of Amazonia. In W. M. Denevan, ed., *The Native Population of the Americas in 1492*, pp. 205–233. Madison: University of Wisconsin Press.

Ducke, A. and G. A. Black. 1954. Notas sobre a fitogeografia da Amazônia Brasileira. *Boletim Técnico do Instituto Agronômico do Norte* (IAN, Belém) 4:1–40.

Ewel, J. J. 1977. Differences between wet and dry successional tropical ecosystems. *Geo-Eco-Trop* 1(2):103–111.

Fearnside, P. M. 1982. Deforestation in the Brazilian Amazon: How fast is it occurring? *Interciencia* 7(2):82–88.

Fearnside, P. M. 1985. Environmental change and deforestation in the Brazilian Amazon. In J. Hemming, ed., *Change in the Amazon Basin: Man's Impact on the Forest and Rivers*, pp. 70–89. Manchester, England: Manchester University Press.

Gomez-Pompa, A., C. Vazquez-Yanes, and S. Guevara. 1972. The tropical rainforest: A nonrenewable resource. *Science* 117:762–765.

Goodland, R. J. and H. S. Irwin. 1975. *Amazon Jungle: Green Hell to Red Desert?* New York: Elsevier.

Goulding, M. 1980. *The Fishes and the Forest: Explorations in Amazonian Natural History*. Berkeley: University of California Press.

Gradwohl, J. and R. Greenberg. 1988. *Saving Tropical Forests*. London: Earthscan Publications Ltd.

Haffer, J. 1969. Speciation in Amazonian forest birds. *Science* 165:131–137.

Hecht, S. B. 1982. Agroforestry in the Amazon Basin: Practice, theory and limits of a promising land use. In S. B. Hecht, ed., *Amazonia: Agriculture and Land Use Research;* pp. 331–371. Cali, Colombia: Centro Internacional de Agricultura Tropical (CIAT).

Hecht, S. B. 1985. Environment, development and politics: Capital accumulation and the livestock sector in eastern Amazonia. *World Development* 13(6):663–684.

Hecht, S. B., A. B. Anderson, and P. May 1988. The subsidy from nature: Shifting cultivation, successional palm forests, and rural development. *Human Organization* 47(1): 25–35.

Hecht, S. B., R. B. Norgaard, and G. Possio. 1988. The economics of cattle ranching in eastern Amazonia. *Interciencia* 13(5):233–240.

Hemming, J. 1978. *Red Gold.* London: Macmillan.

INPE. 1989. Avaliação da Alteração da Cobertura Florestal na Amazônia Legal Utilizando Sensoriamento Remoto Orbital. São José dos Campos, Brazil: Instituto Nacional de Pesquisas Espaciais.

Janzen, D. H. 1986. *Guanacaste National Park: Tropical Ecological and Cultural Restoration.* San Jose, Costa Rica: Editorial Universidad Estatal a Distancia.

Mahar, D. 1979. *Frontier Development Policy in Brazil: A Study of Amazonia.* New York: Praeger Publishers.

Mahar, D. 1988. *Government Policies and Deforestation in Brazil's Amazon Region.* Washington DC: World Bank Environment Department Working Paper No. 7.

Meggers, B. J. 1985. Aboriginal adaptation to Amazonia. In G. T. Prance and T. E. Lovejoy, eds., *Key Environments: Amazonia,* pp. 307–327. New York: Pergamon Press.

Moran, E. F. 1981. *Developing the Amazon.* Bloomington: Indiana University Press.

Myers, N. 1979. *The Sinking Ark.* New York: Pergamon Press.

Myers, N. 1980. *Conversion of Tropical Moist Forests.* Washington, DC: National Academy of Sciences.

Myers, N. 1984. *The Primary Source: Tropical Forests and Our Future.* New York: Norton.

Myers, N. 1986. Tropical forests: Patterns of depletion. In G. T. Prance, ed., *Tropical Rain Forests and the World's Atmosphere,* pp. 9–22. Boulder, CO: Westview Press.

Nair, P. K. R. 1985. Classification of agroforestry systems. *Agroforestry Systems* 3:97–128.

Oren, D. C. 1988. Uma reserva biologica para o Maranhão. *Ciência Hoje* 8(44):36–45.

Pires, J. M. and G. T. Prance 1985. The vegetation types of the Brazilian Amazon. In G. T. Prance and T. E. Lovejoy, eds., *Key Environments: Amazonia,* pp. 109–145. New York: Pergamon Press.

Posey, D. A. 1983. Indigenous knowledge and development: An ideological bridge to the future. *Ciencia e Cultura* 35(7):877–894.

Postel, S. and L. Heise. 1988. Reforesting the earth. In L. R. Brown, ed., *State of the World 1988: A Worldwatch Report on Progress Toward a Sustainable Society.,* pp. 83–100. New York: Norton.

Prance, G. T. 1985. The changing forests. In G. T. Prance and T. E. Lovejoy, eds., *Key Environments: Amazonia,* pp. 146–165. New York: Pergamon Press.

Rankin, J. M. 1985. Forestry in the Brazilian Amazon. In G. T. Prance and T. E. Lovejoy, eds., *Key Environments: Amazonia,* pp. 360–392. New York: Pergamon Press.

Salati, E. 1985. The climatology and hydrology of Amazonia. In G. T. Prance and T. E. Lovejoy, eds., *Key Environments: Amazonia,* pp. 18–48. New York: Pergamon Press.

Schmidt, R. C. 1987. Tropical rain forest management. *Unasylvia* 156(39):2–17.

Setzer, A. W., M. C. Pereira, A. C. Pereira Jr., and S. A. O. Almeida. 1988. *Relatório de Atividades do Projeto IBDF-INPE Ano 1987.* São José dos Campos, Brazil: Instituto Nacional de Pesquisas Espaciais (INPE) Report Number INPE-4534-RPE/565.

Silveira, E. A. de and W. Nestlehner. 1987. Cerco de labaredas. *Isto E,* 9 September 1987, pp. 30–33.

Sioli, H. 1973. Recent human activities in the Brazilian Amazon region and their ecological effects. In B. J. Meggers, E. S. Ayensu, and W. D. Duckworth, eds., *Tropical Forest Ecosystems in Africa and South America: A Comparative Review*, pp. 321–324. Washington, DC: Smithsonian Institution Press.

Sioli, H. 1984. The Amazon and its main affluents: Hydrology, morphology of the river courses, and river types. In H. Sioli, ed., *The Amazon: Limnology and Landscape Ecology of a Mighty Tropical River and its Basin*, pp. 127–165. Dordrecht, The Netherlands: Dr. W. Junk.

Smith, N. J. H. 1982. *Rainforest Corridors: The Transamazon Colonization Scheme*. Berkeley: University of California Press.

Spears, J. S. 1984. Role of forestation as a sustainable land use strategy option for tropical forest management and conservation and as a source of supply for developing country wood needs. In K. F. Wiersum, ed., *Strategies and Designs for Afforestation, Reforestation and Tree Planting*, pp. 29–47. Wageningen, The Netherlands: Pudoc.

Tardin, A. T., D. C. L. Lee, R. J. R. Santos, O. R. de Assis, M. P. dos Santos Barbosa, M. de Lourdes Moreira, M. T. Pereira, D. Silva, and C. P. dos Santos Filho. 1980. *Subprojeto Desmatamento*. São José dos Campos, Brazil: Instituto Nacional de Pesquisas Espaciais (INPE) Report Number INPE-1649-RPE/103.

Uhl, C. 1983. You can keep a good forest down. *Natural History* 4(83):71–79.

Uhl, C. and R. Buschbacher. 1985. A disturbing synergism between cattle ranching burning practices and selective tree harvesting in the Eastern Amazon. *Biotropica* 17(4): 265–268.

Uhl, C. R. Buschbacher, and A. Serrão. 1988. Abandoned pastures in eastern Amazonia. I: Patterns of plant succession. *Journal of Ecology* 76:663–681.

Uhl, C. and G. Parker. 1986. Is a quarter-pound hamburger worth a half-ton of rain forest? *Interciencia* 11(5):210.

Weaver, P. 1979. Agri-silviculture in tropical America. *Unasvlva* 31(26):2–12.

Wood, C. and M. Schmink. 1978. Blaming the victim: Small farmer production in an Amazon colonization project. *Studies in Third World Societies* 7:77–93.

WRI. 1985. *Tropical Forests: A Call for Action*. Washington, DC: World Resources Institute (WRI).

WRI. 1986. *World Resources 1986*. New York: Basic Books.

2

Studies of Ecosystem Response to Natural and Anthropogenic Disturbances Provide Guidelines for Designing Sustainable Land-Use Systems in Amazonia

■

CHRISTOPHER UHL

DANIEL NEPSTAD

ROBERT BUSCHBACHER

KATHLEEN CLARK

BOONE KAUFFMAN

SCOTT SUBLER

ABSTRACT

The study of Amazon rain forest ecosystems reveals that natural disturbances of both small (e.g., treefalls) and large scale (e.g., wildfires) have been common throughout history. Now, because of the recent dramatic increase in human activities in Amazonia, anthropogenic disturbances (e.g., shifting cultivation and pasture clearings) have become even more common than natural disturbances in many areas. The Amazonian flora has several regeneration strategies that ensure forest regrowth after natural disturbances, but recovery following anthropogenic disturbances is frequently slow and in some cases succession is deflected to a nonforest end point.

Research on plant succession following natural disturbances (treefalls and fires) indicates that forest management techniques that mimic natural disturbances in size, duration, and frequency will protect the functional integrity of Amazonian ecosystems while providing modest profits. Likewise, research on succession following the anthropogenic disturbance of slash-and-burn agriculture illustrates the feasibility of agroforestry systems that retain nutrients and protect fragile soils while providing steady yields. Finally, research on nonregenerating, abandoned cattle pastures (large-scale anthropogenic disturbance) is providing opportunities to elucidate barriers to tree establishment on derelict lands and to develop technologies to restore these lands to a forested state.

A half a century ago, most people only dimly recognized the existence of tropical forests and knew little of their biological richness or complex structure and function; nor was there much cognizance of their impending peril. Now, Jari's financial status, the potential ecological effects of the ambitious Carajas iron-ore project, and the sustainability of Amazon ranching are discussed worldwide. Moreover, it is now recognized that the ramifications of tropical deforestation will surely extend beyond the tropics. One need only reflect on how tropical deforestation could increase atmospheric CO_2 levels and thereby contribute to global warming, or how forest destruction could decrease biological diversity and thereby impoverish crop-species germplasm banks, to sense everyone's ties to the well-being of tropical lands.

Through all this there is a tendency to consider that the Amazon rain forest has existed in a pristine, cathedral-like state for tens of thousands—or even millions—of years, and that this forest is just now being disturbed for the first time by modern humans' "development" activities. However, natural perturbations (e.g., in the form of flooding, wind storms, fire, etc.) have always been an ecological component of the Amazon Basin.

The study of ecosystem disturbances, both past and present, is very relevant to considerations of Amazon land use because almost all land-use schemes result in disturbance. Indeed, it is the act of forest disturbance that leads to temporarily elevated levels of nutrients and reduced levels of competition that, in turn, make agriculture possible.

In this paper we first illustrate how anthropogenic disturbances differ from natural disturbances in terms of scale, duration, and frequency. Next, we describe the ecological response of Amazonian ecosystems to two common natural disturbances (treefalls and forest fires) and to two important anthropogenic disturbances (short-term farming in small clearings and long-term ranching in large clearings). Specifically, we consider how the study of these disturbances offers guidelines for the management of natural forests, as well as for the wise use of deforested lands. Overall, we aim to provide a conceptual framework for the papers that follow by linking ecological processes in natural and disturbed ecosystems to the broader issues of sustainable land use in Amazonia.

Classifying Disturbances

The natural and anthropogenic disturbances occurring in Amazonia can be classified by scale as follows:

Natural Disturbances

1. Small scale

These are the frequent small-scale (0.01–10 ha) disturbance events, such as treefalls, that have occurred for millennia in Amazonian forests.

2. Large scale

These are the infrequent, but nonetheless significant, large-scale (1–100,000 km²) disturbance events, such as floods or fires, that have occurred throughout Amazon history at intervals of hundreds or perhaps thousands of years.

Anthropogenic Disturbances

1. Small scale

These are the frequent, small-scale (0.1–10 ha) disturbance events, such as slash-and-burn agriculture, that have only become common since humans entered the Amazon landscape several thousand years ago.

2. Large scale

These are the grand (1–100 km²) disturbance events, such as the conversion of forest tracts to pasture, that have only become an ingredient of Amazon disturbance history in this century.

Disturbance Continua

In this classification, we use the word "disturbance" to refer to any event that creates an opening in the forest canopy. For each of our four categories of disturbance, there are several types of events that could lead to canopy openings. For example, small-scale natural canopy openings might result from wind throws, insect-mediated defoliation, or senescence of canopy trees. In a like manner, small-scale anthropogenic canopy openings result from selective logging or slash-and-burn agriculture, but not from the tapping of latex or harvesting of nuts from natural stands of rubber or Brazil nut trees, because these human activities do not lead to canopy openings.

While it is possible to classify disturbances in categories when we discuss causality (natural vs. anthropogenic) or scale (small vs. large), it is also helpful to envision disturbances as falling along continua with respect to scale, duration, and frequency. We place examples of natural and anthropogenic disturbances along such continua in figure 2.1. Considering scale first (figure 2.1A), both natural and anthropogenic disturbances in our small-scale category are usually less than 2 ha in size, whereas the large-scale disturbances are usually >100 ha in size. Of course, there is a middle ground (e.g., a 10 ha pasture clearing or a 10 ha swath of forest toppled in a wind storm). The disturbance-scale continuum (figure 2.1A) accom-

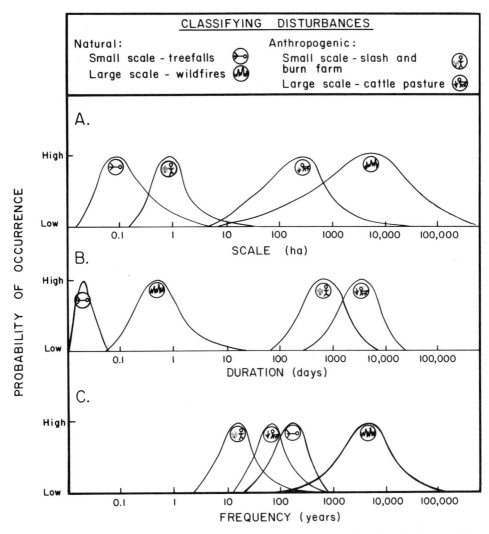

FIGURE 2.1. A classification of both small- and large-scale natural and anthropogenic disturbances with respect to (a) scale; (b) duration; and (c) frequency.

modates this variation by relating the relative probability of occurrence to scale for each of the disturbance types. Disturbances can also be placed along a "duration" continuum (figure 2.1B). Natural disturbances are characteristically short-lived—the disturbance event being measured in seconds, minutes, or days; whereas anthropogenic disturbances usually persist for years. Disturbance return-intervals (frequencies) for a given plot of ground (figure 2.1C) may also differ, with natural disturbances tending to recur on the order of hundreds (treefalls) or thousands (fires) of years and anthropogenic disturbances recurring on the same plot at perhaps 50–200 year intervals.

Disturbance Regimes

We can combine these concepts of disturbance scale, duration, and frequency to envision the "disturbance regime" for a region. The natural disturbance regime will change as climate changes. For example, during the Pleistocene, when Amazonian climate was drier, savanna vegetation occupied large expanses of what is now forest (Van der Hammen 1972). This drier climate probably led to a disturbance regime characterized by frequent fires and severe droughts. When conditions turned wet again, flooding and wind storms may have become elements of the disturbance regime with fire and drought receding in importance. In the more recent past, humans have entered Amazonia, and are adding wholly new elements to the disturbance regime. There were no past disturbances quite like modern-day selective logging, slash-and-burn agriculture, or cattle ranching.

One distinguishing characteristic of these anthropogenic disturbances is the abruptness with which they have become common. In the past, changes in disturbance regimes were probably more gradual, allowing opportunities for species to adapt to changing conditions; now, whole biotas can be imperiled within a few decades, a time period shorter than the life span of many of the resident organisms. A second hallmark of anthropogenic disturbances is their long duration relative to natural disturbances. This allows time for nutrient loss and erosion (i.e., site degradation) to occur. Hence, in the modern era, we are truly witnessing a grand experiment in Amazonia as we unwittingly ask: How much disruption can Amazonian ecosystems withstand before they are irreparably damaged? By considering how Amazon ecosystems respond to both natural and anthropogenic disturbances, we can address this question while providing guidelines for the sustainable use of Amazonian lands.

Plant Succession Following Natural Disturbances

Natural, Small-Scale Disturbance—Treefalls

Research over the last decade has elucidated the dynamic nature of tropical rain forests (reviewed by Whitmore 1983; Brokaw 1985; and Denslow 1987). As an example, in a 1-ha forest plot near San Carlos de Río Negro, in the Amazonian region of Venezuela, mean annual mortality for trees ≥ 10 cm dbh is 1.2 percent and stand half-life (*sensu* Lieberman et al. 1985) is 58 years (Uhl et al. 1988). These results and others like them (Hartshorn 1980; Putz and Milton 1982) illustrate that small-scale natural disturbances are common in tropical forests.

At San Carlos, most tree deaths result in the formation of small (50–100 m^2) canopy gaps. Approximately 4–6 percent of the forest area is usually in this "gapped" condition at any one time. Recently formed light gaps are dominated by tree and liana seedlings, and older gap patches by pole-sized trees. The patch reaches a mature phase when it contains a mix of large trees, poles, and seedlings. It is possible to walk through the Amazon rain forest and detect these young, middle-aged, and mature-phase patches—testimony to past disturbances and to the dynamic nature of tropical forest ecosystems.

Regeneration Pathways. Because treefalls have undoubtedly been the most common type of disturbance throughout Amazon forest history, they have much to teach us about how this ecosystem responds to disturbance. The plants that grow up in treefall gaps or in any other disturbance come from four possible sources. First, the seedlings and saplings present in the forest understory can, if relatively undamaged, quickly gain control of site resources (i.e., the advance-regeneration pathway). In Amazonia, one square meter of forest floor often supports about 10–20 seedlings and small saplings (less than 2 m tall) (Uhl et al. 1988). These seedlings and saplings can persist in the understory for years in a state of arrested development, and they grow rapidly when sunlight becomes available.

A second avenue of plant regeneration is sprouting. The capacity to produce sprouts from stem bases or roots following destruction of aboveground parts is common among Amazonian tree species. Third, plants can recolonize disturbed sites by the germination of seeds buried in the soil. From 200 to 1000 seeds may lie dormant in each square meter of soil in the Amazon forest. Almost all of these seeds are of pioneer tree species (that is, fast-growing, light-demanding species that specialize in taking over disturbed areas) (Uhl and Clark 1983). The fourth mechanism of regeneration is through the arrival of seeds. Seeds of surrounding trees can simply fall into the disturbed area. Seeds of more distant trees can be dispersed by wind, birds, bats, rodents, and other mammals.

Through long-term treefall studies at San Carlos in the Venezuelan Amazon, we have found that the advance regeneration pathway plays the dominant role in treefall gap succession. Four years after gap formation, advance regeneration accounted for more than 95 percent of all trees ≥ 1 m tall in a sample of five treefall gaps. Almost all trees were of primary forest species; pioneer trees comprised only a small fraction of the regrowth. Advance regeneration was also abundant in two other tierra firme forest stands we surveyed in the Brazilian Amazon (Uhl et al. 1988). These results indicate that many Amazonian tree species have a remarkable ability to persist as advance regeneration in a semi-arrested state of development. Height growth is usually only a few centimeters per year for this advance regeneration and leaf retention frequently exceeds 4 years (C. Uhl and K. Clark, unpublished data), but when treefalls occur, growth rates improve dramatically.

Importance of Plant Nutrients. The speed of recovery following a treefall or any other disturbance will depend not only on the presence of colonizing vegetation but also on the availability of resources (i.e., light, water, and nutrients) necessary for plant growth. In the highly weathered soils of Amazonia, nutrient availability frequently limits plant growth.

Studies of treefall gap disturbances have also taught us about the nutrient economy of Amazon ecosystems. Roughly 1–2 percent of total forest nutrient stocks reach the forest floor in treefalls each year. One question that has intrigued us is the effect of this concentration of debris on nutrient loss from these already nutrient-impoverished ecosystems. We created experimental treefall gaps at San Carlos to measure nutrient loss from gaps. Our measurements revealed no improvement in soil fertility nor any substantial increases in nutrient concentration of leachate water in these experimental treefall gaps as compared to forest controls (Uhl et al. 1988). At La Selva, Costa Rica, Parker (1985) also found that nutrient concentrations of leachate water did not differ following forest treefalls compared to undisturbed forest. By inference, we conclude that nutrients released from the decomposition of treefall debris in treefall gaps must move quickly into the extant vegetation.

Overall, it appears that treefall gaps are a rejuvenating disturbance because the light and nutrients critical for plant growth become available through the fall and decomposition of the gap-maker tree(s). A good stock of advance regeneration quickly shoots up and plants arising as sprouts, from seed-bank seeds, or from dispersed seeds fill in any open places. The result is a quick return to forest with very little nutrient loss.

Natural, Large-Scale Disturbance—Fire

In contrast to the frequent and nondisruptive nature of natural, small-scale disturbances (e.g., treefalls), natural, large-scale disturbances are infrequent and potentially very destructive. For example, extensive landslides in mountainous areas of Central America expose the subsoil, resulting in the loss of all local sources of colonizing plants and substantial nutrient export from the ecosystem. Not surprisingly, recovery proceeds slowly. Hurricane damage may also destroy large expanses of tropical forest (e.g., in the Caribbean), but in contrast to landslides, the destroyed vegetation rebounds quickly because of abundant regenerating material (e.g., advance regeneration, sprouts, etc.) and because nutrients are available. In Amazonia, fire has probably been the most important natural, large-scale disturbance over the last several thousand years and we center our discussion on it.

The evidence for past fires comes from the abundance of charcoal in Amazonian soils. In the Upper Río Negro region of the Venezuelan Amazon, charcoal is frequently found in the soils and radiocarbon dating of charcoal from different depths within any one soil profile usually shows that several fires have occurred at that spot during the past 6000 years (Sanford et al. 1985; Saldarriaga 1986). Indeed, the radiocarbon dates correspond roughly with what are believed to have been dry periods (based on palynological evidence) during recent Amazon history (Absy 1982; Markgraf and Bradbury 1982). Amazon researchers from the Empresa Brasileira de Pesquisa Agropecuária (EMBRAPA) and Instituto Nacional de Pesquisas de Amazonia (INPA) in Brazil concur that charcoal is common in the soils of the central and eastern Amazon (pers. comm.). Indeed, in much of Amazonia, it is difficult to find soils that are not studded with charcoal.

Moreover, in the decades ahead, human disturbances will dramatically increase the likelihood of fire in Amazonia through four interrelated phenomena:

1. human activity generally involves fire in one way or another and, thus, ignition potential increases (Uhl and Buschbacher 1985);

2. forest cutting for any purpose leaves slash on the ground and, thus, increases fuel loads (Kauffman, Uhl, and Cummings 1988);

3. opening of the forest canopy, by increasing the amount of radiation reaching the forest floor and decreasing relative humidity, allows fuels to quickly dry to the ignition point (Uhl, Kauffman, and Cummings 1988);

4. deforestation, at the Basinwide level, changes overall climatic patterns—decreasing evapotranspiration, total precipitation, and mean relative humidity—and thereby increases fire likelihood (Dickinson 1987).

Regeneration Pathways. Given the prevalence of fire in Amazon forest history, how does Amazon vegetation respond to fire disturbances? Fires usually kill all the saplings and seedlings (advance regeneration) that are so important in treefall gap succession, but other avenues of regeneration are possible. For example, in studies of forest succession following the cutting and burning of 0.5–1.0-ha plots at San Carlos, Uhl and Jordan (1984) found that vegetation regrowth was vigorous on lightly burned sites, with 10 mt ha^{-1} yr^{-1} of biomass accumulating during the early years of recovery. The regrowth was composed of plants that arose from seeds in the seed bank (the usual case), or as vegetative sprouts (also common), or from seeds dispersed to the site after the fire (occasionally).

More severe fires would result in greater mortality of live trees and seed-bank seeds than that reported by Uhl and Jordan (1984), and, as a result, forest regeneration would be slower and less predictable. Indeed, the possibility of severe fires may already exist in Amazonia. For example, in the Brazilian state of Pará, surface fires, associated with selective logging, leave a high volume of standing dead trunks (i.e., most trees and vines between 1–10 cm dbh are killed in these fires but remain standing; Uhl and Buschbacher 1985), which could promote more severe subsequent fires capable of killing the remaining large canopy trees. Even in the absence of an initial surface fire, we have observed that selective logging encourages the growth of vines. These vines, by providing continuous fuel ladders from ground to canopy, may, likewise, create conditions favorable for more severe forest fires.

Overall, fire appears to be the most important natural, large-scale disturbance in Amazonia. The ability of many rain forest species to rebound following fire, either through sprouting or the buried seed strategy, may be the result of natural selection (i.e., fire may have been a selecting agent for these characteristics). Because of its long history of occurrence, fire should not necessarily be viewed as a dangerous and destructive force. For example, when fires are of low severity they can act as stimulants: both nutrients and plant colonists are readily available and regrowth is vigorous. This more balanced view of fire has become predominant in temperate-zone forest management over the past few decades (Pyne 1984).

Management Guidelines from Studies of Succession Following Natural Disturbances

Treefalls and fires are part of the natural disturbance regime of Amazonia and, probably for this reason, vegetation recovery after these disturbances is quick. To the extent that disturbances provoked by forest exploitation mimic these natural disturbances in size, duration, and frequency, the functional integrity of the ecosystem should be protected.

In many respects timber management via selective logging (e.g., the harvest of only those species with desirable commercial properties) creates disturbances akin to natural treefalls—canopy openings that stimulate the growth of advance regeneration. Foresters recognize the importance of advance regeneration in treefall gap succession and have developed systems of forest management, such as the tropical shelterwood system, explicitly to stimulate the growth of this pool of saplings and seedlings (Pitt 1960; Baur 1964; Carvalho et al. 1984; Jonkers and Schmidt 1984; de Graaf 1986).

However, these systems of natural forest management have not always been successful. Failures result from a combination of factors. First, while advance regeneration may be abundant, desirable species may not predominate. Second, unless great care is exercised in harvesting, damage to advance regeneration and to the residual canopy trees can be considerable. For example, in a preliminary study of seven hectares of selectively logged forest in the eastern Amazon, we found that, although only 1 percent of the trees greater than 10 cm diameter were harvested, 11 percent were uprooted by bulldozers (in the establishment of logging roads and trails), 12 percent were crushed by the fall of harvested trees, and 3 percent suffered extensive bark removal (Uhl and Vieira, unpublished data). Additional harmful effects may not become apparent until several years after logging—as forest structure begins to deteriorate. Trees that were scraped and wounded during logging sometimes succumb to pathogen attack. Other trees that no longer have neighbors to shelter them are prone to windthrow. Those canopy trees that survive often become overgrown with vines. While this scenario may not typify all sites, it does describe the process of stand degradation that occurs following the careless practices that occur in the eastern Amazon. In short, while the management of natural forest stands is possible using the gap-succession model, selective logging *per se* does not necessarily mimic the natural treefall disturbance regime. Rather, considerable care must be exercised in tree selection and extraction procedures if natural forest management is to succeed.

Our research on forest regeneration following fire suggests that intensive methods of Amazon forest management might be appropriate under some circumstances. For example, where the expertise to manage the natural forest does not exist, it may make more sense to cut the residual stand (after selective logging) and then lightly burn the site (e.g., after a 2- to 3-day rainless period). Such a treatment would result in an even-aged stand of vigorously growing pioneer trees of perhaps 10–20 species such as *Bagassa guianensis* Aubl., *Didymopanax morototoni* (Aubl.) Decne. et Planch., and *Goupia glabra* Aubl. These and other pioneer species tend to have good form and sawing properties. Moreover, stands of species with similar wood properties (e.g., wood specific gravity of this pioneer group is usually between 0.45 and 0.65) are well suited for chipping operations, an important attribute since wood products of the future will increasingly be made from pressed wood chips. Such an approach to forestry, using insights from natural forest succession following fire disturbances, merits further study.

In the essays that follow on natural forest management (papers 3–8), the authors provide examples of research illustrating that the management of natural forests is, indeed, a viable alternative to deforestation.

Plant Succession Following Anthropogenic Disturbances

Anthropogenic, Small-Scale Disturbance—Shifting Cultivation

Humans cause small-scale disturbances (i.e., canopy openings) by either cutting individual trees for fiber needs or cutting and burning small patches of forest to make farm clearings. We will focus here on the disturbance of slash-and-burn agriculture. Until recently, no other human activity affected more land in Amazonia or was more critical to human well-being than slash-and-burn agriculture.

The essential characteristics of shifting cultivation are that an area of forest is cut and burned and used to grow subsistence crops such as cassava, plantains, corn, rice, beans, and fruits for several years without tilling the soil. Two or sometimes three crops are produced on a site before it is abandoned. While the site is being actively farmed, it must be weeded two to three times a year to prevent second-growth vegetation from taking over.

Forests regrow on abandoned Amazon farms only because the resident flora has (1) regeneration mechanisms that ensure that its germplasm will be present, and (2) growth requirements that can be satisfied by the low-nutrient soils characteristic of abandoned farms.

Regeneration Pathways. To assess the effects of slash-and-burn agriculture on the regeneration mechanisms of the resident flora, it is helpful to consider this type of farming as a series of disturbances. Each stage—cutting, burning, and weeding—has distinct effects on the regeneration mechanisms of plant species. The drastic increase in irradiance reaching the ground after felling can cause the death of advance regeneration. The effects of burning on regeneration mechanisms are even more dramatic. Above-ground temperatures during fires may exceed 590° C and soil temperature at 1 cm depth may exceed 170° C (Uhl et al. 1981). Many of the shoots that have sprouted from tree stumps before burning are killed by fires and few of these reappear. Moreover, high burn temperatures reduce the soil seed bank.

Despite the adverse effects of cutting and burning, the natural vegetation does not lose all its ability to recover. Succession begins and is curtailed through farm-plot weeding many times before farms are abandoned. These repeated weedings cause striking shifts in the composition of the regrowth (Uhl et al. 1982). Most notably, the number of woody pioneer species declines after each weeding while the density of herbs increases. Forbs and grasses are able to germinate, flower, and set seed in the interval between weedings and, therefore, can build up high densities and large seed banks. In contrast, the woody pioneer species, which establish from the seeds surviving the burn, are weeded from the site before they have time to produce seeds locally.

Since cutting, burning, and weeding greatly diminish on-site mechanisms of regeneration, the principal way for woody species to reestablish is by seed dispersal. Because slash-and-burn clearings are small (usually ≤1 ha), seed dispersal distances are short. Our experiments on one abandoned farm revealed that, after one year of succession, areas in the shade of isolated fruit trees or under slash had significantly more woody colonizers than did more open areas (Uhl 1987). The relatively high densities of colonizing trees under fruit trees and slash may be due, in part, to differential seed dispersal. Higher numbers of seeds (from the native flora) are found in the soil under cultivated fruit trees, presumably because bats and birds are attracted and defecate seeds there (Uhl et al. 1982). Once the seeds germinate, shade may protect seedlings from direct heating, and leaf and branch litter may provide nutrients.

Availability of Plant Nutrients. The most likely cause of declining crop productivity as Amazon farms age is nutrient limitation. Soil nutrient concentrations at farm abandonment in our Río Negro work and in other studies have usually declined to the low values typical of mature forest (Nye and Greenland 1964; Denevan 1971; Harris 1971; Scott 1974; Uhl, Jordan, and Montagnini 1983). Successional vegetation thrives on sites where crop plants can no longer grow, because, relative to crops, many successional species: 1) allocate more energy to root production; 2) take up nutrients even when soil-solution nutrient concentrations are very low; and 3) use nutrients efficiently (e.g. produce long-lived, insect-resistant leaves that have relatively low concentrations of nutrients; Uhl 1987).

Long-Term Succession. Surveys of abandoned farm sites of different ages in the Upper Río Negro region are enabling us to put together a picture of the entire succession from farm to forest. When farm sites are abandoned, they are first dominated by grasses and herbs, but within a year trees become common. Almost all the trees present on recently abandoned farm sites are pioneer species. These trees begin to die after about ten years and are gradually replaced by a somewhat slower growing, more long-lived grouping of tree species. This second cohort of species lives for about 50–100 years, gradually yielding to the final residents, a group of shade-tolerant, slow-growing species. Saldarriaga (1986) estimated that 200 or more years are required for a farm site to pass through these successional stages and be considered as full-grown, mature forest. Of course, most abandoned farms are cut long before they reach mature forest status (see Fearnside, this volume).

While slash-burn agriculture does dramatically alter site structure, ecosystem function does not appear to be severely disrupted during the recovery phase. Productivity is probably the best integrator of ecosystem function, and above-ground production is equal or somewhat greater on regenerating farms, at least during the early years of succession, as compared to mature forests (Uhl 1987).

Management Guidelines from Studies of Farm Succession

Research on how tropical forests develop on abandoned farm sites can aid in the design of ecologically sustainable uses of rain forest lands for human ends. One possible approach would be to design a sustained-yield agroecosystem modeled after successional processes (i.e., to mimic the natural process of succession by substituting plants useful to humans at each stage). This natural succession-mimic approach is practiced by farmers of Japanese descent who have been slowly immigrating to Amazonia since the 1920s (see Subler and Uhl, this volume).

The present-day Japanese-settler agroecosystems are remarkably complex, incorporating annual crops, perennial tree crops, and perennial vine crops. The perennial and annual crops are planted together after forest clearing. Gradually, farms develop into mixed-perennial polycultures. The overstories are dominated by rubber, mango, Brazil nut, andiroba, and other lesser known species valued for their timber and/or fruit. The understories are composed of shade-tolerant trees such as coffee, cacao, guaraná, and cupuaçu. Vines of vanilla and other species move from understory to canopy adding still more complexity. These agroecosystems often incorporate fish culture and chicken and hog production. There is a high level of horizontal integration with waste or refuse from one operation forming a subsidy (fertilizer, mulch, food) for other operations.

Overall, this approach offers promise because it can reduce many of the problems that plague annual cropping systems (e.g., pests, weeds, loss of nutrients). Tree crops protect the soil from degradation caused by leaching, erosion, and compaction, and they frequently have a higher tolerance to soil acidity and aluminum toxicity than annual crops. They also make relatively low demands on soil nutrients because of efficient nutrient recycling, and because the mass of harvested products is low. Indeed, critical to the success of these systems is their choice of products that have very high commercial value per unit of harvested mass. Finally, this approach is labor-, rather than energy-intensive, an important consideration in a region scarce in economic resources.

The recognition that the natural process of plant succession can provide a model for the design of sustainable agricultural systems and that there are already working examples of such systems is encouraging. Indeed, a whole research agenda is now emerging (see papers 9–11, this volume) aimed at orchestrating plant succession through the design of agroforestry systems.

Anthropogenic, Large-Scale Disturbance—Pasture

During the last century, and particularly within the last twenty years, large areas of the Amazon Basin have been converted to pasture. Toledo and Serrão (1982) estimated that about six million ha of Amazonian land are in pasture, and by the close of the 1980s, this figure could easily exceed ten million hectares. Planners had hoped that Amazon pastures would have sustained yield, but generally, these cleared lands have been productive for only four to eight years before they have had to be abandoned. Hence, there are now millions of hectares of abandoned pastures in Amazonia.

Regeneration Pathways. Will forest species regrow on abandoned Amazon pastures and, if so, at what rate? We addressed this question by studying vegetation composition, structure, and biomass accumulation on thirteen forest sites that had been cut and burned, used as pasture, and then abandoned in the eastern

Amazon near the town of Paragominas in the Brazilian state of Pará (Uhl, Busch-bacher, and Serrão 1988).

The study sites were classified by past history into three use-intensity classes: 1) light use—sites with poor grass establishment, light grazing, and short-use pe-riod (typical of perhaps 20 percent of the region's pastures); 2) moderate use—sites with good grass establishment, regular grazing, frequent weeding, and final abandonment after 6–10 years (typical of maybe 70 percent of the region's pas-tures); and 3) heavy use—sites with good grass establishment, regular grazing, weed control through mowing and/or herbiciding, and final abandonment after 12–20 years (typical of 10 percent or less of the region's pastures).

Abandoned pastures subjected to light use (four study sites) exhibited vigor-ous forest regeneration. Aboveground biomass accumulation averaged 10 t ha^{-1} yr^{-1} or 80 t after eight years (roughly one-third of mature forest biomass levels). Tree species richness was also high: approximately 20 tree species were present per 100 m^2 with many individuals originating via sprouting. Abandoned pastures subjected to moderate use (six study sites) were also developing forest character-istics but biomass accumulation was only 5 t ha^{-1} yr^{-1} (one-half the rate for the light-use sites). Individuals arose via sprouting, from seed bank seeds, or dispersed seeds, but tree species richness was also lower than on light-use sites and the number of forest trees was less. Abandoned pastures subjected to heavy use (3 sites) had the least distinct patterns of succession. The single eight-year-old site was dominated by grasses and forbs with fewer than one tree per 100 m^2 and an aboveground biomass accumulation of 0.6 t ha^{-1} yr^{-1}, a value only about 6 percent of that found on light-use sites. Most colonizing plants established via dispersed seeds.

Overall, our results show that Amazon ecosystems generally can recover for-est structure after large-scale pasture disturbances. Only in cases where the land has been used very abusively for long periods is reforestation uncertain, but prob-ably less than 10 percent of the pasture land in the eastern Amazon has degraded to this level at present. However, as pressure on Amazonian lands continues, non-regenerating sites are certain to become more common.

Impediments to Forest Regeneration on Nonregenerating Pastures. It is clearly important that we understand the factors that restrict forest regeneration in highly disturbed Amazon landscapes if we are to: 1) predict the capacity of other Amazon ecosystems to recover from severe disturbances, and 2) develop techniques to pro-mote recovery of degraded Amazonian ecosystems. We are currently addressing this topic by examining the obstacles to forest tree establishment in an abandoned pasture with a history of "heavy-use" near Paragominas, Pará, Brazil.

Our data (see Nepstad, Uhl, and Serrão, this volume) show that forest trees have difficulty establishing in highly degraded pastures because of: 1) low dis-persal of forest tree seeds into pasture environments; 2) high predation on the seeds that do arrive; and 3) high mortality of seedlings due to competition with the existing herbaceous vegetation for light and water.

Management Guidelines from Studies of Pasture Succession

The results of our basic studies provide guidelines for reforestation of degraded pastures. For example, by coupling precise descriptions of pasture environments (in terms of barriers to tree species dispersal, germination, and establishment) with a knowledge of tree morphology and physiology, tree species can be selected for introduction into degraded pastures based on characteristics such as dispersibility, distastefulness to predators, capacity to penetrate compacted soil horizons, drought tolerance, and competitive ability.

Overall, our results reveal that survival and growth are extremely low in small-seeded, colonizing species—the group most readily dispersed to degraded pastures. These pioneer-type species lack the endosperm reserves to get their stems above the matrix of competing herbaceous vegetation and their roots below the drought-plagued surface soil. To ensure establishment, they must be protected from predators and pampered through their first year of life by providing shade and water and removing competitors. Other species require less vigilance. Tough coated, large-seeded species sometimes establish because they are too big for seed predators to handle and because their ample endosperm gives them the reserves needed to grow large enough to effectively compete with the existing herbaceous vegetation.

Hence, the critical first step in forest restoration will be to foster the establishment of predator-resistant, stress-tolerant tree species. Deep-rooted species that are able to extract water and nutrients from the lower soil horizons would be particularly appropriate. Once a few scattered trees are present in these pastures, subsequent phases of forest development may occur naturally because isolated trees attract bird and bat seed vectors and provide favorable establishment microsites.

A thorough treatment of the questions and approaches in restoration ecology is provided in subsequent essays (see papers 12–14, this volume).

Conclusions

Earlier we posed the question: How much disruption can Amazonian ecosystems withstand before they are irreparably damaged? We conclude that these ecosystems are not defenseless. The resident species have many responses to disturbance including the ability to persist as advance regeneration or as buried seed, the capacity to sprout following stem damage, and the ability to disperse their seeds throughout the landscape via animal vectors. As disturbances become larger and more prolonged, soil nutrient impoverishment occurs (figure 2.2A) and these regeneration strategies are slowly eliminated (figure 2.2B). Because natural disturbances are either small-scale or short-lived (or both), postdisturbance regeneration is rapid (figure 2.2C). However, recovery following anthropogenic disturbances tends to be slow (e.g., slash-and-burn agriculture) or in some cases uncertain (e.g., abandoned pastures after heavy use).

Our four-part classification of Amazon disturbance types and responses is also useful when considering alternatives to Amazon deforestation (figure 2.3). Our treefall studies demonstrate the dominant role played by advance regeneration and the nutrient retentiveness of Amazonian forests following natural, small-scale disturbances. Our fire studies (natural, large-scale disturbance) reveal that, while natural forest fires are rare at present, historically fire has been a common feature of the Amazonian disturbance regime and that increased human disturbances are now dramatically increasing the likelihood of fire in Amazonia. Our slash-and-burn studies (anthropogenic, small-scale disturbance) reveal that successional species can thrive on lands that will no longer support crops because these species are less demanding of nutrients, but that the recovery process back to forest takes

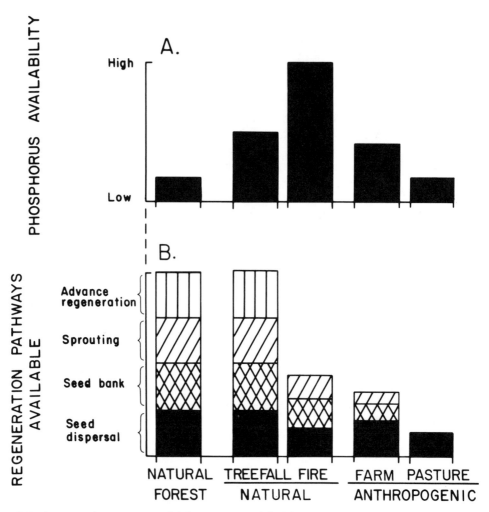

FIGURE 2.2. A) Nutrient availability, as exemplified by phosphorus, is elevated after natural disturbances but can decline to the low levels characteristic of native forest, as in the case of prolonged anthropogenic disturbances (e.g., cattle pastures). B) As disturbances increase in size and/or intensity, mechanisms of natural regeneration are gradually lost. In

a hundred years or more (and millennia may be required to reestablish the original predisturbance complement of plant and animal species). Our pasture studies (anthropogenic, large-scale disturbance) reveal that excessively abused Amazonian lands sometimes form semistable shrublands not only because of nutrient impoverishment, but also because seed paucity, seed and seedling predation, and drought stress retard tree establishment.

At the applied level, each of these disturbance vignettes has management implications (figure 2.3). First, treefalls and fires are part of the natural disturbance regime of Amazonia, and probably for this reason, vegetation recovery after these disturbances is quick. It follows that forestry operations that mimic these natural disturbances in size, duration, and frequency should protect the functional integrity of Amazon ecosystems (see papers 3–8, this volume). The applied side of our farm succession research is in the development of agroforestry systems based on

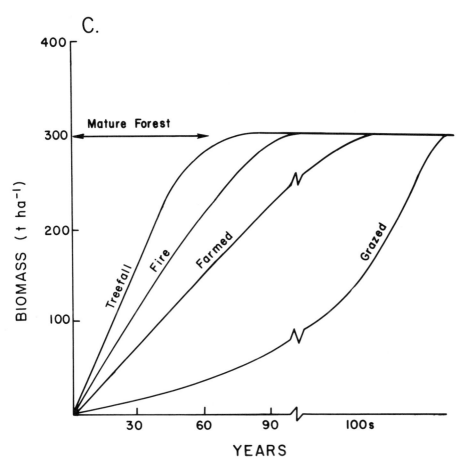

the most severe case, the only hope for tree establishment is by long-distance dispersal of seeds. C) Both the availability of nutrients and regeneration mechanisms influence the speed of forest regeneration after disturbed sites are abandoned. Recovery is relatively rapid following natural disturbances as compared with anthropogenic disturbances.

NATURAL DISTURBANCES

Small Scale (e.g., Treefalls)

Observations:
   —a good stock of suppressed advance regeneration is available to ensure both quick regrowth and high nutrient retention after natural treefalls.

Management implications:
   —careful natural forest management using the gap-succession model, with advance regeneration capitalizing on resources made available in small-scale disturbances, will ensure the health and vigor of forest ecosystems.

Large Scale (e.g., Wildfires)

Observations:
   —fire has been a part of the Amazon disturbance regime for millennia.
   —regeneration following low intensity fires is rapid because of high nutrient availability and vigorous resprouting.

Management implications:
   —indiscriminate use of fire will lead to gradual deterioration of Amazonian ecosystems.
   —properly timed, low-intensity fires could lead to rapid development of even-aged forest stands.

SUSTAINABLE ALTERNATIVES TO DEFORESTATION

Small Scale (e.g., Shifting Cultivation)

Observations:
   —native species can thrive on lands that no longer support crops because these wild species are well adapted for nutrient uptake and retention under low nutrient conditions.

Management implications:
   —natural plant succession following farming can provide a model for the design of sustainable agricultural systems (e.g., agroforestry) that retain nutrients and protect fragile soils while providing steady yields.

Large Scale (e.g., Pastures)

Observations:
   —on highly disturbed Amazonian sites, forest regeneration is uncertain because of biotic limitations, such as lack of seed dispersal and seed and seedling predation, and abiotic limitations, such as drought stress.

Management implications:
   —by first determining the ecological limitations to forest regeneration on degraded lands, natural resource managers will be in a position to develop high-information, low-cost restoration strategies that overcome regeneration barriers.

ANTHROPOGENIC DISTURBANCES

FIGURE 2.3. A summary of guidelines for substainable land-use emerging from studies of both small- and large-scale natural and anthropogenic disturbances in the Amazon Basin.

natural succession models that retain nutrients and protect fragile soils while providing steady yields (see papers 9–11, this volume). Finally, the pasture research prompts us to contemplate the emergence of a synthetic discipline: restoration ecology. Degraded lands can be revived with human assistance but, to be successful, we need to become students of the ecology of degraded lands. Only when we understand how these new ecosystems function will we know how to remold them into forest (see papers 12–14, this volume).

REFERENCES

Absy, M. L. 1982. Quaternary palynological studies in the Amazon Basin. In G. T. Prance, ed., *Biological Diversification in the Tropics.* New York: Columbia University Press.

Baur, G. N. 1964. The ecological basis of rainforest management. Sydney, Australia: Forestry Commission of New South Wales.

Brokaw, N. V. L. 1985. Treefalls, regrowth, and community structure in tropical forests. In S. T. A. Pickett and P. S. White, eds., *The Ecology of Natural Disturbance and Patch Dynamics.* New York: Academic Press.

Carvalho, J. O. P. de, J. N. M. Silva, J. do C. A. Lopes, and H. B. da Costa. 1984. Manejo de florestas naturais do tropico úmido com referência especial à Floresta Nacional do Tapajós no Estado do Pará. EMBRAPA-CPATU *Documentos*, 26, Belém.

Denevan, W. M. 1971. Campa subsistence in the Gran Pajonal, Eastern Peru. *Geographical Review* 61:496–518.

Denslow, J. S. 1987. Tropical rainforest gaps and tree species diversity. *Annual Review of Ecology and Systematics* 18:431–451.

Dickinson, R. E. 1987. Introduction to vegetation and climate interactions in the humid tropics. In R. E. Dickinson, ed., *The Geophysiology of Amazonia.* New York: Wiley.

Graaf, N. R. de. 1986. *A Silvicultural System for Natural Regeneration of Tropical Rain Forest in Suriname.* Wageningen, The Netherlands: Agricultural University.

Harris, D. R. 1971. The ecology of Swiden cultivation in the upper Orinoco rain forest, Venezuela. *Geographical Review* 61:475–495.

Hartshorn, G. S. 1980. Neotropical forest dynamics. *Biotropica* 12, Supplement, 23–30.

Jonkers, W. B. J. and P. Schmidt. 1984. Ecology and timber production in tropical rainforest in Suriname. *Interciencia* 5:290–297.

Kauffman, J. B., C. Uhl, and D. L. Cummings. 1988. Fire in the Venezuelan Amazon 1: Fuel biomass and fire chemistry in the evergreen rainforest of Venezuela. *Oikos* 53:167–175.

Lieberman, D., M. Lieberman, R. Peralta, and G. S. Hartshorn. 1985. Mortality patterns and stand turnover rates in a wet tropical forest in Costa Rica. *Journal of Ecology* 73:915–924.

Markgraf, V. and J. P. Bradbury. 1982. Holocene climatic history of South America. *Striae* 16:40–45.

Nye, P. H. and D. J. Greenland. 1964. Changes in the soil after clearing tropical forest. *Plant and Soil* 21:101–112.

Parker, G. 1985. The effect of disturbance on water and solute budgets of hill-slope tropical rainforests in northeastern Costa Rica. Ph.D. Thesis, University of Georgia at Athens.

Pitt, C. J. W. 1960. Report to the government of Brazil on the application of silvicultural methods to some of the forests of the Amazon. FAO/ETAP Report 1337.

Putz, F. E. and K. Milton. 1982. Tree mortality rates on Barro Colorado Island. In E. G. Leigh, A. S. Rand, and D. M. Windsor, eds., *The Ecology of a Tropical Forest: Seasonal Rhythms and Long-Term Changes.* Washington, DC: Smithsonian Institution Press.

Pyne, S. J. 1984. *Introduction to Wildland Fire: Fire Management in the United States.* New York: Wiley.

Saldarriaga, J. G. 1986. Forest succession in the Upper Río Negro of Columbia and Venezuela. Ph.D. Thesis, University of Tennessee at Knoxville.

Sanford, R. L., Jr., J. Saldarriaga, K. Clark, C. Uhl, and R. Herrera. 1985. Amazon rain-forest fires. *Science* 227:53–55.

Scott, G. A. J. 1974. Effects of shifting cultivation in the Gran Pajonal, Eastern Peru. *Proceedings of the Association of American Geographers* 6:58–61.

Toledo, J. M. and E. A. S. Serrão. 1982. Pasture and animal production in Amazonia. In S. B. Hecht, ed., *Amazonia: Agriculture and Land-Use Research.* Cali, Colombia: Centro Internacional de Agricultura Tropical (CIAT).

Uhl, C. 1987. Factors controlling succession following slash-and-burn agriculture in Amazonia. *Journal of Ecology* 75:377–407.

Uhl, C. and R. Buschbacher. 1985. A disturbing synergism between cattle ranch burning practices and selective tree harvesting in the eastern Amazon. *Biotropica* 17:265–268.

Uhl, C., R. Buschbacher and E. A. S. Serrão. 1988. Abandoned pastures in eastern Amazonia. I. Patterns of plant succession. *Journal of Ecology* 76:663–681.

Uhl, C. and K. Clark. 1983. Seed ecology of selected Amazon Basin successional species. *Botanical Gazette* 144:419–425.

Uhl, C., H. Clark, K. Clark, and P. Maquirino. 1982. Successional patterns associated with slash-and-burn agriculture in the Upper Río Negro region of the Amazon Basin. *Biotropica* 14:249–254.

Uhl, C., K. Clark, H. Clark, and P. Murphy. 1981. Early plant succession after cutting and burning in the Upper Río Negro region of the Amazon Basin. *Journal of Ecology* 69:631–649.

Uhl, C., K. Clark, N. Dezzeo, and P. Maquirino. 1988. Vegetation dynamics in Amazonian treefall gaps. *Ecology* 69:751–763.

Uhl, C. and C. F. Jordan. 1984. Succession and nutrient dynamics following forest cutting and burning in Amazonia. *Ecology* 65:1476–1490.

Uhl, C., C. F. Jordan, and F. Montagnini. 1983. Traditional and innovative approaches to agriculture on Amazon Basin tierra firme soils. In R. Lowrance, R. Todd, L. Asmussen and R. Leonard, eds., *Nutrient Cycling in Agricultural Ecosystems.* Special Publication 23. University of Georgia at Athens, College of Agriculture Experimental Station.

Uhl, C., J. B. Kauffman, and D. L. Cummings. 1988. Fire in the Venezuelan Amazon 2: Environmental conditions necessary for forest fires in the evergreen rainforest of Venezuela. *Oikos* 53:176–184.

Van der Hammen, T. 1972. Changes in vegetation and climate in the Amazon Basin and surrounding areas during the Pleistocene. *Geol. en Mijnbouw.* 51:641–643.

Wadsworth, F. H. 1987. Applicability of Asian and African silviculture systems to naturally regenerated forests of the Neotropics. In F. Mergen and J. R. Vincent, eds., *Natural Management of Tropical Moist Forests.* New Haven CT: Yale University.

Whitmore, T. C. 1983. Secondary succession from seed in tropical rain forests. *Forestry Abstracts* 44:767–779.

2
NATURAL FOREST MANAGEMENT

2. Natural Forest Management.—The so-called *buriti* palm (*Mauritia flexuosa* L. f.) flourishes in freshwater swamps, forming extremely dense stands that can extend over hundreds of square kilometers. In the Amazon estuary, natural stands of *buriti* are managed for production of edible fruits and fibers, and they provide shade and organic material for understory plantations of cacau.

3

Traditional Management of Tropical Forests in Mexico

■

ARTURO GÓMEZ-POMPA

ANDREA KAUS

ABSTRACT

Some outstanding characteristics of the tropical forests of Mexico are discussed in relation to the impact of modern and ancient societies. It is noted that before the European conquest the forests coexisted for millennia with civilizations of high population densities without a known loss of biological diversity. Traditional farmers are still using techniques today that hold great potential for future forest management, such as the management of fallow succession, the use of trees in kitchen gardens, agroforestry systems, and the setting aside of special areas of semimanaged forest. These techniques are discussed separately, but we believe that in the past they were an integral part of forest management systems for entire regions. Results from a survey show that the same or closely related species are used or managed by traditional groups in other tropical regions of the world. Integrating our modern knowledge with that of present-day traditional farmers who still use these techniques can provide alternatives for the wiser management of tropical resources.

Tropical deforestation leads to loss of forest resources, reduction of biological diversity, and impoverishment of rural people. Throughout most of the American tropics deforestation is associated with a pervasive cycle of initial timber extraction followed by shifting cultivation, land acquisition, and subsequent conversion to pasture (Nations and Nigh 1978; Partridge 1984). Unfortunately, it is the poor landless farmers, with their techniques of shifting cultivation, who are frequently blamed for deforestation, when in fact they are only the visible agents of a much deeper problem.

In tropical areas of Mexico, the root causes of deforestation are not population growth or shifting cultivation; archaeological evidence and the current composition of mature forests suggest that numerous regions once supported dense human populations without known detrimental impact on forest ecosystems. Instead, tropical deforestation in Mexico is due to neglect of traditional people's vast experience with resource management. Failure to consult this untapped "library" has resulted in policies allowing timber extraction, settlement by landless farmers from other regions, and conversion of formerly forested lands to pastures. One alternative to deforestation involves learning traditional methods that permit simultaneous use and management of tropical forests.

Historical Evidence of Tropical Forest Management

Since colonial times, human disturbance in tropical forests has been a well-established fact (Parsons 1975). Yet archaeological evidence points to interactions between humans and forests that extend far into the past. In some tropical regions, population densities were actually higher in the past than they are today (Meggers 1971; Bennett 1975b; Parsons 1975). Denevan (1976) cites estimates of dense populations in Central America before or at the time of European contact, including one estimate by H. O. Wagner of 8 million inhabitants in the Yucatán, and his own estimate of 1.2 million for eastern Peru and northeastern Bolivia and 6.8 million for greater Amazonia.

Recent studies show the existence of some ancient civilizations in Mexico with high population densities that were integrated with the forest ecosystems. Examples can be found in the Olmec and the Maya civilizations of southeastern Mexico. Both cultures developed in the tropical high forest environments of southern Mexico and Central America and occupied that region for a combined period of at least 3000 years, reaching peak population densities of 400–500 people per km^2 in rural areas (Turner 1976).

Similar to the rise and fall of many other cultures throughout the world, these civilizations had fluctuations in population and power. The Olmec thrived in the tropical lowlands on the coast of the Gulf of Mexico for at least 1000 years before disappearing mysteriously almost 2000 years ago (Soustelle 1984). They were then replaced by the Maya, who took over as a dominant culture in similar environments during a period from A.D. 300 to 900. During this period, according to Coe (1984:61), they "reached intellectual and artistic heights which no others in the New World, and few in the Old, could match at that time." This was followed by a well-known collapse of the urban centers, a subsequent recovery, and then another population collapse from disease and war during the European conquest. The population density in the rural Maya area today is only about 5 people per km^2, but evidence for the much higher density of the old civilization is pervasive. Hardly any region exists without archaeological remains in the lowland tropics of Mesoamerica.

These findings indicate that extensive areas of tropical forests which our own civilization has cut in the last fifty years were not untouched environments but the result of the last cycle of abandonment. The effect of past civilizations on the structure and composition of today's forests is more than just an intriguing question: it is important to the current concern over deforestation. Even with modern-day scientific knowledge, our generation has failed to maintain the tropical biological diversity left us by previous generations. The persistence of forest resources and ecosystems following widespread human intervention indicates that a knowledge of the management techniques practiced by ancient civilizations could help in reverting current processes of landscape degradation in the tropics.

Traditional Farmers and Forest Management Techniques

Traditional farmers are, by definition here, those agriculturalists that have lived in the same region for generations. They are recipients of a long heritage based on an extended interaction with the local environment, and they have thus accumulated considerable knowledge concerning the environment and available natural resources. Although farmers within a traditional community may share a common "knowledge set" about the environment, it is important to understand that all farmers are individuals who make decisions based on trial and error. Each farmer also possesses a unique set of information obtained from other people in both verbal and written form that supplements the shared cultural knowledge of the community. That is, each small set of individual knowledge may be added, in part, to the general knowledge of the community, building a cumulative set of ideas and techniques that have withstood the test of time. In communities of great age, the result is a variance in agricultural techniques by individual farmers, built on a common "library" of shared cultural knowledge. It is this library, the decisions made from it, and the long-term effect on the environment that interest us here.

The successes and failures of traditional farmers can be used as the experimental fieldwork of folk "scientists." Their experimental results are living agroecosystems, where success is measured by the ability to sustain the biodiversity and productivity of the land over time. At present, Mexico has several million farmers who belong to over fifty ethnic groups, all of which still speak their own languages and practice many ancient traditions that persist despite efforts to "modernize" rural Mexico. It is a challenge to the scientific community in the natural and social sciences to evaluate the land-use history and processes of these people in the context of modern science. They deserve serious consideration, not as curious techniques of "primitive" people, but as an enormous source of unwritten knowledge that should be integrated into our universal cultural heritage.

With these ideas in mind we will review some traditional management techniques of forest resources in tropical Mexico and discuss their implications for enhancing forest conservation and management.

Shifting Agriculture

This system of agriculture is practiced by many farmers in tropical Mexico. The basic sequence involves cutting down the large trees in a given area, slashing the small trees and shrubs, burning the resultant slash, cultivating the cleared area for a few years, and, as crop productivity declines, moving on to another location to repeat the process. The abandoned area is then left fallow for a variable period of years, depending on the region or specific system, after which the farmer may return to the same spot and begin again. This is a well-known system of many agriculturalists in tropical areas and good general descriptions and documentations of its variability are available (Conklin 1954; Hernández-Xolocotzi 1959; Remakrishnan 1984).

An important part of the system as it relates to forest management is that, if given a choice, farmers generally prefer secondary to primary forests. Even in areas where mature forests are available, a preference for secondary forests can be observed (Nations and Nigh 1978). This is logical as it is easier to cut and slash a secondary forest than a mature forest. In addition, a choice of secondary over primary forest does not necessarily result in a loss of productivity. Many secondary tropical forests of ten or more years have already recovered their nutrient stocks (Jordan and Kline 1972), and the seed bank for weeds may also be considerably reduced.

Some traditional shifting cultivators in Mexico practice several techniques specifically related to trees. When cutting forests they leave some useful trees standing (Edwards 1986), which provide a variety of uses depending on the individual perceptions and needs of the farmers who decide to spare them. These uses may include edible fruits, seeds, or leaves; medicine; construction; nectar production; soil improvement; religion; ornamentation; or shade, among others (Illsley 1984; Alcorn 1987). In addition, relic trees play a very important role in the regeneration process during the fallow period. The local authorities of some Maya communities even reinforce the social and biological value of many trees by prohibiting the cutting of economically useful species such as *Brosimum alicastrum* Sw., *Talisia olivaeformis* Radlk., *Sabal* spp., *Achras sapota* L., *Malphigia glabra* L., and *Acrocomia mexicana* Karw. ex Mart. (Illsley 1984).

The trees spared from cutting in the shifting cultivation plot ("milpa") must also be able to survive subsequent agricultural practices, especially burning. In many cases the fire may go to the crown of selected trees and burn them completely. Yet many tree species survive burning and provide important resources during the subsequent fallow (see Dubois, this volume). Coppicing is common in fire-tolerant tree species, and local farmers frequently make use of this characteristic. When they slash, farmers leave stumps of many species that may serve as support for cultivated vine-beans or for accelerating forest fallow succession. In addition, since they sprout from the base, the aerial portion of the stumps may be cut for firewood purposes.

In some cases, plantations of trees are mixed with understory crops. In other cases, seeds of trees present in the soil or dispersed from adjacent forests or agroecosystems may germinate in the milpa and be protected. These include fruit trees (e.g., oranges or different species of "sapotes"), timber trees (e.g., *Cedrela*), or cash crops (e.g., legume trees shading coffee plantations).

The application of fallow management techniques may seem simple, but in practice it is not. Unpredictable events can occur such as hurricanes, diseases, escaped fires, or invasions by aggressive weeds that take over the fallow succession. The "ideal" managed fallow containing only useful species may never occur. However, as demonstrated by traditional farmers, it is possible to manipulate succession at least partially, and traditional farmers have learned from long experience that any approximation to a managed succession is better than none at all.

The possibility of fallow management is one of the most promising alternatives for biological conservation and reforestation in the tropics (Ewel 1979; Hart 1980; Amo 1984). Yet there is currently little research on this topic. One of the most difficult constraints is the high biological diversity characteristic of traditional agroecosystems in the tropics. However, the rewards and potentials for this type of research are high, as it represents a potentially sustainable system already practiced by millions of agriculturalists around the world.

Forest Gardens

There is increasing evidence that during prehispanic times, cultivation and management of native trees were common land-use practices among the cultures that flourished in the lowland tropics of Mexico (Puleston 1968; Wilkerson 1983; Alcorn 1984; Dahlin 1985; Medellin-Morales 1986; Gómez-Pompa 1987a). Many early chroniclers marvelled at the cultivation of trees by indigenous peoples. In 1588, Landa described in his "Relaciones" many useful species of trees that were cultivated ("criados"), exclaiming that "they have so many kinds of trees for all services and uses that it is frightening (y tienen otros tantos arboles y de todo servicio y provecho, que espanta)" (Landa 1984). In fact, the Maya may have had extensive areas of managed forests from which they derived basic subsistence products (Gómez-Pompa 1987a). This is attested by the important work by Puleston (1968) regarding the "ramón" tree as a basic subsistence food of the Maya and the newer contribution of Peters (1983) on the ecology of "ramón."

From the practices of traditional farmers who still cultivate and manage native trees in forest gardens within tropical Mexico today, we are deducing the past practices of the ancient Maya and interpreting their effects on present-day forest composition. The term "forest gardens" ("selvas-huertos") is used here to refer to managed forest communities containing high densities of useful native trees. Management of these forest gardens consists of human interventions such as planting, protecting, or sparing desirable species.

Kitchen Gardens. After shifting agriculture, kitchen gardens (also known as home gardens, dooryard gardens, "solares," or "huertos familiares") are the most important agroecosystems of traditional farmers in Mexico as well as of traditional societies in most tropical countries (Brownrigg 1985). Yet, in comparison with Asia, research on these important systems is very scarce in Mexico and, more generally, in tropical America as a whole. A literature review of the most important studies on dooryard gardens in the American tropics has been prepared by Alcorn (1987).

Trees are the most important component of these gardens, since they require little attention and provide shade, food, and firewood. Most of the plants are native species. In the Maya area of the Yucatán Peninsula, for example, Barrera-Marín (1981) calculated that 61 percent of the most frequently found trees in the kitchen gardens were natives of the Peninsula, while 13 percent originated from other neotropical regions and 26 percent from the Old World tropics.

Despite their ubiquity, the procedures for establishing kitchen gardens have rarely been documented. Decisions have to be made in creating and maintaining a kitchen garden: 1) the tree species to be planted or, if already present, to be selected; and 2) the architectural arrangement of the individual trees.

It is clear that additional interdisciplinary research on kitchen gardens is needed. Available knowledge already indicates the great potential of these agroecosystems as well as possibilities for their improvement. For instance, the use of improved varieties of fruit or timber trees is a high priority, because it takes equal effort to plant and care for a good tree as for a bad one, yet the rewards obtained from the former are far greater. More research in the selection of tropical trees for different purposes is needed, and traditional kitchen gardens already provide a highly diversified gene pool for selection. Another possibility for improvement lies in the careful architectural design of kitchen gardens to optimize space. Trees and shrubs of different light and soil requirements can be used to suit the ecological characteristics of specific sites as well as the needs of families and local markets.

Other Forest Gardens. Well-kept plantations of trees were found by the Spanish upon their arrival in the tropics of Mexico. Among the most interesting prehispanic forest gardens were the cacao plantations, which were planted under the shade of legume trees. Cardós (1978:20) mentioned that the chronicler Herrera described cacao as "a tree so delicate that it will die from any extreme, the care of which requires planting a mother tree for protection from sun and air (es un árbol tan tierno que con cualquier extremo se pierde y seca para cuidarle es menester ponerle otro que llaman madre, que le ampare del sol y del aire)." Cacao probably represents the most highly sophisticated arboricultural system of the ancient Maya; seeds of this species were even used as money in prehispanic Mexico.

A remnant of this ancient system of tree cultivation can be found in the poor farmers' coffee and cacao plantations (figure 3.1), which still use native legume trees for shade in addition to many other useful tree species. Some traditional farmers cultivate these shade species within native secondary forests, as has been found among the Huastec Indians (Alcorn 1984) and in a general survey of coffee agroecosystems in the east coast of Mexico (Gómez-Pompa and Jiménez-Avila 1982).

A variety of shade trees is used for coffee, ranging from species in native forests to plantations comprised mainly of legume trees. This variety is probably also a reflection of the ancient techniques of cultivating cacao, which varied from introductions in semimanaged forests to completely managed agroforestry systems. Similar methods were followed for other shade species, such as allspice

A Persea americana Miller (aguacate)
B Coffea arabica L. (café)
C Inga leptoloba Schlechter (chalahuite)
D Xanthosoma sp. (makal)
E Musa sapientum L. (plátano)
F Citrus aurantium L. (naranja)
G Zea mayz L. (maíz)
H Phaseolus vulgaris L. (trijol)
I Mangifera indica L. (mango)
J Ananas comossus (L.) Merril (piña)
K Hortaliza
L Psidium guajava L. (guayaba)

@Vicia faba L.
Capsicum annuum L.
Cucurbita pepo L.
Sida rhombifolia L.
Paspalum conjugatum Bergius
Phytolacca icosandra L.
Commelina diffusa Burm F.
Solanum nigrum L.
Saracha procumbens (Cav.) Ruiz & Pavón
Acalypha sp.

FIGURE 3.1. Ancient system of tree cultivation.

(*Pimenta dioica* L.), edible palms (e.g., *Chamaedorea* spp.), and probably also vanilla (*Vanilla planifolia* Andr.).

The use of shade-tolerant species in forest management has great potential since they occupy an "empty" niche. However, there are very few new useful species that can be accommodated within this niche, and it is significant that the only shade species currently used were also the product of observation and experimentation by old tropical cultures.

Some traditional farmers also set aside special forests that have been managed for generations. Management in such cases consists of selection of certain useful species, elimination of others, introduction of useful species from outside sources, and protection of the forest from fire and destructive uses. These forests have been found in the Totonacan area (Medellin-Morales 1986), in the Huastecan region under the name "te lom" (Alcorn 1983), and in the Maya area where they are known as "tolché" (Flores and Ek 1983). The same type of forests, called "pet kot," were developed by the Maya in the past (Gómez-Pompa, Flores, and Sosa 1987).

The basic structure of these "artificial forests" is very similar: an upper canopy dominated by a few useful species, shade canopies with a mixture of useful species and tolerated or encouraged wild species of lesser value, and the rest of the life forms (herbs, lianas and epiphytes) composed of mainly wild species. The structure of these managed forests provides many interesting possibilities for future reforestation projects.

It is likely that in prehispanic times large expanses of land were dedicated to these forest gardens (Puleston 1968; Wiseman 1978; Gómez-Pompa 1987a), which provided food and many other products for people. Forest subsistence systems apparently occupied all areas not dedicated to shifting cultivation or other agricultural systems. Past forest gardens were probably as diverse as the ones we have described and likewise provided niches for a great number of wild species. The diversification of tree plantations by traditional farmers has been recently studied by Ewel (1984) among present-day traditional farmers in the Puuc region of Yucatán, where a monocultural citrus program of the federal government was transformed by Maya farmers into forest gardens dominated by citrus.

Past Practices and Present Tropical Vegetation

All of the techniques we have discussed add up to a forest management strategy for entire regions, not just for cultivated areas. A growing body of evidence suggests that the composition of present-day tropical forests in Mexico may have been strongly influenced by such management in the past (Gómez-Pompa 1987a; Gómez-Pompa and Kaus 1987). Thus, for example, many tropical forests are dominated by one or two economically important tree species. This dominance has long been recognized by traditional farmers who use it in their own nomenclature of forest communities, and local recognition of vegetation units is a basic component in some widely used vegetation methods in Mexico (Bartlett 1935; Miranda, Gómez-Pompa, and Hernandez 1967). Folk nomenclature has frequently been used to name towns where the forest communities occur, such as "ojital," "cedral," "zapotal," or "mezquital," among others. In addition, a number of economically important species are dominant in different vegetation types. An outstanding example is the "rámon" tree, *Brosimum alicastrum* Sw. which is dominant in various vegetation types of almost all humid and subhumid regions in the lowland tropics of Mexico (Gómez-Pompa 1965). A similar distribution pattern can be found for other species such as *Manilkara achra* (Mill.) Fosberg, *Ceiba pentandra* Gaertn., *Swietenia humilis* Zucc., and *Enterolobium cyclocarpum* Griseb. Even in drier climates, a similar pattern occurs where the same species may be abundant or dominant in different climatic and soil conditions. A few examples of these are *Piscidia piscipula* Sarg., *Prosopis juliflora* DC., *Cordia dodecandra* DC., and *Byrsonima crassifolia* H.B.K. Many of these species are used or managed by present-day traditional farmers (table 3.1). The fact that remnants of mature forests are still dominated today by many species that are protected, used, and managed by present-day traditional farmers is excellent evidence of the anthropogenic origin of these forests.

In an ongoing literature survey of managed forests in other tropical regions of the world, we have already found some evidence outside the Maya area of protection and enrichment of tropical forest resources by indigenous peoples. Within Latin America, many researchers (Harris 1971; Gordon 1982; Posey 1984; Balée

TABLE 3.1. The Uses of Some of the Trees Abundant in the Mature Vegetation of Mexico.

Species[a]	Family	Region (and Cultural Groups)	Uses (and Reported Management)	References
Astronium graveolens Jacq.	Anacardiaceae	Mexico and Central America	medicinal, construction	INIREB,[b] Standley 1937
Brahea prominens L.H. Bailey	Palmae	Mexico	thatch	INIREB
Brosimum alicastrum Swartz	Moraceae	Mexico and Central America (Maya, Terraba)	edible fruit and seeds, fodder, medicinal, latex for chicle, [planted, protected]	INIREB, Lundell 1937, Standley and Record 1936
[acutifolium] Hub.		Bolivia (Chacobó)	edible fruit	Boom 1987
[costaricanum] Liebm.		Mexico and Central America	edible seed, fodder	Standley 1937
[gaudichaudii] Trécul		Brazil	fruit for gum	Mors and Rizzini 1966
[lactescens] (S. Moore) C.C. Berg		Bolivia (Chacobó)	edible fruit	Boom 1987
[potabile] Ducke		Brazil	drinkable latex	Mors and Rizzini 1966
[ovatifolium] Ducke		Brazil	drinkable latex	Mors and Rizzini 1966
[utile] (H.B.K.) Oken		Central America (Boruca, Guaymí)	drinkable latex, chicle, bark cloth	Allen 1954, Boom 1987, Standley 1937
Bucida macrostachya Standley	Combretaceae	Mexico	wood for fencing and boats	INIREB
Bursera aloexylon (Schiede) Engl.	Burseraceae	Mexico	medicinal, aromatic	INIREB, Uphof 1959
bipinnata (Sesse et Moc.) Engl.		Mexico	utility wood, ceremonial, glue	INIREB
jorullensis Engl.		Mexico	medicinal, aromatic, glue	INIREB, Uphof 1959
odorata Brandg.		Mexico	medicinal, glue, tanning	INIREB, Uphof 1959
simaruba (L.) Sarg.		Mexico and Central America (Maya)	glue, medicinal, aromatic [planted]	INIREB, Standley 1937, Steggerda 1943

TABLE 3.1. (continued)

Species	Family	Region (and Cultural Groups)	Uses (and Reported Management)	References
Byrsonima crassifolia (L.) Kunth	Malpighiaceae	Mexico and Central America (Maya)	edible fruit, medicinal, charcoal, construction	Standley 1937, Uphof 1959
Caesalpinia eriostachys Benth.	Leguminosae	Mexico and Central America	fodder, bark for stupifying fish	INIREB, Uphof 1959
velutina Standley		Mexico	carpentry	INIREB
[*leiostachya*] [Benth.] Ducke		Brazil	carpentry	Mors and Rizzini 1966
Ceiba acuminata Rose	Bombaceae	Mexico	stuffing from seed floss	Uphof 1959
aesculifolia (H.B.K.) Bretton et Baker		Mexico (Maya)	edible fruit and seed, stuffing from seed floss, oil	INIREB, Steggerda 1943
[*pentandra*] (L.) Gaertn.		Tropical America (Guaymí, Maya, Zenu)	edible fruit and seed, stuffing from seed floss, oil, medicinal, sacred (planted, protected)	INIREB, Gordon 1982, Standley 1937
Chlorophora tinctoria (L.) Gaudich	Moraceae	Tropical America (Maya)	dye, medicinal, carpentry (planted)	Boom 1987, Lundell 1939, Standley 1937, Standley and Record 1936, Uphof 1959
[*Chlorophora excelsa*] Welw.	Moraceae	Africa (Ashanti, Igbo)	sacred, medicinal, construction, (planted, spared, protected)	Dalziel 1937, Rattray 1916, Uphof 1959
Coccoloba barbadensis Jacq.	Polygonaceae	Mexico and Central America	medicinal	INIREB
Cordia dodecandra A.DC.	Boraginaceae	Mexico and Guatemala	medicinal, edible fruit, carpentry (planted)	INIREB, Uphof 1959
gerascanthus L.		Mexico and West Indies	carpentry	INIREB, Uphof 1959

				INIREB
Crescentia alata H.B.K.	Bignoniaceae	Mexico	edible fruit and seeds, medicinal	INIREB
cujete L.		Tropical America (Kuikuru, Maya)	edible fruit and seeds, medicinal, gourd for container (planted)	INIREB, Carneira 1978, Steggerda 1943, Uphof 1959
Curatella americana L.	Dilleniaceae	Tropical America (Kuikuru, Maya)	leaves for sanding, carpentry, medicinal, tanning	Carneira 1978, Lundell 1939, Uphof 1959
Dialium guianense (Aubl.) Sandwith [quineense]	Leguminosae	Mexico and Central America (Maya)	edible fruit pulp, construction	INIREB, Standley and Record 1936
Diospyros cuneata Standl.	Ebenaceae	Nigeria (Igbo, Yoruba)	edible fruit	Kennedy 1936
digyna Jacq.		Mexico (Maya)	edible fruit, firewood	INIREB, Steggerda 1943 Lundell 1939, Standley 1937
[*mespiliformis*] Hochst. ex A.DC.		Mexico and Central America (Maya)	edible fruit, carpentry, construction (planted)	Campbell 1987, MacGregor 1934
		Tropical Africa (Yoruba)	edible fruit (protected)	INIREB, Uphof 1959
Enterolobium cyclocarpum (Jacq.) Griseb	Leguminosae	Mexico and Central America	carpentry, edible pods, soap, medicinal, forage, gum	INIREB
Eysenhardtia adenostylis H.B.K.	Leguminosae	Mexico	construction, medicinal	INIREB, Standley 1937
Ficus glabrata H.B.K.	Moraceae	Tropical America	edible fruit, medicinal, latex, construction	Peters et al. 1987
tecolutensis (Liebm.) Miq.		Mexico (Otomí)	paper-making	
[*Ficus spp.*]		Pantropical (Aztec, Chacobo, Jicaque, Kuuku-ya'a, Maring, Maya, Yoruba, . . .)	edible fruit, bark cloth, paper bark, sacred, shade (planted, protected)	Boom 1987, Clarke 1971, Corner 1960, Hynes and Chase 1982, Kennedy 1936, Standley 1937, Von Hagen 1943
Gyrocarpus americanus Jacq.	Hernandiaceae	Mexico	medicinal, varnish, wood for toys	INIREB, Uphof 1959
Guaiacum sanctum L.	Zygophyllaceae	Tropical America	resin, medicinal, carpentry	INIREB, Uphof 1959
Haematoxylon campechianum L.	Leguminosae	Mexico and Central America (Maya)	dye, medicinal	INIREB, Standley and Record 1936

TABLE 3.1. (continued)

Species	Family	Region (and Cultural Groups)	Uses (and Reported Management)	References
Hura polyandra Baillon	Euphorbiaceae	Mexico	medicinal, poison, construction, ornamental	INIREB, Uphof 1959
Hymenaea courbaril L.	Leguminosae	Tropical America (Bora, Chacobó, Kuikuru)	edible fruit, beverage, resin, thatch, wood for artifacts, canoes (planted, protected)	Boom 1987, Carneiro 1978, Denevan et al. 1984, Mors and Rizzini 1966
Leucaena glauca (L.) Benth.	Leguminosae	Mexico	edible fruits, medicinal, construction, firewood	INIREB
Lucuma campechiana H.B.K.	Sapotaceae	Mexico, Guatemala	edible fruit, latex for chicle	INIREB, Lundell 1939
Lysiloma bahamensis Benth.	Leguminosae	Mexico	construction	INIREB
divaricata (Jacq.) Macbr.		Mexico	construction, tanning	INIREB, Uphof 1959
Malmea depressa (Baillon) R.E. Fries	Annonaceae	Mexico	medicinal	INIREB
Manilkara zapota (L.) Van Royen	Sapotaceae	Mexico and Central America (Maya)	edible fruit, chicle, medicinal, construction (planted)	Lundell 1937, 1939; Steggerda 1943
[*bidentata*] (DC.) Chev.		Tropical America (Guaymí)	edible fruit, drinkable latex, balata rubber	Gordon 1982, Mors and Rizzini 1966
[*kauki*] Dub.		Australia	edible fruit	Hynes and Chase 1982
[*spectabilis*] Standley		Costa Rica	construction	Standley 1937
Myroxylon balsamum (L.) Harms	Leguminosae	Tropical America	medicinal, ornamental, shade	Levingston and Zamora 1982, Uphof 1959
Parmentiera aculeata (H.B.K.) Seeman	Bignonaceae	Mexico	edible fruit, medicinal, artisan	INIREB
Piscidia piscipula (L.) Sarg.	Leguminosae	Mexico	construction, medicinal	INIREB

Species	Family	Distribution	Uses	References
Plumeria rubra L.	Apocynaceae	Mexico	medicinal, ornamental	INIREB
Poulsenia armata (Miq.) Standley	Moraceae	Mexico and Central America	bark for clothes, hammocks, mats	INIREB, Uphof 1959
Protium copal (Schlechtendal et Cham.) Engl.	Burseraceae	Mexico and Central America (Maya)	aromatic resin	Popenoe 1919, Standley 1937
[*costaricense*] Engl.		Costa Rica	resin	Standley 1937
[*panamense*] I.M. Johnston		Panama (Guaymí)	resin	Gordon 1982
[*unifoliolatum*] Engl.		Bolivia (Chacobó)	edible fruit, resin as poultice	Boom 1987
Pseudolmedia oxyphyllaria Donn. Smith	Moraceae	Mexico and Central America	edible fruit, latex, construction	INIREB, Standley 1937
[*laevis*] Macbr.		Bolivia (Chacobó)	edible fruit	Boom 1987
[*macrophylla*] Tréc.		Bolivia (Chacobó)	edible fruit, medicinal	Boom 1987
[*spuria*] (Sw.) Griseb.		Central America	edible fruit, bark cloth (planted, spared)	Lundell 1937, 1939; Gordon 1982
Pseudosmodingium perniciosum Engl.	Anacardiaceae	Mexico	medicinal, resin	INIREB
Psidium guajava L.	Myrtaceae	Mexico and Central America (Maya, Jicaque)	edible fruit, medicinal, firewood (planted)	Lundell 1939, Standley 1937, Steggerda 1943, Von Hagen 1943
[*sartorianum*] (Bergius) Nied		Mexico and Central America (Maya)	edible fruit, medicinal, carpentry	Standley 1937, Steggerda 1943
[*friedrichsthalianum*] Ndz.		Mexico and Central America (Cabecar)	edible fruit (planted)	Standley 1937, Hazlett 1986
[*guajaba*]		Honduras (Jicaque)	edible fruit (planted)	Von Hagen 1943
[*guajava*] L.		Bolivia (Chacobó)	edible fruit and leaves, medicinal (planted)	Boom 1987
[*quineense*] Swartz		Tropical America (Kayapo)	edible fruit and flower	Posey 1983, Standley 1937
[*savannarum*] Donnell Smith		Costa Rica (Bribri, Terraba)	edible fruit	Standley 1937

TABLE 3.1. (continued)

Species	Family	Region (and Cultural Groups)	Uses (and Reported Management)	References
Quararibea funebris (Llave) Vischer	Bombacaceae	Mexico	construction, condiment	INIREB
Sabal mexicana Martius	Palmae	Mexico, Guatemala (Maya)	thatch, edible shoots, medicinal, construction (planted)	INIREB, Lundell 1939
[mayarum] H.H. Bartlett		Guatemala (Maya)	thatch (spared)	Lundell 1939
Scheelea liebmanii Becc. lundellii Bartl.	Palmae	Mexico	thatch, construction, fodder	INIREB
[martiana] Burret		Mexico, Guatemala (Maya)	thatch, construction, fodder	INIREB, Lundell 1939
[gomphococca] Burret		Brazil	oil from kernel	Mors and Rizzini 1966
		Costa Rica	thatch	Standley 1937
Sideroxylon tempisque Pittier	Sapotaceae	Mexico	edible fruit, construction	INIREB
Sterculia apetala (Jacq.) Karsten	Sterculiaceae	Mexico and Central America	edible seed, construction	INIREB, Standley 1937
Swietenia macrophylla King	Meliaceae	Mexico and Central America	construction (spared)	Lundell 1937, Standley 1937
Tabebuia guayacan (Seemann) Hemsley	Bignoniaceae	Mexico	construction, carpentry	INIREB, Uphoff 1959
Talisia olivaeformis (Kunth) Radlk.	Sapindaceae	Mexico and Central America (Jicaque, Maya)	edible fruit, medicinal (planted)	INIREB, Lundell 1939, Von Hagen 1943
Terminalia amazonia (J. F. Gmel.) Excell	Combretaceae	Mexico	construction	INIREB
[catappa] L.		Belize	edible seed, shade (planted)	Standley and Record 1936
[obovata] Cambess.		Belize	construction	Standley and Record 1936
Virola spp.	Myrsticaceae	Tropical America (Bora, Chacobó)	narcotic, hallucinogen, construction	Denevan et al. 1984, Mors and Rizzini 1966, Boom 1987

Vochysia hondurensis Sprague [*ferruginea* Mart.]	Vochysiaceae	Mexico, Belize	construction	INIREB, Standley and Record 1936
Zuelania guidonia (Swartz) Britton et Millsp.	Flacourtiaceae	Panama (Guaymí)	wood for canoes (spared)	Gordon 1982
		Mexico	medicinal	INIREB

[a]Dominant or abundant species in tropical vegetation of Mexico based on Gómez-Pompa (1965, 1973), Miranda (1975), and Rzedowski (1978); [ ] indicates related species which have been reported to be useful.
[b]Instituto Nacional de Investigaciones Sobre Recursos Bioticos (INIREB): Useful Plants of Mexico Database.

1987) suggest that high species dominance is a reflection of past management practices, including the equivalent of forest gardens and the planting of useful species along well-used trails. Similar situations are reported for tropical regions in Southest Asia and Oceania (Corner 1960; Clarke 1971; Kunstadter 1978), and Africa (Sykes 1930; Jones 1956; Campbell 1987).

The systems of forest exploitation that predominate today in the tropics are generally shaped by modern technology rather than by the experience of traditional farmers, whose cultural transmission of knowledge has largely ceased. The current cycle of land—based on perpetual movement from degraded to mature forests—is not sustainable in the long run, as it requires a constant supply of forests and will eventually result in the depletion of its own economic base.

One alternative available to us is to bridge the gap between ancient and modern forms of land use by consulting with present-day traditional farmers. Unfortunately, the "libraries" contained in the cultural practices of these farmers are undergoing a process of depletion equivalent to that of tropical forests. Many traditional groups have few legal rights of ownership and even fewer options to develop their own initiatives for the use of the forest regions in which they live. They are often pushed out of their homelands by modern business interests or, in other instances, relocated to unfamiliar environments or incorporated into the modern cycle of forest use. With this loss of knowledge, we are losing our cultural as well as environmental resources and decreasing the range and diversity of management choices available to us (Bennett 1975a).

Conclusions

Despite current advances in science and technology, we have failed to develop methods of forest management that allow growing human populations and tropical forest ecosystems to coexist as we believe occurred previously in ancient civilizations. Like other tropical countries, Mexico has been incapable of formulating development policies that ensure a better quality of life for impoverished rural populations. Nor has it been able to implement viable mechanisms for conserving biological diversity in tropical forests. Little support for conservation efforts exists in the population as a whole and even less in the government (Gómez-Pompa et al. 1976; Halffter 1983; Gómez-Pompa 1987b).

The combination of modern science and folk science may provide a basis for managing tropical resources on behalf of both people and the forests. An integrated effort in research, education, and extension is needed to develop ecologically sound land-use alternatives that are based on the needs as well as the knowledge of rural inhabitants.

ACKNOWLEDGMENTS

We would like to thank Dr. Kathleen Truman and Elizabeth J. Lawlor from the Department of Anthropology at the University of California, Riverside, for their useful comments and suggestions on this paper.

REFERENCES

Alcorn, J. B. 1983. El te'lom huasteco: Presente, pasado y futuro de un sistema de silvicultura indigena. *Biotica* 8(3):315–331.

Alcorn, J. B. 1984. *Huastec Maya Ethnobotany.* Austin: University of Texas Press.

Alcorn, J. B. 1987. Indigenous agroforestry systems in the Latin American tropics. In M. Altieri and S. B. Hecht, eds., *Agroecology and Small Farm Development.* Boca Raton, FL: CRC Press.

Allen, P. H. L. 1954. The cow tree. *Natural History* 63(1):41–43.

Amo, del S. 1984. Manejo de la sucesion secundaria. In *Proceedings on the UNESCO Conference on "Tropical Forest Regeneration and Management."* Paris: UNESCO.

✗ Balée, W. C. 1987. Cultural forests of the Amazon. *Garden* 11(6):12–14, 32.

Barrera-Marin, A. 1981. La unidad de habitación tradicional campesina y el manejo de los recursos bióticos en el area maya yucatanense. *Biotica* 5(3):115–128.

Bartlett, H. H. 1935. A method of procedure for field work in tropical American phytogeography based upon a botanical reconnaissance in parts of British Honduras and the Peten Forests in Guatemala. In *Botany of the Maya Area.* Carnegie Institution of Washington Publication 461:1–26.

Bennett, C. F. 1975a. The advantages of cultural diversity. *Unasylva* 27(110):11–15.

Bennett, C. F. 1975b. *Man and Earth Ecosystems.* New York: Wiley.

Boom, B. 1987. Ethnobotany of the Chácobo Indians, Beni, Bolivia. *Advances in Economic Botany* 4. Bronx: New York Botanical Garden.

Brownrigg, L. 1985. *Home Gardening in International Development: What the Literature Shows.* Washington, DC: League for International Food Education.

Campbell, B. M. 1987. The use of wild fruits of Zimbabwe. *Economic Botany* 41(3):375–385.

Cardós, A. 1978. El comercio entre los Mayas antíguos. *Acta Antropológica* 2:50.

Carneiro, R. L. 1978. The knowledge and use of rain forest trees by the Kuikuru Indians of Central Brazil. In R. I. Ford, ed., *Status of Ethnobotany.* Museum of Anthropology, *Anthropological Papers* 67:201–216.

Clarke, W. C. 1971. *Place and People: An Ecology of a New Guinean Community.* Berkeley: University of California Press.

Coe, M. D. 1984. *Mexico.* New York: Thames and Hudson.

Conklin, H. C. 1954. An ethnoecological approach to shifting agriculture. *Transactions of New York Academic of Science* 2(17):133–142.

Corner, E. J. H. 1960. Botany and prehistory. In *Symposium on the Impact of Man on Humid Tropics Vegetation,* pp. 38–41. Sponsored by Administration of the Territory of Papua and New Guinea and UNESCO Science Co-operation Office for South East Asia.

Dahlin, B. H. 1985. La geografia histórica de la antígua agricultura maya. In T. Rojas and W. T. Sanders, eds., *Historia de la Agricultura: Epoca Prehispánica—Siglo XVI,* pp. 125–196. Mexico, D. F.: Colección Biblioteca del Instituto Nacional de Antropologia e Historia.

Dalziel, J. M. 1937. *The Useful Plants of West Tropical Africa. An Appendix to the Flora of West Tropical Africa,* vols. 1–2. London: The Crowns Agent for the Colonies.

Denevan, W. M., ed. 1976. *The Native Population of the Americas in 1492.* Madison: University of Wisconsin Press.

Denevan, W. M., J. M. Treacy, J. B. Alcorn, C. Padoch, J. Denslow, and S. F. Paitan. 1984. Indigenous agroforestry in the Peruvian Amazon: Bora Indian management of swidden fallows. *Interciencia* 9(6):346–357.

Edwards, C. R. 1986. The human impact on the forest in Quintana Roo, Mexico. *Journal of Forest History* 30(3):120–127.

Ewel, J. 1979. Crossroads for tropical biology. *Mosaic* 10:10–18.

Ewel, P. T. 1984. Intensification of peasant agriculture in Yucatan. *Agricultural Economics Research* 84(4):1–233. Ithaca: Cornell University.

Flores, J. S. and E. Ucan Ek. 1983. Nombres usados por los mayas para designar la vegetación. *Cuadernos de Divulgación INIREB* 10:1–33.

Gómez-Pompa, A. 1965. La vegetación de México. *Boletin de la Sociedad Botánica de México* 29:76–120.

Gómez-Pompa, A. 1987a. On Maya silviculture. *Mexican Studies* 3(1):1–17.

Gómez-Pompa, A. 1987b. Tropical deforestation and Maya silviculture: An ecological paradox. *Tulane Studies in Zoology and Botany* 26(1):19–37.

Gómez-Pompa, A., J. S. Flores, and V. Sosa. 1987. The "pet kot": A man-made tropical forest of the Maya. *Interciencia* 12(1):10–15.

Gómez-Pompa, A., G. Halffter, R. Casco, and E. Leff. 1976. Desarrollo del trópico mexicano. *Ciencia y Desarrollo* 1(6):17–21.

Gómez-Pompa, A. and E. Jiménez-Avila, eds. 1982. *Estudios Ecológicos en el Agroecosistema Cafetalero.* México: CECSA-INIREB.

Gómez-Pompa, A. and A. Kaus. 1987. The conservation of resources by traditional cultures in the tropics. *Proceedings of World Wilderness Congress* (in press).

Gordon, B. L. 1982. *A Panama Forest and Shore: Natural History and Amerindian Culture in Bocas del Toro.* Pacific Grove, CA: Boxwood Press.

Halffter, G. 1983. Colonización y conservación de los recursos en el trópico. *Cuadernos de Divulgación INIREB* 1:1–31.

Harris, D. R. 1971. The ecology of swidden cultivation in the Upper Orinoco rain forest, Venezuela. *The Geographical Review* 61(4):475–495.

Hart, R. D. 1980. A natural ecosystem analog approach to the design of a successional crop system for tropical forest environments. *Biotropica* 12(2):93–82.

Hazlett, D. L. 1986. Ethnobotanical observations from Cabecar and Guaymi settlements in Central America. *Economic Botany* 40(3):339–352.

Hernández-Xolocotzi, E. 1959. La agricultura. *Publicaciones Instituto Mexicano de Recursos Renovables* 3:3–57.

Hynes, R. A. and A. K. Chase. 1982. Plants, sites and domiculture: Aboriginal influences upon plant communities in Cape York Peninsula. *Archaelogia Oceania* 17:38–50.

Illsley, C. 1984. Vegetación y produción de la Milpa Bajo Roza, Tumba y Quema en el ejido de Yaxcabá, Yucatán, México. Tesis profesional, Escuela de Biologia, Universidad Michoacana de San Nicolás de Hidalgo.

Jones, E. W. 1956. Ecological studies on the rain forest of southern Nigeria. IV. The plateau forest of the Okumu forest reserve. *Journal of Ecology* 44:83–117.

Jordan, C. F. and J. R. Kline, 1972. Mineral cycling: Some basic concepts and their application in a tropical rain forest. *Annual Review of Ecology and Systematics* 3:33–50.

Kennedy, J. D. 1936. *Forest Flora of Southern Nigeria.* Lagos, Nigeria.

Kunstadter, P. 1978. Ecological modificaton and adaptation: An ethnobotanical view of Lua' swiddeners in northwestern Thailand. *Anthropological Papers* 67:169–200.

Landa, D. de. 1984. *Relación de las Cosas de Yucatan.* Yucatán, México: Producción Editorial Dante, S.A.

Levingston, R. and R. Zamora. 1982. Medicine trees of the tropics. *Unasylva* 35(140):7–10.

Lundell, C. L. 1937. *The Vegetation of Peten.* Washington, DC: Carnegie Institute.

Lundell, C. L. 1939. Plants probably used by the old empire Maya of Peten and adjacent lowlands. *Papers Michigan Academy of Science, Arts and Letters* 24:37–56.

MacGregor, W. D. 1934. Silviculture of the mixed deciduous forests of Nigeria with special reference to the south-western provinces. *Oxford Forestry Memoirs* 18.

Medellín-Morales, G. 1986. Uso y manejo de las especies vegetales comestibles, medicinales, para construccion y combustibles en una comunidad totonaca de la costa (Plan de Hidalgo, Pap., Ver., Mex.). INIREB, manuscript.

Meggers, D. J. 1971. *Amazonia: Man and Culture in a Conterfeit Paradise.* New York: Aldine-Atherton.

Miranda, F., A. Gómez-Pompa, and E. Hernández X. 1967. Un método para el estudio ecológico de las zonas tropicales. *Anales Instituto Biologia UNAM, Série Botánica* 38(1):203–250.

Mors, W. B. and C. T. Rizzini. 1966. *Useful Plants of Brazil.* San Francisco: Holden-Day.

Nations, J. D. and R. B. Nigh. 1978. Cattle, cash, food, and forest. *Bull. of the Anthropological Study Group on Agrarian Ssytems* 6.

Parsons, J. R. 1975. The changing nature of New World tropical forests since European Colonization. In *The Use of Ecological Guidelines for Development in the American Humid Tropics,* pp. 28–38. Caracas, Venezuela, 20–22 Feb. 1974. IUCN Publications New Series No. 31.

Partridge, W. L. 1984. The humid tropics cattle ranching complex: Cases from Panama reviewed. *Human Organization* 43(1):76–80.

Peters, C. M. 1983. Observations on Maya subsistence and the ecology of a tropical tree. *American Antiquity* 48:610–615.

Peters, C. M., J. Rosenthal, and T. Urbina. 1987. Otomi bark paper in Mexico: Commercialization of a pre-hispanic technology. *Economic Botany* 41(3):423–432.

Popenoe, W. 1919. Useful plants of copan. *American Anthropologist* 21:125–138.

Posey, D. A. 1983. Indigenous knowledge and development: An ideological bridge to the future. *Ciencia e Cultura* 35(7):876–894.

Posey, D. A. 1984. A preliminary report on diversified management of tropical forest by the Kayapó Indians of the Brazilian Amazon. In G. T. Prance and J. A. Kallunki, eds., *Ethnobotany in the Neotropics,* pp. 112–126. Bronx: New York Botanical Garden.

Puleston, D. E. 1968. *Brosimum alicastrum* as a subsistence alternative for the classic Maya of Central Southern lowlands. Master's thesis. Ann Arbor: University Microfilms International.

Ramakrishnan, P. S. 1984. The science behind rotational bush fallow agricultural system (jhum). *Proceedings Indian Academy Science (Plant Science)* 93(3):379–400.

Rattray, R. S. 1916. *Ashanti Proverbs (The Primitive Ethics of a Savage People).* Oxford: Clarendon Press.

Soustelle, J. 1984. *The Olmec.* New York & London.

Standley, P. C. 1937. Flora of Costa Rica. *Field Museum of Natural History.* Publication No. 392.

Standley, P. C. and S. J. Record. 1936. The forest and flora of British Honduras. *Field Museum of Natural History.* Publication No. 350.

Steggerda, M. 1943. Some ethonological data concerning one hundred Yacatan plants. *Bureau of American Ethnology Bulletin* 136:189–226.

Sykes, R. A. 1930. Some notes on the Benin forests of Southern Nigeria. *Empire Forestry Journal* 9:101–106.

Turner, B. L. II. 1976. Population density in the classic Maya lowlands: New evidence for old approaches. *Geographical Review* 66(1):73–82.

Uphof, J. C. T. 1959. *Dictionary of Economic Plants.* New York: Hafner.

Von Hagen, V. W. 1943. The Jicaque (Torrupan) Indians of Honduras. *Indian Notes and Monographs* No. 53, New York Museum of the American Indian Heye Foundation.

Wilkerson, S. J. K. 1983. So green and like a garden: Intensive agriculture in ancient Veracruz. In J. P. Darch, ed., *Drained Field Agriculture in Central and South America,* pp. 55–90. Bar International Series.

Wiseman, F. M. 1978. Agricultural and historical ecology of the Maya lowlands. In P. D. Harrison and B. L. Turner II, eds., *Prehispanic Maya Agriculture,* pp. 63–115. Albuquerque: University of new Mexico Press.

4

Extraction and Forest Management by Rural Inhabitants in the Amazon Estuary

■

ANTHONY B. ANDERSON

ABSTRACT

Although traditional inhabitants of tropical regions frequently possess a profound knowledge concerning natural resources and their sustained use, such knowledge has been rarely documented in Amazonia. This paper describes the use of forest resources among descendents of Amerindians (known regionally as "caboclos" or "ribeirinhos") in the floodplain forests of the Amazon estuary. Relatively high accessibility and high concentraton of resources have made these forests a historical source of timber, edible fruits, fibers, latex, and medicinals. Although the caboclos' use of these forests is usually viewed as mere extraction, it in fact frequently involves subtle forms of management. Common practices include favoring highly desirable species and eliminating or thinning less desirable competitors, while maintaining the essential forest structure and composition. These practices, which I refer to as "tolerant" forest management, facilitate access to and exploitation of forest resources, and they are simple and inexpensive to implement. This case study illustrates how traditional inhabitants can utilize Amazonian forests in ways that conserve natural resources and at the same time generate moderate economic returns.

Extraction can be defined as the withdrawal of natural resources with no provision for their replacement. In the Amazon Basin, the term has become historically associated with resource depletion, environmental degradation, socioeconomic disruption, and cultural decimation. Since the arrival of the first European traders in the late sixteenth century, extraction has been the basis for virtually all major economic activities in the region and continues to be so today. Even in the case of potentially renewable resources such as fisheries and forests, extraction remains the rule in Amazonia (Goudling 1980; Rankin 1985)—and it is largely responsible for the current degradation of these resources in the region.

Yet in spite of its sordid reputation in Amazonia and in other tropical regions, extraction has occasionally been coupled with sustained management of natural resources (e.g., Fox 1977; Posey et al. 1984). Such coupling not only promotes resource conservation but may eliminate many of the socioeconomic ills associated with purely extractive forms of resource exploitation.

This paper examines one such case of extraction and forest management by rural inhabitants (known as "caboclos" or "ribeirinhos") in the floodplain of the Amazon estuary. Extractive forms of production predominate in this area because both ecological and socioeconomic factors have undermined conventional forms of agriculture. After briefly analyzing these factors, I examine in detail how rural inhabitants integrate extractive and management practices within floodplain forests. Finally, I conclude with an attempt to identify ecological and socioeconomic factors that could permit such integration in other settings.

I believe this study is of special interest for several reasons. First, it involves the Amazon floodplain ("várzea"), a zone known for its high agricultural potential (e.g., Meggers 1971; Roosevelt 1980) but not generally recognized as favorable for long-term forest management. Second, it involves caboclos, a group generally maligned for its purported lack of industry, "collecting mentality," Indian blood, and "primitive" land-use practices (cf. Ross 1978:193). Although caboclos are acknowledged to be the cultural representatives of the Amazon region since the early 19th century (Parker 1985), most documented case studies of sustained land-use management in Amazonia have involved Indians (e.g., Denevan et al. 1984; Posey 1983; but see Moran 1977; Parker 1985). Finally, this study shows that extraction, despite its historical defects, has the potential to be incorporated into economically and ecologically rational forms of land use.

The Setting

Floodplain forests of the Amazon estuary cover an area estimated at 25,000 km^2 (Calzavara 1972). Although this area has supported relatively dense human populations for millennia, the native forest structure is surprisingly intact, as revealed in a recently completed survey of forest cover in the Brazilian state of Pará (IBDF-SUDAM 1988). For example, in two municipalities (i.e., counties) lying mostly in the floodplain of the Amazon estuary, the percentage of total forest area altered was found to be only 1.7 percent (Afuá) and 0.8 percent (Gurupá) by the end of 1986. In contrast, the figures were found to be far greater in more recently settled municipalities with relatively small areas of floodplain, such as Conceição de Araguaia (33.4%), Redenção (39.3%), Xinguara (47.6%) and São João de Araguaia (54.9%).

The most obvious cause for these differences in deforestation is that recent frontier expansion—in the form of road construction, land speculation, influx of settlers, etc.—has been minimal in the former municipalities and of major significance in the latter. I believe, however, that other factors account for the high degree of resource conservation characteristic of long-settled floodplain areas in the Amazon estuary. These factors, which include both ecological and cultural components, are briefly examined below.

The Estuarine Floodplain

The floodplain of the Amazon River and its white-water tributaries has long been recognized as among the most suitable sites for agriculture in Amazonia, primarily due to its abundant and nutrient-rich sediments (e.g., Meggers 1971; Roosevelt 1980). This suitability, however, varies considerably along the course of the major white-water rivers. For example, sediment concentrations as well as pH decline markedly between the Upper Amazon and the estuary (Lima 1956; Falesi 1974; Irion 1984); this decline can be attributed to the low suspension loads of most of the tributaries in the middle and lower sections of the Amazon. Pronounced variations in flood duration also occur between upriver areas and the estuary. As the river widens downstream and tidal influences increase, flooding becomes less pronounced but more frequent. The combination of these factors produces soils that are not only poor in nutrients compared with upriver areas, but excessively humid during most of the year.

Conditions for agriculture thus appear to be less favorable in the estuarine floodplain, and agricultural production is, in fact, chronically low (Lima 1956). This precarious agricultural base supports a rural population that lives for the most part in isolated dwellings or in hamlets perched along the river banks.

Production Systems

Prior to European contact, human population densities along the major rivers of Amazonia were far greater than they are today (Carvajal, Rojas, and de Azuña 1941; Denevan 1976). These populations appear to have been supported by a complex food production system, characterized by intensive seed crop cultivation on bottomlands in the floodplain, manioc cultivation on the terra firma, and animal capture in both zones (Roosevelt 1980; Denevan 1984). These systems were in turn administered by relatively complex societies: the chiefdoms that once proliferated along the major rivers of the Amazon valley.

Nearly four centuries of colonization effectively destroyed these societies by turning a subsistence economy based on food production into a predominantly market economy geared toward extraction of forest and riverine products (Ross 1978). The contemporary residents of the floodplain—known as "caboclos," or Portuguese-speaking rural inhabitants of Amerindian, Portuguese, and African descent (Parker 1985)—have adapted logical responses to the economic demands of an extractive economy. The scattered settlement pattern of contemporary inhabitants promotes efficient extraction of natural resources, while at the same time effectively impedes agricultural development. Likewise, much of the indigenous knowledge of natural resources inherited by the caboclo contributes toward maintaining an essentially extractive economy.

The Floodplain Forest

In the floodplain of the Amazon estuary, not only the local inhabitants but their very environment seem to be eminently suited to the demands of an extractive economy. The intricate network of rivers and canals in this landscape has facilitated wood extraction for centuries (Huber 1943). The flooding cycle, which produces waterlogged soils over extensive portions of the year, also accounts for the peculiar composition and dynamics of floodplain forests in the Amazon estuary. In this ecosystem, lack of soil oxygen probably represents the key limiting factor to plant growth. Few species can thrive under waterlogged conditions, and as a result these forests exhibit relatively low biological diversity and pronounced dominance by few tree species, many of which are of economic importance (Anderson and Jardim 1989; table 4.1). Flooding also appears to have a dramatic effect on forest dynamics in this ecosystem. Shallow root systems due to impeded drainage, combined with constant soil movement associated with flooding, result in a high frequency of tree falls, and abundant light gaps provide ample opportunities for forest regeneration. With a high concentration of economic species and quick recovery following disturbance, these forests appear to be able to support short-cycle extraction on a sustainable basis.

"Tolerant" Forest Management

Whereas extraction is an unambiguous term, management seems to mean different things to different people (e.g., Alcorn 1981; Posey 1985; Anderson et al. 1985). I define management as the conscious manipulation of the environment to promote the maintenance and/or productivity of natural resources. According to this definition, the manipulation should be conscious: controlled burns, for example, constitute management, whereas human-induced wildfires are mere accidents. By the same token, management should have an objective: promoting maintenance and/or productivity of natural resources. Management is not limited to forests; it can be carried out in cities or farms, coral reefs or lakes: the term "environment" encompasses these entities.

The above definition provides a point of reference when examining the often subtle forms of floodplain forest management practiced in the Amazon estuary. The following description is based on an in-depth case study (Anderson et al. 1985), comparative field research at diverse locales (figure 4.1), and reconnaissance trips throughout the area.

Land-Use Units

Around the isolated dwellings of rural inhabitants in the floodplain of the Amazon estuary, one can observe a recurring pattern of land-use units. A house garden ("terreiro") typically surrounds the dwelling. This intensively managed, relatively open zone is used for raising domesticated animals and cultivating a wide variety of exotic and native plants. Here one frequently encounters herbs and shrubs that

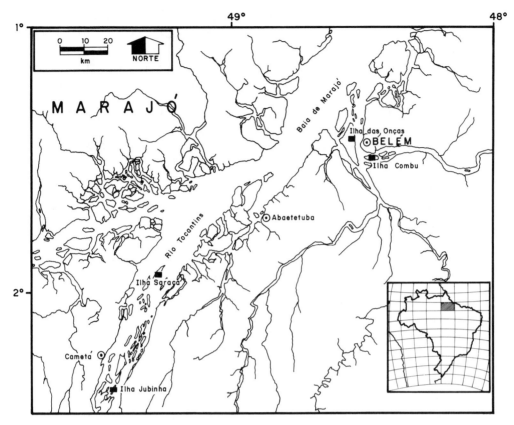

FIGURE 4.1. Map showing southeastern portion of the Amazon estuary. Squares indicate study sites.

are used as condiments, remedies, and ornaments; these plants are often cultivated on elevated platforms to protect them from flooding. The house garden,
which is usually less than one hectare in area, contrasts sharply with the far denser
and more extensive dense floodplain forest ("mata de várzea"), which is covered
by a closed canopy of trees and is not subject to discernible management as defined above. This last unit is used primarily for gathering forest products and for
hunting. Gathered forest products include fruits, palm heart, latex, wood, fertilizer, ornamental plants, fibers, honey, oilseeds, medicines, and utensils. Game
such as pacas, agoutis, porcupines, sloths, and feral pigs may be locally abundant
and are routinely hunted. At scattered locations within the dense floodplain forest, small (usually less than one hectare) swidden plots ("roças") are cut for cultivation of annual subsistence crops such as rice, corn, and beans; cash crops, such
as sugarcane and rice, are sometimes grown on a more extensive scale. Swidden
plots are usually located far from the household to minimize intrusions by domesticated animals. Although continuous cultivation appears to be possible, most
farmers fallow their plots after a short period of cultivation, citing weed invasion
and incursions of feral pigs as principal causes.

The three major land units described above—house garden, dense floodplain forest, and swidden plot—are easily distinguishable entities that are clearly designated by local terms. Additional zones grade into the units described above and are consequently less distinguishable. These zones occupy a variety of locations in relation to the household, originate by different means, and are designated by a variety of terms.[1] Despite the variable nature of these transition zones, they have an important element in common: they are all subject to long-term forest management. For purposes of simplicity, I refer to these various zones as "managed forests" and distinguish them from dense floodplain forest that is not subject to discernible management, which I call "unmanaged forest."

The so-called managed forests exhibit a number of distinctive features in relation to the other land-use units described above. For example, they typically contain a more or less continuous tree cover, in contrast to the relatively open house garden or swidden plot; conversely, the vegetation is considerably more dense in unmanaged forest. Managed forests are also subjected to less intensive management than either the house garden or the swidden plot, where weeding is a more or less constant activity. Weeding does take place in managed forests but to a lesser degree, as their relatively deep shade effectively reduces weed establishment and growth. By contrast, unmanaged forests are by definition not subjected to weeding or other discernible forms of management.

Managed forests exhibit considerable variability in structure and composition. At one extreme, they may appear as orderly plantations of exotic trees on sites where the original floodplain forest has been completely removed. Alternatively, they may be almost indistinguishable from the native floodplain forest and comprised entirely of native forest species that are only subject to occasional thinning. These two extremes reflect contrasting management strategies. I refer to the first extreme as "intrusive" forest management, in which the native vegetation is replaced by tree plantations that are maintained by long-term care. The second extreme exemplifies "tolerant" forest management, in which the native vegetation is largely conserved or reconstituted through successional processes. The degree to which the intact native forest is preserved in these systems is inversely related to the intensity of human interference.

Management Strategies

A managed forest studied in detail on the Ilha das Onças ("Jaguar Island"), adjacent to the city of Belém (Anderson et al. 1985; figure 4.1), illustrates the principal features of tolerant forms of forest management. This zone consists of a 1.1-ha area located adjacent to a house garden (figure 4.2); according to informants, this area has been subjected to intermittent management since at least the beginning of this century.

Local residents implement two basic management strategies in this zone. The first strategy is to favor desirable species indirectly by weeding or thinning less

FIGURE 4.2. Map of vicinity of household studied on Ilha das Onças (Anderson et al. 1985), showing major land-use units.

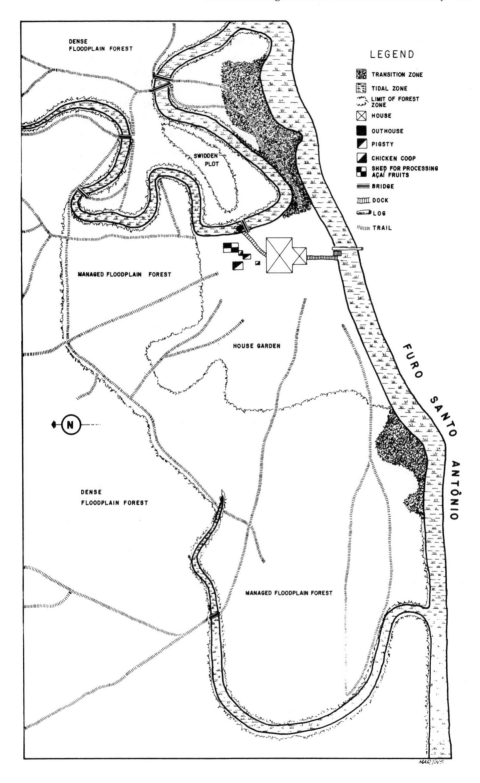

LEGEND

TRANSITION ZONE

TIDAL ZONE

LIMIT OF FOREST ZONE

HOUSE

OUTHOUSE

PIGSTY

CHICKEN COOP

SHED FOR PROCESSING AÇAÍ FRUITS

BRIDGE

DOCK

LOG

TRAIL

DENSE FLOODPLAIN FOREST

SWIDDEN PLOT

MANAGED FLOODPLAIN FOREST

HOUSE GARDEN

DENSE FLOODPLAIN FOREST

MANAGED FLOODPLAIN FOREST

FURO SANTO ANTÔNIO

N

MARTINS

desirable competitors, such as vines and tree species that are used only for timber or fuel. Large trees are frequently ringed rather than felled, so as to minimize damage to the surrounding forest. Selective elimination not only favors desirable species by reducing competition, but also promotes the regeneration of such species by selectively sparing their seedlings. Many species are neither eliminated nor subsequently favored by discernible management practices. These so-called "tolerated" species are important sources of extracted products: examples within the managed forest under consideration include "taperebá" (*Spondias mombin* Urb.), "ingá" (*Inga* spp.), and "miriti" (*Mauritia flexuosa* L.f.), which bear edible fruits and also attract game; and "seringueira" (*Hevea brasiliensis* (Willd. ex A. Juss.) M. Arg.), which provides latex used to make rubber. Such species are a key feature in forests subjected to tolerant forms of management, whereas they are virtually absent in systems characterized by intrusive management.

The second management strategy is to favor desirable species directly by promoting their maintenance and/or productivity. This strategy is implemented in a number of ways. Local residents introduce seeds of desirable species by conscious planting or seeding or, alternatively, by unconscious dispersal of propagules. They also introduce species by planting or transplanting seedlings and cuttings. For example, consciously planted species in the managed forest under consideration include cacao (*Theobroma cacao* L.), "cupuaçu" (*Theobroma grandiflorum* (Willd. ex Spreng.) K. Schum.), coconut (*Cocos nucifera* L.), genipap (*Genipa americana* L.), and mango (*Mangifera indica* L.); several varieties of banana (*Musa* spp.) have also been introduced. In addition, the "açaí" palm (*Euterpe oleracea* Mart.) is frequently seeded in house gardens and fallows. Species that are propagated by unconscious human dispersal probably include açaí, mango, ingá, and annatto (*Bixa orellana* L.). Seedlings of desirable species (e.g., cacao, cupuaçu, and coconut) are actively protected by more intensive weeding and construction of improvised fences (frequently made of palm leaves or stems) in the vicinity. Organic material, usually comprised of decaying inflorescences and leaves of the extraordinarily abundant açaí palm, is concentrated at the base of favored plants. The stems of fruit trees such as mango and genipap are often scored with a number of shallow cuts, which is claimed to promote fruit production. Local residents regularly prune the multistemmed açaí to harvest palm heart for sale to local industries. They report that when carried out selectively, this practice enhances fruit production in the remaining stems. The fruits of açaí are used to make a thick beverage that is widely consumed throughout the Amazon estuary.

Effects of Management

The effects of these practices can be seen by comparing areas of managed and unmanaged floodplain forests on the Ilha das Onças. The most notable difference between these two zones is the much higher biomass of the unmanaged forest. An examination of forest profiles and crown projection (figures 4.3 and 4.4) reveals a far greater density of vegetation on the unmanaged site, especially in the lower and middle levels. Comparison of basal areas on the two sites (tables 4.1 and 4.2)

FIGURE 4.3. Profile and crown projections of all plants with DHB ≥ 2 cm in a 60 × 10 m area of unmanaged floodplain forest on Ilha das Onças, following methodology of Hallé, Oldeman, and Tomlinson (1978). *Euterpe oleracea* Mart. is not numbered, 1 = *Pterocarpus officinalis* Jacq., 2 = *Spondias mombin* Urb., 3 = *Pithecellobium latifolium* (L.) Benth., 4 = *Carapa guianensis* Aubl., 5 = *Astrocaryum murumuru* Mart., 6 = *Hevea brasiliensis* (Willd. ex A. Juss.) M. Arg., 7 = *Cynometra marginata* Benth., 8 = *Macrolobium angustifolium* (Benth.) Cowan, 9 = *Inga* cf. *alba* Willd., 10 = *Pentaclethra macroloba* (Willd.) Kuntze, 11 = *Quararibea guianensis* Aubl., 12 = *Crudia* sp., 13 = *Mora paraensis* Ducke, 14 = *Virola surinamensis* (Rol.) Warb., 15 = *Symphonia globulifera* L., 16 = *Pithecellobium* cf. *cauliflorum* (Willd.) Benth., 17 = *Rheedia macrophylla* Pl. et Tr., 18 = *Virola* cf. *michelli* Heckel, 19 = *Eschweilera* cf. *alba* Kunth., 20 = *Posoqueira* sp., 21 = *Parinari excelsa* Sabine, 22 = *Ocotea caudata* Mez, 23 = *Richardella glomerata* (Miq.) Baehni, 24 = *Licania* sp., 25 = *Swartzia racemosa* Benth., 26 = *Aegiphila* sp., 27 = *Socratea exhorriza* (Mart.) H. Wendl., 28 = *Herrania mariae* (Mart.) DC., 29 = *Swartzia polyphylla* DC., 30 = *Couepia* sp., 31 = *Inga* sp.

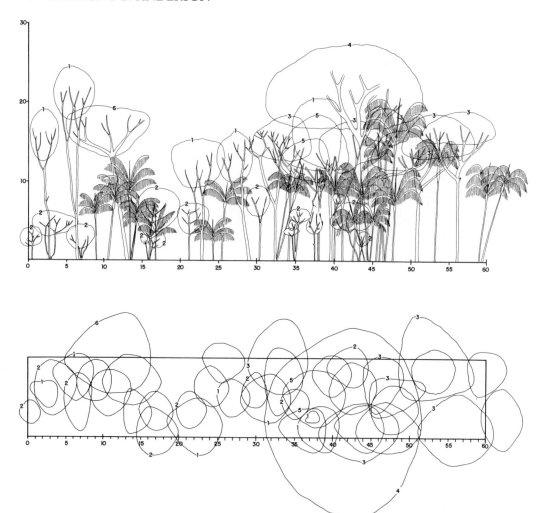

FIGURE 4.4. Profile and crown projections of all plants with DBH ≥ 2 cm in a 60 × 10 m area of managed floodplain forest on Ilha das Onças, following methodology of Hallé, Oldeman, and Tomlinson (1978). *Euterpe oleracea* Mart. is not numbered, 1 = *Hevea brasiliensis* (Willd. ex A. Juss.) M. Arg., 2 = *Theobroma cacao* L., 3 = *Inga edulis* Mart., 4 = *Spondias mombin* Urb., 5 = *Inga* cf. *alba* Willd., and 6 = *Genipa americana* L.

indicates that roughly one quarter of the total forest biomass was eliminated through selective thinning.

Species diversity, in addition to biomass, is reduced substantially in the managed forest. In the 0.25-ha samples, for example, I found a total of 52 species with DBH ≥ 5 cm in the unmanaged forest, compared with only 28 in the managed forest. As a result of lower diversity, species are also more concentrated in the managed forest (table 4.3), thus facilitating their exploitation.

Comparing the relative importance of resources in the forest types, sources of food and drink have a considerably higher (>10%) relative importance on the

TABLE 4.1. Species With DBH 2.5 cm, Collected in a 0.25-ha Area of Unmanaged Floodplain Forest on Ilha das Onças with Scientific and Vernacular Names, and Data on Ecology and Uses.

N	SCIENTIFIC NAME	FAM	VERNACULAR NAME	ABUN-DANCE		FRE-QUENCY		DOMI-NANCE		IMPOR-TANCE	USES
				n	%	n	%	cm²	%	%	
	Euterpe oleracea Mart.	PAL	açaí	100	38.3	10	7.9	13,814	13.8	20.0	F,M,W,G,U,X
1405	*Pterocarpus officinalis* Jacq.	LEG	mututi	6	2.3	5	4	21,408	21.5	9.3	E,G,U
1437	*Spondias mombin* Urb.	ANA	taperebá	4	1.5	3	2.4	16,770	16.8	6.9	F,E,G
1402	*Pithecellobium latifolium* (L.) Benth.	LEG	jarandeua	23	8.8	9	7.1	1,587	1.6	5.8	E
	Carapa guianensis Aubl.	MEL	andiroba	8	3.1	6	4.8	6,357	6.4	4.8	M,W,G
	Astrocaryum murumuru Mart.	PAL	murumuru	12	4.6	7	5.6	2,223	2.2	4.1	F,G,U
1417	*Hevea brasiliensis* (Willd. ex A. Juss.) M. Arg.	EUP	seringueira	5	1.9	4	3.2	4,844	4.9	3.3	G,X
1424	*Cynometra marginata* Benth.	LEG	maraximbe	4	1.5	3	2.4	5,430	5.4	3.1	W,E
1416	*Inga* cf. *alba* Willd.	LEG	ingá branco	8	3.1	5	4	2,143	2.1	3.1	F,E,G,X
1413	*Macrolobium angustifolium* (Benth.) Cowan	LEG	ipê	4	1.5	4	3.2	4,343	4.4	3.0	W,E
1404	*Matisia paraensis* Huber	BOM	cupuaçurana	6	2.3	5	4	2,333	2.3	2.9	E
1408	*Pentaclethra macroloba* (Willd.) Kuntze	LEG	pracaxi	6	2.3	4	3.2	3,259	3.3	2.9	E
1412	*Quararibea guianensis* Aubl.	BOM	inajarana	6	2.3	4	3.2	1,155	1.2	2.2	M,W,E
1420	*Dalbergia monetaria* L. f.	LEG	verônica vermelha	7	2.7	4	3.2	235	0.2	2.0	M
1411	*Protium* cf. *polybotrium* (Turcz.) Engl.	BRS	breu branco	7	2.7	3	2.4	989	1	2.0	E,G
1414	*Terminalia dichotoma* G. Meyer	CMB	cuiarana	2	0.8	2	1.6	3,740	3.7	2.0	W,E,U

TABLE 4.1. (continued)

N	SCIENTIFIC NAME	FAM	VERNACULAR NAME	ABUN-DANCE		FRE-QUENCY		DOMI-NANCE		IMPOR-TANCE	USES
				n	%	n	%	cm²	%	%	
1427	Derris cf. negrensis Benth.	LEG	cumacaí	4	1.5	4	3.2	126	0.1	1.6	M,U
1432	Crudia sp.	LEG	———	2	0.8	2	1.6	1,955	2	1.5	E
1410	Mora paraensis Ducke	LEG	pracuúba	1	0.4	1	0.8	2,463	2.5	1.2	M,W,G
1438	Symphonia globulifera L.	GUT	anani	3	1.1	2	1.6	186	0.2	1.0	M,W
1428	*Virola surinamensis (Rol.) Warb.	MYS	ucuúba vermelha	2	0.8	2	1.6	612	0.6	1.0	M,W,E,G,X
1419	Adenocalymma cf. inundatum Mart. ex DC.	BIG	graxamã da branca	2	0.8	2	1.6	82	0.1	0.8	———
1422	Crudia oblonga Benth.	LEG	———	1	0.4	1	0.8	1,176	1.2	0.8	E
———	Cydista sp.	BIG	———	2	0.8	2	1.6	102	0.1	0.8	
1436	Eschweilera cf. alba Kunth.	LCY	matá-matá branco	2	0.8	2	1.6	99	0.1	0.8	M,W,E,G,X
1441	Rheedia macrophylla Pl. et Tr.	GUT	bacuri	2	0.8	2	1.6	88	0.1	0.8	F,W,E,G
———	Unidentified Vine No. 1	———	———	2	0.8	2	1.6	99	0.1	0.8	———
1406	Machaerium leiophyllum (DC.) Benth.	LEG	ingá pretinho (?)	3	1.1	1	0.8	162	0.2	0.7	E
1463	Uncaria guianensis (Aubl.) Gmel.	RUB	jupinda do vermelho	3	1.1	1	0.8	93	0.1	0.7	U
1425	Sterculia cf. elata Ducke	STR	capoteiro do duro	1	0.4	1	0.8	693	0.7	0.6	E
1445	Swartzia polyphylla A.DC.	LEG	pitaíca	1	0.4	1	0.8	293	0.3	0.5	E,U
1415	Allantoma cf. lineata (Mart. ex Berg.) Miers	LCY	xuru	1	0.4	1	0.8	52	0.1	0.4	W,E,G,U
1409	Arrabidaea sp.	BIG	———	1	0.4	1	0.8	18	0	0.4	———
1426	Bauhinia guianensis Aubl.	LEG	escada de jabuti	1	0.4	1	0.8	26	0	0.4	M
1495	Caraipa grandifolia Mart.	GUT	ipê do duro	1	0.4	1	0.8	108	0.1	0.4	W,E,X
1450	Cecropia concolor Willd.	MOR	imbaúba branca	1	0.4	1	0.8	64	0.1	0.4	E,G

Number	Species	Family	Common name								Uses
1446	*Couepia* sp.	CHB	tamaquaré	1	0.4	1	0.8	71	0.1	0.4	W,E
1424	*Cynometra* cf. *martiana* (Hayne) Macbr.	LEG	maraximbe	1	0.4	1	0.8	26	0	0.4	W,E
1431	*Ficus trigona* L. f.	MOR	apuí	1	0.4	1	0.8	16	0	0.4	G
1403	*Guarea kunthiana* A. Juss.	MEL	boloteiro	1	0.4	1	0.8	64	0.1	0.4	E
1449	*Licania heteromorpha* Benth.	CHB	mucucu do vermelho	1	0.4	1	0.8	21	0	0.4	E
1443	*Lophostoma* sp.	THI	cipó de fogo	1	0.4	1	0.8	15	0	0.4	—
1423	*Machaerium macrophyllum* var. *brevialatum* Rudd.	LEG	—	1	0.4	1	0.8	28	0	0.4	—
1439	*Ocotea caudata* Mez	LAU	louro preto	1	0.4	1	0.8	17	0	0.4	—
1448	*Paragonia* cf. *pyramidata* (L. Rich.) Bur.	BIG	graxamã da branca	1	0.4	1	0.8	61	0.1	0.4	—
1429	*Parinari excelsa* Sabine	CHB	tamaquaré	1	0.4	1	0.8	66	0.1	0.4	W,E
1442	*Richardella glomerata* var. *glomerata*	SPT	canela de velho	1	0.4	1	0.8	34	0	0.4	F,E,G
—	*Socratea exorrhiza* Mart.	PAL	paxiúba	1	0.4	1	0.8	102	0.1	0.4	M,W,U
1401	*Sterculia pruriens* (Aubl.) Sch.	STR	capoteiro	1	0.4	1	0.8	52	0.1	0.4	E,U
—	Unidentified Vine No. 2		—	1	0.4	1	0.8	21	0	0.4	—
—	Unidentified Vine No. 3		—	1	0.4	1	0.8	17	0	0.4	—
—	Unidentified Vine No. 4		—	1	0.4	1	0.8	25	0	0.4	
1444	*Virola* cf. *michellii* Heckel	MYS	ucuúba branca	1	0.4	1	0.8	24	0	0.4	M,W,E,G,X
	TOTAL			261	100.5	126	100.6	99,787	100.1	99.8	

NOTE: Numbers [N] refer to collections of A. B. Anderson et al. Asterisks indicate species also present in the inventory of managed floodplain forest on Ilha das Onças (Table 4.2). F = food, M = medicine, W = wood for construction or furniture, E = energy in the form of firewood or charcoal, G = game attractant, U = utensils, X = other uses.

TABLE 4.2. Species With DBH ≥5 cm, Collected in a 0.25-ha Area of Managed Floodplain Forest on Ilha das Onças with Scientific and Vernacular Names, and Data on Ecology and Uses.

N	SCIENTIFIC NAME	FAM	VERNACULAR NAME	ABUN-DANCE		FRE-QUENCY		DOMI-NANCE		IMPOR-TANCE	USES
				n	%	n	%	cm^2	%	%	
1066	*Euterpe oleracea Mart.	PAL	açaí	163	50.5	24	19.2	11,919	15.2	28.4	F,M,W,U
1083	*Hevea brasiliensis (Willd. ex A. Juss.) M. Arg.	EUP	seringueira	27	8.4	15	12.0	23,746	30.2	16.9	M,G,X
1129	Theobroma cacao L.	STR	cacau	48	14.9	18	14.4	2,359	3.0	10.8	F
1095	Inga edulis Mart.	LEG	ingá cipó	27	8.4	13	10.4	8,009	10.2	9.7	F,E,G
1084	*Spondias mombin Urb.	ANA	taperebá	5	1.6	5	4.0	9,526	12.1	5.9	F,M,W,E,G
1201	Ficus cf. paraensis (Miq.) Miq.	MOR	apuí	1	0.3	1	0.8	8,511	10.8	4.0	G
1152	*Inga cf. alba Willd.	LEG	ingá xichica	8	2.5	6	4.8	2,724	3.5	3.6	F,G,E
1137	Cordia cf. bicolor A. DC.	BOR	—	5	1.6	5	4.0	1,064	1.4	2.3	E
1171	*Pentaclethra macroloba (Willd.) Kuntze	LEG	pracaxi	5	1.6	5	4.0	1,035	1.3	2.3	M,E,X
1056	Cecropia cf. obtusa Tréc.	MOR	imbauba	3	0.9	3	2.4	2,229	2.8	2.0	M,E,G
1128	Theobroma grandiflorum (Willd. ex Spreng.) K. Schum.	STR	cupuaçu	3	0.9	3	2.4	1,215	1.6	1.6	F
1085	*Astrocaryum murumuru Mart.	PAL	murumuru	3	0.9	3	2.4	721	0.9	1.4	F,E,G,X
1200	Guarea cf. guidona (L.) Sleumer	MEL	boloteiro	2	0.6	2	1.6	1,324	1.7	1.3	E
1146	*Pithecellobium latifolium (L.) Benth.	LEG	jarandeua	3	0.9	3	2.4	102	0.1	1.1	M
1166	Allophyllus mollis Radlk.	SAP	—	3	0.9	3	2.4	236	0.3	1.1	—
1074	Genipa americana L.	RUB	genipapo	1	0.3	1	0.8	1,176	1.5	0.9	F,M,W,U

	Species	Family	Common name								Uses
—	*Mangifera indica* L.	ANA	manga	2	0.6	2	1.6	487	0.6	0.9	F,M,G
1131	*Aqiphila* cf. *arborescens* Vahl	VER	—	2	0.6	2	1.6	146	0.2	0.8	—
1140	*Mauritia flexuosa* L.f.	PAL	miriti	1	0.3	1	0.8	951	1.2	0.8	F,W,G,U
1150	*Virola surinamensis* (Rol.) Warb.	MYS	ucuúba branca	2	0.6	2	1.6	129	0.2	0.8	M,W,E,G,X
1142	*Carapa guianensis* Aubl.	MEL	andiroba	1	0.3	1	0.8	269	0.3	0.5	M,W,E,G
1148	*Miconia* sp.	MLT	—	2	0.6	1	0.8	55	0.1	0.5	—
1133	*Cedrela odorata* L.	MEL	cedro	1	0.3	1	0.8	119	0.2	0.4	W
1159	*Guarea trichilioides* L.	MEL	—	1	0.3	1	0.8	35	0.0	0.4	W
1067	*Psidium guajava* L.	MYR	goiaba	1	0.3	1	0.8	121	0.2	0.4	F,E,G
1079	*Gustavia augusta* L.	LCY	geniparana	1	0.3	1	0.8	20	0.0	0.4	E
—	*Eugenia* sp.	MYR	—	1	0.3	1	0.8	26	0.0	0.4	W
—	*Tetrapterix* sp.	MPH	—	1	0.3	1	0.8	24	0.0	0.4	W
	TOTAL			323	100.0	125	100.0	78,296	99.6	100.0	

NOTE: Numbers (N) refer to collections of A. B. Anderson et al. Asterisks indicate species also present in the inventory of managed floodplain forest on Ilha das Onças (Table 4.1). F = food, M = medicine, W = wood for construction or furniture, E = energy in the form of firewood or charcoal, G = game attractant, U = utensils, X = other uses.

managed site, conversely, sources of wood (i.e., timber) and fuel (i.e., firewood and charcoal) have a higher relative importance on the unmanaged site (table 4.3). As mentioned previously, trees that provide fuel are selectively eliminated when floodplain forests are subjected to management. Due to the exceptional abundance and economic importance of the açaí palm, trees that branch at a height of ca. 8–15 m and consequently interfere directly with mature crowns of this species are especially prone to thinning. Examples of such trees indicated by informants include *Pithecellobium latifolium* (L.) Benth., *Pentaclethra macroloba* (Willd.) Kuntze, *Matisia paraense* Huber, *Quararibea guianensis* Aubl., and *Protium* cf. *polybotrium* (Turez.) Engl.; all of these species provide firewood, and all have reduced (or no) representation in the managed forest (tables 4.1 and 4.2).

According to local informants, one of the principal motives for subjecting floodplain forests to tolerant management is to make natural resources more accessible. As shown above, forest thinning results in a considerable reduction of biomass, and selective elimination of vines and understory vegetation results in vastly improved access. Local residents carry out periodic cleaning of managed forests to remove obstacles, reduce the occurrence of spines (especially those of the abundant palm, *Astrocaryum murumuru* Mart.), and eliminate hiding places of poisonous snakes.

Tolerant forms of forest management also provide improved conditions for consciously favored species. Various cultigens such as mango, cacao, and coconut are introduced as seeds or seedlings in the understory and are subsequently favored by concentrating organic material at their bases and eliminating forest competitors. Tolerant forms of forest management also preserve a wide range of tolerated species, many of which are economically useful as sources of extractive products such as fruit trees and rubber. The latter species is especially important in floodplain forests of the Amazon estuary, where it abounds over widespread

TABLE 4.3. Relative Importance of Species and Resources in Areas of Managed and Unmanaged Floodplain Forests on the Ilha das Onças.

	IMPORTANCE	
ITEM	*Managed Forest*	*Unmanaged Forest*
Species (20)	96.4	84.9
Food	64.0	40.1
Drink	48.4	33.8
Medicine	59.2	55.1
Wood	36.8	52.5
Game Attractant	46.0	36.2
Energy	29.3	47.0
Fertilizer	29.3	27.1
Utensils	30.1	38.1
Fibers	29.2	27.1
Other Uses	21.4	10.3

SOURCE: Data summarized from tables 4.1 and 4.2.

areas. Although informants report that rubber is not planted or consciously favored, it is roughly five times more abundant in the managed forest than in the unmanaged forest (tables 4.1 and 4.2). This greater abundance is probably the result of long-term tolerance of seedlings and saplings, combined with selective elimination of competitors. Other tolerated species include fruit trees such as taperebá, ingá, and miriti. Although important sources of timber such as "andiroba" (*Carapa guianensis* Aubl.) and "ucuuba" (*Virola* spp.) are not abundant, seedlings of these species are also reportedly tolerated by local inhabitants.

Most of the species utilized in the managed forest under consideration are not planted, much less tended, in ways commonly associated with more intrusive forms of land use. In fact, the very nature of management in this forest is frequently elusive. For example, a species such as rubber is hardly managed in a conventional sense. Yet its tolerance in a managed zone appears to lead to higher representation than in an unmanaged zone. Is this species undergoing management or mere extraction?

The Value of Management

Although often difficult to detect, tolerant forms of forest management appear to be economically rational. A field experiment was carried out on Ilha das Onças to assess the effects of forest management practices on the ecologically and economically important açaí palm (Anderson and Jardim 1989). The experimental treatments—selective thinning of competitors and pruning of açaí stems—duplicated tolerant management practices utilized by rural inhabitants. Average annual fruit yields of açaí per hectare were found to increase from 1,158.8 kg on control plots to 1,854.8 kg on plots subjected to thinning and pruning; in economic terms, gross annual returns per ha from açaí fruit production increased 58.0 percent, from U.S. $235.25 to U.S. $371.58. Discounting estimated costs of implementing management, net annual gains per hectare were U.S. $109.83.

This analysis does not take into account the value of other forest products extracted during thinning and pruning operations, such as palm heart and timber. Nor does it consider the greater facility of obtaining these and other forest products on managed sites, as compared with sites not subjected to management. The analysis only covers the first year: in subsequent years, site preparation costs should decline while returns from fruit yields are likely to remain constant.

Finally, although net returns per unit area from other land uses such as swidden agriculture may be higher over the short term, such land uses require considerable labor and material inputs, can only be practiced on a relatively small scale, and are rarely (if ever) practiced continuously at a given site. In contrast, the forest management practices described above require few inputs, can be carried out over extensive areas, and are likely to be sustainable indefinitely. Although far from comprehensive, this cost-benefit analysis illustrates that tolerant forest management practices are simple, apparently sustainable, and—in the long run—economically competitive.

The forest management practices described above are an integral part of other land uses commonly practiced in the floodplain of the Amazon estuary. Managed forests may originate from a house garden or a swidden plot through selective control of regeneration; when regeneration ceases to be controlled, they revert to unmanaged forest (figure 4.5). The dynamic linkages between managed forests and other forms of land use—all within close proximity to rural households—seem to be part of a general strategy to maximize opportunities for resource exploitation. These opportunities include domestic and recreational activities; fishing, hunting, and raising of livestock; and use of fruits, palm heart, wood, fertilizer, ornamental plants, fibers, latex, honey, oilseeds, medicinals, and utensils. No single land unit offers all these opportunities, but a combination of units does.

Finally, the foregoing discussion illustrates that systems of forest management are transitional in nature and consequently difficult to distinguish. Such transitional land units have historically been viewed as useless, unowned, or abandoned, and are consequently anathema to agronomists, planners, and policymakers committed to more intrusive forms of land management (cf. Dove 1983). It is thus no surprise that caboclos are often overlooked in policies aimed at developing the economic potential of the Amazon floodplain.

Extraction and Forest Management Reconsidered

Extraction and management seem to be irreconcilable land-use strategies. Yet in describing a so-called tolerant strategy of forest management, I have entered domains that many would consider closer to extraction. Although I am not certain where management ends and extraction begins in tolerant land-use systems, both processes clearly coexist within the floodplain forest sites described in this paper.

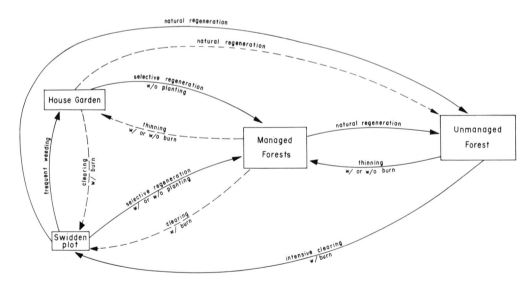

FIGURE 4.5. Flowchart of major land-use units associated with forests subjected to tolerant forms of management in the floodplain of the Amazon estuary (Anderson et al. 1985). Solid arrows indicate processes visibly documented by author; dashed arrows indicate processes surmised by author or suggested by informants.

I would suggest that such systems occupy a middle ground between conventional, intrusive land uses on the one hand, and exclusively extractive land uses on the other.

Reconciliation of extraction and forest management can probably occur only under certain circumstances. Integration of these activities is facilitated in forests that contain a relatively high concentration of economic species, such as the floodplain forests of the Amazon estuary. The dynamic nature of these ecosystems likewise produces optimal conditions for sustained, short-cycle extraction of forest products.

In traditional indigenous cultures, where intrusion of external markets is minimal, extraction and forest management may coexist under a wide variety of ecological conditions (e.g., Posey 1983). Where market economies predominate and indigenous traditions fade, however, one would expect that the opportunities for such reconciliation are reduced. Yet the results reported here and those of Padoch et al. (1985) show that near major Amazonian cities such as Belém and Iquitos, rural communities comprised of deculturated indigenous descendents have evolved market-oriented land-use systems that successfully integrate extraction and forest management.

These considerations lead me to conclude that the essential ingredient for reconciling extraction and forest management is a rural population with both a knowledge of and respect for forest resources. The Amazon caboclo, often marginalized by both academics and policymakers, has developed sophisticated systems of land use that appear to be both ecologically sustainable and economically profitable.

ACKNOWLEDGMENTS

A preliminary version of this paper was presented in November, 1986, at the Man and the Biosphere (MAB) Workshop on Regeneration and Management of Tropical Forests, in Guri, Venezuela, under the title "Forest Management Strategies in the Amazon Estuary." The research for this paper was supported by the Ford Foundation, the World Wildlife Fund, and the Conselho Nacional de Desenvolvimento Cientifico e Tecnológico. I express my gratitude to Anne Gély, Bill Balée, Darrell Posey and Janis Alcorn for their helpful comments on earlier drafts of this paper.

ENDNOTE

1. One such zone commonly occurs in the vicinity of rural dwellings and represents a transition between the house garden and the dense floodplain forest. At such locales this zone is considered to be an extension of the house garden and is likewise called "terreiro," although it is structurally and functionally quite distinct. (Alternatively, both the house garden and the adjacent managed forest are called "sítio," a term roughly equivalent to homestead.) Other, less distinguishable zones are relatively distant from the household and are frequently surrounded by dense forest. These zones may originate through thinning of the forest, regeneration of a swidden plot, or long-term cultivation of trees on a formerly cleared plot. According to their origin and current structure, they may be referred to as a gap or clearing ("clareira"), a fallow ("capoeira"), a cultivated field ("roça"), or a plantation ("plantio").

REFERENCES

Alcorn, J. B. 1981. Huastec noncrop resource management: implications for prehistoric rain forest management. *Human Ecology* 9(4):395–417.

Anderson, A. B., A. Gély, J. Strudwick, G. L. Sobel, and M. G. C. Pinto. 1985. Um sistema agroflorestal na várzea do estuário amazônico (Ilha das Onças, Município de Barcarena, Estado do Pará). *Acta Amazonica*, Supplement, 15(1–2):195–224.

Anderson, A. B. and M. A. G. Jardim. 1989. Costs and benefits of floodplain forest management by rural inhabitants in the Amazon estuary: A case study of açaí palm production. In J. Browder, ed., *Fragile Lands of Latin America: The Search for Sustainable Uses.* Boulder, Colo.: Westview Press.

Calzavara, B. B. G. 1972. As possibilidades do açaizeiro no estuário amazônico. *Boletim da Fundação de Ciências Agrárias do Pará* 5:1–103.

Carvajal, G. de, A. de Rojas, and C. de Azuña. 1941. *Descobrimentos do Rio das Amazonas.* São Paulo: Editora Nacional.

Denevan, W. M. 1984. Ecological heterogeneity and horizontal zonation of agriculture in the Amazon floodplain. In M. Schmink and C. H. Wood, eds., *Frontier Expansion in Amazonia*, pp. 311–336. Gainesville: University of Florida Press.

Denevan, W. M., J. M. Treacy, J. B. Alcorn, C. Padoch, J. Denslow, and S. F. Paitan. 1984. Indigenous agroforestry in the Peruvian Amazon: Bora Indian management of swidden fields. *Interciencia* 9(6):346–357.

Dove, M. 1983. Theories of swidden agriculture and the political economy of ignorance. *Agroforestry Systems* 1:85–99.

Falesi, I. C. 1974. Soils of the Brazilian Amazon. In C. Wagley, ed., *Man in the Amazon*, pp. 201–229. Gainesville: University of Florida Press.

Fox, J. J. 1977. *Harvest of the Palm.* Cambridge: Harvard University Press.

Goulding, M. 1980. *The Fishes and the Forest.* Berkeley: University of California Press.

Hallé, F., R. A. A. Oldeman, and P. B. Tomlinson. 1978. *Tropical Trees and Forests: An Architectural Analysis.* New York: Springer-Verlag.

Huber, J. 1943. Contribuição à geografia física da região dos furos de Breves e da parte ocidental da Ilha do Marajó. *Revista Brasileira de Geografia* 5(3):449–474.

IBDF-SUDAM. 1988. *Levantamento da Alteração de Cobertura Natural.* Instituto Brasileiro de Desenvolvimento Florestal and Superintendência de Desenvolvimento da Amazônia, Belém, Brazil.

Iron, G. 1984. Sedimentation and sediments of Amazonian rivers and evolution of the Amazonian landscape since Pliocene times. In H. Sioli, ed., *The Amazon: Limnology and Landscape Ecology of a Mighty Tropical River and Its Basin*, pp. 201–214. Dordrecht, The Netherlands: Dr. W. Junk.

Lima, R. R. 1956. A agricultura nas várzeas do estuário do Amazonas. *Boletim Técnico do Instituto Agronômico do Norte* 33:1–164.

Meggers, B. J. 1971. *Amazonia: Man and Culture in a Counterfeit Paradise.* Chicago: Aldine-Atherton.

Moran, E. F. 1977. Estratégias de sobrevivência: O uso de recursos ao longo da Rodovia Transamazônica. *Acta Amazonica* 7(3):363–379.

Padoch, C., J. Chota Inuma, W. de Jung, and J. Unruh. 1985. Amazonian agroforestry: A market-oriented system in Peru. *Agroforestry Systems* 3:47–58.

Parker, E. P. 1985. Cabocloization: The transformation of the Amerindian in Amazonia 1615–1800. E. P. Parker, ed., *The Amazon Caboclo: Historical and Contemporary Perspectives*, pp. xvii–1i. Studies in Third World Societies Publication Series, vol. 29. Williamsburg, Va: William and Mary Press.

Posey, A. D., J. Frechione, J. Eddins, F. S. Silva with D. Myers, D. Case, and P. Macbeath. 1984. Ethnoecology as applied anthropology in Amazonian development. *Human Organization* 43(2):95–107.

Posey, D. A. 1983. Indigenous knowledge and development: An ideological bridge to the future. *Ciência e Cultura* 35(7):877–894.

Posey, D. A. 1985. Indigenous management of tropical forest ecosystems: The case of the Kayapó Indians of the Brazilian Amazon. *Agroforestry Systems* 3:139–158.

Rankin, J. M. 1985. Forestry in the Brazilian Amazon. In G. T. Prance and T. E. Lovejoy, eds. *Amazonia*, pp. 369–392. Oxford, England: Pergamon Press.

Roosevelt, A. C. 1980. *Parmana: Prehistoric Maize and Manioc Subsistence along the Amazon and Orinoco*. New York: Academic Press.

Ross, E. B. 1978. The evolution of the Amazon peasantry. *Journal of Latin American Studies* 10(2):193–218.

5

Population Ecology and Management of Forest Fruit Trees in Peruvian Amazonia

■

CHARLES M. PETERS

ABSTRACT

Monodominant forests of native fruit trees extend over thousands of square kilometers in Peruvian Amazonia. Long-term demographic studies were conducted in two of these forests, one dominated by Myrciaria dubia, *the other by* Grias peruviana. *Both of these species produce fruit of economic importance. The* M. dubia *study population contained 3050 adult trees/ha and produced from 9.5 to 12.6 mt of fruit/ha/yr. The* G. peruviana *study population contained 248 adults trees/ha and produced 2.3 mt of fruit/ha/yr. Transition matrix analyses of the demographic data collected for* G. peruviana *indicate that intensive fruit harvests have little impact on the long-term regeneration of this species in the forest. Increasing the exploitation of wild fruit trees offers a unique opportunity to integrate the utilization and conservation of Amazonian forests.*

Current efforts to develop the native fruit resources of Amazonia are focused almost exclusively on cultivation. The agronomic characteristics of a growing number of native fruits are being assessed at research stations throughout the Amazon Basin (Clement et al. 1982), and single or mixed plantings of many species have already been established. The areal extent of commercial fruit plantations is expected to increase dramatically in the next decade (Alvim 1981). Clearly, there are strong economic arguments for growing fruit trees in high-density plantations. The inherent problem with this form of management is that plantation establishment inevitably entails forest clearing. Given existing rates of deforestation in Amazonia, alternative management strategies are urgently needed.

Although the fact is seldom emphasized in most of the literature on Amazonian fruits, many economic species occur naturally in dense populations. Monodominant forests of fruit trees extend over thousands of square kilometers in Amazonia, these communities usually being confined to extremely adverse or stressed habitats where severe flooding or shallow soils preclude the formation of species-rich forest. The occurrence of natural "monocultures" of fruit trees offers a unique opportunity to integrate the utilization and conservation of Amazonian forests. However, before promoting the increased exploitation of wild fruit trees, two fundamental questions must be addressed: 1) do natural populations produce enough fruit to warrant commercial harvesting? and 2) how much fruit can be harvested from the forest each year without damaging the long-term regeneration of the species?

This paper examines the ecology and management potential of natural populations of fruit trees in Peruvian Amazonia. A brief description is presented first of the native species known to form monodominant forests in this region. The structure and yield of natural populations of two of these species, *Myrciaria dubia* (H.B.K.) McVaugh and *Grias peruviana* Miers, are then discussed in detail based on the results of a three-year ecological study. Finally, a simple matrix model is used to evaluate the sustainability of annual fruit harvests.

Monodominant Forests of Native Fruit Trees

The distribution and habitat of six native fruit species that form dense, natural populations in Peruvian Amazonia are listed in table 5.1. All of the species are exploited commercially to varying degrees; the two palms were listed in the U.S. National Academy of Science report on economically promising tropical plants (NAS 1975). General information about the characteristics and use of each species can be found in the classic works of Le Cointe (1934) and Cavalcante (1972, 1974, 1979).

Mauritia flexuosa L.f. attains dominance in permanently flooded backwater swamps along low upland terraces. Pure stands of this palm occupy at least a million hectares in the Peruvian lowlands (Malleux-Orjedo 1975). *Jessenia bataua* (Mart.) Burret, another common Amazonian palm, forms dense populations in upland sites on poorly-drained, gleyic podzols. Both *M. flexuosa* and *J. bataua* produce edible fruit and yield a high-quality vegetable oil (Balick 1979). *Quararibea cordata* (H. B.) Vischer is frequently cultivated in household gardens in Peruvian Amazonia; the species is a dominant component of upland forests along high terraces.

High-density populations of fruit trees also occur in forest subject to periodic flooding. *Myrciaria dubia*, a common riparian shrub, forms pure stands along the banks of the tributaries and ox-bow lakes of the Amazon River. Of great potential importance, the fruits of this species contain the highest concentration of vitamin C of any plant known to man (Ferreyra 1959; Peters and Vazquez 1987). Although

TABLE 5.1. Nomenclature, Distribution, and Habitat of Six Forest Fruit Trees that Form Dense, Natural Populations in Peruvian Amazonia.

Species	Local Name	Distribution	Habitat
Mauritia flexuosa L.f. PALMAE	aguaje (PE) buriti (BR)	Amazonia, Guianas	Swamp forest on distric histosols
Jessenia bataua (Mart.) Burret PALMAE	ungurahui (PE) patauã (BR)	Amazonia	Upland forest on gleyic podzols
Quararibea cordata (H.B.) Vischer BOMBACACEAE	sapote (PE) sapota (BR)	Western Amazonia	Upland forest on ferric luvisols; also cultivated
Myciaria dubia (H.B.K.) McVaugh MYRTACEAE	camu-camu (PE) caçarí (BR)	Northwest Amazonia	Riparian fluvisols
Grias peruviana Miers LECYTHIDACEAE	sacha mangua (PE)	Northwest Amazonia	Lowland forest on eutric fluvisols
Theobroma cacao L. *STERCULIACEAE*	cacao (PE) cacau (BR)	Amazonia	Lowland forest on eutric fluvisols; also cultivated

NOTE: Local names in Peru (PE) and Brazil (BR) based on personal observations; distributional patterns compiled from personal observations and examination of herbarium specimens (AMAZ, NY). Habitat designations represent areas within which a species was most frequently observed to attain local dominance; the same species may occur at lower densities in other environments. Soil descriptions follow FAO-UNESCO (1971) classification.

somewhat limited in distribution, *Grias peruviana* is an abundant understory species in many lowland forests. The fruits of this small, monopodial tree are rich in vitamin A (INDDA 1984) and contain an edible oil. Interestingly, even *Theobroma cacao* L., probably the best known and most widely appreciated of all Amazonian fruits, forms dense (semi-wild?) groves in the flooded forests of Peruvian Amazonia.

Structure and Yield of Forest Populations

To assess the feasibility of managing wild populations of fruit trees on a sustained-yield basis, ecological studies of *M. dubia* and *G. peruviana* were initiated in 1984. These two species were selected for study based on their natural abundance and superior nutritional characteristics. Local markets also exist for each fruit. Fieldwork on both species was based out of the Instituto de Investigaciones de la Amazonia Peruana (IIAP) research station at Jenaro Herrera (73° 40′W, 4° 55′S), Department of Loreto, Peru. The small village of Jenaro Herrera is located on the eastern bank of the Ucayali River, approximately 165 km from the city of Iquitos. Annual rainfall in the region averages 2889 mm; mean annual temperature is 25.9° C (unpublished IIAP records). The local vegetation is classified as "tropical wet forest" (Holdridge et al. 1971), and contains both upland and seasonally flooded forest formations.

The *M. dubia* study population is located along the eastern margin of Sahua cocha, an 80-ha ox-bow lake of the Ucayali River near Jenaro Herrera. Although *M. dubia* is clearly the dominant plant in this riparian habitat, associated species include *Eugenia inundata* D.C., *Symmeria paniculata* Benth. and *Laetia americana* L. The vegetation bordering the lake is usually flooded for six to seven months each year. *Grias peruviana* was studied in a tract of floodplain forest near the mouth of the Iricahua River, a small black water tributary of the Ucayali. Dominant canopy species in the forest include *Maguira coriacea* (Karst.) C. C. Berg, *Hura crepitans* L., and *Ceiba samauma* (Mart.) K. Schum.; palms of the genera *Euterpe*, *Astrocaryum* and *Scheelea* are especially prevalent. The forest floods to a depth of about 1.5 m each year during April and May.

Population Structure

In September of 1984 during low-water level, a series of 10 × 10 m permanent study plots was established in the *M. dubia* population bordering Sahua cocha. All *M. dubia* individuals in each plot were measured for height and basal diameter, and their position mapped to the nearest 0.5 m. Each individual was permanently numbered with a metal tag. In response to the continual rise in water level of Sahua cocha, the inventory was suspended after completing 10 plots (1000 m^2).

The density and size-class structure of the *G. peruviana* population was determined through systematic inventories of fifteen 20 × 20 m plots (6000 m^2). Within each plot, all *G. peruviana* individuals were labelled, measured, and mapped. Seedlings and saplings less than 1.5 m tall were measured for height; both height and diameter (DBH) were measured for juveniles and adults.

Including seedlings, saplings, juveniles, and adults, the *M. dubia* and *G. peruviana* study populations contain 12,310 and 2007 individuals/ha, respectively. The size-class distribution of these two populations is shown in figure 5.1, the number of individuals in each class being plotted on a log scale. It should be noted that the data presented for *M. dubia* represents the number of genetically distinct individuals in the population, or "genets" (*sensu* Harper 1977), and not the total number of stems or "ramets." This is an important distinction given the profuse basal branching exhibited by the species. If ramets are also included, the density estimate for the *M. dubia* population surpasses 15,000 stems/ha. The dotted vertical line shown in figure 5.1 reflects the division between juvenile and adult trees in each population.

A common characteristic of the size-class distributions of many tropical trees is a pronounced absence of saplings and juveniles (Richards 1952; Whitmore, 1975; Sarukhan, 1980). This type of size structure results when the regeneration of a species is severely limited for some reason, most seedlings dying before becoming established. The size-class distributions of *M. dubia* and *G. peruviana*, however, display a smooth decrease in the number of individuals from the smaller to the larger size classes, and the intermediate classes are well-represented. Both histograms closely approximate a negative exponential distribution, which several authors (e.g., Meyer 1952; Leak 1965) have reported to be characteristic of stable, self-maintaining plant populations. Although it is difficult, and sometimes misleading, to draw conclusions about the dynamics of a plant population based on its size structure, both species appear to be actively regenerating.

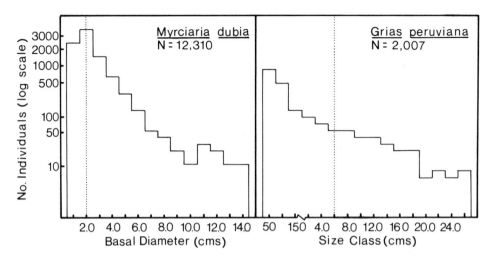

FIGURE 5.1. Size-class distribution of individuals in *Myrciaria dubia* and *Grias peruviana* study populations. Note log scale on y-axis. Size classes used for *Grias peruviana* are based on both height and diameter (DBH); transition occurs at 150 cm height class as indicated by break in scale. Dotted vertical line shown in each histogram reflects the division between juvenile and adult trees.

Reproductive Phenology

The *M. dubia* study population contains 3050 adults/ha; there are 248 adults/ha in the *G. peruviana* population. Adult trees of both species produce flowers and fruits on an annual basis, yet there are distinct differences between species in the timing and duration of each reproductive event. A graphic representation of the reproductive phenology of *M. dubia* and *G. peruviana* is shown in figure 5.2 together with water level data for the Ucayali River at Jenaro Herrera (unpublished IIAP records). Phenological patterns were compiled from weekly observations of marked adult trees in each study population.

Myciaria dubia initiates flowering at the end of August when the Ucayali River is at low-water level and all plants are on dry land. Flowering continues in distinct pulses until all trees are completely flooded, usually some time in February. Rising water levels apparently have little effect on anthesis, plants with over 95 percent of their crown underwater continuing to produce new flowers. Mature fruit start to form during the last weeks of October. The actual duration of the fruiting cycle in any given year is controlled by the flood cycle of the Ucayali. The longer that flooding is delayed, the longer *M. dubia* continues to produce fruit.

The reproductive phenology of *G. peruviana*, in contrast, is more aseasonal, this species maintaining a low level of flower and fruit production over an eight-month period (early September–late April). There is a slight peak in fruit production from January to March. Water from the Ucayali begins to flood the forest in late April or early May; flower and fruit production cease during peak flooding.

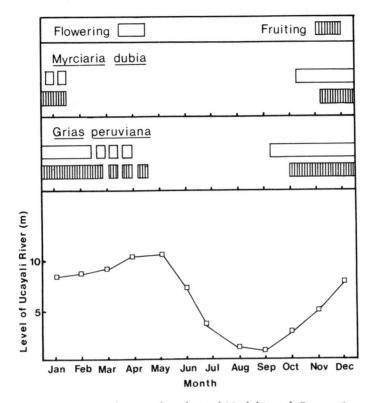

FIGURE 5.2. Reproductive phenology of *M. dubis* and *G. peruviana.*

Adult trees remain reproductively inactive for two to three months following flooding, the first new flowers being produced in early September.

Total Fruit Yield

The reproductive output from a forest population is determined by the density of adult trees and the rate of fruit production per tree. Given information on the size structure of natural populations of *M. dubia* and *G. peruviana*, size-specific rates of fruit production were measured for a subsample of adult trees on each study site. Regression equations relating fruit production to tree diameter were then derived for each species, and a fecundity value was calculated for every adult tree in the population based on its diameter. Summing these values provided an estimate of total population fruit production.

Fruit production by *M. dubia* was measured using 25 adult trees ranging in basal diameter from 2.0 to 14.0 cm. By means of a small boat, all mature fruits produced by each sample tree were periodically harvested, counted, and weighed until its crown was completely flooded. Measurements were continued over two fruiting seasons (1984 and 1985), the same 25 individuals being monitored each year.

Bi-weekly censuses of 15 adult trees of differing size were used to quantify fruit production rates for *G. peruviana*. Although some of the sample trees were over 15 m tall, all fruits were accessible from a ladder owing to the cauliflory exhibited by the species. At each sampling period, the total number of mature fruit present on each tree was counted, and all fruits were marked with paint to avoid duplication in subsequent counts. The censuses were continued for one complete year (1985–1986).

Size-specific fruit production rates for *M. dubia* and *G. peruviana* are shown in figure 5.3. Given the range in values and the exponential nature of the relationship between tree size and fecundity, fruit production data are plotted on a log scale. Least-squares linear regression using log-transformed fruit production data showed that fecundity was significantly related to diameter in both *M. dubia* (1984 data $r^2 = 0.973$, $p < 0.01$; 1985 data $r^2 = 0.991$, $p < 0.001$) and *G. peruviana* ($r^2 = 0.865$, $p < 0.05$). An increase in diameter results in an exponential increase in the number of fruits produced by each species.

Summing the individual fecundities of every adult tree in the population, *M. dubia* was estimated to produce between 1,200,000 (1984 results) and 1,600,000 (1985 results) fruits/ha/yr at Sahua cocha. Given an average fruit weight of 7.91 ± 0.23 g (N = 500) for this species, the total fruit yield in 1984 and 1985 is equivalent to 9.5 and 12.6 mt/ha, respectively. Using a similar analysis, total fruit production for the *G. peruviana* population at Iricahua was estimated at 8500 fruits/ha/yr. As a single mature fruit weighs 271.1 + 5.1 g (N = 42), this figure represents a total annual yield of 2.3 mt/ha.

Potential for Sustained-Yield Management

Natural populations of *M. dubia* and *G. peruviana* produce a prodigious amount of fruit. It should be realized, however, that these fruits contain the seeds that are essential for the continued regeneration of each species. If too many fruits are harvested from the forest each year, population recruitment could be severely affected. New seedlings would not be available to replace the growth and mortality of individuals in the larger size classes, the size-class distribution of the population would become progressively skewed toward adults, and with time, the species would disappear from the forest. As the sustainability of fruit collections from natural forests is contingent on the population maintaining an adequate level of regeneration, the determination of a maximum allowable harvest is a critical management problem.

Demography and Life Table Construction

The change in numbers a population experiences over time is a direct result of birth and death processes. The population grows when the recruitment of new individuals exceeds the number of deaths, and the population diminishes in size when mortality is greater than the number of births. Population stability, the goal of sustained-yield management, is reached when birth rates are exactly balanced

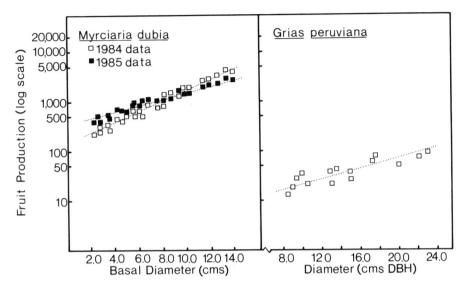

FIGURE 5.3. Size-specific fruit production ratios for *M. dubia* and *G. peruviana*.

by death rates. Given a knowledge of initial population size and size-specific birth, death, and growth rates, future changes in the structure and size of the population can be predicted with reasonable precision. Furthermore, by altering specific birth and death parameters, a sensitivity analysis can be performed to determine the demographic impact of a particular management practice.

The results from the inventory of the *M. dubia* and *G. peruviana* study sites furnish baseline data on population structure, and the studies of fruit yield provide detailed information on size-specific fecundity, or birth rates. What is lacking is to quantify the mortality and growth of individuals at different stages in the life cycle. These data were collected by periodically remeasuring all of the marked individuals in the *M. dubia* and *G. peruviana* populations. At each sampling period, the number of individuals in each size class that had died was recorded, height growth was measured for seedlings and saplings, and diameter growth was measured for larger individuals. The *M. dubia* population was monitored before and after flooding for two consecutive years; mortality and growth for *G. peruviana* were recorded bimonthly for 16 months.

To illustrate the potential utility of a demographic approach to forest management, life table data for the *G. peruviana* population is shown in table 5.2. For simplicity, the population has been grouped into nine life cycle stage (s_0 to s_8). The prereproductive phase of the life cycle is represented by seeds (s_0), seedlings (s_1), saplings (s_2 and s_3), and juveniles (s_4); adults are stratified into four different size classes (s_5 to s_8). The first column of this table shows the number of individuals (N) at each stage; columns two and three describe the annual growth and mortality of each stage. The proportion of individuals moving from or remaining in a given size class after one year was calculated using average growth rates and the height/diameter class interval. For example, small saplings (stage s_2) grow 12.0 cm/yr. Given a class interval of 50 cm, 4.2 yr would be required to move all of

TABLE 5.2. Life Table Data for *Grias peruviana* growing at Iricahua River, Loreto, Peru.

Size Class	Stage	N	Survival	Growth	% Moving	% Remaining	Fecundity
Seeds	s_0	8,581	0.525		1.000	0.000	—
Seedlings (0–50 cm tall)	s_1	997	0.124	7.9	0.158	0.842	—
Small saplings (50–100 cm tall)	s_2	463	0.682	12.0	0.240	0.760	—
Large saplings (100–150 cm tall)	s_3	167	0.877	17.2	0.344	0.656	—
Juveniles (1–5 cm DBH)	s_4	132	0.965	0.21	0.052	0.948	—
Adults (5–10 cm DBH)	s_5	118	0.978	0.26	0.053	0.947	16
Adults (10–15 cm DBH)	s_6	82	0.978	0.15	0.031	0.969	34
Adults (15–20 cm DBH)	s_7	35	0.978	0.19	0.038	0.962	59
Adults (20+ cm DBH)	s_8	13	0.978	0.18	0.000	1.000	97

NOTE: All rates expressed on a yearly basis; growth rate units are cm/yr for both height and diameter classes. See text for sources and calculations.

these individuals to the next stage (s_3). Assuming a homogenous size distribution within the class, 24.0 percent of the small saplings would advance to stage s_3 each year, while 76.0 percent would remain in stage s_2 until some future time period.

Matrix Models of Population Growth

Before the dynamics of the *G. peruviana* population can be analyzed, some means of tabulating and manipulating the demographic data shown in table 5.2 is needed. Matrix models are particularly useful for this purpose, and have been used to study the population dynamics of several tropical tree species (Hartshorn 1975; Enright and Ogden 1979; Bullock 1980). The basic model was initially developed by Leslie (1945) to predict the structure and growth rate of populations grouped into age classes. Given the difficulty of accurately determining the age of many organisms (e.g., tropical trees), this model was subsequently modified by Lefkovitch (1965) to utilize size-class data. The classes do not necessarily have to be of equal size, and even broad life stages such as seedlings, saplings, and adults may be used.

The basic structure of the model can be expressed in matrix notation as:

$$n_{t+1} = Mn_t$$

where n_t is a column vector containing s life cycle stages that represents the structure of the population at a given moment in time. M is a square matrix of order *s* that defines the movement of individuals from one stage to the next in a unit time period. Specifically, the transition matrix, *M*, contains transfer rates from one stage to the next, and mortality and fecundity data for each life cycle stage. Multiplying the transition matrix by the column vector yields the size and stage structure of the population at one time interval in the future.

Given that *M* is a square matrix with *s* rows and columns, repeated multiplication by the column vector will eventually produce the dominant latent root, or λ, of the matrix. As Leslie (1945), Lefkovitch (1965), Usher (1966), and other workers have shown, the dominant latent root of a transition matrix is equal to e^r, or the finite rate of increase of a population. This is a very important parameter, because it can be used to assess the stability, growth, or decline of a study population. For example, a λ greater than 1.0 indicates that the population is increasing in size, while a λ less than 1.0 shows that the population is decreasing in size. A λ equal to 1.0 indicates that birth and death rates are exactly balanced so that the population remains stable.

Matrix Projections and Sensitivity Analysis

Arranging the life table data for *G. peruviana* in a matrix format yields the transition matrix shown in table 5.3. The top row of the matrix lists the size-specific fecundity values for adults. The principal diagonal gives the proportion of individuals that remain in a given stage. This element takes into account both mortality and growth, and is equal to the proportion of individuals that remain in a given stage multiplied by the survivorship of that stage. Similarly, the subdiagonal lists the proportion of individuals that move into the next stage.

Exponentiation was used to calculate the dominant latent root of the transition matrix constructed for *G. peruviana*. The matrix was sequentially expo-

TABLE 5.3. Transition Matrix for *Grias peruviana* Population at Iricahua River, Loreto, Peru.

				STAGE				
s_0	s_1	s_2	s_3	s_4	s_5	s_6	s_7	s_8
0	0	0	0	0	16	34	59	97
0.52	0.10	0	0	0	0	0	0	0
0	0.02	0.52	0	0	0	0	0	0
0	0	0.16	0.57	0	0	0	0	0
0	0	0	0.30	0.91	0	0	0	0
0	0	0	0	0.05	0.93	0	0	0
0	0	0	0	0	0.05	0.95	0	0
0	0	0	0	0	0	0.03	0.94	0
0	0	0	0	0	0	0	0.04	0.98

NOTE: Top row gives fecundity values for adults; principal diagonal lists proportion of individuals staying in a stage; subdiagonal lists proportion of individuals moving from one stage to the next. Transition probabilities have been rounded off to two digits. See text for explanation of parameter estimation.

nentiated to the kth power of two until a constant value of λ was reached, stable values usually being obtained at a k of 256. The BASIC program used to manipulate the matrix was originally developed by Enright and Ogden (1979).

Using this procedure, a dominant latent root of 1.018 was calculated for the matrix. Although this λ is extremely close to the theoretical value of 1.0 expected for stable populations, the slight departure from unity indicates that the density of *G. peruviana* in the forest near Iricahua is increasing slightly. In the absence of exogenous disturbance, the population consistently maintains a level of seedling establishment that is more than sufficient to compensate for mortality in the larger size classes.

Given the balance between mortality and seedling establishment, what happens to the *G. peruviana* population if a large quantity of fruit is harvested each year? To simulate annual fruit collections, fecundity coefficients in the transition matrix were reduced in a stepwise fashion for all adult stages. Dominant latent roots were then calculated for each new matrix to determine the harvest intensity necessary to drive the λ value below 1.0. The results from this analysis are presented in figure 5.4, which shows the dominant latent roots derived from matrices in which fruit production parameters have been reduced from 10 to 90 percent. The dotted, horizontal line at 1.0 represents the value of a stable population. As indicated in the figure, latent roots greater than 1.0 are maintained under all harvest intensities up to 80 percent. If more than 80 percent of the fruit produced each year is harvested, however, λ values drop below 1.0, indicating that the existing level of regeneration is insufficient to balance natural mortality rates.

Based on these results, natural populations of *G. peruviana* can be exploited on a sustained-yield basis if at least 20 percent of the annual fruit crop is left in

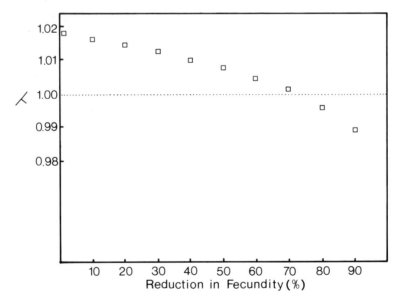

FIGURE 5.4. Dominant latent roots derived from matrixes in which fruit reproduction parameters were reduced from 10 to 90 percent.

the forest. Two different management strategies could be used to regulate fruit collections. Given their high individual fecundity, adult trees greater than 20 cm DBH (stage s_8) produce approximately 30 percent of the total fruit crop each year. The individuals in this class, however, represent only 5 percent of the total number of adults. Marking these trees and leaving them unharvested would ensure that an adequate amount of fruit were left in the forest. A second approach would be to divide the forest into five parcels, each parcel containing more or less the same number of adult trees. Only four parcels would be harvested in a given year, the fifth being left "fallow" to permit seedling recruitment. Especially vigorous or productive individuals could also be left to regenerate for several years to enhance the genetic composition of the population.

The increased use of monodominant forests of native fruit trees is obviously not a panacea for the innumerable problems facing resource managers in Amazonia. These forests represent a very small percentage of the total forest area, and are formed by only a select group of species. The sustainable exploitation of forest fruit trees, however, does provide one promising alternative to deforestation. Clearly, the structure and function of wild populations of fruit trees merit much further study. Before promoting the extensive cultivation of native fruit trees, it would seem logical to first assess the growth and yield of these species in their natural habitat. Man has been trying to establish monocultures in Amazonia for several centuries without realizing that, for some species, nature has already done the job for him.

ACKNOWLEDGMENTS

This study was conducted as part of a cooperative agreement between the Instituto de Investigaciones de la Amazonia Peruana (IIAP) of Iquitos, Peru, and the Institute of Economic Botany of the New York Botanical Garden. The support of both these institutions is gratefully acknowledged. Special thanks to Dr. Jose Lopez Parodi and the technical staff at the Jenaro Herrera field station for providing logistic help and a comfortable working environment. Humberto Pacaya, Manual Chota, and Elysa J. Hammond gave invaluable assistance in the field. Funding for the Native Fruits of Peruvian Amazonia project was provided through a generous grant from the Exxon Corporation.

REFERENCES

Alvim, P. de T. 1981. A perspective appraisal of perennial crops in the Amazon Basin. *Interciencia* 6(3):139–145.

Balick, M. 1979. Amazonian oil palms of promise: A survey. *Economic Botany* 33(1): 11–28.

Bullock, J. 1980. Demography of an undergrowth palm in littoral Cameroon. *Biotropica* 12:247–255.

Cavalcante, P. 1972. *Frutas Comestíveis da Amazônia*, vol. 1. Belém: Museu Paraense Emílio Goeldi.

Cavalcante, P. 1974. *Frutas Comestíveis da Amazônia*, vol. 2. Belém: Museu Paraense Emílio Goeldi.

Cavalcante, P. 1979. *Frutas Comestíveis da Amazônia*, vol. 3. Belém: Museu Paraense Emílio Goeldi.

Clement, C. R., C. H. Muller, and W. B. Chavez Flores. 1982. Recursos genéticos de espécies frutíferas nativas da Amazônia Brasileira. *Acta Amazonica* 12(4):677–695.

Enright, N. and J. Ogden. 1979. Application of transition matrix models in forest dynamics; *Araucaria* in Papua New Guinea and *Nothofagus* in New Zealand. *Australian Journal of Ecology* 4:3–23.

FAO–UNESCO. 1971. *Soil Map of the World,* vol. 4, South America. Paris: United Nations Educational, Scientific and Cultural Organization.

Ferreyra, R. 1959. Camu-camu, nueva fuente de vitamina C. *Boletin Experimental Agropecuaria* 7(4):28.

Harper, J. L. 1977. *Population Biology of Plants.* London: Academic Press.

Hartshorn, G. S. 1975. A matrix model of tree population dynamics. In F. Golley and E. Medina, eds., *Tropical Ecological Systems: Trends in Terrestrial and Aquatic Research,* pp. 41–51. New York: Springer-Verlag.

Holdridge, L. R., W. C. Grenke, W. H. Hatheway, T. Liang, and J. A. Tosi. 1971. *Forest Environments in Tropical Life Zones: A Pilot Study.* Oxford: Pergamon Press.

INDDA. 1984. Unpublished laboratory results. Laboratorio de Bromatología Instituto Nacional de Desarrollo Agroindustrial, Lima.

Leak, W. B. 1965. The J-shaped probability distribution. *Forest Science* 11:405–419.

Le Cointe, P. 1934. *Arvores e Plantas Uteis (Indígenas e Aclimadas): Nomes Vulgares, Classificacão Botanica, Hábitat, Principais Aplicações e Propriedades.* Belém: Libreria Clássica.

Leslie, P. H. 1945. On the use of matrices in certain population mathematics. *Biometrika* 35:183–212.

Lefkovitch, L. P. 1965. The study of population growth in organisms grouped by stages. *Biometrics* 21:1–18.

Malleux-Orjedo, J. 1975. *Memoria Explicativa: Mapa Forestal de Peru.* Lima: Universidad Nacional de Agronomía, La Molina.

Meyer, H. A. 1952. Structure, growth and drain in balanced, uneven-aged forest. *Journal of Forestry* 50:85–92.

NAS. 1975. *Underexploited Tropical Plants with Promising Economic Value.* Washington, DC: National Academy of Sciences.

Peters, C. and A. Vazquez. 1987. Estudios ecológicos de camu-camu (*Myrciaria dubia*) I. Producción de frutos en poblaciones naturales. *Acta Amazonica* 16(17):161–173.

Richards, P. W. 1952. *The Tropical Rain Forest.* Cambridge: Cambridge University Press.

Sarukhan, J. 1980. Demographic problems in tropical systems. In O. Solbrig, ed., *Demography and Evolution of Plant Populations,* pp. 168–188. Berkeley: University of California Press.

Usher, M. B. 1966. A matrix approach to the management of renewable resources, with special reference to selection forests. *Journal of Applied Ecology* 3:355–367.

Whitmore, T. C. 1975. *Tropical Rain Forests of the Far East.* Oxford: Claredon Press.

6

Seed and Seedling Availability as a Basis for Management of Natural Forest Regeneration

■

VIRGÍLIO M. VIANA

ABSTRACT

The technical success of forest management based on natural regeneration ultimately depends on the availability of seeds and seedlings of desirable species. Recent advances in tropical ecology can have practical value in terms of predicting this availability. Four general patterns of seed and seedling availability are recognized in space (isolated and overlapping) and time (transient and persistent). These patterns vary in a predictable fashion along a successional gradient.

Seed and seedling availability of Vochysia maxima *in a Central Amazonian secondary forest is examined.* V. maxima *is a gap opportunist species that is promising for management through natural regeneration. Seed availability in the soil is restricted to seven weeks after seed dispersal and most seeds fall in the vicinity (≤60 m) of parent trees. Seedlings persist under the forest canopy for more than 1 year, and their distribution decreases sharply beyond 50 m from parent trees. Because mature trees of* V. maxima *occur at high density in this secondary forest, seed and seedling banks originating from different trees tend to overlap. Due to their long-term availability, seedlings and not seeds should be targeted for management. To obtain continuous regeneration, parent tree density should be greater than 1.5 trees/ha.*

Understanding the patterns of seed and seedling availability provides a basic tool to increase the density of desirable species as well as the predictability of forest composition in silvicultural systems.

Tropical forests are rarely managed in a sustainable fashion by nontraditional populations in Amazonia (Rankin 1985). To guarantee large-scale forest cover outside national parks, there is a compelling need for forest management systems that are socioeconomically and ecologically sound (Gomez-Pompa, Vazquez-Yanes, and Sada 1972; Dubois 1974; Ewel 1977; Cardoso and Müller 1978; Homma 1982; Salati et al. 1983). Forest management, however, will be a viable form of land use only if it offers greater economic returns than more conventional alternatives, such as pastures or cropping (de Graaf 1986; de Graaf and Poels, this volume).

Early efforts in management of tropical forests in various parts of the world were based on trial and error, as there was insufficient understanding of how different forest ecosystems respond to random and systematic disturbance (Kio and Ekwebelam 1987). Thanks to recent developments in tropical ecology (e.g., Janzen 1983; Medina, Mooney, and Vazquez-Yanes 1984; Brokaw 1985; Gomez-Pompa and Del Amo 1985; Sioli 1984; Whitmore 1985; Estrada and Fleming 1986; Jordan 1987), we now have the opportunity to draw on more extensive ecological data to develop more predictable systems of tropical forest management.

A promising silvicultural system for tropical regions such as Amazonia is forest management through natural regeneration (MNR). The objective of MNR is to maximize natural regeneration while minimizing management costs, by manipulating tree populations through careful logging and thinning operations (Baur 1964). The main advantages of MNR are its low investment requirements and minimal environmental impact compared with other forms of land use. MNR is a socially flexible system: it can be practiced by both large and small farmers. It is particularly promising on low-fertility soils that dominate the Amazonian landscape (Jordan 1985).

Unfortunately, attempts to establish management systems based on natural regeneration in tropical forests have been undermined by a variety of technical problems (Whitmore 1985; Leslie 1987; Tang 1987), of which the following are particularly critical to Amazonian forests: 1) low density of desirable species, and 2) low predictability of forest composition after logging. Understanding the dynamics of seed and seedling availability can contribute toward solving these problems. In this chapter, I first discuss how seed and seedling availability varies among tropical tree species. I then present data on seed dispersal, longevity, and recruitment of *Vochysia maxima* Ducke, a promising species for MNR in Central Amazonia. Finally, I close this chapter by discussing the implications of seed and seedling availability to MNR.

Natural Seed and Seedling Availability of Tropical Trees

A forest management system based on natural regeneration must deal with two basic ecological variables: 1) potential for regeneration, largely determined by availability of seeds and seedlings; and 2) potential for growth, largely determined by availability of light and nutrients. This chapter examines the first of these variables.

Seed and seedling availability vary predictably among ecological species groups (Gomez-Pompa and Vazquez-Yanes 1982; Whitmore 1983; Bazzaz 1984; Vazquez-

Yanes and Orozco-Segovia 1984), which are defined according to habitat requirements for regeneration. Natural regeneration of tropical trees occurs in a wide range of habitats, from sunny treefall gaps to shady forest understory.

Species that require large gap environments (high irradiance, high red/far red ratios, high temperatures) for germination and establishment are usually referred to as *pioneers* (Martinez-Ramos 1985). An example of such species is *Cecropia obtusifolia* Bertol., which depends on colonization of treefall gaps for regeneration (Vazquez-Yanes and Orozco-Segovia 1986). To colonize these gaps, pioneer species have evolved mechanisms to maintain dormant seeds in the soil and/or disperse seeds over long distances from parent trees (Vazquez-Yanes and Smith 1983; Murray 1988). In treefall gaps, pioneer species exhibit very fast growth (Ashton 1978; Bazzaz and Pickett 1980; Brokaw 1985).

Species that do not require gaps for regeneration are *shade tolerant species* (Schulz 1960; Hutchinson 1987). Shade tolerant species such as *Ocotea rubra* Mez do not depend on colonization of scattered gaps for germination and seedling growth: they grow continuously under the canopy (Schulz 1960). Seeds of shade tolerant species are often too heavy to have long-distance wind dispersal, or too big to have long-distance dispersal by animals. Dispersal in space represents mostly a mechanism of predator or pathogen avoidance (Janzen 1970; Connell 1971; Hubbell 1980).

Shade tolerant and pioneer species represent extremes of a continuum (Baur 1964; Bazzaz and Pickett 1980). There is a large number of intermediate species that germinate under the closed forest canopy but require varying degrees of canopy opening for seedling survival and growth. These are *gap opportunist species* (Hutchinson 1987). Regeneration of gap opportunist species such as the Light Red Meranti *Shorea* spp. (*Dipterocarpaceae*) depends on gap openings for seedling and sapling growth, but not for germination (Nicholson 1965; Whitmore 1985). These species have evolved mechanisms to promote regeneration in time by having extended seedling survivorship under closed canopy conditions. When a treefall occurs, these seedlings are "released" and experience rapid growth. Because of their high seedling density, fast growth, and economic value, these species are very promising for MNR (Whitmore 1985; Asabere 1987).

Availability in Time

The availability of seeds and seedlings on the forest floor varies in time and space. Seed availability in the soil varies in time, depending on 1) timing and length of fruiting season, 2) rate of loss of seed viability, 3) timing and intensity of predation and diseases, and 4) timing of germination. As a consequence, a species' seed bank may be persistent or transient (Grime 1979). Species with prolonged fruiting and/ or long-lived seeds have *persistent seed banks*. A species' seed bank is persistent if seed longevity is greater than the time interval between fruiting events. In this case, regeneration from seeds is not necessarily limited in time (fig. 6.1A).

Many pioneer species in the tropics have persistent seed banks. Some of these species have seeds that may remain dormant in the soil for months or even years, others fruit for several months or continuously throughout the year, and few ex-

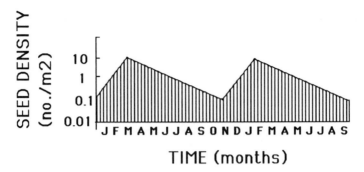

FIGURE 6.1A. A hypothetical representation of a persistent seed bank. Each peak represents a fruiting event. In this case, seed longevity in the soil is longer than the time between fruiting events. Thus, seed availability does not limit regeneration in time.

hibit both high seed longevity and prolonged fruiting (Lebrón 1979; Vazquez-Yanes and Smith 1983; Vazquez-Yanes and Orozco-Segovia 1986). Because of their high seed production, long fruiting periods, and long dormancy, pioneer species dominate soil seed banks in tropical forests (e.g., Symington 1933; Guevara and Gomez-Pompa 1972; Holthuijzen and Boerboom 1982; Putz 1983; Uhl and Clark 1983; Enright 1985).

Species that have a short dispersal season and short seed longevity have *transient seed banks*. A species' seed bank is transient if seed longevity is shorter than the time interval between fruiting events. In this case, regeneration from seeds is necessarily limited in time (fig. 6.1B). In the tropics, seeds of most forest species are short-lived (Ng 1978, 1983; Vazquez-Yanes and Orozco-Segovia 1984), and dispersal occurs during a short period of time (SUDAM 1979; Carvalho 1980; Garwood 1983; Murray 1988). Consequently, most tropical forest species have transient seed banks. These species (mostly gap opportunists and shade tolerant species) are underrepresented in soil seed banks because of their low seed pro-

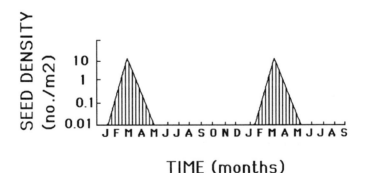

FIGURE 6.1B. A hypothetical representation of a transient seed bank. In this case, seed longevity in the soil is shorter than the time interval between fruiting events. Thus, seed availability limits regeneration in time.

duction, infrequent fruiting periods of short duration, and short longevity in the soil.

Like seeds, seedlings form populations that vary in time and can also be seen as a "bank," with inputs and outputs. Seedling availability is dependent on the time of 1) seed germination, 2) seedling mortality, and 3) seedling growth. The temporal variation in seedling availability is similar to seeds in the sense that it can also form *persistent* and *transient seedling banks*. For example, *Cedrela odorata* L. and *Tabebuia serratifolia* (Vahl.) Nichols. have transient seedling banks: They produce successive waves of short-lived (1/2 to 1 year) seedlings that die unless there happens to be a suitable gap (Schulz 1960). In contrast, seedlings of *Pentaclethra macroloba* (Willd.) Kuntze have high survivorship under shade and form a persistent seedling bank (Hartshorn 1975).

Availability in Space

Seed availability in the soil varies in space, depending on the 1) density and distribution of parent trees, 2) distance and shape of the dispersal curve, and 3) pattern of mortality around parent trees. As a result, soil seed banks may be isolated or overlapping. Species with high densities of mature trees and/or long distance dispersal have *overlapping seed banks*. A species' seed bank is overlapping if the dispersal distance is greater than half of the distance between trees (fig. 6.2A). In this case, regeneration from seeds is not necessarily limited in space.

Some pioneer and gap opportunist species may form stands of high density in disturbed forests (Silva et al. 1985a) and also have long-distance dispersal (Murray 1988). Such species often form overlapping seed banks. This is the case in the secondary forest at Belterra for *Vochysia maxima* (see next section) and *Jacaranda copaia* (Aubl.) D. Don (Viana, unpublished data), both wind-dispersed. Wind-dispersed species tend to build more uniform seed banks, in which seed density tends to decrease monotonically with distance away from parent trees. Animal-dispersed species such as *Didymopanax morototoni* (Aubl.) Decne. et Planch. (Viana, unpublished data) tend to form patchy seed shadows as a result of the spatial pattern of animal defecation and regurgitation. The seed banks of animal-dispersed species are likely to be discontinuous, unless densities of dispersal agents and trees are extremely high. Low densities of animal populations are likely to increase clumping of seeds around parent trees.

In most tropical tree species, seed dispersal distances tend to be short (Howe and Smallwood 1982; Augsburger 1983), and individuals generally occur at low densities and exhibit clumped distributions (Hubbell 1979; Silva and Lopes 1982; Carvalho 1983). Data on the spatial characteristics of seed dispersal in tropical trees are, however, limited to a small number of species (e.g., Estrada and Fleming 1986). Additional information is needed, especially for more complex patterns of animal-dispersed species, which depend on animal behavior and digestive habits (e.g., Murray 1988).

Species that have low density and short dispersal distances have *isolated seed banks*. A species' seed bank is isolated if the dispersal distance is shorter than half the distance between trees (fig. 6.2B). Many tropical species, especially those

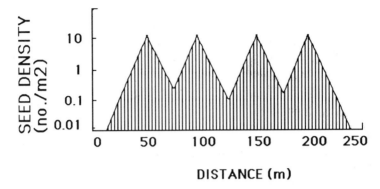

FIGURE 6.2A. A hypothetical representation of an overlapping seed bank. Each peak represents a fruiting tree. In this case, seed dispersal distance is greater than half of the distance between trees. Thus, seed availability does not limit regression in space.

that do not have high density and are not clumped, are likely to have isolated seed banks because of their short seed dispersal distance. Natural regeneration of these species is limited in space.

If mortality is complete near the parent tree (Janzen 1970; Connell 1971), or if recruitment occurs only in gaps, then seeds and seedlings are available only at some distance away from the tree. Conversely, if mortality is not complete near the tree, then seed and seedling availability tends to be concentrated near the seed source (Hubbell 1980). Similar to seed, seedling banks of tropical tree species tend to be more *isolated* than *overlapping*.

A Case Study

Although knowledge concerning seed and seedling availability of desirable species is essential for management of natural forest regeneration in the tropics, surpris-

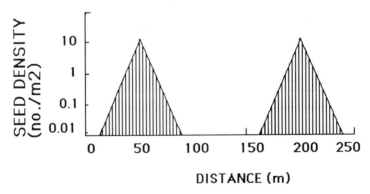

FIGURE 6.2B. A hypothetical representation of an isolated seed bank. In this case, seed dispersal distance is shorter than half of the distance between trees. Thus, seed availability limits regeneration in space.

ingly little is currently known. This is especially the case in Amazonia, where studies of natural forest management have a relatively short and discontinuous history (Rankin 1985).

Here I present a case study of *Vochysia maxima* Ducke (*Vochysiaceae*). This species produces light wood (0.55 g/cm³) which has wide use in construction and carpentry (SUDAM 1979). "Quaruba verdadeira," as it is usually known, is today one of the most used species in sawmills of the Tapajós region. Natural populations of *V. maxima* are found in terra firma forests south of the Amazon River, in the basins of some of its major tributaries: Tapajós, Xingú, and Tocantins (SUDAM 1979). *V. maxima* is a gap opportunist species, in which seeds are dispersed by wind and germinate under closed canopy but release of seedlings depends on canopy opening. Trees are 25–40 m in height when mature, reaching the top of the canopy. Tree density is usually much higher in secondary than in primary forests. The occasional high density of natural regeneration of *V. maxima* in secondary forests, coupled with its fast growth, make it one of the most promising species for MNR in Amazonia (Pitt 1969; Silva et al. 1985a).

Despite its silvicultural potential, very little is known about the reproductive biology of this species. In Central Amazonia, seed dispersal occurs during April–May, at the end of the rainy season (Pitt 1969, SUDAM 1979, Carvalho 1980). An ongoing phenological study being conducted at the Tapajós National Forest will reveal between-year variation in flowering, fruiting, and leafing patterns (Leão et al., unpublished data). At the same site, I have studied seed dispersal and seedling establishment around parent trees and in natural gaps.

Study Site

This study was conducted in Belterra, 02°38′S and 54°7′W, located in Central Amazonia. The altitude is 175 m and the climate is Ami (Köppen), with average annual precipitation of 2100 mm and less than 60 mm of rain during the four-month-long dry season (Yared and Carpanezzi 1981). The forest has a basal area of about 35 m²/ha and a stem volume of 220 m³/ha (Silva et al. 1985b). Following Pires and Prance's (1985) classification, this is a "dense terra firma forest."

A natural population of *Vochysia maxima* was studied in a late successional terra firma forest in a 132-ha secondary forest reserve at Belterra. This area was cleared by the Ford Motor Company in 1934 to establish a rubber plantation (Costa 1981). The rubber plantation was gradually abandoned in the late 1950s, when maintenance decreased significantly (Sr. Mário Cunha, pers. comm.). The reserve, currently managed by Empresa Brasileira de Pesquisas Agropecuárias, is located at the NW edge of the plantation, and was bordered by primary forests that were undisturbed until recently. *V. maxima* is a codominant species in the secondary forests at this reserve that comprises 18.2 percent of the total basal area above 20 cm DBH (10.2 m²/ha). Other dominant species are *Jacaranda copaia*, *Hevea* sp., and *Didymopanax morototoni*, with 17.7, 13.5, and 4.8 percent of the basal area, respectively (Silva et al. 1985a).

The objective of this study was to address the problem of unpredictability of regeneration density of *Vochysia maxima*. The hypothesis is that regeneration is limited in time and space because of seed and seedling availability, thus requiring appropriate timing and intensity of logging to obtain high regeneration densities. The data presented here are part of an ongoing research project that also includes *Jacaranda copaia* and *Didymopanax morototoni*.

Material and Methods

Natural seed longevity was studied by burying seed in neutral nylon bags under the forest litter. Seeds were collected from five trees and were stored in darkness until the beginning of the experiment. Bags had 50 seeds each and three bags were recovered and put to germinate at 3, 5, 7, and 9 weeks after burial. Seeds were put to germinate in a nursery under moderate shade and on forest topsoil substrate. Germinating seeds were removed and final germination was scored.

Seed dispersal was studied around three mature trees, isolated by at least 120 m from a conspecific fruiting individual. Seeds were collected twice a week in 1 m² nylon traps, laid down along transects in N, S, E, W directions, at 5, 10, 20, 40, and 60 meters from the base of each tree, giving a total of 20 traps per tree.

Seedling recruitment was surveyed around six isolated mature trees. Starting from the bole of an individual tree, a wedge of 10° was laid down along an E–W orientation (following the direction of prevailing winds), 60 meters from the base of the tree. Total area per transect was 312.7 m². This method results in a constant increase of the area sampled as the distance from tree increases: sampling intensity remains constant (Howe et al. 1985).

Results

The availability of seeds of *Vochysia maxima* was limited in time because of this species' short fruiting period and short seed longevity in the soil. Fruiting in 1987 was restricted to the second half of the rainy season (fig. 6.3), similar to the period described by Pitt (1969) and Carvalho (1980). Seed longevity in the soil was likewise short: under nine weeks (fig. 6.4). Seeds germinate right after dispersal, in forest shade, forming dense seedling populations. *V. maxima* consequently has transient seed banks.

Seed availability in space was limited to the vicinity of parent trees. Although seeds may occasionally fall further than 40 m from the tree, most seeds fall in the vicinity of the tree (fig. 6.5). A similar distribution of seeds is found for other tropical forest trees (Cremer 1966; Augsburger 1983; Castilho 1986). However, since tree density in this secondary forest is very high (15.8 trees/ha; Silva et al. 1985a), and average distance between trees is 25 m, *Vochysia maxima* often forms overlapping seed banks.

Seedling availability was greater in the vicinity of parent trees, with a marked decrease beyond 50 m (fig. 6.6). The average seedling density at 50 m from parent trees was 0.127 (±0.054) seedling/m² and at 60 m it was 0.024 (±0.017) seedling/

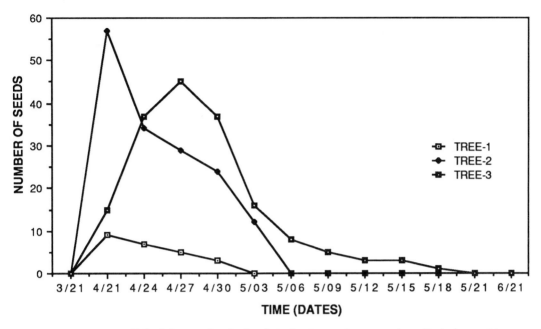

FIGURE 6.3. Seedfall of three individuals of *Vochysia maxima* over time. Each data point represents the total number of seeds collected in 20 traps around individual trees at a particular time.

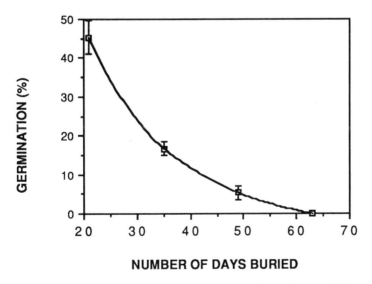

FIGURE 6.4. Germination of seeds of *Vochysia maxima* buried tropical forest soil as a function of time. Seed samples were recovered from the soil at the times stated. Data points represent final germination, and bars represent their respective standard errors.

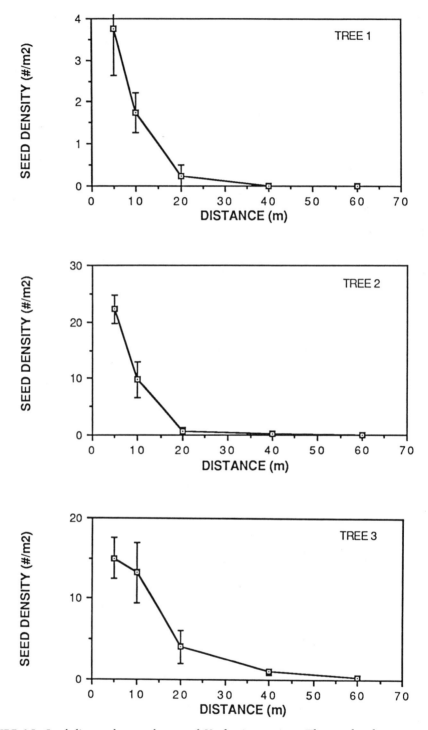

FIGURE 6.5. Seed dispersal around trees of *Vochysia maxima.* The graphs show average seed densities and respective standard errors.

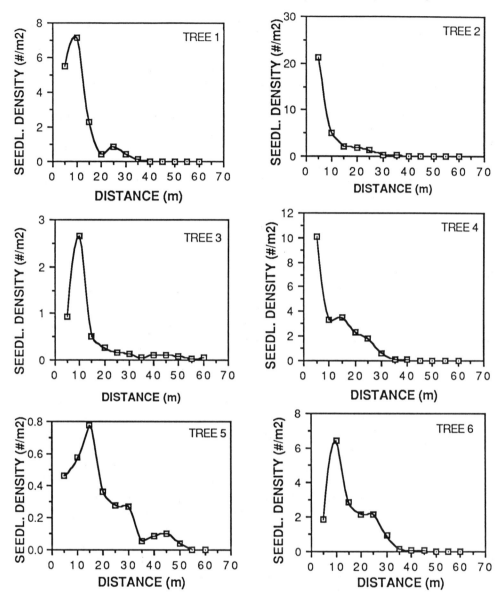

FIGURE 6.6. Seedling recruitment of *Vochysia maxima* around parent trees. The graphs illustrate seedling distribution at 5 m distance intervals along east-west transects.

m^2. There were two basic patterns of seedling recruitment. In the first, represented by trees 2 and 4, seedling density fell exponentially from the base of the tree. In the second, represented by trees 1, 3, 5, and 6, seedling density was low in the vicinity of the tree, peaked at 10–20 m from the base of the tree, and fell exponentially thereafter. This second pattern indicates the occurrence of density-dependent mortality around parent trees. It appears that most seedling death was caused by pathogens, as there was no evidence of intense herbivory on seedlings around parent trees.

These results indicate that seedling distribution of *Vochysia maxima* at Belterra conformed to Hubbell's (1980) model, which predicts clumping of regeneration around parent trees. Seedling mortality was not complete near the seed source and seedling regeneration was concentrated near parent trees.

At Belterra, regeneration of *Vochysia maxima* from seedlings was not limited in time, but seedling density was observed to be highest in months following seed dispersal. Seedlings persisted well under forest shade, but growth was higher in treefall gaps. In the secondary forest studied, the death of senescent rubber trees generated a high frequency of small canopy gaps, which in turn has promoted the regeneration of this species.

Discussion

Natural regeneration of *Vochysia maxima* from seeds is limited in time but not in space in this secondary forest. Although seed dispersal is limited to the vicinity of parent trees, the high tree density allows for the formation of overlapping seed banks of *V. maxima* in the secondary forest studied. Seed availability is very short and limited to the second half of the rainy season. Seed availability in the soil is further reduced by between-year variations in fruit production (pers. obs.). Natural regeneration from seeds in the soil is not dependable because *V. maxima* has transient seed banks.

In contrast to seeds, natural regeneration from seedlings is not limited in time. Seedlings establish on the forest floor before the end of the rainy season and survive through the dry season, until the next fruiting period. These are persistent seedling banks in which regeneration from seedlings can occur all year.

Because seed availability is limited in time and seedling availability is not, management of *Vochysia maxima* through natural regeneration (MNR) should target seedlings rather than seeds. High regeneration densities can be obtained in years of high seed production, and in months following seed dispersal. High regeneration densities can also be obtained if reproductive and prereproductive trees are maintained at densities high enough to offset the relatively short seed dispersal distance. Logging intensities of *V. maxima* trees have to be such that a minimum density of trees is maintained in order to guarantee successful regeneration and sustainability of timber production.

Seedling availability showed a marked decrease beyond 50 m. Considering 50 m as a limit to natural regeneration around parent trees, the minimum distance between trees would have to be 100 m, or about 1.5 tree/ha (based on a hexagonal pattern), to guarantee spatially continuous regeneration of *Vochysia maxima*. Assuming even distribution, this means that in the secondary forest of Belterra where tree density is 15.8 trees/ha (Silva et al. 1985a), a minimum density of about 1.5 trees/ha should be kept after logging. The more clumped trees are, the greater will be the required tree density. In primary forests such as the Tapajós National Forest, where density of *V. maxima* trees bigger than 15 cm DBH is 0.3/ha (Carvalho 1981), only overmature (senescent) trees should be logged in the first cycle of conversion to managed natural forests dominated by *V. maxima*. Maintaining nonlogged trees should be considered as part of the cost of implementing a sustainable system of forest management.

Conclusions

Seed and seedling availability sets limits to natural regeneration of tropical forests. Understanding the patterns of seed and seedling availability is a necessary step toward developing viable systems of management through natural regeneration. It provides a basic tool to increase the density of desirable species and predictability of forest composition. Without adequate densities of seeds and seedlings of desirable species, management will not be sustainable.

Valuable gap opportunist species such as *Vochysia maxima* are particularly promising for MNR. Regeneration from their persistent seedlings banks make them easy to manipulate silviculturally. Logging and thinning operations can be carried out throughout the year, giving a desirable flexibility to silvicultural operations.

Since *Vochysia maxima* should be managed in conjunction with other species, basic data on other species are necessary (especially pioneers and gap opportunists). These data should encompass not only the availability of seeds and seedlings but also growth under various levels of light and nutrients. The response of seedlings and saplings to various levels of canopy opening is of crucial importance in determining finely tuned silvicultural operations. We can, however, make use of general predictions that apply to most tropical species prior to obtaining detailed data on all desirable species (e.g., Bazzaz 1986).

Future success of MNR will not depend solely on an understanding of the critical ecological variables involved. A clear understanding of local problems and socioeconomic, political, and cultural variables is also necessary (Gomez-Pompa 1985; Buschbacher 1987; Wyatt-Smith 1987; Schmink 1987; Solbrig 1988). Therefore, greater interaction between foresters, ecologists, and social scientists is necessary to obtain a practical as well as a theoretical basis for tropical forest management.

ACKNOWLEDGMENTS

The author thanks D. Ackerly, A. Anderson, P. S. Ashton, F. A. Bazzaz, W. Bossert, J. O. P. Carvalho, C. Castro, D. Foster, P. Y. Kageyama, C. Klink, J. C. Lopes, A. Moreira, D. Napstad, C. Samper, J. N. M. Silva, O. T. Solbrig, and L. Taylor for critical comments on various versions of this manuscript, and J. A. G. Yared for his support in Brazil. This research was supported by grants of EMBRAPA/CPATU/PNPF, CNPq, and the Atkins Fund of Harvard University.

REFERENCES

Asabere, P. K. 1987. Attempts at sustained yield management in tropical high forests of Ghana. In F. Mergen and J. R. Vincent, eds., *Natural Management of Tropical Moist Forests*, pp. 47–70. New Haven: Yale University Press.

Ashton, P. S. 1978. Crown characteristics of tropical trees. In P. B. Tomlinson and M. H. Zimmerman, eds., *Tropical Trees as Living Systems*, pp. 519–615. Cambridge, England: Cambridge University Press.

Augsburger, C. 1983. Seed dispersal of a neotropical tree, *Platinopodium elegans*, and the escape of its seedlings from fungal pathogens. *Journal of Ecology* 71:759–772.

Baur, G. N. 1964. *The Ecological Basis of Rain Forest Management*. New South Wales, Australia: Forestry Commission.

Bazzaz, F. A. 1984. Dynamics of wet tropical forest and their species strategies. In E. Medina, H. A. Mooney, and C. Vazquez-Yanes, eds., *Physiological Ecology of Plants in the Wet Tropics*, pp. 233–244. Boston: Dr. W. Junk.

Bazzaz, F. A. 1986. Regeneration of tropical forests: Physiological responses of secondary species. Paper presented at the International Workshop on Rainforest Regeneration and Management, Guri, Venezuela.

Bazzaz, F. A. and S. T. A. Pickett. 1980. Physiological ecology of tropical succession: A comparative review. *Annual Review of Ecology and Systematics* 11:287–310.

Brokaw, N. V. L. 1985. Gap-phase regeneration in a tropical rain forest. *Ecology* 66(3): 628–687.

Buschbacher, R. J. 1987. Ecological analysis of natural forest management in the humid tropics. Paper presented at the symposium "The Application of Ecology to Enhancing Economic Development in the Humid Tropics," American Institute of Biological Sciences.

Cardoso, F. H. and G. Müller. 1978. *Amazônia: Expansão do Capitalismo*. 2nd ed. São Paulo: Editora Brasiliense.

Carvalho, J. O. P. 1980. *Fenologia de Espécies Florestais que Ocorrem na Floresta Nacional do Tapajós*. Boletim de Pesquisa no. 20. Belém: Centro de Pesquisa Agropecuária do Trópico Húmido (EMBRAPA/CPATU).

Carvalho, J. O. P. 1981. *Distribuição Diamétrica de Espécies Comerciais e Potenciais em Floresta Tropical Umida Natural na Amazônia*. Boletim de Pesquisa no. 23. Belém: Centro de Pesquisa Agropecuária do Trópico Húmido (EMBRAPA/CPATU).

Carvalho, J. O. P. 1983. *Abundância, Frequência e Grau de Agragação de Pau-Rosa (Aniba duckei Kostermans) na Floresta Nacional do Tapajós*. Boletim de Pesquisa no. 53. Belém: Centro de Pesquisa Agropecuária do Trópico Húmido (EMBRAPA/CPATU).

Castilho, C. A. R. 1986. Dispersão anemochórica das sementes de paineira (*Chorisia speciosa* St. Hil.) na região de Bauru, Estado de São Paulo. Ms Thesis. Piracicaba: Universidade de São Paulo.

Connell, J. H. 1971. On the role of natural enemies in preventing competitive exclusion in some marine animals and in rain forest trees. In P. J. Den Boer and G. Gradwell, eds., *Dynamic of Populations*, pp. 298–312. Wageningen, The Netherlands: PUDOC.

Costa, F. A. 1981. Capital estrangeiro e agricultura na Amazônia: A experiência da Ford Motor Company (1922–1945). Ms. Thesis. Rio de Janeiro: Fundação Getúlio Vargas.

Cremer, K. W. 1966. Dissemination of seeds from *Eucalyptus regnans*. *Australian Forester:* 30(1):33–37.

Dubois, J. L. C. 1974. *Prioridades e Coordenação das Pesquisas Florestais na Amazônia Brasileira*. Miscellaneous publication. Belém: Instituto Brasileiro de Desenvolvimento Florestal (IBDF-PRODEPEF).

Enright, N. 1985. Ecology of a soil seed bank under rain forest in New Guinea. *Australian Journal of Forestry:* 10:67–71.

Estrada, A. and Flemming, T., eds. 1986. *Frugivores and Seed Dispersal*. Boston: Dr. W. Junk.

Ewel, J. 1977. Secondary forests: The tropical wood resource of the future. In M. Chavarria, ed, *Simposio Internacional sobre las Ciencias Forestales y su Contribucion al Desarollo de la America Tropical.* San José, Costa Rica: Editorial EUNED.

Garwood, N. C. 1983. Seed germination in a seasonal tropical forest in Panama: A community study. *Ecological Monographs:* 53(2):159–181.

Gomez-Pompa, A. 1985. *Los Recursos Bioticos de Mexico: Reflexiones.* Mexico D. F.: Alhambra.

Gomez-Pompa, A. and C. Vazquez-Yanes. 1982. Successional studies of a rain forest in Mexico. In D. C. West, H. H. Shugart, and D. C. Botkin, eds., *Forest Succession,* pp. 246–266. New York: Springer-Verlag.

Gomez-Pompa, A., C. Vazquez-Yanes, and S. Sada. 1972. The tropical rain forest: A nonrenewable resource. *Science* 177:762–765.

Gomez-Pompa, A. and S. Del Amo, eds. 1985. *Investigaciones Sobre la Regeneracion de Selvas Altas en Veracruz, Mexico.* Mexico D. F.: Alhambra.

Graaf, N. R. de. 1986. *A Silvicultural System for Natural Regeneration of Tropical Rain Forest in Suriname.* Wageningen, The Netherlands: Agricultural University.

Grime, J. P. 1979. *Plant Strategies and Vegetation Processes.* New York: Wiley.

Guevara, S. S. and A. Gomez-Pompa. 1972. Seeds from surface soils in a tropical region of Veracruz, Mexico. *Journal of the Arnold Arboretum:* 53:313–335.

Hartshorn, G. S. 1975. A matrix model of tree population dynamics. In F. B. Golley and E. Medina, eds., *Tropical Ecology Systems,* pp. 41–52. New York: Springer-Verlag.

Holthuijzen, A. M. A. and J. H. A. Boerboom. 1982. The *Cecropia* seed bank in the Surinam lowland rain forest. *Biotropica:*14(1):62–68.

Homma, A. K. O. 1982. Uma tentativa de identificação teórica do extrativismo amazônico. *Acta Amazonica:* 12(2):251–255.

Howe, H. F. and J. Smallwood. 1982. Ecology of seed dispersal. *Annual Review of Ecology and Systematics:* 13:201–228.

Howe, H. F., E. W. Schupp, and L. C. Westley. 1985. Early consequences of seed dispersal for a neotropical tree (*Virola surinamensis*). *Ecology:* 66 (3):781–791.

Hubbell, S. 1979. Tree dispersion, abundance and diversity in a tropical dry forest. *Science* 2003:1299–1309.

Hubbell, S. P. 1980. Seed predation and coexistence of tree species in tropical forests. *Oikos* 35:214–229.

Hutchinson, I. 1987. Improvement thinning in natural tropical forests: Aspects and institutionalization. In F. Mergen and J. R. Vincent, eds., *Natural Management of Tropical Moist Forests,* pp. 113–134. New Haven: Yale University Press.

Janzen, D. H. 1970. Herbivores and number of trees in tropical forests. *American Naturalist:*104:501–528.

Janzen, D. H., ed. 1983. *Costa Rican Natural History.* Chicago: Chicago University Press.

Jordan, C. 1985. *Nutrient Cycling in Tropical Forest Ecosystem.* New York: Wiley.

Jordan, C., ed. 1987. *Amazonian Rain Forests: Ecosystem Disturbance and Recovery,* New York: Springer-Verlag.

Kio, P. R. O. and S. A. Ekwebelam. 1987. Plantations versus natural forests for meeting Nigeria's wood needs. In F. Mergen and J. R. Vincent, eds., *Natural Management of Tropical Moist Forests,* pp. 149–176. New Haven: Yale University Press.

Lebrón, M. L. 1979. An autoecological study of *Palicourea riparia* Bentham as related to rain forest disturbance in Puerto Rico. *Oecologia* 42:31–46.

Leslie, A. J. 1987. The economic feasibility of natural management of tropical forests. In F. Mergen and J. R. Vincent, eds., *Natural Management of Tropical Moist Forests,* pp. 177–198. New Haven: Yale University Press.

Martinez-Ramos, M. 1985. Claros, ciclos vitales de los arboles tropicales y regeneracion natural de selvas altas perennifolias. In A. Gomez-Pompa and S. Del Amo, eds., *Investigaciones Sobre la Regeneracion de Selvas Altas en Veracruz, Mexico*, pp. 191–240. México, D. F.: Alhambra.

Medina, E., H. Mooney, and C. Vazquez-Yanes, eds. 1984. *Physiological Ecology of Plants of the Wet Tropics*. Boston: Dr. W. Junk.

Murray, K. G. 1988. Avian seed dispersal of three neotropical gap-dependent plants. *Ecological Monographs* 58(4):271–298.

Ng, F. S. P. 1978. Strategies and establishment in Malayan forest trees. In P. B. Tomlinson and M. H. Zimmerman, eds., *Tropical Trees as Living Systems*, pp. 129–162. Cambridge, England: Cambridge University Press.

Ng, F. S. P. 1983. Ecological principles of rain forest conservation. In S. L. Sutton, T. C. Whitmore, and A. C. Chadwick, eds., *Tropical Rainforest Ecology and Management*. Oxford, England: Blackwell.

Nicholson, D. I. 1965. A review of natural regeneration in the dipterocarp forest of Sabah. *Malayan Forester:* 28:4–26.

Pires, J. M. and G. T. Prance. 1985. The vegetation types of the Brazilian Amazon. In G. T. Prance and T. E. Lovejoy, eds., *Amazonia*, pp. 109–145. Oxford, England: Pergamon Press.

Pitt, J. 1969. *Relatório ao Governo do Brasil sobre Aplicação de Métodos Silviculturais a Algumas Florestas da Amazônia*. Belém: Superintendência do Desenvolvimento da Amazônia (SUDAM).

Putz, F. E. 1983. Treefall pits and mounds, buried seeds, and the importance of soil disturbance to pioneer trees on Barro Colorado Island, Panama. *Ecology* 64(5):1069–1074.

Rankin, J. M. 1985. Forestry in the Amazon. In G. T. Prance and T. E. Lovejoy, eds., *Amazonia*, pp. 369–392. Oxford, England: Pergamon Press.

Salati, E., H. O. R. Schubart, W. Junk, and A. E. Oliveira. 1983. *Amazonia: Desenvolvimento, Integração e Ecologia*. São Paulo: CNPQ/Ed. Brasiliense.

Schmink, M. 1987. The rationality of tropical forest destruction. In J. C. Figueiroa Colon, F. H. Wadsworth, and S. Brannan, eds., *Management of Forests in Tropical America: Prospects and Technologies*. Rio Piedras, Puerto Rico: Institute of Tropical Forestry, USDA Forest Service.

Schulz, J. P. 1960. *Ecological Studies on a Rain Forest in Northern Suriname*. Amsterdam, The Netherlands: N.V. Noord-Holladsche Uitgevers Maatschappij.

Silva, J. N. M. and J. C. A. Lopes. 1982. *Distribuição Espacial de Arvores na Floresta Nacional do Tapajos*. Circular Técnica no. 26. Belém: Centro de Pesquisa Agropecuária do Trópico Húmido (EMBRAPA/CPATU).

Silva, J. N. M., Carvalho, J. O. P., Lopes J. C. A. and L. H. Montagner. 1985a. Regeneração natural de *Vochysia maxima* em floresta secundária no planalto do Tapajós, Belterra, PA. *Boletim de Pesquisa Florestal* 10(11):1–37.

Silva, J. N. M., Carvalho, J. O. P., Lopes, J. C. A., and H. B. Costa. 1985b. Inventário florestal de uma área experimental na Floresta Nacional do Tapajós *Boletim de Pesquisa Florestal* 8(9):50–63.

Sioli, H., ed. 1984. *The Amazon: Limnology and Landscape Ecology of a Mighty Tropical River and its Basin*. Boston: Dr. W. Junk.

Solbrig, O. T. 1988. Destruicion o transformacion del paisaje tropical sudamericano? *Interciencia:* 13(2):79–82.

SUDAM 1979. *Pesquisas e Informaçoes sobre Espécies Florestais da Amazônia*. Belém: Superintendência do Desenvolvimento da Amazônia (SUDAM).

Symington, C. D. 1933. The study of secondary growth on rain forest sites in Malaya. *Malayan Forester* 2:107–117.

Tang, H. T. 1987. Problems and strategies for regenerating dispterocarp forests in Malaysia.

In F. Mergen and J. R. Vincent, eds., *Natural Management of Tropical Moist Forests*, pp. 23–46. New Haven: Yale University Press.

Uhl, C. and K. Clark. 1983. Seed ecology of selected Amazon Basin successional species. *Botanical Gazette* 144(3):419–425.

Vazquez-Yanes, C. and H. Smith. 1983. Phytochrome control of seed germination in the tropical rain forest pioneer trees *Cecropia obtusifolia* and *Piper auritum* and its ecological significance. *New Phytologist*: 92:477–485.

Vazquez-Yanes, C. and A. Orozco-Segovia. 1984. Ecophysiology of seed germination in the tropical humid forests of the world: A review. In E. Medina, H. A. Mooney, and C. Vazquez-Yanes, eds., *Physiological Ecology of Plants in the Wet Tropics*, pp. 35–50. Boston: Dr. W. Junk.

Vazquez-Yanes, C. and A. Orozco-Segovia. 1986. Dispersal of seed by animals: Effect on light controlled dormancy in *Cecropia obtusifolia*. In A. Estrada, and T. Flemming, eds., *Frugivores and Seed Dispersal*, pp. 71–80. Boston: Dr. W. Junk.

Whitmore, T. C. 1983. Secondary succession from seed in tropical rain forest. *Forestry Abstracts*: 44(12):767–779.

Whitmore, T. C. 1985. *Tropical Rainforests of the Far East*, 2nd ed. Oxford, England: Clarendon Press.

Wyatt-Smith, J. 1987. Problems and prospects for natural management of tropical moist forests. In F. Mergen and J. R. Vincent, eds., *Natural Management of Tropical Moist Forests*, pp. 5–22. New Haven: Yale University Press.

Yared, J. A. and A. A. Carpanezzi. 1981. *Conversão de Capoeira Alta em Povoamento de Produção de Madeira: O Método "Recru" e Espécies Promissoras*. Boletim de Pesquisa no. 25. Belém: Centro de Pesquisa Agropecuária do Trópico Umido (EMBRAPA/CPATU).

7

The Celos Management System: A Polycyclic Method for Sustained Timber Production in South American Rain Forest

■

N. R. de GRAAF

R. L. H. POELS

ABSTRACT

The Celos Management System (CMS) was developed for timber production in natural high forest, based on long-term research in Suriname. The key aspect of this system is the maintenance of high levels of nutrients in the forest vegetation throughout all timber harvesting and silvicultural operations. CMS allows harvesting of 20 to 30 m^3/ha of high-quality timber during each 20-year cycle, in a highly mechanized and strictly controlled operation. Under CMS, growth rates of commercial timber species after harvesting increase by a factor of four. Sustainable timber production under CMS could lead to a more stable forest industry, better land use, and permanent jobs in industry and forest management.

When defining optimal land-use systems for tropical rain forest areas, economic, sociological, and ecological factors must be taken into consideration. The type of land use discussed in this chapter is an extensive one, requiring large stretches of unbroken forest or at least more or less continuously forested land, with only a sparse population. It is obviously not suitable in areas where many small farmers are already practicing shifting cultivation. In such areas, plantation forestry is a more appropriate system for timber production.

In sparsely populated areas where a wider range of land-use options is available, the production of quality timber and plywood in large economic units may be an attractive way of improving the regional economy, with products aimed for export as well as for local industries. When using the natural forest, it is possible to leave much of the original ecosystem intact and to utilize many timber species that cannot be grown in plantations.

The idea of seminatural forestry, with polycyclic felling (rather than clear-cutting) and manipulation of the original forest, is far from new. But the testing of such an idea in the tropical rain forests of South America, with long-term assessment of the possibilities and problems involved, was never done before (Boxman et al. 1985).

The Celos Management System was developed from field experiments and trials between 1965 and 1983. The name "Celos" is the Dutch abbreviation for Centre for Agricultural Research in Suriname, where the system was developed. The CMS has been tested only over a few hundred hectares, which is not an economically viable scale; research had to be stopped in 1983 for political reasons unrelated to forestry or scientific research.

Principles of the Celos Management System

The Celos Management System consists of two parts: the Celos Harvesting System (CHS) and the Celos Silvicultural System (CSS). Because effective silviculture on sites subjected to selective felling is impossible unless harvesting is controlled, this two-part approach is essential. In other words, the first priority is to domesticate the logger, whereupon it is possible to domesticate the forest.

CMS is a management system for natural, nonflooded forests in which 1) sustained yields of high-quality timber are produced by strictly controlled, polycyclic harvests; and 2) growth of commercial trees is increased by killing competing noncommercial species. Detailed descriptions of the harvesting and silvicultural aspects of CMS are provided by Hendrison (in prep.) and de Graaf (1986a), respectively. The general principles of the Celos Management System are as follows (de Graaf and Hendrison 1987):

1. Harvesting operations and silvicultural treatments are integrated.

2. Forest inventory is the basis for planning harvesting operations and silvicultural treatments, and for control of stand development, logging impact, and treatment effects.

3. Timber extraction is restricted in order to maintain the ecological functioning of the forest, thus reducing logging damage and export of nutrients.

4. The system is polycyclic, with rotations of 15–25 years, depending on the growth rates attained and timber dimensions expected.

5. Management units function as forest districts with an infrastructure of multipurpose roads and settlements for laborers.

6. A strict forest law safeguards the legal position of management units.

Characterization of the Celos Management System

The Celos Harvesting System (CHS)

Under concession systems, timber harvesting from tropical rain forest is usually done without concern for sustained yield, since only current timber yield—and not what remains of the forest—is of interest. The concession system puts final responsibility with the government issuing concessions, but this does not result in adequate measures to guarantee conservation or sustained productivity. Local industries, which are dependent on forest resources for the many years during which their investments in infrastructure and machinery have to be written off, are likely to be more interested in conservation than expatriate loggers that leave the country when the forests have been stripped of commercial timber. Regulation of harvesting thus starts with enhancing the interests of local forest industries.

Logging damage is traditionally viewed as the main bottleneck in polycyclic systems. This view originated from experience in African forests, in which much larger trees are harvested than is usually the case in South America (Dawkins 1958). Removal of very large trees does indeed cause large gaps, which are difficult to regenerate into productive forest. But if our results from Suriname can be extrapolated, the situation appears to be less extreme in most South American forests.

CHS differs from conventional logging methods in its care for the remaining forest ecosystem, its meticulous organization of labor, its use of special logging techniques, and its emphasis on inventory as an essential planning tool. In the research done at the CELOS on logging damage, it was found that felling as well as skidding damage could be reduced considerably by careful organization of operations. The following sequence of operations is provided by de Graff and Hendrison (1987).

1. *Inventory.* This consists of terrain reconnaissance and enumeration of commercial trees, at least one year prior to logging. These activities are part of a larger inventory program, which consists of stock and increment assessment and monitoring of logging and treatment effects.

2. *Planning.* This phase consists of demarcating harvesting units and delimiting silvicultural treatments. The felling units and the road and skid trail network are set out on working maps.

3. *Determination of the felling.* Trees to be felled are selected according to harvesting requirements and silvicultural and ecological considerations. Allowable harvest may vary from unit to unit, depending on stand quality and terrain conditions.

4. *Preharvesting preparations.* Forest roads and skid trails are established to be used over successive cycles. Damage can be controlled effectively if these preparations are done before felling starts.

5. *Organized felling.* The skid trail network, designed for efficient log transport, is the framework for proper felling. In spite of limited possibilities for uniformly directional felling in tropical rain forest, a method was developed to establish a regular felling pattern that increases the efficiency of skidding logs from stump to landing. Felling is done by well-trained crews of three men in a job rotation system with the skidding crew.

6. *Winch skidding.* The crawler tractor that collects the logs should use its winch whenever possible to haul logs from the stump to the skid trail. Doing so reduces the movement of the tractor in the stand. Maximum distance for winching was found to be 50 meters.

7. *Terrain transport.* The wheeled skidders used for long-distance transport on the preestablished skid trails should keep to these trails, thus restricting soil damage.

8. *Log registration.* Logs are numbered at stump with metal discs and measured by the felling crew. Simple record forms are used to collect these data. Registration is continued by skidding and road transport crews up to the processing center.

9. *Job rotation.* To promote responsibility for the whole harvesting operation, job rotation is recommended.

Although the care used in logging would seem to increase the cost of operations, in fact the reverse has been the case in the CELOS project. The cost of increased control and planning was fully compensated by increased productivity and efficiency in the use of the expensive machinery.

The Celos Silvicultural System (CSS)

After controlled logging, the partly disturbed and damaged ecosystem starts to recover. Harvesting selectively reduces the population of commercial tree species. Long-term research at the CELOS shows that, without silvicultural treatment, recovery of this group is too slow for good economic results in a polycyclic system. Forest gaps formed by logging are filled by establishing young trees from below and by expanding crowns from neighboring trees, but most of these are of noncommercial species. Annual production of commercial timber volume was less than 0.5 m^3/ha in the control plots (without silvicultural treatment), and the number of trees of commercial species in the lowest diameter classes declined over the years.

To increase the representation of commercial species, the noncommercial species must be reduced in numbers and volume. The definition of commercial species depends on market critieria and the technological qualities of the wood; in Suriname the list consists of some 40–50 species. Reduction of noncommercial species is done in a simple silvicultural operation called refinement. Most large trees considered nondesirable are killed, keeping a lower diameter limit of 20–40 cm at breast height (dbh). Such a refining limit reduces total basal area above 5 cm dbh from about 31 to 12–16 m^2/ha, and eliminates about half to two-thirds of the standing stem volume of all species.

Killing is done by cutting around the stem bases and spraying arboricide in the notches. Such refinement drastically reduces competition, resulting in greatly increased growth of most of the remaining individuals in the forest. These include seedlings, saplings, and medium-sized trees of undesirable species. Most benefit, however, goes to the now-dominant medium-sized and large trees of commercial species. As a result of refinement, the increment of commercial timber volume increases by a factor of at least four, from about 0.5 to 2 m^3 or more per hectare per year. Better stocked parts of the forest produce more than less well-stocked areas.

Table 7.1 shows bole volume distribution during the first years in an experimental forest stand after silvicultural treatment. The commercial species gained 12 m^3/ha over six years, mostly in the size classes above 30 cm dbh.

This releasing effect slows down markedly after eight to ten years, first for the smaller trees, then for the dominant and co-dominant trees. The refinement should then be repeated, with somewhat different limits and criteria for eliminating trees.

Following the second refinement, the commercial species gain dominance over the noncommercial species. The extent to which this happens can be determined by the forest manager. Complete elimination of all noncommercial tree species is probably damaging to the ecosystem: The ecological effects of such elimination should be tested in the field over a long period.

In a cycle of 20–25 years, a third intervention may be desirable to prepare the forest for the next harvest. The purpose of the third intervention is to kill lianas that increase felling damage and eliminate small trees of undesirable species, which may supplant smaller individuals of commercial species in the gaps created during the second harvest.

The effects of these interventions on the forest are illustrated by figures 7.1 and 7.2, in which the commercial species are hatched and the noncommercial species left blank. The profiles illustrate the constant presence of forest cover,

TABLE 7.1. Bole Volume Distributions (in m^3/ha) of All Species and of a Group of 30 Commercial Species, in a 16 ha Plot, Just Before Silvicultural Treatment in 1975 and Afterwards. (Adapted from de Graaf 1986a).

	DIAMETER CLASS (cm)[a]							
	1	*2*	*3*	*4*	*5*	*6*	*7*	*Total*
All species, 1975	17	59	69	60	63	31	9	308
All species, 1979	15	44	31	15	6	1	1	113
Commercial spp., 1976	—	4.1	9.1	6.1	2.0	0.4	0.5	22.2
Commercial spp., 1982	—	4.5	15.0	10.4	3.1	1.1	0	34.1

[a]Class 1, 5.0–14.9 cm dbh; class 2, 15.0–29.9 cm dbh; class 3, 30.0–44.9 cm dbh; class 4, 45.0–59.9 cm dbh, etc.

comprised of trees of highly variable size, age, and composition. The forest remains rich in species and phytomass is kept high during all stages of the cycle, important factors for sustained yield (de Graaf 1986a; Poels 1987).

The refinements make the forest much more productive in an economic sense, permitting a second harvest of about 30 m^3/ha after 15–25 years. The cost of silviculture was estimated in Suriname as half a man-day plus a few liters of arboricide mixture per m^3 of timber grown. This cost would probably decline markedly in future cycles.

Ecological and Socioeconomic Impacts of CMS and Alternative Land Uses

Management

The idea of utilizing the wood of noncommercial species by careful harvesting has won many supporters in South America. It seems wasteful to kill trees and leave them to rot in the forest, especially given the increased demand for energy in market as well as subsistence economies. Mass harvesting for fuelwood is seen as a viable land-use alternative in rain forest areas, and may soon be implemented within the Grande Carajás Program in Brazilian Amazonia (Fearnside, this volume).

The chief objection against mass harvesting is that nutrient exports become quite large. Because the unit value of this wood is low, considerable quantities must be harvested per unit area to be economical, and transport costs are high for such raw material. An alternative strategy is to harvest only products with a high unit value and a relatively low nutrient content, such as quality timber logs in restricted quantities. Forest plantations, with application of fertilizers, are probably a better option for production of fuelwood.

In contrast, the ecological impacts are minimal in forest under CMS. Hydrology is influenced not so much by logging and silviculture as by roadmaking, which may cause erosion at crossings with creeks and in hilly terrain. The elimination of large individuals of noncommercial tree species can lead to local decline or extinction of various tree-dwelling animal species, but this is likely to occur only after repeated applications of intensive refinement. Pressure on such specialized species could be reduced by leaving unrefined areas around treated forest units.

The use of arboricides is a controversial subject. Professional management is needed to train labor and to control the use of chemicals. Safe arboricides are not cheap, and this in itself will help to prevent abuse. Quantities used are small in relation to area and biomass influenced, and claims of calamities when such chemicals are used often come from people inexperienced with the actual procedures.

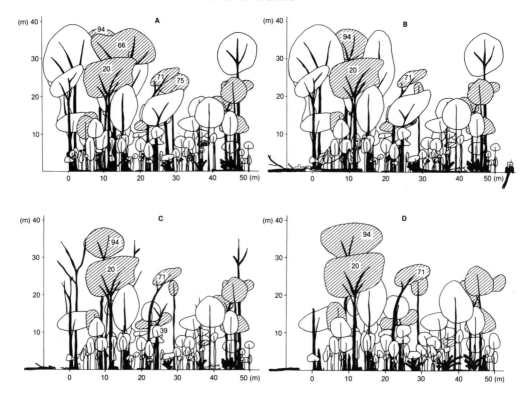

FIGURE 7.1. Hypothetical forest profile diagrams for the first felling cycle under CMS, years 0–7. (Source: de Graaf 1986a.) A = prior to harvesting (year 0); B = after felling of two trees (year 0); C = after initial refinement (year 2); D = prior to second refinement (year 7). Crowns of economic species are shaded.

Nutrients

A key issue in evaluating CMS is its ecological sustainability. On the oligotrophic soils characteristic of a major portion of the humid tropics, most of the potentially limiting nutrients are stored in the living forest biomass. Long-term conservation of this biomass is consequently a major factor in determining site productivity.

The long-term effects of CMS on biomass and nutrients were evaluated between 1977 and 1983 on yellow oxisols (Ultic Haplorthox) in north-central Suriname. Nutrient content of the soil on this site was extremely low: Cation exchange capacity (CEC) in the subsoil was about 2 me/100 g clay, and available nutrients in the mineral soil to 120 cm depth were much less than those contained in the organic matter. The mineral soil was largely comprised of quartz sand and kaolinitic clay.

The experimental treatment consisted of timber harvesting and poisoning unwanted trees, which killed about half of the biomass. The effects of CMS on biomass over a 5-year period are illustrated in fig. 7.3. During the first two years, an enormous loss (232t/ha) of living biomass resulted from the treatment. A minor

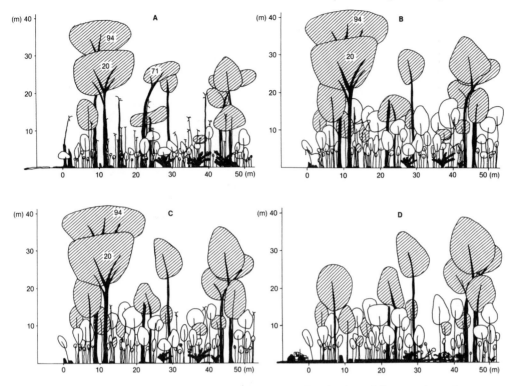

FIGURE 7.2. Hypothetical forest profile diagrams for the first felling cycle under CMS, years 9–20. (Source: de Graaf 1986a.) A = after second refinement (year 9); B = prior to third (light) refinement (year 15); C = after third refinement (year 17); D = after second felling (year 20). Crowns of economic species are shaded.

amount of living was extracted as timber (15 t/ha), while substantial quantities were converted to litter (165 t/ha) and soil organic matter (44 t/ha). In undisturbed forest, the decomposition of organic matter was equal to litter production $(24 \text{ t ha}^{-1} \text{ yr}^{-1})$. Treatment increased litter amount and thus decomposition; nutrients released during this accelerated decomposition are susceptible to leaching. During the first two years, extra decomposition was only 8 t/ha. Between years 2 and 5, living biomass increased again (93 t/ha), and the extra decomposition likewise increased (37 t/ha), posing a potential danger to nutrient conservation within the ecosystem. Over the entire five-year period, nutrient losses from the ecosystem (vegetation plus soil to 120 cm depth) were 340 kg N, 717 kg Ca, 63 kg Mg, 328 kg K, and 28 kg P.

Table 7.2 reports the nutrient content in soil, litter, and vegetation on experimental plots under the following treatments: 1) undisturbed forest (control); 2) forest under CMS; 3) agricultural land directly after clearing and burning of the forest; and 4) the same land 4 years after clearing, subjected to continuous cropping. Only Ca, Mg, K, and P were considered as they are believed to be the most limiting in this forest ecosystem. The supply of nitrogen to the forest does not appear to be limiting, because concentrations of this element in the soil and veg-

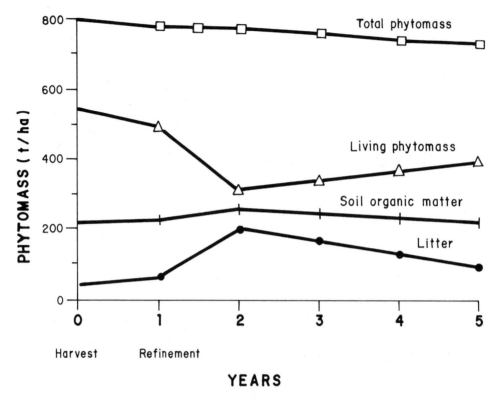

FIGURE 7.3. Simulated changes in total and living phytomass, resulting from harvest and refinement. (Source: Poels 1987.)

etation were relatively high and because the forest ecosystem has many mechanisms for fixing atmospheric sources.

Removal of forest for agriculture resulted in a loss of approximately 5200 kg nutrients (Ca + Mg + K + P) per hectare in 4 years, equivalent to a fertilizer value of about U.S. $1350. Including nitrogen losses of approximately 2700 kg/ha, the total fertilizer value of lost macronutrients was approximately U.S. $2800 per hectare.[1] Nutrient losses in forest under CMS were relatively small and the forest can probably recover part of the nutrients that have been leached to depths greater than 120 cm. Nepstad, Uhl, and Serrão (this volume) report rooting depths of up to 12 m under mature tropical forest in Brazilian Amazonia.

On this and other nutrient-poor soils, site quality is highly dependent on maintenance of biomass. The above data illustrate how reduction in biomass can result in considerable nutrient losses, especially of Ca and K. The low CEC of the soil, combined with a low pH, prevent the readsorption of these cations. Agricultural experiments show that practically all nutrients tied up in the biomass disappear upon clearing and that application of fertilizers is necessary soon thereafter.

These results suggest that maintenance of forest biomass is essential for long-term conservation of nutrients. However, sustainability is rarely taken into ac-

TABLE 7.2. Total Nutrient Content (kg/ha of Ca + Mg + K + P) in Vegetation, Litter, and Soil under Different Land Uses.

	LAND USE			
	Undisturbed Forest	*Forest Under CMS*	*Directly after Clearing and Burning*	*Four Years after Clearing*
Vegetation	5034	3791	0	0
Litter	299	309	0	0
Soil	3152	3250	6900	3300
Total	8485	7350	6900	3300

NOTE: Nutrients are combined for simplicity. Average ratios of Ca:Mg:K:P are about 18:2:10:1 for vegetation and litter and 5:2:4:1 for soil. For more complete information see Poels (1987).

count when assessing alternative land uses. For example, the dramatic release of nutrients in the forest biomass provides an essential subsidy for agricultural land uses. When comparing the economics of forestry and agriculture, however, it would be more correct to measure agricultural yields on land cleared some years previously. As the nutrients accumulated during a long forest fallow are depleted within a few years after clearing (table 7.2), such delayed measurement would provide a better long-term indication of how agricultural yields compare with those from forestry.

People

Socioeconomic aspects may be more decisive than ecological considerations for implementation of systems like CMS. What are the implications of this type of land use for people?

The rapid rates of forest clearing caused by shifting cultivation are largely due to the fact that farmers produce agricultural products not only for themselves but for urban markets in exchange for monetary income. One alternative is to provide income from jobs in timber production instead of food production (de Graaf 1986b). This alternative is less damaging to the land and could provide local people with money earned in forestry jobs.

Instead of applying agricultural or plantation forestry techniques that may be unsuitable to the ecological characterstics of tropical rain forest areas, CMS manipulates the natural forest to produce the products desired. The ecosystem is thus left largely intact, and people promote production of forest commodities rather than forest destruction. Controlled hunting and gathering are still possible, thus enabling people to benefit directly from forest conservation.

CMS provides about one job per 250–500 ha of managed forest area for silvicultural and harvesting operations together. The people most suited for such jobs are those who have experience in the rain forest, like the Amerindians and the Bushnegros in Suriname. The system is reasonably simple to apply and organize, but efficiency is also dependent on the natural resource knowledge of the native labor force.

To work optimally, CMS should be applied over forest management areas of several tens of thousands of hectares of potentially productive forest. This might require two or more times as big an area to be reserved, since not all forest types are fit for such timber production. In the Mapane area in Suriname, it is estimated that only half of the closed high forest land has enough potential to be permanently managed for timber. The rest might be harvested once but then should be left to recover without further interference, as the necessary input for management would probably not be compensated by returns. Such a policy would leave large areas in which rare species suffer minimal interference from forest management practices, as long as hunting is controlled.

In an area contemplated for such a forestry system, one third of the land could be allocated for strict nature reserves or only hunting and gathering, one third for CMS, and one third (the best soils) for intensive land uses such as agricultural and forest plantations. This area could support a well-situated forest industry with a planned village nearby. Transportation distances would be reduced for raw material such as logs, and the people employed in the industry would live as nearby as possible. Labor transport heavily burdens the budget of forestry operations, especially as the humid climate often prohibits work during periods of heavy rains. The village could have some agricultural land, but self-sufficiency should not be pursued at all cost. Staple food may be cheaper to import from regions more fit for food production, such as areas with fertile alluvial soils. Transport of food is probably not a major problem, as the timber transport system provides opportunities to import goods from elsewhere.

In summary, CMS should be considered as a land-use option in heavily forested tropical rain forest areas on poor acid soils that still contain low population densities. This land use offers long-term jobs and income from sustained-yield forestry, instead of short-term gains from land uses that cannot be sustained.

ENDNOTE

1. For the calculation, the following fertilizer prices (in US$ per kg element) were used: $0.54 (N), $1.02 (P), $0.31 (K), $0.19 (Ca), and $0.31 (Mg).

REFERENCES

Boxman, O., N. R. de Graaf, J. Hendrison, W. B. J. Jonkers, R. L. H. Poels, P. Schmidt, and R. Tjon Lim Sang. 1985. Towards sustained timber production from tropical rain forests in Suriname. *Netherlands Journal of Agricultural Science* 33:125–132.

Dawkins, H. C. 1958. *The Management of Natural Tropical High-Forest with Special Reference to Uganda.* Oxford: Imperial Forestry Institute, University of Oxford.

Graaf, N. R. de 1986a. *A Silvicultural System for Natural Regeneration of Tropical Rain Forest in Suriname (Ecology and Management of Tropical Rain Forests in Suriname, 1).* Wageningen, The Netherlands: Agricultural University.

Graaf, N. R. de. 1986b. Natural regeneration of tropical rain forest in Suriname as a land-use option. *Netherlands Journal of Agricultural Science* 35:71–74.

Graaf, N. R. de and J. Hendrison. 1987. Algunas notas sobre al manejo del bosque alto seco en Suriname. *Actas del Primer Seminario Internacional sobre Manejo de Bosque Tropical Humedo en la Region de Centro America.* Siguatepeque, Honduras: ESNACIFOR.

Hendrison, J. (in prep.). *Damage-controlled Logging in Managed Tropical Rain Forest in Suriname.* Wageningen, The Netherlands: Agricultural University.

Poels, R. L. H. 1987. *Soils, Water and Nutrients in a Forest Ecosystem in Suriname (Ecology and Management of Tropical Rain Forests in Suriname, 2).* Wageningen, The Netherlands: Agricultural University.

8

Natural Forest Management by the Yanesha Forestry Cooperative in Peruvian Amazonia

■

GARY S. HARTSHORN

ABSTRACT

Five native communities of Amuesha (Yanesha) Indians in the Palcazú valley of eastern Peru formed a forestry cooperative to manage their natural production forests on a sustained-yield basis. Long, narrow (30–40 m wide) strips are clear-cut to maximize utilization of timber and to facilitate natural regeneration of trees. The strip clear-cuts are rotated through a production forest so that uncut primary forest or advanced secondary forest borders a harvested strip. The clear cutting of narrow strips in a production forest promotes excellent natural regeneration of hundreds of native tree species. Local processing of timber for sawwood, preserved posts and poles, and charcoal adds considerable value to the native forest products. Timber production from Amuesha forest lands, local processing (sawmill and preservation plant), and marketing of forest products are vertically integrated through the operations of the Yanesha Forestry Cooperative. Net returns (after local processing) are projected to be $3500 per hectare harvested.

Tropical deforestation often occurs on soils that cannot sustain intensive agriculture. The inexorable advance of the agricultural frontier on forest lands not only destroys vast quantities of wood; it also rapidly exhausts the natural productivity of the system, usually leading to abandonment or conversion to extensive pasture. Wherever virgin lands are accessible by roads for oil exploration, logging, or other activities, strong socioeconomic and political pressures lead to spontaneous or directed colonization, which in turn promotes deforestation.

Peru's Pichis-Palcazú Special Project (PEPP), with the financial and technical support of the United States Agency for International Development (USAID), is addressing the problems of inappropriate land use and uncontrolled agricultural colonization through an innovative approach to rural development (Dickinson et al. 1981). The Central Selva Resources Management project (figure 8.1) is implementing sustained-yields management of natural forests as the principal development activity in the lower Palcazú valley (about 100,000 ha), while protecting the traditional culture of the local Amuesha (Yanesha) Indians. In addition to community-based production forestry, the Palcazú development project includes social, agriculture, and livestock components.

The Tropical Science Center (TSC) provides technical assistance to the forestry and land-use components of the Palcazú development project. TSC designed a vertically integrated system for local processing and national marketing of wood products, with management of native forests based on natural regeneration and sustained yields (Tosi 1982; Hartshorn, Simeone, and Tosi 1987). PEPP and USAID assisted with the formation of the Yanesha Forestry Cooperative and financed construction of a timber processing center at Shiringamazú for the Indian cooperative.

The three principal objectives of the Yanesha Forestry Cooperative are: 1) to provide a source of employment for members of the native communities, 2) to manage the communities' natural forests for sustained yields of forest products, and 3) to protect the cultural integrity of the Amuesha people. By integrating intensive forest exploitation, local processing of timber, and natural regeneration of native trees, the forest management component is expected to maximize sustainable productivity of the forest resources and to increase the income and social well-being of the indigenous communities in the valley (Stocks and Hartshorn 1988).

The Area

The small Palcazú valley is at the eastern base of the Peruvian Andes. The Palcazú watershed (189,200 ha) is formed by the rugged Yanachaga range (3800 m above sea level) to the west and the lower San Matías range (1200 m) to the east (figure 8.1). The Palcazú River flows north, where it joins the Pozuzo River, both of which are tributaries of the Pachitea River. Base elevations vary from approximately 270 m at the northern end of the valley to 350 m in the southern foothills. Forestry development activities are limited to the lower valley, generally below 500 m in elevation.

As part of the Central Selva Resources Management Project, USAID assisted in the creation of the Yanachaga-Chemillén National Park (122,000 ha) and the San Matías Protection Zone (33,000 ha). These conservation units (Aguilar 1986) encompass most of the protection forests on the west and east slopes of the upper Palcazú watershed.

The population of the Palcazú valley is estimated to be 6000 inhabitants, including 3500 Amuesha Indians. Most of the Amueshas live in twelve native communities (figure 8.1), where they practice traditional shifting cultivation of man-

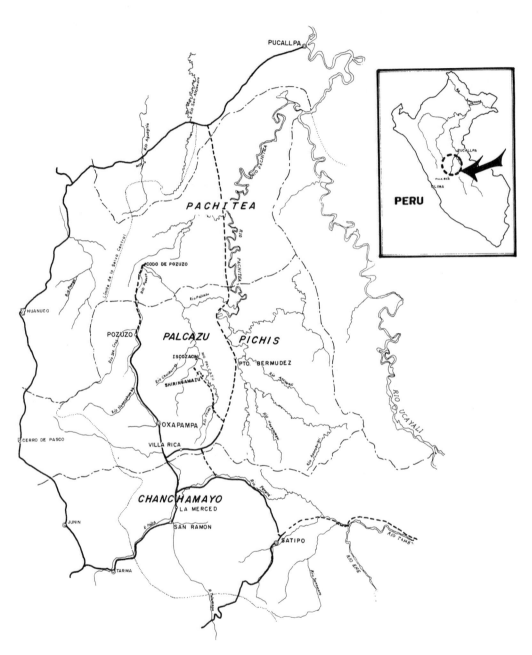

SELVA CENTRAL, PERU.

FIGURE 8.1. Location of Amuesha Native Communities in the lower Palcazú valley, Peru (inset).

ioc, maize, and upland rice on small plots, alternating these short-term crops with longer periods of bush or forest fallow. As part of the Palcazú project, the twelve native communities in the Palcazú valley have been officially recognized and granted property titles by the Peruvian government. The rest of the valley's population is made up of Ladino (mestizo) settlers, some Campa Indians, and a significant component of cattle ranchers descended from German, Swiss, and Austrian immigrants attracted by the turn-of-the-century rubber boom.

Although the lower valley was originally classified as tropical moist forest life zone (ONERN 1976), recent studies indicate that the lower valley is much wetter. Detailed mapping of life zones indicates that 85 percent of the lower valley is in the tropical wet forest life zone (Bolanõs and Watson 1981). Weather data taken by the Palcazú project (since 1984) give annual averages of 23.6° C biotemperature (*sensu* Holdridge 1967) and 6300 mm rainfall, which puts the lower Palcazú valley in the tropical premontane rain forest life zone (J. A. Tosi, pers. comm.). Such high rainfall and the lack of an effective dry season produce natural vegetation commonly called tropical rain forest.

Approximately 75 percent of the lower valley (i.e., roughly between 300 and 500 m elevation) retains its coverage of primary forests. Most of the deforested areas are along the rivers and on the low hills close to these rivers. The Palcazú valley appears to be especially rich in native plant species, including medicinal plants (e.g., Gentry and Cook 1984; Gentry and Wettach 1986). I estimate there are at least 1000 native tree species in the lower Palcazú valley (G. Hartshorn, unpublished data).

The Palcazú valley's soils are notoriously poor. The red clay soils of the extensive rolling hills in the lower valley are extremely acidic (pH 3.8–4.5), with an abundance of aluminum. Furthermore, these soils are highly leached and almost devoid of major nutrients, especially calcium, phosphorus, and potassium. Also present in the valley are old riverine terraces with white sandy-clay loam soils that are even less fertile than the red clay soils. As the Amueshas do not use the old terraces for shifting cultivation, these poor soils usually have well-developed primary forests (Hartshorn 1981), with an abundance of valuable trees such as rubber (*Hevea brasiliensis* (Willd. ex A. Juss.) M. Arg., Euphorbiaceae), and "tornillo" (*Cedrelinga catenaeformis* Ducke, Mimosaceae).

Because of high rainfall and rolling-to-steep terrain, the red clay soils are highly erodible when cleared of their protective forests and used for agriculture or pasture. A survey of the land-use capability in the lower valley indicates the following distribution of maximum sustainable use: 7.6 percent suitable for annual or seasonal crops, 13.3 percent for pasture, 14.4 percent for perennial crops, 46.2 percent for production forestry, and 18.6 percent in protection forests (Tosi 1981). In this classification system, less intensive use is permissible, such as production forestry on lands suitable for agriculture or grazing. But the opposite (pasture on forestry land, for example) is not sustainable and should be avoided. The project includes a program for mapping land-use capability in the lower valley, as well as actual land use in the lower valley, with a view to adjusting current land-use practices to sustainable use of natural resources. Thus, some 44,000 ha of remaining forests in the lower Palcazú valley should be under permanent management for production forestry.

Forest Management

Numerous efforts to manage heterogeneous tropical forests have failed due to difficulties such as: 1) the low volume of commercial woods per unit area, with as many as 200 tree species in one hectare; 2) very high extraction costs associated with the practice of high-grading only the quality timber; 3) lack of understanding about the dynamic nature of most tropical forests; 4) a general lack of information about the regeneration requirements and silvics of canopy tree species; 5) government policies (e.g., short-term concessions for large volumes, large minimum diameters for cutting) that discourage sustained-yield forest management or make it economically unattractive; 6) national and international agencies that promote agricultural colonization on lands that cannot sustain agriculture or cattle ranching; and 7) agencies in charge of forestry that may not have the resources to define and protect permanent forest lands for timber production.

These complex factors have given rise to a pervasive attitude among forestry professionals, development agencies, and the public in general that it is economically unjustifiable and ecologically impossible to manage tropical forests (Leslie 1977). Nonetheless, significant economic changes in the demand for tropical woods and recent advances in our understanding of tropical forest dynamics have reawakened interest in the potential for managing tropical forests for sustained production of wood, without resorting to plantation forestry (Leslie 1987a, 1987b; Schmidt 1987; Hartshorn in press).

Perhaps the most important change has been the dramatic opening of national markets to a much wider range of timber species. National markets traditionally accepted only the finest woods, which often meant only 10 to 50 of the thousands of native tree species. However, in the past decade, as high-grading has depleted stocks of premium timber and deforestation has destroyed substitute species, national markets are opening to timber species than were heretofore unacceptable. Where timber is scarce, as in much of Central America and the Andean highlands, local markets now accept any log of adequate size and decent form (Greub 1985). Generally, many tree species are marketed under a single generic name, for example "common oak" in Chanchomayo, Peru, or "mountain oak" in central Ecuador. Market acceptance of a large number of native species literally opens the door to intensive management of tropical forests as an alternative to the selective exploitation of a few species.

The incredible richness and diversity of tree species in tropical forests have long been formidable obstacles to economic management of these forests. Most previous attempts at forest management failed because they focused on one or a few quality timbers (e.g, cedar, ebony, mahogany), which are usually scarce in primary forest. Due to the great complexity of most tropical forests, the competition of one species against hundreds of others was doomed ecologically, or was prohibitively expensive to control.

Forest Dynamics

During the last decade, some researchers working independently in Southeast Asia and in Tropical America discovered that tropical forests are very dynamic (Hartshorn 1978; Oldeman 1978; Whitmore 1978). This means that rapid renewal of the primary forest generally occurs with the fall of large trees and their replacement by young, fast-growing trees. One of the key components of this natural renewal is a surprisingly high dependency of tree species on natural openings (gaps) in the canopy for successful regeneration (Hartshorn 1980). At the La Selva Biological Station in northeastern Costa Rica, for example, 50 percent of the native tree species require gaps for regeneration (Hartshorn 1978). If we consider only the tree species that compose the forest canopy, 63 percent are gap species. The shade-intolerant species that colonize gaps are fast-growing trees that fill a gap within a few years and reach the canopy in 20–30 years. In the La Selva primary forest, the median life span of trees greater than 10 cm dbh is just 34 years (Lieberman et al. 1985). Forest renewal through gap-phase dynamics, which is the principal pattern of natural regeneration in most tropical forests, is the key to our management plan for natural forests in the Palcazú valley.

Management Plan

TSC designed a forest management plan based on the above-mentioned ecological factors (Tosi 1982). Timber exploitation is limited to long, narrow clear-cuts interspersed in the natural forest. Each strip clear-cut is 30 to 40 m wide, with the length determined by topography and logistics (figure 8.2). Where feasible, strips 200–500 m in length will be oriented with the topography to minimize crossing ridges and streams. In effect, each strip is an elongated gap, bordered on each side by intact forest, which is the source of seeds for natural regeneration of trees in each clear-cut strip. In successive years, new strips will be located at least 100 m from recently cut strips, so as to ensure adequate stocks of reproductive trees to repopulate the harvested strips. TSC is projecting a 30- to 40-year rotation between the successive harvests of a specific site in this strip shelterbelt system.

Two demonstration strips were harvested in 1985, the first (20 × 75 m) in April–May and the second (50 × 100 m) in October–December. As the 20-m wide strip proved too narrow for large-crowned trees and it was feared that the 50-m wide strip would promote regeneration of weedy species, the first production block consists of strips 30–40 m wide.

Although the great quantity of organic matter substantially delayed initial colonization, the natural regeneration of trees is striking. In addition to abundant regeneration from seed, many stumps have vigorous sprouts; even some of the very dense, beautiful hardwoods like *Tabebuia obscura* (Bur. et K. Schum.) Sandw., *Myrocarpus* sp. and *Vatairea* sp. (both Fabaceae) have abundant stump sprouts on the demonstration strips. In a complete inventory of regeneration in the first strip 15 months after harvest, we found approximately 1500 individuals (>50 cm tall), representing 132 tree species. At 27 months, there were 155 tree species with

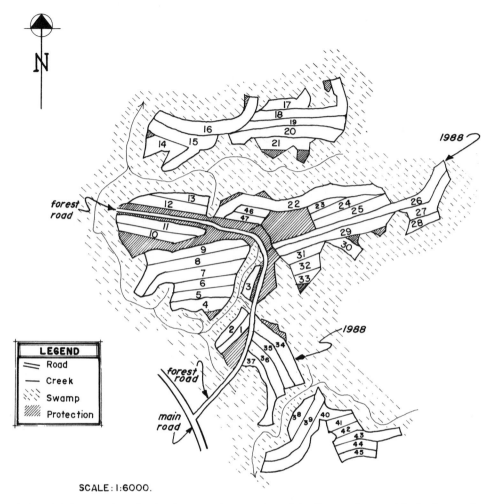

FIGURE 8.2. Location of strip clear-cuts in a portion of the first production block of natural forests, Shiringamazú Native Community.

saplings more than 1 m tall. This wealth of tree species regenerating on the first demonstration strip is more than double the number of tree species initially harvested from the same strip (0.15 ha). The proximity of seed sources and the absence of burning and cropping are probably critical factors in the abundant natural regeneration of trees on the strip clear-cuts.

The forest management plan also includes silvicultural treatments. Once the young trees have formed a closed canopy (at about 5 m), the competitive equilibrium can be adjusted to favor particularly desirable individuals or to eliminte undesirable trees. In the second year the number of sprouts is reduced to one or two per stump, depending on the size of the stump. As the canopy closes, climbers are cut to prevent lianas from overtopping or damaging the young trees. To allow natural suppression of weeds and vines, thinning of trees will not be initiated until after the canopy is fully closed.

Wood Uses

The harvesting and processing of timber are integral components of forest management. To promote natural regeneration of shade-intolerant tree species, the canopy opening must be sufficient to allow sunlight to reach the forest floor. Thus the management plan requires clear-cutting and use of almost all the cut biomass. All trunks and large branches are extracted, leaving only the small branches and leaves on the ground to provide nutrients for the regenerating forest.

Draft animals (such as oxen or water buffaloes) are used to extract the logs, poles, posts, and fuelwood. The few exceptionally large logs are sawn lengthwise to facilitate extraction. The logs are moved by draft animals to a roadhead for transport to the local processing center. The use of such simple technology to extract logs is feasible because extraction is concentrated in a small area (<2 ha) and the distances are not great. Extraction of logs is considerably cheaper—and logging and skidding damage to soil much less—with draft animals than with articulated tractors or skidders.

Processing of the wood is done locally in the valley, at an integrated processing center organized cooperatively by the producers of the raw materials. This arrangement ensures that the added value from processing accrues to the timber producers. The wood preservation plant, sawmill, administrative offices, and support facilities were constructed on land ceded by the Shiringamazú Native Community to the Yanesha Forestry Cooperative. The portable sawmill was installed in 1987 and the wood preservation plant began operation in February 1988.

Membership in the Yanesha Forestry Cooperative has increased to eight native communities and 125 individual members. The cooperative has identified approximately 8500 ha of production forests and is developing operational plans for the first production blocks to be harvested according to the strip clear-cut forest management system (e.g., Sanchoma et al. 1986). The Yanesha Forestry Cooperative plans to involve all the native communities of the Palcazú valley and bring under sustained-yield management their 25,000 hectares of natural forests suitable for production forestry.

Economic Aspects

Inventories of the lower valley forests carried out by the project's forestry unit indicate that there is an average of 150 m^3/ha of timber in saw logs, plus 90 m^3/ha of roundwood for poles and posts. The inventory data do not include branchwood, which can be sawn for specialty items or converted to charcoal. Thus, the total harvested wood from the first demonstration strip was equivalent to 350 m^3/ha. Much of the smaller-dimension timber is marketable as utility poles and posts, which is treated with a preservative (CCA) to increase longevity and value. Much of the nonresistant sawnwood will also be treated with a preservative for use as form lumber in construction. The untreated hardwoods are sold in specialized markets based on their specific wood properties and workability, which are determined by laboratory tests and trials in a local carpentry shop. Timber that cannot be transformed into sawn products or preserved poles and posts will be converted to charcoal, for which there is considerable demand wherever energy sources are scarce, such as the high Andes and coastal deserts of Peru.

The first processing center located in Shiringamazú has a "Mighty-Mite" portable sawmill and a bank of 44 PresCaps (figure 8.3) for preserving roundwood (Krones 1987). With this first stage, the cooperative can process twelve hectares of timber per year. For 1988–89 there are plans to diversify and expand the processing center's productive capacity by adding a band resaw, an automatic sharpener, two miter saws, one table saw, one molder, two driers, three duplicating lathers, two sanders, 50 PresCaps, and a complete "slurry seal" system for preserving sawnwood.

Our economic calculations indicate that the limited capacity of the existing processing center (portable sawmill, 44 PresCaps and a portable charcoal kiln) will produce net returns of $3500 per hectare of forest harvested and processed locally. The planned diversification and expansion of the local processing center at Shiringamazú should increase net returns to $27,500 per hectare worked (Simeone et al. 1986). These estimated profits to the Yanesha Forestry Cooperative are based on current market values and transport costs for wood products in Peru; start-up costs covered by USAID or the Peruvian government are not included in these calculations. Once local processing is available, this integrated forest management system is expected to produce attractive profits beginning in the first year

FIGURE 8.3. PresCap for replacing the sap with chemical preservatives. A combination of rubber and metal rings fits over the log and inside the PresCap to provide a tight seal. Air pressure is used to force in the preservative.

of operation, which should encourage sustained production of timber from managed natural forests.

Clearly, the most important aspect of the Palcazú project is the opportunity and potential for sustainable development of tropical forests. Instead of the typical pattern of temporary prosperity for a few years based on traditional high-grading of the forest followed by expansion of the agricultural frontier, sustained-yield forest management will generate incomes adequate for local communities to realize their development priorities. If the Palcazú project is successful, sustained exploitation and integrated-management forests should become a more attractive development option for tropical forests that are suitable only for production forestry. Sustained-yield management of tropical forests could diminish the growing pressures to convert forests into agricultural lands or pastures, and thus reduce the rate of tropical deforestation.

REFERENCES

Aguilar, D., P. R. 1986. Yanachaga-Chemillén: Futuro parque nacional en la Selva Central del Perú. *Boletin Lima* 45:7–21.

Bolanõs M., R. and V. Watson, C. 1981. Report on the ecological map of the Palcazú valley. In Dickinson et al. 1981, Appendix C.

Dickinson, J., M. Dourojeanni, D. McCaffrey, D. Pool, and R. C. Smith. 1981. Central Selva Natural Resources Management Project: USAID Project No. 527-0240. McLean, VA: JRB Associates, 2 vols.

Gentry, A. H. and K. Cook. 1984 *Martinella* (Bignoniaceae): A widely used eye medicine of South America. *Journal of Ethnopharmacology* 11:337–343.

Gentry, A. H. and R. H. Wettach. 1986. *Fevillea*—a new oil seed from Amazonian Peru. *Economic Botany* 40(2):177–185.

Greub, H. 1985. Primer informe preliminar sobre productos forestales y mercadeo. Tropical Science Center report no. 036-C.

Hartshorn, G. S. 1978. Tree falls and tropical forest dynamics. In P. B. Tomlinson and M. H. Zimmermann, eds., *Tropical Trees as Living Systems*, pp. 617–638. Cambridge, England: Cambridge University Press.

Hartshorn, G. S. 1980. Neotropical forest dynamics. *Biotropica* 12 (Suppl.):23–30.

Hartshorn, G. S. 1981. Forestry potential in the Palcazú valley, Peru. In Dickinson et al. 1981, Appendix G.

Hartshorn, G. S. In press. Tropical forest management based on gap theory. *Ecology* (Special Feature on Forest Dynamics).

Hartshorn, G. S., R. Simeone, and J. A. Tosi, Jr. 1987. Manejo para rendimiento sostenido de bosques naturales: Um sinopsis del proyecto de desarrolo del Palcazú en la Selva Central de la Amazonía Peruana. In J. C. Figueroa Colón, F. H. Wadsworth, and S. Branham, eds., *Management of the Forests of Tropical America: Prospects and Technologies*, pp. 235–243. Rio Piedras, Puerto Rico: Institute of Tropical Forestry.

Holdridge, L. R. 1967. *Life Zone Ecology.* San José, Costa Rica: Tropical Science Center.

Krones, M. 1987. Informe final sobre las actividades desarrolladas en la implementación y puesta en marcha del primer nucleo de transformación en la cooperativa forestal "Yanesha." Tropical Science Center report no. 114-C.

Leslie, A. J. 1977. When theory and practice contradict. *Unasylva* 29(115):2–17.

Leslie, A. J. 1987a. The economic feasibility of natural management of tropical forests. In F. Mergen and J. R. Vincent, eds., *Natural Management of Tropical Moist Forests: Sil-*

vicultural and Management Prospects of Sustained Utilization, pp. 177–198. New Haven, Connecticut: Yale University School of Forestry and Environmental Studies.

Leslie, A. J. 1987b. A second look at the economics of natural management systems in tropical mixed forests. *Unasylva* 39 (155):46–58.

Lieberman, D., M. Lieberman, R. Peralta, and G. Hartshorn. 1985. Mortality patterns and stand turnover rates in wet tropical forest in Costa Rica. *Journal of Tropical Ecology* 73(3):915–924.

Oldeman, R. A. A. 1978. Architecture and energy exchange of dicotyledonous trees in the forest. In P. B. Tomlinson and M. H. Zimmermann, eds., *Tropical Trees as Living Systems,* pp. 535–560. Cambridge, England: Cambridge University Press.

ONERN. 1976. *Mapa Ecológico del Peru: Guia Explicativa.* Lima, Peru: Oficina Nacional de Evaluación de Recursos Naturales (ONERN).

Sanchoma, R. E., R. Simeone, G. M. Velis, and H. Vilchez B. 1986. Plan de manejo forestal: Bosque de producción de la Comunidade Nativa Shiringamazú, 1987–1989. Tropical Science Center report no. 105-C.

Schmidt, R. 1987. Tropical rain forest management. *Unasylva* 39(156):2–17.

Simeone, R., W. Aspinall, M. Krones, and H. Greub. 1986. Propuesta para la ampliación del centro de transformación integral de productos forestales en el valle del Palcazú. Tropical Science Center report no. 083-C.

Stocks, A. and G. Hartshorn. 1988. The Palcazú project: Forest management and native Amuesha communities. In S. Hecht and J. Nations, eds., *The Social Dynamics and Alternatives to Deforestation in Latin America.* Ithaca, New York: Cornell University Press.

Tosi, J. A. 1981. Land use capability and recommended land use for the Palcazú valley. In Dickinson et al. 1981, Appendix N.

Tosi, J. A. 1982. Sustained yield management of natural forests: Forestry sub-project, Central Selva Resources Management Project, Palcazú Valley, Peru. Report to USAID/Peru.

Whitmore, T. C. 1978. Gaps in the forest canopy. In P. B. Tomlinson and M. H. Zimmermann. eds., *Tropical Trees as Living Systems,* pp. 639–655. Cambridge, England: Cambridge University Press.

3
AGROFORESTRY

3. *Agroforestry.*–Yams are an important tuber crop among Indian tribes throughout Amazonia. The species illustrated here (*Dioscorea trifida* L. f.) is frequently grown in forest fallows long after annual crops have ceased producing. This agroforestry technique represents one way of extending the cultivation cycle in swidden systems.

9

Indigenous Agroforestry Strategies Meeting Farmers' Needs

■

JANIS B. ALCORN

ABSTRACT

Indigenous farmers offer an alternative to deforestation—"managed deforestation." Forests meet farmers' needs for a variety of goods and services, and farmers use agroforestry strategies to insure that the forest is not destroyed. Seven characteristics of indigenous agroforestry strategies are discussed. These strategies: 1) take advantage of native trees and native tree communities; 2) rely on native successional processes; 3) use natural environmental variation; 4) incorporate numerous crop and native species; 5) are flexible; 6) spread risks by retaining diversity; and 7) maintain a reliable back-up to meet needs should other sources fail. Specific examples from the sequential agroforestry and forest grove systems of Mexican Huastec and Peruvian Bora farmers demonstrate how indigenous strategies are used by farmers. By understanding the needs, the knowledge, and the successful strategies of traditional farmers, agronomists and agroforesters can develop new, imaginative alternatives for managing deforestation.

Managed deforestation, as carried out by indigenous agroforestry systems, is an alternative to uncontrolled deforestation. Indigenous systems are often built around patchy, pulsed deforestation—systems based on removal of trees but not of the forest. Total removal of the forest makes no sense to those who have tried for generations to make a living in areas of tropical moist forest. Indigenous farmers do not want to deforest, because they value the natural processes of the forest that they can harness. To them, the forest is not just trees, but rather it is the natural regenerative processes, the successional stages, the forest animals, the timber, and the other useful plants.

In addition to producing products of value to the local and national economies, these systems enable farmers to rely on nature, not the state, for subsidy and insurance. The farmers' land is kept productive by the regenerative forces of the forest, and the farmer is thereby maintained as a contributing member of society. If we are interested in successfully promoting agroforestry for reasons we deem important (e.g., conservation of forest resources, sustained productivity of the land, timber production, water resource protection), it behooves us to look at how and why farmers have integrated trees into their existing agroecosystems—how forests have been managed to meet farmers' needs within agroecosystems that have been shaped to succeed under farmers' socioeconomic and environmental constraints.

In this essay, I will first outline the characteristics of indigenous agroforestry strategies. Then I will describe some of the structures created by farmers using these strategies and discuss the needs met by these structures. I will primarily draw on my experience with Huastec farmers in Mexico and Bora farmers in Peru. I am not suggesting that these structures should be adopted wholesale by colonists. I am suggesting, however, that by adopting indigenous strategies and by understanding the reasons behind the success of indigenous systems, agronomists and agroforesters will be better able to design modernized systems that meet farmers' needs. I believe that agronomists and agroforesters who understand the knowledge and strategies used by traditional farmers can develop new, imaginative alternatives to deforestation.

Characteristics of Indigenous Strategies

Indigenous agroforestry strategies share seven attributes. First, farmers incorporate native species into their systems. To have access to these species, they rely on natural succession to make available communities of associated species that arise predictably after a given type of disturbance—as after slashing, burning, and weeding a plot. Farmers also protect or plant native plants so that individuals may be found in sites where they would not have grown without human intervention. Often, particular native species are favored because they serve multiple uses. Indigenous agroforestry systems commonly terminate in a successional forest community. The second attribute then, is that, instead of viewing secondary succession solely as a weed problem, farmers rely on the successional process to produce resources, improve and protect soils, and reduce pest problems.

Thirdly, farmers use natural environmental variation. They recognize numerous biotopes (specific natural environments and their associated biota, related to topographic variation) and follow various farming options to use the different natural resources associated with a given biotope. In addition, they use different species mixtures in smaller patches within a given field according to microenvironmental differences.

Fourthly, farmers incorporate numerous species in their system—staple crops, minor crops that vary from region to region, and native species. Risk avoidance, pest control, and production of a wide range of products are the advantages of this strategy. Each farmer in a given cultural group is free to choose species mixtures according to household needs and resources. While a traditional pattern of farming is followed, farmers experiment with new mixtures and new cultivars, and they choose among traditional options. Thus, a fifth attribute is that strategies are flexible and personalizable. The same initial steps create structures than can be modified to develop in different directions several years later. The structures produced by a farmer vary from year to year and field to field.

Diversification is the sixth mark of the indigenous strategy. Farmers integrate agroforestry into diversified farmsteads—shaped by a need for self-insurance. Farmers work to spread risks and produce many commodities, and agroforestry is just one of the ways in which they do this. One of the major objectives of land-use decisions is to insure themselves against failure of one crop. In addition to labor-intensive structure, farmers include low-labor field types for insured subsistence in the case of illness, disability, or opportunities of off-farm labor that prevent meeting the labor requirements for some crops.

Seventh, agroforestry strategies work to ensure independent survival given the resources available to the farmers' community. Farmers design their land use given that they can utilize, in addition to their family's labor resources, certain resources available on their own lands, their neighbors' lands, and the forested wildlands that have traditionally been part of their local community's resource base—stands of trees that can be regarded as agroforestry adjuncts to more intensively managed fields. The means by which these community resources can be accessed shape farmers' land-use decisions.

Indigenous strategies work to manage deforestation in two basic systems: 1) sequential agroforestry systems that integrate secondary successional vegetation, and 2) managed forest grove systems. Farmers' strategies are developed within the context of these traditional systems, which are to a large extent carried out unconsciously as custom (Alcorn 1989a). In the next two sections, I will use specific examples, primarily drawn from the activities of Mexican Huastec and Peruvian Bora farmers, to demonstrate how indigenous strategies are applied in sequential agroforestry and forest grove systems.

Sequential Agroforestry Systems

The Huastec Maya (population 65,000) farm the foothills of the Sierra Madre Oriental of Mexico, southwest of Tampico. They support themselves through wage labor and the sale of household-produced raw sugar supplemented by subsistence products derived from their lands (Alcorn 1989b). Huastec couple low labor-intensive agroforestry with more labor-intensive profitable activities. Compared to Bora, Huastec have limited access to mature forest and have focused part of their attention toward manipulating and using younger successional forest. Currently each family lives on its own farmstead, although there are government programs to encourage families to move into concentrated population centers. Huastec lands are held in communally-owned chunks (400 to 1000 ha) that exist as islands in a sea of mestizo-owned pastures. The climax forest of the region is tropical moist forest, but the area has been disturbed for many centuries. Rainfall varies widely across the region but averages approximately 2300 mm per year. More detail on the Huastec and their environment can be found in Alcorn (1984a).

Bora (population approximately 500) manage lands along the Ampiyacu and Yaguasyacu rivers north of Pebas, Peru, and between the Putumayo and Caquetá rivers in Colombia. In this area, tropical moist forest covers an undulating terrain criss-crossed by many small streams. Rainfall averages over 2400 mm per year. Bora gain most of their subsistence from hunting, fishing, and farming. Families share use rights to all the available land and forest. Cash for salt, shotgun shells, clothing, and plastic goods is obtained primarily from the sale of fruits, fariña, pelts, and handicrafts. Compared to the Huastec, the Bora are less tightly linked to the global economy. Further details on the Bora system are available elsewhere (Denevan et al. 1984; Denevan and Padoch 1987; Guyot 1975).

Both Huastec and Bora use traditional, sequential agroforestry systems. The Huastec use a system known as "milpa," which is widespread in Middle America (for a review see Alcorn 1989c). The milpa system produces maize, beans, assorted other crops, fruits, firewood, livestock feed, wild game, honey, and wood products. It creates a mosaic of maize fields, gardens, fallow thickets, and forested plots. The Huastec use a short fallow version of milpa—maize is generally planted on the site every four to eight years. Bora follow a traditional South American system known variously as "chacra," "roça," or "conuco." The chacra yields a range of products similar to the milpa, but the staple produced is manioc, and the minor crops are drawn from a different set of species from those of the milpa. The Bora agroecosystem is a mosaic of different-aged manioc fields, garden-orchards, fallows, and old growth forest of various types. The Bora system is long fallow—gardens are reestablished every 20 or more years.

When talking about farming, Huastec describe it as "tohonal an ts'uleel," which translates as "working succession." I do not speak Bora so I cannot say anything about how they discuss farming. But looking at Bora farming patterns I believe they would agree with the Huastec analysis of their work. These farmers do not actively attempt to mimic the forest or the systems that keep the forest alive. From the farmer's perspective, he or she is following a way of farming that uses nature, not one that mimics it. The system is elaborated around deforestation and forest recovery. Management involves much more than simply slashing, burning, planting, weeding, and fallowing.

The cycle is initiated by selectively cutting down and burning forest. When Huastec prepare their site, they spare scattered individuals of useful trees (e.g., for house posts), which then continue to grow among the maize plants. They may also selectively pollard saplings useful for firewood production so that the young, limbless trees can support climbing beans, and firewood production is accelerated. Bora, on the other hand, rarely spare individual trees in their chacras since they have relatively unlimited access to forest.

Fire is set in the plot after the slashing back is complete. A slashed but unburned perimeter usually surrounds the field to be planted. In the Bora case, the unburned perimeter includes an unslashed area into which large trees were felled. Thus, after burning, the site contains a border of undisturbed forest; interior to that lies an unburned, unslashed area disturbed by falling trees; interior to that is an area of unburned slash; and most interior is the burned area littered by charred tree branches and trunks. The length of the hiatus between slashing and burning affects yields. Huastec prefer to allow three weeks between slashing and burning in order to get optimum maize yields. They believe pre-burn decomposition is responsible for this difference.

While this initial stage may be labeled deforestation, for the farmer it is a harvest of firewood, forest products, and accumulated nutrients liberated for use by the crops. Firewood harvesting procedures vary. Some firewood is removed before the burn; other firewood or construction wood, charred by the burn, is left lying in the field and picked up when needed. Harvest of firewood requires no labor beyond picking up the pieces because slashing to prepare the site for planting also accomplishes the first step of firewood harvest. Among other groups, there are variations on this basic plan. Alternative options include the Yucatec Mayan practice of leaving firewood trees uncut until after the burn so less wood is destroyed by the fire (Sanabria 1986). Yucatec Maya also plant climbing beans among unburned slash at the edges of a new milpa clearing and then harvest firewood from this zone after harvesting the beans.

After burning the site, farmers do not till the soil, but rather they plant their propagules in the forest rootmat that holds the bare soil in place. Thus the forest trees, even after their tops have been removed, play an important role in maintaining the site for future farming. Rotting tree roots also release nutrients for crops during the cropping phase of these systems. In the milpa system, stumps begin to sprout even as maize leaves emerge. Weeding is done only once, when the maize is six weeks old, and is accomplished by cutting new growth off near ground level. The slash is used to mulch the maize plants. Manioc cultivation, on the other hand, entails systematic disturbance of the soil as manioc plants are uprooted to harvest the tubers. The remains of uprooted manioc plants and any regrowth vegetation are burned in small piles during manioc harvest. This process enriches the soil, but it also tends to eliminate tree seedlings so that grasses become a much more important component of the noncrop vegetation in comparison with the Huastec milpa system. (A few scattered seedlings of useful wild trees are spared during weeding, however.) In the case of the chacra, forest regeneration begins on the edges and moves inward across the unburned slash areas and into spots where manioc is not replanted after being harvested. By the fourth or fifth year, the only area being weeded is a nucleus of fruit trees that were planted at the chacra's initiation. Thus the agroforestry sequence in some spots is a manioc (and other minor crops) stage slowly replaced by secondary woody vegetation. In other areas of the site, a fruit tree stage follows the manioc stage, but ultimately, after eight to ten years, the entire site becomes dominated by regrowth forest. Fifteen to twenty years after the site is burned, it is deemed ready to be recycled again.

A garden nucleus, not unlike the Bora orchard nucleus in so far as it is a small part of the initial clearing, is sometimes created in a milpa after maize is harvested. Most of the milpa field is fallowed, but one area is selectively cleared and replanted in maize and other minor crops without burning. Over the next three to seven years, during which the larger initial clearing is left to relatively undisturbed natural succession, farmers transform this smaller area into a complex garden containing spared and transplanted native species, as well as garden crops and fruit trees. The crop and native species mixture created here varies from farmer to farmer and from garden to garden of the same farmer.

The fallow stage can be managed more intensively. For example, neighbors of the Huastec, the Totonac, produce vanilla in the secondary thickets of fallows. When the site is cleared for planting maize, farmers spare many saplings to support vanilla vines. The Totonac also enrich their fallows by planting cuttings of *Bursera simaruba* (L.) Sarg. (a native species) and *Gliricidia sepium* (Jacq.) Steud. (an introduced species) around the edges of a new milpa for increased firewood production, and by transplanting wild seedlings of commercially valuable, native allspice, *Pimienta dioca* (L.) Merrill, among the maize (Medellín-Morales 1986). Farmers of another Mayan group, Yucatec Maya, selectively remove from fallowed areas trees that are not of value to bees (Sanabria 1986).

There is also potential for greater tree crop production within the chacra system. The Bora dooryard garden that surrounds the communal dwelling ("maloca") is created just as a chacra, but more fruit trees and "pejibaye" (*Bactris gasipaes* H.B.K.) are included. Bora indicate, however, that tree roots compete with manioc, and therefore they do not scatter fruit trees all over their gardens, because they want good manioc yields from those gardens. Bora squatting on land near Iquitos are using 12-year cycles in which they primarily slash and burn an orchard of fruit trees (cultivated for Iquitos markets) to reinitiate the chacra cycle. Mestizo river-dwellers have also intensified the chacra system for greater production from certain trees (Padoch and de Jong 1987), but it is not clear how this affects the capacity for forest regeneration in a given area.

Managed Forest Grove Systems

Both Bora and Huastec farmers maintain more permanently forested zones within their agroecosystems. In the Bora case, forested zones cover seasonally flooded spots and follow the creeks that often separate garden sites. These zones are maintained for the useful species found in these low areas, as well as for the reason that the areas are not deemed good for manioc cultivation. The distribution of gardened areas and uncut forest have not been mapped, and I am unable to comment further on how uncut forest zones are integrated into the maintenance of the total agroecosystem. To my knowledge, forested areas are not actively managed but fruits, wood, and game are harvested from these areas. I did notice that Bora pay close attention to the locations and growth of particular individual trees in forested zones.

Forested zones are more actively managed by the Huastec and other groups in Central and South America (Alcorn 1989c), as well as in other parts of the world (Olofson 1983). Following is a summary of more detailed accounts of the Huastec-managed forest system (the te'lom), its advantages, its products, and its component species that have been published in Spanish and English (Alcorn 1983, 1984a, 1984b).

In the Huastec case, 25 percent of a community's land is typically under te'lom groves. The te'lom patches are preferentially sited along creeks or on steep slopes where they prevent soil erosion and protect watersheds. Each farmer's te'lom is not large (1 to 3 ha), but, because of siting parameters, individual farmers' forest patches and communally owned patches generally border one another to create contiguous patches covering 25 or more hectares. Parts of these groves are occasionally put into the milpa cycle, but most are at least 80 years old (i.e., had the same location within living memory). They are managed by a combination of arboriculture and natural forest management to create a mixture of native species of primary and secondary forest and introduced species. A typical te'lom plot contains over 300 species. Ninety percent have known uses (as food, construction material, medicine, firewood, and livestock forage)—aside from the ecological services they provide. In addition, small gardens of other, less shade-tolerant species are found in small gaps within the te'lom and around its edges. The species composition of a given farmer's te'lom depends on historical, topographical, personal, and market-related factors. Some te'loms have been called rustic coffee plantations—plantations with a dense canopy of scattered native trees that are only weeded when farmers expect a coffee harvest of sufficient value to merit the work (Fuentes Flores 1979). Others risk being classified by government workers as "unused land," because they do not produce significant amounts of any particular commercial product.

The te'lom structure is created by casual management. The primary technique used is selective removal of unwanted individuals of native species. But this does not mean intensive weeding. The individuals removed are those that are unproductive, those that hamper the growth of other desirable species, and tall, old trees that might destroy other resources if they are felled by high winds. Trees are valued, and therefore not removed, for their products and for the ecological services they provide. For example, in areas where winter temperatures occasionally drop to near freezing, farmers preserve whichever native saplings and trees are present in order to maintain a dense canopy over coffee to protect it from the low temperatures (Barradas and Fanjul 1984). Farmers rely on birds, bats, and other animals to "plant" most of the grove. If sufficient individuals of a given species do not volunteer, seedlings of desired species are transplanted, or propagules are planted, into the grove. Useful species native to other ecological zones and locally rare trees are maintained in this way. Huastec families with the largest te'loms are usually those who pursue more off-farm income and prefer the low labor requirements of this system.

Te'lom groves are quite heterogeneous. Farmers often manage different areas within a te'lom for different purposes; some for coffee, some for firewood, others for avocado or mangos, and a section for lianas used in house construction. But each section contains a mixture of other species in addition to the focal species. Some parts of the te'lom are of different ages as new sections are created or put into a long fallow cycle. Thus a given farmer's grove often contains smaller subunits of different types, and one farmer's grove differs somewhat from those of other farmers.

Agroforestry Mosaics

Traditional agricultural systems such as that of the Bora and Huastec create a mosaic of eco-units (an eco-unit being defined as "a unit of vegetation which started its development at the same moment and on the same surface," Oldeman 1984:76). Both Bora and Huastec initiate milpa and chacra cycled fields every year, at any time of the year, often two or three times per year. Such patches, and subpatches within the patches, are cultivated and planted for varying lengths of time, and then secondary succession is allowed to proceed for varying lengths of time. Patches and greenbelts of less disturbed forest, and patches of more intensively farmed plots (e.g., sugarcane, pasture) complete the landscape. Each of these contain eco-units of different ages and species constitution.

By maintaining such forest patches over time and across space, indigenous agroforestry systems keep forest regeneration as part of their system. The farmers have opened lands for raising sun-loving crops, but they have kept the forest, its species and its regenerative processes, as well. At any given time, secondary successional species are reproducing somewhere in this mosaic, and mature forest species are reproducing somewhere else in the mosaic. In this way, the elements necessary to regenerate forest are retained in the system. Although such a system does not protect all forest species, it does provide a measure of protection for many species. The Huastec system today includes virtually no unmanaged forest, yet it remains fairly rich in species. Forests have been retained despite the fact that the Huastec region has supported relatively dense human populations for many centuries (Alcorn 1984a). (In the past 50 years, however, large mammals, such as monkeys, deer, paca, and jaguar, have disappeared from the region—probably as a result of hunting with guns.)

Conclusions

Indigenous agroforestry strategies are not primitive attempts to make a living with crude tools. They are sophisticated management systems using biological processes as tools to meet farmers' needs for desired products, nutrient concentrators, soil and water protectors, and a variety of other goods and services. Indigenous systems accomplish these goals given the restrictions faced by peasant farmers the world over: limited available labor, limited land base, low available capital, limited availability of artificial inputs (improved seed, fertilizer, alternative crops), unpredictable markets, and competing space and time requirements of other systems that are part of the farm enterprise.

But indigenous farmers are increasingly hampered by identification with a dominant culture that does not value natural processes but favors artificial, man-made items. This attitude prevents colonist farmers from taking advantage of the resources they have available to them (Moran 1979), and it is leading to the demise of indigenous managed groves, because forested lands are classified as "unused" (Dewalt 1982). Members of dominant, urban-oriented cultures (cultures shaped by other socioeconomic, historical, and environmental forces) need to take another look at how trees and forests have met farmers' needs in tropical moist areas.

Traditional agroforestry systems have been undervalued by outsiders. From the indigenous farmers' perspective, agroforestry systems do not merely produce items for a market. Unlike most modern agroforestry or social forestry systems promoted in developing countries (Shiva 1987), traditional systems meet many needs. For example, they meet needs generated by other farm enterprises. They concentrate nutrients for crops, prevent erosion, protect soil structure, control crop pest outbreaks, and provide microclimates for sheltering other crops. Livestock and game production are supported by forage and shelter provided by tree components of the agroecosystem. Farmers recognize that forest protects water sources basic to a farm's future. Fruits meet the farm family's basic needs for a nutritionally balanced diet and for snacks while traveling to and from work. Construction materials, craft items, and medicines are harvested "free" from forested tracts. Forest products generate income to supplement cash gained from other sources for the purchase of needed salt, rope, buckets, shotgun shells, radios, batteries, shoes, books, and other basic needs. Also from an economic perspective, low capital-input and low labor-input forest structures enable farmers to take advantage of other high-yielding labor opportunities while ensuring them subsistence when jobs are unavailable, or when they are disabled by illness and unable to rely on their own labor for support. In addition, the complex, user-managed systems I have described offer dignity to farmers. Each farmer has the opportunity to function as a self-sufficient individual applying his own management skills and knowledge to meet his family's changing needs.

A farmer's identity is bolstered by cultural judgments of the proper ways to farm. The modern farmer's identity and standing in the community are now being bolstered by different cultural judgments from those that shaped the traditional farmer. If members of the dominant culture would acknowledge the work of traditional farmers as worthy of emulation, as something they would like to learn how to do, this would be a major shift in attitude. Such a shift in attitude would enable indigenous farmers, extension agents, agricultural researchers, and development planners to enter as equals into a dialogue sharing knowledge to generate acceptable, viable alternatives to deforestation.

ACKNOWLEDGMENTS

This paper is based on fifteen months research among the Huastec and six weeks research among the Bora. I am grateful to the Huastec and Bora farmers who guided my research. Research among the Huastec from 1978 to 1983 was supported by NSF Dissertation Improvement Grant DEB 78-05968, a Social Science Research Council International Doctoral Research Fellowship, an E. D. Farmer International Fellowship, The University of Texas Institute of Latin American Studies, The University of Texas Office of Graduate Studies, The University of Texas International Student and Faculty Exchange Office, and a Tinker postdoctoral fellowship administered through the Mesoamerican Ecology Institute of Tulane University. Research among the Bora in 1981 was supported by a MAB grant to W. M. Devevan and C. Padoch of the University of Wisconsin at Madison and S. Flores Paitan of the Universidad Nacional de la Amazonia Peruana in Iquitos. Library research on agricultural use of secondary succession was supported by a grant from the American Philosophical Society. I alone, however, am reponsible for the contents of this paper.

REFERENCES

Alcorn, J. B. 1983. El te'lom huasteco: Presente, pasado y futuro de un sistema de silvicultura indígena. *Biótica* 8:315–331.

Alcorn, J. B. 1984a. *Huastec Mayan Ethnobotany.* Austin: University of Texas Press.

Alcorn, J. B. 1984b. Development policy, forests, and peasant farms: Reflections on Huastec-managed forests' contributions to commercial production and resource conservation. *Economic Botany* 38:389–406.

Alcorn, J. B. 1989a. Process as resource: The agricultural ideology of Bora and Huastec resource management. In D. A. Posey and W. Balee, eds., *Natural Resource Management by Indigenous and Folk Societies in Amazonia* (in press). New York: New York Botanical Garden.

Alcorn, J. B. 1989b. An economic analysis of Huastec Mayan forest management. *In* J. Browder, ed., *Fragile Lands in Latin America: The Search for Sustainable Uses* (in press). Boulder, CO: Westview.

Alcorn, J. B. 1989c. Indigenous agroforestry systems in the Latin American tropics. In M. Altieri and S. Hecht, eds., *Agroecology and Small Farm Development* (in press). Boca Raton, FL: CRC Press.

Barradas, V. L. and L. Fanjul. 1984. La importancia de la cobertura arborea en la temperatura del agroecosistema cafetalero. *Biótica* 9:415–421.

Denevan, W. M., J. M. Treacy, J. B. Alcorn, C. Padoch, J. Denslow, and S. Flores Paitan. 1984. Indigenous agroforestry in the Peruvian Amazon: Bora Indian management of swidden fallows. *Interciencia* 9:346–357.

Denevan, W. M. and C. Padoch, eds. 1987. *Swidden-Fallow Agroforestry in the Peruvian Amazon.* Bronx: New York Botanical Garden.

Dewalt, B. 1982. The big macro connection: Population, grain, cattle in S. Honduras. *Culture & Agriculture* 14:1–12.

Fuentes Flores, R. 1979. Coffee production systems in Mexico. In G. de las Salas, ed., *Agroforestry Systems in Latin America,* pp. 60–72. Turrialba, Costa Rica: CATIE.

Guyot, M. 1975. Le système cultural Bora-Miranta. In P. Centlivres, ed., *Culture sur brûlis et évolution de milieu forestier en Amazonie de Nord-Quest,* pp. 93–109. Geneva, Switzerland: Musée d' Ethnographie.

Medellín-Morales, S. G. 1986. *Uso y Manejo de las Especies Vegetales Comestibles, Medicinales, para Construcción y Combustibles en una Comunidad Totonaca de la Costa (Plan de Hidalgo, Papantla, Veracruz, México).* Xalapa, Veracruz, México: Programa Formación de Recursos Humanos, INIREB.

Moran, E. F. 1979. The Trans-Amazonica: Coping with a new environment. In M. L. Margolis and W. E. Carter, eds., *Brazil, Anthropological Perspectives,* pp. 133–159. New York: Columbia University Press.

Oldeman, R. A. A. 1984. The design of ecologically sound agroforests. In P. A. Huxley, ed., *Plant Research and Agroforestry,* pp. 75–121. Nairobi: ICRAF.

Olofson, H. 1983. Indigenous agroforestry systems. *Philippine Quarterly of Culture & Society* 11:149–174.

Padoch, C. and W. de Jong. 1987. Traditional agroforestry practices of native and ribereño farmers in the lowland Peruvian Amazon. In H. Gholz, ed., *Agroforestry: Realities, Possibilities, and Potentials,* pp. 179–194. Dordrecht, The Netherlands: Martinus Nijhoff.

Sanabria, O. L. 1986. *El Uso y Manejo Forestal en la Comunidad de Xul, en el Sur de Yucatán.* Etnoflora Yucatanese Fasciculo 2, Xalapa, Veracruz, Mexico, INIREB.

Shiva, V. 1987. Forestry myths and the World Bank. *The Ecologist* 17:142–149.

10

Japanese Agroforestry in Amazonia: A Case Study in Tomé-Açu, Brazil

■

SCOTT SUBLER

CHRISTOPHER UHL

ABSTRACT

Japanese colonists have been farming the remote forest regions of the Amazon Basin since the late 1920s. Over time they have developed from purely subsistence farmers into commercial agriculturalists fully integrated into local, national, and world markets. In contrast to extensive forms of land use common to the region, such as traditional slash-and-burn agriculture and cattle production, the Japanese farmers rely primarily on the intensive cultivation of relatively small plots of land, producing a diversity of high-value cash crops through mixed cropping of perennial plants. These farm systems require fairly heavy inputs of chemical and organic fertilizers, although amounts tend to decrease as the crop systems reach more mature tree-based stages. Labor requirements are high: a typical farm with about 20 ha in cultivation uses approximately six to eight full-time laborers. Due to large labor and material inputs, capital investments are also high. Constant experimentation with innovative techniques and a cooperative marketing system appear to play important roles in the success of these systems. Capital and technical requirements serve as barriers to the adoption of these systems by other rural Brazilians.

There is widespread acknowledgment of the lack of sustainability and destructive consequences of current major forms of Amazonian land use: slash-and-burn agriculture, cattle production, and logging (see Uhl et al., Fearnside, this volume).

With this comes a search for alternative land-use systems that combine economic and ecological sustainability while conserving Amazonian forest and soil resources. A major difficulty associated with this search is our presently limited vision of appropriate models for land use.

Much has been said about the promise of agroforestry—production systems that incorporate trees or tree crops—as a viable alternative (Hecht 1982; Altieri 1983; Huxley 1985; Nair 1985; Padoch et al. 1985; Ewel 1986), although specific examples of the functioning of these types of systems within Amazonia are uncommon. Extensive systems of forest management such as the extractive activities of flooded-forest inhabitants and indigenous groups are currently being examined and are beginning to provide a wealth of knowledge about the management and ecology of native flora (see papers by Anderson and Alcorn, this volume). However, intensive systems of agroforestry that are well integrated into national and international market economies are relatively unstudied.

This chapter provides an introduction to one such system: the agroforestry system developed by Japanese immigrants to Amazonia. Japanese immigrants and their descendants have been farming the remote forest regions of the Amazon Basin since the late 1920s. Over time they have developed from purely subsistence farmers into commercial agriculturalists fully integrated into national and world market economies. The Japanese farmers rely primarily on the intensive cultivation of relatively small plots of land, producing a variety of high-value cash crops through the mixed cropping of perennial and annual plants.

There are some important contrasts between the agroforestry systems of the Japanese and those of indigenous groups in Amazonia. The Japanese systems are new, have developed only in the past 20 to 30 years, and are still in the early stages of development. They replace the forest vegetation with both native and exotic species of economic value. The Japanese systems are intensive, requiring large inputs of labor, materials (in the form of inorganic and organic fertilizers), and capital investment per unit land area. The Japanese agriculture is well integrated into local, national, and international market economies, relying on the purchase of farm equipment and supplies, and providing food and other agricultural products for local consumption and for export to other regions of Brazil and the world. What do the Japanese farms look like? How do they overcome soil and pest problems? What are their labor and capital requirements? What are the prospects for adoption of these systems by other groups in Amazonia? These are the questions that will be addressed in this essay.

Research Approach

This paper presents preliminary information resulting from ongoing research in the oldest and largest Japanese agricultural colony in Amazonia—Tomé-Açu, in the state of Pará, Brazil (figure 10.1). During the past year we have been interviewing farmers in Tomé-Açu to determine the types of crops used, management techniques, and the allocation of labor, material, and capital resources on their farms. On three farms we have been keeping daily quantitative records of all farm activities, including planting, application of fertilizers and biocides, weeding,

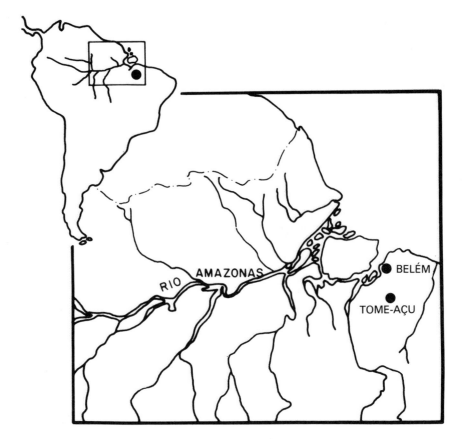

FIGURE 10.1. Locaton of Tomé-Açu.

pruning, harvesting, and processing of farm products, as well as monetary transactions. Additional information comes from interviews with officials of the Tomé-
Açu Agricultural Cooperative (CAMTA) and examination of records on farm production and CAMTA activities.

Early Japanese Settlement

The colony of Tomé-Açu is located approximately 115 km due south of Belém,
the capital city of the state of Pará, and is currently connected by partially paved
highways to Belém in the north and the Belém-Brasilia Highway in the south.
The land is primarily terra firma with highly weathered acid Oxisol soils characterized by low nutrient supplying and retention capabilities (Falesi, dos Santos,
and Vieira 1964; Sanchez 1976). The area annually receives an average of 2600
mm of rain and has a five-month period with reduced rainfall in which water
deficits may occur in the soil (Bastos 1972; Moraes and Bastos 1972). The original
tropical moist forest (Holdridge 1978) contained many species of economic value

including Brazil nut (*Bertholletia excelsa* H.B.), "maçaranduba" (*Manilkara huberi* Standl.), "pau santo" (*Zollernia paraensis* Hub.), "pau amarelo" (*Euxylophora paraensis* Hub.), and "acapú" (*Vouacapoua americana* Aubl.) (Falesi, dos Santos, and Vieira 1964). Remnants of the original forest still exist in small islands throughout the colony, especially on rocky soils, but most of the commercially valuable timber has been extracted from the region.

Tomé-Açu has served as a focal point for Japanese immigration to the Brazilian Amazon since 1929. The history of the colony has been discussed by various authors (see Cruz 1958; Valverde and Dias 1967; Staniford 1973; Rocque 1976; Flohrschütz et al. 1983; Uhl and Subler 1988). In 1929 the first 43 families of Japanese immigrants arrived in Tomé-Açu. They were sponsored by a large Japanese textile company interested in the settlement of the Amazon region as a means of relieving population pressure in their home district in Japan. Early attempts to establish cacao (*Theobroma cacao* L.) plantations in Tomé-Açu failed due to a poor understanding of management techniques. With large debts to the colonization company and no source of income to purchase food and supplies, the early settlers had to resort to subsistence agriculture similar to that practiced by the local Brazilians.

In addition to the traditional crops of rice, corn, beans, and manioc, the Japanese also planted vegetable crops that they brought with them from Japan, including tomatoes, bell peppers, cucumbers, radishes, and turnips. Although most of the food they produced was for their own consumption, they attempted to sell the surpluses in Belém. At first this was difficult since Brazilians were unaccustomed to the types of produce offered. The Japanese formed a cooperative marketing system based on models in their homeland to increase marketing efficiency, and their products gradually gained acceptance in the Brazilian marketplace.

Between 1929 and 1938, a total of 325 families and 28 single men arrived in Tomé-Açu. Economic crises resulting from the overproduction of vegetables and rice, poor infrastructure, and frequent outbreaks of malaria and yellow fever led to a large emigration of Japanese from Tomé-Açu. By 1942 only 98 of the original 353 households remained in Tomé-Açu.

During the Second World War Tome-Açu was designated as an enemy alien relocation center and many of the Japanese who had left were forced to return. The cooperative was disbanded and transport of produce to Belém was halted, leaving the Japanese farmers cut off and virtually self-sufficient. As Staniford (1973) points out, this period of internment served to reunite Tomé-Açu families with those who had greater experience with the Brazilian language and culture, and provided them with time to initiate a restructuring of their cooperative system.

In the years immediately following the war the Japanese at Tomé-Açu discovered that the exotic, perennial vine, black pepper (*Piper nigrum* L.), could be profitably grown in the region and the entire community began cultivating this crop. In 1949 the Tomé-Açu Agricultural Cooperative was founded to handle the marketing of pepper and other less important crops. Tomé-Açu became the first region in the western hemisphere to produce significant quantities of black pepper and by 1961, 3200 tons, representing more than 5 percent of the total world production of pepper (56,400 t), came from the community of less than 500 Japanese families (Staniford 1973).

Between 1953 and 1960 about 360 new Japanese families immigrated to Tomé-Açu and the community entered a new period of growth and prosperity. However, the "pepper boom" in Tomé-Açu quickly turned into a "pepper crisis" following a drastic fall in world pepper prices in the early 1960s, coupled with the spread of a *Fusarium* fungus, which wiped out or reduced the productive life of existing pepper plantations and made it impossible to replant pepper in contaminated soils. This spurred a new exodus of Japanese farmers from Tomé-Açu to plant pepper in other regions not yet contaminated by the fungus. Other farmers decided to remain in Tomé-Açu, adapting to the new conditions imposed by the fungal disease, and began to diversify their farms, planting cacao, passion fruit (*Passiflora edulis* Sims), papaya (*Carica papaya* L.), rubber (*Hevea brasiliensis* (Willd. ex A. Juss.) M. Arg.), and an assortment of other crops.

Structure of Japanese Farms in Tomé-Açu

There are currently about 280 Japanese farm households in Tomé-Açu. Almost all farms are operated by single families. The average farm size is between 100–150 ha but an average of only about 20 ha is in cultivation per farm (Flohrschütz et al. 1983). The remaining farm area is generally secondary forest regeneration following pepper field abandonment or previous slash-and-burn activity, or is undisturbed forest.

The Japanese farmers in Tomé-Açu specialize in the production of perennial cash crops: black pepper, cacao, passion fruit, rubber, African oil palm (*Elaeis guineensis* Jacq.), citrus and other fruit trees, and a variety of economically valuable forest tree species such as "cedro" (*Cedrela odorata* L.), "freijó" (*Cordia goeldiana* Hub.), "paricá" (*Schizolobium amazonicum* Hub.), and "parapará" (*Jacaranda copaia* D. Don). However, the Japanese farms in Tomé-Açu are not just scaled-down plantations: They exhibit a unique degree of diversity and management intensity that is uncommon in larger plantations specializing in single crops (Hecht 1982).

A wide variety of crops are produced by the Japanese in Tomé-Açu in addition to those mentioned above. Between 1984 and 1987 over 55 different crop products, representing annual as well as perennial crops, were sold through CAMTA. In 1986 each cooperative member marketed an average of three to four crops. Table 10.1 shows crop products received and sold by CAMTA in 1987. Black pepper, cacao, and passion fruit were its most important crops. Table 10.2 lists selected crop plants found on Japanese farms in Tomé-Açu.

Interplanting of crops is a common practice in Tomé-Açu. Stolberg-Wernigerode and Florschütz (1982) reported that over 70 percent of the farmers interviewed in Tomé-Açu had economic species in mixed culture; 34 species were involved in over 69 different combinations, making up about one-third of the cultivated area.

Insight into the ways that the Japanese farmers combine crops on their land can be gained by examining their overall strategy of land use. Short-lived perennials such as passion fruit or papaya are generally planted early after the clearing of forest or secondary vegetation. Depending upon existing market conditions, the Japanese farmers may plant annuals such as rice, beans, cucumbers, tomatoes, or

TABLE 10.1. Products Received and Sold by the Tomé-Açu Agricultural Cooperative (CAMTA) in 1987.

	RECEIVED BY CAMTA		SOLD BY CAMTA		
Product[a]	Amount (kg)	Producers	Value ($CZ)	Value ($US)[b]	% of Total
Black Pepper	885,093	163	174,802,168.37	3,884,492.63	78.42
Cacao	288,652	138	23,457,000.00	521,266.67	10.52
Passion Fruit	1,870,900	108	16,167,931.04	359,287.36	7.25
Cupuaçu	50,383	30	2,143,191.55	47,626.48	0.96
Rubber (raw)	12,410	13	1,310,611.95	29,124.71	0.59
Papaya	232,067	18	1,216,091.00	27,024.24	0.55
Eggs	—	1	1,011,781.13	22,484.03	0.45
Pumpkin	135,931	37	809,951.18	17,998.92	0.37
Graviola	30,140	10	736,169.96	16,359.33	0.33
Lime	98,740	29	685,978.20	15,243.96	0.31
Cucumber	29,256	4	183,581.63	4,079.59	0.08
Bell Pepper	7,413	7	118,914.48	2,642.54	0.05
Guaraná	1,262	7	56,480.00	1,255.11	0.03
Melon	1,483	3	23,437.32	520.83	0.01
Other[a]	—	—	173,340.76	3,852.02	0.08
	TOTAL	196	222,896,628.57	4,953,258.42	100.00

SOURCE: CAMTA, Collection of Products and Summary Statistics, 1987.

[a]See table 10.2 for further information on agricultural products found in Tomé-Açu.

[b]Based on exchange rate of 45 Cruzados ($CZ) per $US.

leafy vegetables between the rows of perennials. At the same time or soon afterwards, intermediate-lived perennials such as black pepper or fruit trees, or long-lived plants such as cacao, rubber, "capuaçu" (*Theobroma grandiflorum* (Willd. ex Spreng.) K. Schum.), or forest tree species are interplanted. In this way the short-lived crops grow and produce while the longer-lived crops are developing. When the short-lived crops are nearing the end of production the longer-lived crops are ready to begin. There are many variations in the way that this is practiced, but often the result is a temporal sequence of productive crops from short-lived to intermediate-lived to long-lived perennials, with an accompanying change in structure from open, bushy, or vine-like vegetation to a closed, multilayered forest. This sequence is in many ways similar to the natural succession that occurs spontaneously in abandoned clearings (Hart 1980).

A specific example of one farmer's crop sequence follows. In 1983 approximately 7 ha of rubber seedlings were planted in a secondary forest clearing. Half of this area was interplanted with rice and the other half with corn at the same time. After harvesting the grain crops the farmer planted cotton. In 1985, after the cotton was harvested, black pepper and papaya were planted in rows between the rubber trees, followed by a pumpkin crop in 1986. In 1987, the papaya trees finished their productive phase while the black pepper vines began to produce,

TABLE 10.2. Selected Crop Plants Found on Japanese Farms in Tomé-Açu.

Common name	English name	Species	Use
Perennials:			
Trees			
Abacate	Avacado	*Persea americana* Mill.	fruit
Abricó	—	*Mammea americana* L.	fruit
Andiroba	—	*Carapa guianensis* Aubl.	oil
Bacuri	—	*Platonia insignis* Mart.	fruit
Cacau	Cacao	*Theobroma cacao* L.	chocolate
Carambola	Star fruit	*Averrhoa carambola* L.	fruit
Castanha-do-Pará	Brazil nut	*Bertholletia excelsa* H.B.	nut, wood
Cedro	—	*Cedrela odorata* L.	shade, wood
Cupuaçu	—	*Theobroma grandiflorum* (Willd. ex Spreng.) K. Schum.	fruit
Erytrina	—	*Erythrina poeppigiana* (Walp.) O.F. Cook	shade
Freijó	—	*Cordia goeldiana* Hub.	shade, wood
Graviola	Soursop	*Annona muricata* L.	fruit
Ingá	—	*Inga* spp.	fruit
Laranja	Orange	*Citrus sinensis* (L.) Osbeck	fruit
Lima	Lemon	*Citrus limon* (L.) Burm. f.	fruit
Limão	Lime	*Citrus aurantifolia* (Christm.) Swing.	fruit
Mamão	Papaya	*Carica papaya* L.	fruit
Manga	Mango	*Mangifera indica* L.	fruit
Mangostin	Mangosteen	*Garcinia mangostana* L.	fruit
Mogno	Mahogany	*Swietenia macrophylla* King	wood
Palheiteria	—	*Clitoria racemosa* G.Don.	shade
Parapará	—	*Jacaranda copaia* D.Don.	wood
Paricá	—	*Schizolobium amazonicum* Hub.	shade, wood
Pau-d'arco	—	*Tabebuia serratifolia* Nichols.	wood
Piquiá	—	*Caryocar villosum* Pers.	fruit
Seringa	Rubber tree	*Hevea brasiliensis* (Willd. ex A.Juss.) M. Arg.	latex
Tangerina	Tangerine	*Citrus reticulata* Blanco	fruit
Taperebá	—	*Spondias mombin* L.	fruit
Terminalia	—	*Terminalia ivorensis* A. Cheval.	shade, wood
Palms			
Açai	—	*Euterpe oleracea* Mart.	fruit

and the farmer planted *Pueraria phaseoloides* Benth. as a ground cover. The farmer estimates that pepper production will continue satisfactorily for three to four more years and he will begin to harvest latex from the rubber trees when the pepper is finished.

Rather than planting large areas with any single crop or crop mixture, the Japanese farmers generally plant small areas (1–4 ha) at a time. Many cropping

TABLE 10.2. (continued)

Common name	English name	Species	Use
Coco	Coconut	*Cocos nucifera* L.	fruit
Dendê	Oil palm	*Elaeis guineensis* Jacq.	oil
Macaúba	—	*Acrocomia* sp.	fruit
Pupunha	Peach palm	*Bactris gasipaes* H.B.K.	fruit, oil
Shrubs, vines and other perennials			
Abacaxi	Pineapple	*Ananas comosus* (L.) Merr.	fruit
Acerola	Acerola	*Malpighia glabra* L.	fruit
Banana	Banana	*Musa* spp.	fruit
Baunilha	Vanilla	*Vanilla fragrans* (Salisb.) Ames	flavoring
Café	Coffee	*Coffea* spp.	coffee
Cardamomo	Cardamom	*Elettaria cardamomum* Maton	spice
Gengibre	Ginger	*Zingiber officinale* Rosc.	spice
Guaraná	—	*Paullinia cupana* H.B.	flavoring
Maracujá	Passion fruit	*Passiflora edulis* Sims	fruit
Pimenta do reino	Black pepper	*Piper nigrum* L.	spice
Urucú	—	*Bixa orellana* L.	food, dye
Annuals:			
Algodão	Cotton	*Gossypium hirsutum* L.	fiber
Arroz	Rice	*Oryza sativa* L.	grain
Batata doce	Sweet potato	*Ipomea batatas* (L.) Lam.	vegetable
Beringela	Eggplant	*Solanum melongena* L.	vegetable
Cebola	Onion	*Allium cepa* L.	vegetable
Feijão vagem	Cowpea	*Vigna unguiculata* (L.) Walp.	vegetable
Jerimum	Pumpkin	*Cucurbita maxima* Duch. ex Lam.	vegetable
Mandioca	Cassava	*Manihot esculenta* Crantz	tuber
Melão	Melon	*Cucumis melo* L.	fruit
Milho	Corn	*Zea mays* L.	grain
Pepino	Cucumber	*Cucumis sativus* L.	vegetable
Pimentão	Pepper	*Capsicum* spp.	vegetable
Repolho	Cabbage	*Brassica oleracea* L.	vegetable
Soja	Soy bean	*Glycine max* (L.) Merr.	food, oil
Tomate	Tomato	*Lycopersicon esculentum* Mill.	vegetable

SOURCE: Subler, personal observation; CAMTA, Collection of Products, 1984–1987; Stolberg-Wernigerode and Flohrschütz 1982.

systems on different plots of land may be in different stages of the temporal sequence, and the sequence in each may be different. Furthermore, not all planted areas go through a temporal sequence all the way to long-lived crop species. Often plots of land are abandoned and revert to secondary forest, or the sequence is interrupted and land is re-cleared for new crops. All this leads to a spatial mosaic of different crop systems, secondary vegetation, and natural forest patches in different stages of development at any one time. Figure 10.2 shows a map of land use on a representative Japanese farm in Tomé-Açu.

Ecological and Economic Sustainability

There are many potential ecological advantages to diverse agricultural systems including more efficient use of light, water, and nutrient resources, pest protection, and the compensatory growth of some crops under adverse environmental conditions, such as drought, which reduce the growth of other crops (Gleissman, Garcia, and Amador 1981; Altieri and Letourneau 1982; Ewel 1986).

The Japanese themselves acknowledge the economic factors that influence their decisions to increase the diversity and complexity of their farms. They are responding primarily to changes in crop prices and to changes in the costs of labor and material inputs for the production of particular crops. By having a number of perennial crops in different stages of production, they can rely on harvests from three or four crops at any one time, with the option of planting annual crops if the need arises. The farmers are able to reduce overall risk by spreading potential production over a number of crops.

The price the Japanese farmers pay for this flexibility is increased complexity of management, which requires technical knowledge about the management of each individual crop and prevailing economic conditions, in order to make decisions about how to allocate material, land, and labor resources. This complexity of management imposes limits on the size of the area under cultivation by single households (Staniford 1973).

Maintenance of Soil Fertility

The Japanese cropping systems generally require large inputs of organic and chemical fertilizers. The amounts and types depend greatly on the specific requirements of the crops being grown, with some requiring larger and more frequent inputs than others. Quantities applied range from about 4000 kg of organic fertilizers and 1500 kg of chemical fertilizers per ha per year for a well-treated pepper plantation to about 250 kg organic and 400 kg chemical fertilizers per ha per year for a well-treated cacao plantation, although in years with high fertilizer costs and/or low crop prices these amounts may be considerably less.

Although most fertilizer is purchased, there are some examples of the use of organic materials derived from within the farms. Cacao hulls are often composted or burned and returned to cacao plantations. In a plantation that produces 800 kg of dried cacao seeds per ha the hulls could contribute approximately 40 kg of potassium per ha (CEPLAC 1985). Weeds are normally cut and left in place or piled as mulches, recycling nutrients previously removed from the soil. Some farmers make use of nitrogen-fixing leguminous plants as green manures, crops, or shade trees. Common examples include *Pueraria phaseoloides* as a ground cover and green manure, various bean species intercropped with pepper, or the shade tree *Erythrina* in cacao plantations. The latter example is especially interesting

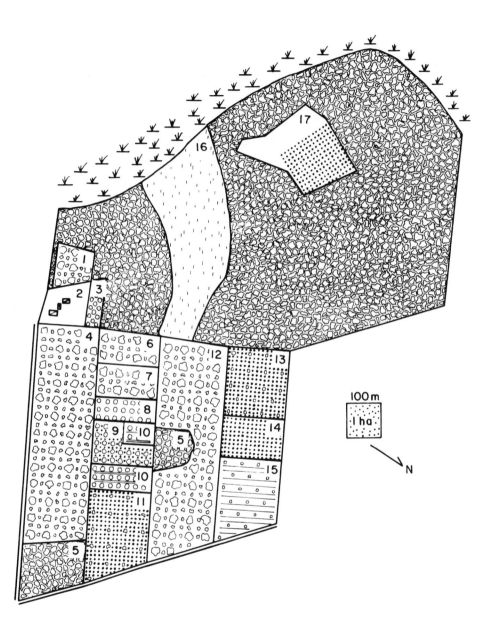

FIGURE 10.2. Map of land use on a representative Japanese farm in Tomé-Açu. 1 = cacao, erythrina; 2 = household area; 3 = coconut, citrus, mangosteen, graviola; 4 = cacao, erythrina, andiroba, Brazil nut; 5 = secondary forest regeneration; 6 = cacao, vanilla, palheteira, freijó; 7 = cacao, paricá; 8 = rubber trees; 9 = rubber trees, black pepper, cacao; 10 = rubber trees, passion fruit; 11 = black pepper, cacao; 12 = cacao, banana, *Cecropia* sp.; 13 = black pepper, cupuaçu; 14 = black pepper; 15 = passion fruit, cupuaçu; 16 = pasture grasses; 17 = black pepper, clearing.

since some farmers claim that their unfertilized cacao plantations with well-established *Erythrina* produce almost as well as nearby fertilized plantations.

The long-term effect of the Japanese crop system and management on changes in soil fertility is currently not well known. However, there is indirect evidence that the soil is not being degraded. Many plots on the Japanese farms have been continuously productive for over 15 years and show no signs of imminent decline in productivity. Compared to traditional slash-and-burn systems that remain productive for only a few years until abandonment, or to typical pasture with a productive life of from four to eight years (Uhl et al., this volume), this is a significant accomplishment. Also, there is a general trend toward the reduction in quantities of fertilizers applied as crop systems mature toward the tree-based stages. The Japanese farmers themselves believe that soil fertility is improved under their management and avow a preference for planting new crops in aging or recently abandoned plots.

Control of Weeds and Pests

The control of weeds represents a large labor input for areas without a closed vegetative cover. In pepper plantations about half of the total labor input, or approximately 70 man-days per ha per year, goes to manual weeding. Mechanical methods such as disking and mowing are employed in some cases, as is chemical control of weeds with herbicides.

Use of chemical pesticides is common on the Japanese farms both as a preventative measure and for the control of specific pest outbreaks. Also common are methods of cultural control through the removal of diseased fruits, limbs, or whole plants. A serious disease problem affecting cacao plantations in this region is caused by the "witch's broom fungus" (*Crinipellis perniciosa*). It attacks both the fruits and the leaves of the cacao plant and can reduce the production of a plantation by more than half. The Japanese farmers control this disease by pruning to remove infected fruits and limbs. In years of especially serious infestation, half of the overall management costs for the cacao plantations may result from this activity.

An interesting technique currently being developed by some farmers is the grafting of branches of cacao trees resistant to the witch's broom fungus to the trunks of cacao trees in established plantations. While the grafted stem is developing, the host plant continues to produce under the traditional management regime. The farmers slowly prune back the branches of the host plant until the grafted stem is fully developed and has replaced the old branches. In this way the farmers hope to increase the resistance of their cacao plantations to fungal attack.

Labor and Capital Requirements

Although most Japanese farmers in Tomé-Açu own at least one tractor, most of the farm work is done manually. An average farm requires the equivalent of about five full-time laborers, or one person for every 3–4 ha under cultivation (Flohrschütz et al. 1983; Subler, unpublished data). Family members contribute an average of about two full-time laborers per farm, but the Japanese role is becoming increasingly supervisory with the Brazilian laborers doing most of the manual work.

Due to the intensive use of materials and labor on the Japanese farms, capital requirements per unit cultivated area are relatively high. In 1985, the costs of material and labor inputs for a single hectare of black pepper, averaged throughout its productive life, was over one thousand U.S. dollars per year. This is close to twice the current minimum annual salary for a wage-laborer in Brazil (January, 1988). This value does not include any of the operational costs of fuel, equipment, and farm maintenance normally incurred by the Japanese farmers.

Sources of capital to finance farm activities currently include credit from CAMTA (credit availability is based on estimates of individual farmers' yearly production) and bank loans. CAMTA has played a central role in the development and success of the agricultural community. The cooperative provides easy access to materials and equipment, credit, technical assistance, and local processing of farm products, and plays an indispensible role in the development of markets for new crops. The cooperative handles the marketing of crops produced by members, and through the cooperative the farmers are able to assert leverage in the marketplace. The cooperative also serves as an important center for information exchange between local farmers and farmers from other regions.

Prospects for Adoption of the Japanese Model by Other Groups

Although it is common to see very small plots of black pepper and sometimes passion fruit on the properties of neighboring Brazilian small producers, there is no indication that they are adopting the types of crop systems and management techniques employed by the Japanese. There are a number of possible explanations for this. Without secure title to the land, it is difficult to risk investment of time, labor, and capital in perennial-based systems that may require a number of years before they even begin to produce. Also, without title to land it is extremely difficult for farmers to receive loans from banks, and even with titled land the large capital investments characteristic of the Japanese systems are beyond the reach of most small producers.

The complexity of management and the level of technical knowledge that the Japanese have obtained through years of experience and research also represent an obstacle to untrained small producers. The few cases we have encountered of Brazilians of non-Japanese descent with farm systems similar to those of the Japanese have been settlers from the south of Brazil who have come from middle-class agricultural backgrounds, bringing with them knowledge of agricultural technology and sufficient capital to invest in their new farms.

Conclusions

The Japanese in Tomé-Açu have, through trial and error, developed a system of agriculture responsive to the environmental and economic constraints of the region. An important question is: What is the potential for the expansion of this form of land use on a wider scale in Amazonia? The sedentary, continuous land use characteristic of Japanese agroforestry systems appears to be conservative of forest and soil resources, requiring relatively small-scale forest clearing and maintaining long-term soil fertility. However, the reliance on fertilizer inputs may play a large role in the maintenance of soil fertility on the Japanese farms. The long-term sustainability of these systems is questionable given the trend toward increasing fertilizer and energy prices.

Problems of transport of equipment, supplies, and crop products were overcome by the establishment of a cooperative in Tomé-Açu. However, the community is located relatively close to a major urban center (Belém). Transportation requirements may represent an obstacle to the development of these systems in more remote areas. As road networks continue to expand in Amazonia, however, large areas of undeveloped land will become increasingly accessible to this form of agriculture.

Rather than displacing rural inhabitants, the Japanese farms utilize local human resources. Although this type of land use may provide employment for rural Brazilians, the high labor requirements make these systems vulnerable to labor shortages and increasing labor costs.

The high prices received for crops such as black pepper, cacao, passion fruit, and rubber make up for the heavy capital investments required for these systems. Yet current prices are based on limited worldwide availability of these products, and there are limits to the expansion in production that can occur before markets become saturated and prices fall (Alvim 1982; Fearnside, this volume). It may be possible to substitute food and oil-producing crops for the "luxury" crops of present-day systems, providing much-needed protein and energy for the expanding population in Amazonia.

The problems associated with the adoption of these systems by rural Brazilians have been discussed. Without some form of institutional support to encourage the adoption of these systems through training, credit, and community services, it appears unlikely that the Japanese agroforestry systems will spread spontaneously to any great extent.

Although no one model may be appropriate for wide-scale adoption in Amazonia, the Japanese in Tomé-Açu demonstrate that small-scale commercial agriculture is possible. Information coming from research on intensive agroforestry systems such as those in Tomé-Açu, and on extensive systems of forest management by indigenous groups and other forest inhabitants, provides promising new directions in the search for ecologically and economically sustainable land-use alternatives for Amazonia.

ACKNOWLEDGMENTS

This research was funded in part by the Jessie Smith Noyes Foundation, the National Science Foundation (BSR-8601333), and through a Garden Club of America Challenge Award. Institutional support was provided by the Museu Emílio Goeldi, Belém. Special acknowledgment goes to the officials of CAMTA and the farmers and community of Tomé-Açu for their cooperation and support.

REFERENCES

Altieri, M. A. 1983. *Agroecology, the Scientific Basis of Alternative Agriculture.* Berkeley, CA: Division of Biological Control.

Altieri, M. A. and D. K. Letourneau. 1982. Vegetation management and biological control in agroecosystems. *Crop Protection* 1:405–30.

Alvim, P. T. 1982. A perspective appraisal of perennial crops in the Amazon Basin. In S. B. Hecht, ed., *Amazonia: Agriculture and Land Use Research,* pp. 311–328. Cali, Colombia: Centro Internacional de Agricultura Tropical (CIAT).

Bastos, T. X. 1972. O estado atual dos conhecimentos da Amazônia Brasileira. *Boletim Técnico* No. 54:68–122. Belém: Instituto de Pesquisa Agropecuária do Norte (IPEAN).

CEPLAC. 1985. *Sistema de Produção do Cacaueiro na Amazônia Brasileira.* Belém, Brazil: Comissão Executiva do Plano de Lavoura Cacaueira.

Cruz, E. 1958. *Colonização do Pará.* Belém, Brazil: Instituto Nacional de Pesquisas da Amazônia.

Ewel, J. J. 1986. Designing agricultural ecosystems for the humid tropics. *Annual Review of Ecology and Systematics* 17:245–71.

Falesi, I. C., W. H. dos Santos, and L. S. Vieira. 1964. *Os Solos da Colônia Agricola de Tomé-Açu.* Boletim Técnico No. 44. Belém: Instituto de Pesquisas e Experimentaçāo Agropecuárias do Norte (IPEAN).

Flohrschütz, G. H. H., A. K. O. Homma, P. C. Kitamura, and A. I. M. dos Santos. 1983. *O Processo de Desenvolvimento e Nivel Technológico de Culturas Perenes: O Caso da Pimenta-do-Reino no Nordeste Paraense.* Documento No. 23. Belém: Centro de Pesquisa Agropecuária do Trópico Umido (EMERAPA-CPATU).

Gleissman, S. R., E. R. Garcia, and A. M. Amador. 1981. The ecological basis for the application of traditional agricultural technology in the management of tropical agroecosystems. *Agro-ecosystems* 7:173–185.

Hart, R. D. 1980. A natural ecosystem analog approach to the design of a successful crop system for tropical forest environments. *Biotropica* 12 (Supplement):73–82.

Hecht, S. B. 1982. Agroforestry in the Amazon Basin: Practice, theory and limits of a promising land use. In S. B. Hecht, ed., *Amazonia: Agriculture and Land Use Research,* pp. 331–371. Cali, Colombia: Internacional de Agricultura Tropical (CIAT).

Holdridge, Leslie R. 1978. *Ecologia: Basada en Zonas de Vida.* San José, Costa Rica: Instituto Interamericano de Ciencias Agrícolas.

Huxley, P. A. 1985. Experimental agroforestry—progress through perception and collaboration? *Agroforestry Systems* 3:129–138.

Moraes, V. H. F. and T. H. Bastos. 1972. Viabilidade e limitações climáticas para as culturas permanentes, semi-permanentes e anuais com possibilidades de expansão na Amazônia Brasileira. *Boletim Técnico* No. 54: 123–153. Belém: Instituto de Pesquisa Agropecuária do Norte (IPEAN).

Nair, P. K. R. 1985. Classification of agroforestry systems. *Agroforestry Systems* 3:97–128.

Padoch, C., J. Chota Inuma, W. De Jong, and J. Unruh. 1985. Amazonian agroforestry: A market oriented system in Peru. *Agroforestry Systems* 3:47–58.

Rocque, C. 1976. História dos municípios do estado do Pará. Belém: *A Provincia do Pará* (Oct. 4, 1976).

Sanchez, P. A. 1976. *Properties and Management of Soils in the Tropics.* New York: Wiley.

Staniford, P. 1973. *Pioneers in the Tropics: The Political Organization of Japanese in an Immigrant Community in Brazil.* London School of Economics Monographs on Social Anthropology, No. 45. London: Athlone Press.

Stolberg-Wernigerode, A. G. and G. H. H. Flohrschütz. 1982. *Levantamento de Plantios*

Mistos na Colônia de Tomé-Açu-Pará. Documento No. 6. Belém: Centro de Pesquisa Agropecuária do Trópico Umido (EMERAPA-CPATU).

Uhl, C. and S. Subler. 1988. Asian farmers: Stewards of Amazonia. *Garden* 12(5).

Valverde, O. and C. V. Dias. 1967. *Rodovia Belém-Brazilia.* Rio de Janeiro: Fundação Instituto Brasileiro de Geografia e Estatística (IBGE).

11

Promoting Agroforestry Practices Among Small Producers: The Case of the Coca Agroforestry Project in Amazonian Ecuador

■

ROBERT B. PECK

ABSTRACT

Oil exploitation and road construction has converted eastern Ecuador into one of the most active areas of colonization in the Amazon Basin. In an effort to make existing farming systems more sustainable, the Coca Agroforestry Project was implemented in 1984 by the Ecuadorian Ministry of Agriculture and the National Forestry Directorate, with financial and technical support of the U.S. Agency for International Development (USAID). Instead of building an extension service to attend approximately 30,000 families, this project promotes agroforestry systems in on-farm demonstrations that are monitored semiannually. On-farm demonstrations are an effective means of communicating to the community at large. Feedback from farmers' experience enables the demonstrations to adopt site-specific components that are not available in experimental station research. By late 1987, over 200 farm demonstrations, ranging from 1–12 ha in size, were promoting 27 native tree species in mixed associations. The project is currently expanding its sphere of influence along new roads being built in the region.

In recent years, agroforestry has received considerable attention as a promising form of land use that is potentially sustainable and highly adaptable to the needs of small-scale producers. In humid tropical areas of Asia and Africa, agroforestry systems are abundant and extremely variable (Nair 1985). In the American tropics, however, these systems are only well-represented among traditional, indigenous communities (Hecht 1982; Posey 1983; Denevan et al. 1984; Padoch et al. 1985; Alcorn, this volume); in rapidly expanding frontier zones, they are relatively rare. This rarity is in large part due to the nature of frontier expansion in the American tropics, where large-scale land uses such as cattle pastures predominate and frequently encroach on small-scale production systems. Practitioners of the latter often originate from other regions and have little prior knowledge of local resources and technologies. Faced with uncertain land tenure, distant markets, and lack of technical support, the small holder is frequently compelled to practice degenerate forms of shifting cultivation for subsistence.

Promoting more sustainable land uses such as agroforestry in frontier zones requires effective extension services aimed at small-scale producers. Yet the obstacles to implementing such a policy are formidable. In general, frontier expansion in the American tropics—and especially in the Amazon Basin—is a rapid and geographically extensive phenomenon that takes place in areas distant from major population centers. In virtually all countries, extension efforts suffer from inadequate personnel, lack of continuity, and insufficient adaptation to local conditions.

This chapter describes an unusual approach to extension that is taking place in Amazonian Ecuador: the Coca Agroforestry Project. The project addresses many of the problems characteristic of extension programs through the use of on-farm demonstrations. These demonstrations effectively promote agroforestry practices in isolated areas, encourage participation and experimentation by resident farmers, and can be periodically modified to suit local needs. The experience gained thus far in this project could provide useful clues for implementation of extension programs elsewhere in the humid tropics.

Regional Production Systems

The Coca Agroforestry Project is located at the confluence of the Coca and Payamino rivers with the Napo River, in the Napo Province of eastern Ecuador, east of the Andes and south of the Equator (figure 11.1). Altitudes in the region range from a minimum of 200 m above sea level in the easternmost portions of the province to a maximum of 600 m above sea level. Rainfall is reported to be approximately 3100 mm annually (Costales et al. 1987); there is no pronounced dry season and precipitation always exceeds potential evapotranspiration (Canadas 1983). The forest vegetation of the eastern lowland forest of the Yasuni National Park was described by Baslev et al. (1987); the vegetation at a higher elevation near Tena was described by Grubb et al. (1963). Because there is no distinct dry season in this region, cut vegetation is not burned but allowed to remain as mulch for cultivated crops (Hiraoka and Yamamoto 1980).

Three perennial production systems are practiced by the residents of this region: swidden agriculture ("chacra"), plantations of robusta coffee, and cattle pastures. All three systems are associated with trees and consequently provide a basis for the design of new agroforestry systems, utilizing improved germplasm and efficient management techniques. Each of the regional production systems is described below.

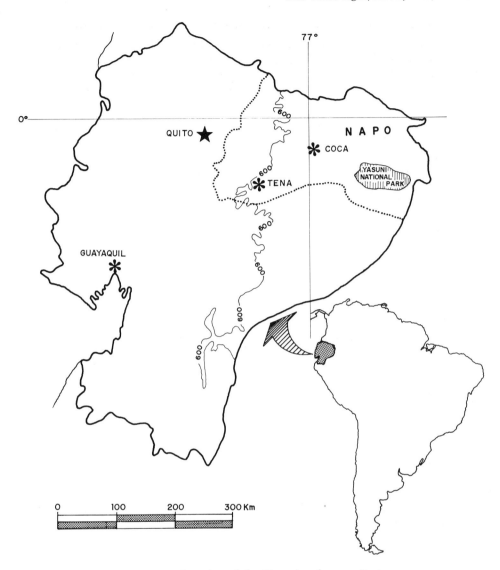

FIGURE 11.1. Location of the Coca Agroforestry Project.

Traditional Production System

Chacra is a perennial production system that has sustained low-density settlements of the lowland Napo Quichuas since before western contact was made in the mid-1500s (Hudelson 1987; Irvine 1987); a similar system was described among the Bora in Amazonian Peru by Denevan et al. (1984).

In the chacra system practiced by the Napo Quichua—referred to as "slash and mulch"—valued trees and palm species are left standing when the forest is first cut. After the harvest of short-cycle crops, the site continues to be used for perennial species. Examples of plant species commonly cultivated or protected in

TABLE 11.1. Commonly Cultivated or Protected Plant Species in the Chacra Production System of the Lowland Napo Quichua, Ecuador (250–600 m above sea level).

| | COMMON NAMES | |
SCIENTIFIC NAME	*Spanish*	*Quichua*
Fruit Trees		
1. *Caryodendron orinocense* Karst.	mani de árbol	inchi huachansu
2. *Inga densiflora* Benth.	ilta	ilta pacai
3. *Inga edulis* Mart.	guaba	pacai suni pacai
4. *Inga spectabilis* Willd.	muchatona	muchetuna pacai
5. *Persea americana* Mill.	aguacate	palta
6. *Pouroma cecropiaefolia* Mart.	uvillia	uvillia
7. *Pouteria caimito* (R. et P.) Radlk.	abiyú	abiyu
8. *Rheedia macrophylla* Planch et Triana	madrono	pungara muyu
9. *Theobroma bicolor* H.B.	cacao blanco	patas yura
Palms		
1. *Astrocaryum chambira* Burret	macora	chambira
2. *Bactris gasipaes* H.B.K.	chonta dura	chunda ruru
3. *Carludovica palmata* R. et P.	pajá toquilla	lisan
4. *Iriartea cornuta* H. Wendl.	pambil	patihua
5. *Jessenia bataua* (Mart.) Burret	mil pesos	ungurahua
6. *Palandra aequatorialis* O.F. Cook	taquá	yarina
Small Trees or Shrubs		
1. *Bixa orellana* L.	achiote	manduru
2. *Brownea* spp.	palo de crúz	cruz caspi
3. *Crescentia cujete* L.	maté	pilchi
4. *Ilex guayusa* Loes	guayusa	guayusa
5. *Lonchocarpus* sp.	barbasco	ambi
Short-Cycle Crops		
1. *Arachis hipogaea* L.	mani	inchi
2. *Carica papaya* L.	papaya	papaya
3. *Gossypium barbadense* L.	algodón	algudun
4. *Manihot utilissima* Pohl.	yuca	lumu
5. *Musa* spp.	plátano	palanda
6. *Renealmia* sp.	platanillo morado	shihuango muyu
7. *Xanthosoma saguttifolium* Schott	papa mandi	papa mandi
8. *Zea mays* Vell.	maíz duro	sinchi sara
Commercial Timber Trees		
1. *Cedrela odorata* L.	cedro	cidra
2. *Cordia alliodora* (Ruiz et Pav.) Oken	laurel	arana caspi
3. *Jacaranda copaia* D. Don	jacarandá	copa
4. *Pollalesta karstenii* (Sch. Bip.) Aristeg.	pigue	piqui

the chacra are provided in table 11.1 Sources of regeneration include residual saplings, sprouts from cut trees, germination of buried and wind-borne seeds, and intentionally planted seeds or seedlings (Irvine 1987); practitioners of chacra alter the proportions of these four sources of regeneration by selecting desirable species and eliminating undesirable plants. As a result, the chacra production system is tightly linked to the natural processes of forest succession (see papers by Anderson and Dubois, this volume). In contrast to shifting cultivation, a chacra is never completely abandoned and provides a continual source of fruits, medicinal, firewood, timber, and even game (cf. Posey 1983). The regeneration strategies promoted in this land-use system have provided a silvicultural basis for some of the management practices recommended in the Coca Agroforestry Project (Peck 1983).

Colonist Production Systems

After oil was discovered and commercially exploited in the early 1970s, construction of roads in the lowlands converted eastern Ecuador into one of the most active centers of colonization in the Amazon Basin. The colonists' first preoccupation was to establish subsistence agriculture for their own needs (González and Ortiz de Villalba 1977), adapting degenerate forms of the indigenous slash-and-mulch production system (Hiroaka and Yamamoto 1980). Together with subsistence agriculture, the colonists developed pastures for cattle ranching, despite persistent pest problems (especially spittlebug) and inadequate knowledge of pasture management. On average, half of the cultivated area in each farm was dedicated to pastures, and the proportion tended to increase as short-cycle subsistence plantations were frequently followed by additional pasture establishment (Uquillas 1984).

Regional land-use patterns, however, were destined to change. Killing frost destroyed coffee plantations in Brazil, and robusta coffee was introduced into eastern Ecuador from coastal plantations established during the 1950s. By 1982, the Napo Province produced 7748 metric tons of coffee from 28,430 ha of plantations; in under a decade, it had become the second coffee producing province in Ecuador.

By the time the Coca Agroforestry Project began in 1984, two market-oriented, perennial crop farming systems—coffee plantations and cattle pastures—had thus become consolidated in the region. Baseline studies conducted prior to initiation of extension services revealed that in the District (or "Cantón") of Francisco de Orellana, the regional headquarters of the project, a total of approximately 3300 colonist families had been settled on 145,500 ha over a fifteen-year period (1972–1986), or an average of 46 ha per homestead. Average areas allocated to the major production systems per homestead are provided in table 11.2; number of trees traditionally associated with each production system is shown in table 11.3.

TABLE 11.2. Average Area of Major Production Systems Per Homestead, Stratified by Soil Type, in the Francisco Orellano District, Napo Province, Ecuador, in 1986. "N" Equals Number of Farms Sampled Per Soil Type.

Characteristic	SOIL TYPE			Mean
	Alluvial (N = 27)	Volcanic (N = 33)	Red Clay (N = 47)	
Area (ha)	45.6	48.1	44.7	46.0
In Crops	6.0	8.5	5.1	6.5
In Pasture[1]	7.0	10.0	4.1	6.6
In Fallow	4.4	4.8	0.4	2.7
Cleared (Total)	17.4	23.3	9.6	15.8

Source: Estrada, Sere and Luzuriaga 1987.

[1]Pasture areas calculated from livestock inventories, assuming a stocking rate of 0.95 animal unit per ha.

Table 11.3. Distribution of "laurel" (*Cordia alliodora*) and "jacaranda" (*Jacaranda copaia*) in Different Cropping Systems in the Francisco de Orellana District, Napo Province, Ecuador, in 1986. Total Sample Size: 107 Farms.

Crop	No. Farms Producing Crop	LAUREL		JACARANDA	
		No. Farms Associating Tree/Crop	No. Trees per Ha	No. Farms Associating Tree/Crop	No. Trees per Ha
Coffee	104	95	19.1	7	6.7
Cacao	16	12	19.3	1	5.0
Corn	23	14	18.3	0	0
"Elefante" grass[a]	47	36	11.9	1	1.3
"Saboya" grass[b]	29	8	8.6	0	0
"Dallis" grass[c]	48	36	14.7	2	4.5
"Kikuyo" grass[d]	11	9	23.1	1	10.0
"Alemán" grass[e]	9	5	7.8	0	0
Fallow	38	38	27.9	4	56.2

Source: Estrada, Sere and Luzuriaga 1987.

[a]*Pennisetum purpureum* Schum.

[b]*Panicum maximum* Jacq.

[c]*Brachiaria decumbens* Stapf.

[d]*Brachiaria humidicola* (Rendle) Schweickt.

[e]*Echinochloa polystrachya* Rojas

Project Activities

In an effort to make existing farming systems more sustainable, the Coca Agroforestry Project was implemented in 1984 by the Ecuadorian Ministry of Agriculture and the National Forestry Directorate, with financial and technical support of the U.S. Agency for International Development (USAID). The town of Coca (figure 11.1) was selected as the headquarters of the project. Located adjacent to the Napo River, Coca is a major commercial center with a population of approximately 10,000. In addition to its strategic location, Coca houses a Ministry of Agriculture field office, as well as two research stations run by the National Institute of Agricultural Research (INIAP).

The project was designed to carry out activities in four broadly defined areas, each of which is described in the following sections.

Promotion of Agroforestry Practices

Promotional activities are carried out using on-farm demonstrations and field trials. The term "demonstration" applies to practices that have proven results, such as the planting of tree species with known silviculture in coffee plantations. The term "field trial" applies to those practices that still must be proven, such as the establishment of multiplication plots of improved grasses, legumes, plantains, or living fence material. Until field trials have been shown to have utility, they are not referred to as demonstrations.

In the Coca Agroforestry Project, demonstrations have focused on agroforestry practices within existing perennial production systems, especially robusta coffee plantations and pastures. The agroforestry practices promoted include introduction of commercial timber species and legume cover crops. In addition to their use in promoting agroforestry practices, demonstrations provide a means of validating the performance of improved germplasm under diverse field conditions.

Demonstrations are established on farms located along the seven principal roads radiating out from the town of Coca. Demonstrations are located on the property of farmers who express interest in receiving technical assistance to increase the number of commercial trees associated with existing production systems. The demonstrations are initially established by the farmer with the help of a project agronomist. This arrangement assures that the demonstration fits into the existing production systems while increasing the probability of successful establishment. Before setting up a demonstration or field trial, the project agronomist makes a farm plan by walking through the farm with the farmer, identifying soil types and farming systems, and sounding out the farmers' needs for different agroforestry practices. The data for each farm are placed in a separate folder, which provides a convenient reference for evaluating results.

By the end of 1987, more than 200 demonstrations had been established on individual farms. Approximately half of these demonstrations (109) are larger than one hectare in area and involve commercial tree species: 75 in association with robusta coffee and 34 within improved grass-legume pastures (composed of

Brachiaria humidicola (Rendle) Schweickt. and *Desmodium ovalifolium* Gull. et Perr.). All silvopastoral demonstrations are initially established with vegetative planting material on small multiplication plots (as small as 10 × 10 m), which are gradually enlarged as the farmer recognizes the merits of a particular species or combination. By late 1987, 188 farms had established multiplication plots composed of improved grass and legume germplasm.

Nursery Production

A 12-ha nursery was established to make agroforestry germplasm available to the general public. The major types of plant material produced in the nursery include: 1) commercial tree species with known silviculture, such as "laurel" (*Cordia alliodora* (Ruiz et Pav.) Oken), "pachaco" (*Schizolobium parahybum* Blake), "jacaranda" (*Jacaranda copaia* D. Don), "cedro" (*Cedrela odorata* L.), and "ahauno" (*Swietenia macrophylla* King) (table 11.4); 2) multiplication plots of perennial food crops such as plantain (*Musa* spp.) and "papa mandi" (*Xanthosoma* spp.); 3) multiplication plots of living fence material for vegetative propagation, such as "mata ratón" (*Lonchocarpus sepium* DC.), "piñon" (*Jatropha curcas* L.) and "lechero" (*Euphorbia cotinifolia* L.) (table 11.5); and 4) multiplication plots for vegetative propogation of grasses and legumes, such as "kikuyo amazónico" (*Brachiaria humidicola*) and "trébol tropical" (*Desmodium ovalifolium*) for well-drained sites and "pasto alemán" (*Echinochloa polystachia* Rojas), "antelope" (*E. pyramidalis* Hitchc. et Chase), and *Desmodium heterophyllum* DC. for poorly drained sites.

The site for the nursery was located close to a stream that provides a reliable water supply throughout the year. Tree species are produced in prepared beds for bare root planting. The nursery beds are rotated each year, and between beds a legume cover crop of perennial peanut (*Arachis* sp.) is planted to control weeds and erosion. After the ends are abandoned, a persistent legume cover crop of *Desmodium ovalifolium* and *Inga edulis* Mart. is established during a 2–3-year fallow for restoring soil fertility. The nursery is surrounded by living fence posts of various species, which provide a source of vegetative propagation for farm demonstrations.

Training

The field staff members of the Coca Agroforestry Project are recruited from local agronomy schools. All recruits have been raised on farms or "comunas" (communal lands belonging to the lowland Napo Quichuas), and all have practical farm experience and know the local crops and their management problems. Formal training focuses on introduction and management of selected germplasm within existing agricultural production systems. Practical field training includes supervised elaboration of farm plans, preparation of planting materials in the nursery, and establishment of on-farm demonstrations.

TABLE 11.4. List of Commercial Timber Species Identified by Farmers and Included in On-Farm Demonstrations in the Coca Agroforestry Project.

		COMMON NAMES	
	SCIENTIFIC NAME	Spanish	Quichua
1.	*Apeiba aspera* Aubl.	prene mono	maccha caspi
2.	*Brosimum utile* (H.B.K.) Pittier	sande	sandi yura
3.	*Cabralea canjerana* Saldanha	batea caspi	batia caspi
4.	*Calycophyllum spruceanum* (Benth.) K. Schum.	capirona	capiruna
5.	*Cedrela odorata* L.	cedro	cedru yura
6.	*Cedrelinga cateniformis* (Ducke) Ducke	chunchu	chunchu
7.	*Chimarrhis glabriflora* Ducke	mecha	intachi
8.	*Clarisia racemosa* R. et P.	moral bobo	moral
9.	*Cordia alliodora* (R. et P.) Oken	laurel	arana caspi
10.	*Didymopanax morototoni* (Aubl.) Decne. et Planch.	fósforo	puma maqui
11.	*Guarea kunthiana* A. Juss.	tocota	tucuta
12.	*Hieronyma chocoensis* Cuatrec.	mascarey	huapa
13.	*Huertea glandulosa* Ruiz et Pav.	bajaya	bajuya
14.	*Jacaranda copaia* D. Don	jacaranda	copa
15.	*Myroxylon balsamum* Drude	bálsamo	balsamu
16.	*Otoba parvifolia* (Mgf.) A. Gentry	sangre de gallina	huapa
17.	*Parkia multijuga* Benth.	cutanga	cutanga
18.	*Platymiscium stipulare* Benth.	coaba veteada	—
19.	*Pollalesta karstenii* (Sch. Bip.) Aristeg.	pigue	pigui
20.	*Schizolobium parahybum* Blake	pachaco	masachi
21.	*Swietenia macrophylla* King	ahuano	ahuano
22.	*Tabebuia chrysantha* Nichols	guayacan	guayanchi
23.	*Virola* spp.	huapa	huapa
24.	*Vitex cymosa* Bert. ex Spreng.	guayacan	pucuna caspi
25.	*Vochysia braceliniae* Standl.	tamboro	tamburu
26.	*Zanthoxylum* spp.	tachuelo	casha caspi

TABLE 11.5. Species Used as Living Fence Posts by Small Holders in the Lowland Tropics of Ecuador.

		COMMON NAMES	
	SCIENTIFIC NAME	Spanish	Quichua
1.	*Citharexylum* sp.[a]	nacadero	pilche caspi
2.	*Erythrina ulei* Harms[a]	porotillo	chucu
3.	*Euphorbia cotinifolia* L.	lechero	puca panga
4.	*Jatropha curcas* L.	piñon	—
5.	*Lonchocarpus* sp.[a]	barbasco	ambi
6.	*Lonchocarpus sepium* DC.	mata ratón	—
7.	*Spondias* sp.[a]	hobos	—
8.	*Spondias lutea* L.	ciruelo	ciruelo muyu

[a]Species recommended by farmers participating in the Caco Agroforestry Project.

Research

In the Coca Agroforestry Project, all research is conducted in collaboration with INIAP. Three lines of basic and applied research are currently being pursued.

1. Two forest reserves have been established at the INIAP stations for determining species composition and forest structure. These studies are carried out in collaboration with the "Flora del Ecuador" project of the Missouri Botanical Garden and the New York Botanical Garden.

2. Research is being conducted to optimize management of robusta coffee in association with a ground cover of *Desmodium*, which should reduce weeding costs and fertilizer requirements.

3. Studies are underway to investigate the viability of introducing tropical hair sheep as an alternative production system for smallholders.

Project Phases

The Coca Agroforestry Project has been carried out in three distinct phases. The first phase (1984–1986) consisted of designing and initiating the various activities of the project summarized above.

During its second phase (1986–1987), the project underwent intensive evaluation. Much of this evaluation was carried out by the participating farmers, who provided crucial feedback on germplasm performance and the efficacy of management practices. Farmers have been helpful in calling attention to additional tree species with promising silvicultural characteristics, and many take an active role in extension through recommendations to others. Another source of feedback has been visitors: By late 1987, the project had a total of 176 visitors from 49 institutions and 14 countries. As a result of these visits, a cooperative baseline study of smallholder production systems in the Napo Province was conceived and carried out in 1986, with the collabotation of six institutions (Estrada, Sere, and Luzuriaga 1987).

Based on the experience to date and feedback from farmers and visitors, the project is developing new initiatives to be carried out during its third two-year phase (1988–1989). These initiatives include:

1. An economic study of inputs and outputs in 20 farms, as a means of evaluating the contribution of agroforestry systems in the farm system economy.

2. Expansion of promotional activities to regional schools, using didactic materials such as an introductory slide show, posters, bulletins, and schoolyard demonstrations of improved germplasm.

3. Expansion of the project's training program to other national programs in ecologically similar regions.

Technical Insights

One of the major conclusions of the baseline study of smallholder production systems in the Napo Province (Estrada, Sere, and Luzuriaga 1987) is that labor constitutes a major constraint. For small-scale producers, adoption of labor-intensive practices requires hiring additional laborers or sacrificing some other activity. In extension projects, recommendations for improved technology must take into account the constraint of labor.

Various lessons have been learned since the Coca Agroforestry Project was initiated in 1984. Some of the key technical insights are described in the following sections.

Establishing a Legume Cover Crop

Desmodium ovalifolium has been found to be the preferred legume cover crop, both in regional cropping systems and in pastures. However, this species establishes slowly, requiring several weeks to form a ground cover. Broadcast seeding on sites with weed competition has been found to be ineffective, and planting of vegetative material at close spacing is extremely time consuming.

An alternative approach that is effective and requires minimal labor is to introduce *Desmodium* and trees simultaneously. Seeds of *Desmodium* can simply be sprinkled on the bare ground around the introduced tree species. One hundred small patches of *Desmodium* per hectare can thus be established successfully with a minimum of labor. The stoloniferous growth habit of this species permits gradual consolidation of the patches, and in pastures, cattle also contribute by consuming seeds and distributing them, scarified and fertilized.

Establishing Trees in Pastures

Experience both in Ecuador and in other areas of the Amazon Basin (see Nepstad, Uhl, and Serrão, this volume) has shown that establishing trees in pastures can be extraordinarily difficult. However, over 100 field trials in the Coca Agroforestry Project have indicated a successful technique.

Survival is greatly enhanced when trees are planted next to natural barriers such as stumps and fallen tree trunks. In the absence of natural barriers, the next best alternative is to make them. During the rainy season, vegetative material of "lechero" (*Euphorbia cotinifolia*) should be introduced around the planted tree; this species forms a protective barrier of leaves that are offensive to cattle. In addition, *Desmodium* can be established around the base of each tree as described previously.

Living Fence Posts

To implement rotational grazing, pastures must be subdivided into various units; one of the major constraints to pasture management is maintaining these subdivisions. The costs and labor of acquiring, transporting, and replacing fence posts are often prohibitively high for small producers.

At the outset of the Coca Agroforestry Project, three living fence post species were identified for testing. In subsequent years, five additional species recommended by participating farmers have been added to the list of species available for living fences (table 11.5).

Restoration of Degraded Pastures

Degradation of pastures can be caused by a number of factors, such as decreasing soil fertility, increasing weed competition, spittlebug infestation, overgrazing, and soil compaction (Serrão and Toledo, this volume). Restoration of degraded pastures is labor-intensive and often unsuccessful. In the eastern lowlands of Ecuador, *Brachiaria humidicola* and *Desmodium ovalifolium* are generally introduced in degraded pastures. Two or three initial weedings are usually required before the grass is sufficiently well established to support grazing, and the legume frequently requires a longer period for establishment.

To reduce the labor costs of pasture restoration, two methods have been developed by farmers participating in the Coca Agroforestry Project. The first method involves application of herbicides, a practice adopted by farmers for controlling weeds in coffee plantations. Two or three days after application of contact and postemergent herbicides, *Brachiaria humidicola* is planted vegetatively. This method assures time for grass establishment, seed set, and initiation of grazing before additional weeding is required.

The second method is to abandon the pasture for a few years, after which the undergrowth is slashed and grass planted under the overstory of secondary forest species. Within several days the overstory is also cut, leaving only valued species such as *Cordia alliodora* and *Jacaranda copaia*.

Advice for Future Extension Projects

The experience gained in designing and implementing the Coca Agroforestry Project provides insights that may be of use in future extension projects.

1. Form a multidisciplinary team for project design and implementation, and use the farming systems approach. These practices help to keep the project objectives from being dominated by a single field of specialization.

2. Build on former project experience and local expertise. For example, prior to establishing the Coca Agrforestry Project, staff members of INIAP had already worked on collection and evaluation of germplasm.

3. Recruit local resident personnel, who tend to be more stable than those brought in from other regions and can more easily establish rapport with farmers.

4. Develop an individual work plan for each farm, and recommend technology that responds to the needs and insights of each farmer. Extension is a highly site-specific process.

5. Build into the project constant self-evaluation. Project personnel should carry out frequent evaluations of on-farm demonstrations so that they can obtain direct feedback from the farmer concerning the pros and cons of recommended practices.

6. Build into the project design linkages with national and international research centers for additional technical support.

7. Design and implement the project within national institutions that can maintain continuity.

ACKNOWLEDGMENTS

I wish to give credit to Dr. John P. Bishop for his insight and 15 years of collaborative work on farming systems research in Ecuador. I also acknowledge the personnel of the Ecuadorian Ministry of Agriculture and particularly the Forestry Directorate for their continuous support during the development of this project. Finally, I am grateful to USAID for its financial support of the project and its contribution to institutional strengthening.

REFERENCES

Baslev, H., J. Luteyn, B. Ollgaard, and L. B. Holm-Nielsen. 1987. Composition and structure of adjacent unflooded and floodplain forest in Amazonian Ecuador. *Opera Botánica* 92:37–57.

Canadas, C. L. 1983. *El Mapa Bioclimático e Económico del Ecuador.* Quito, Ecuador: MAG-PRONARED.

Costales, J., H. D. Caballero, M. Hurtado, and R. Gonzalez 1987. La Amazonia Equatoriana: Investigación en pasturas y diagnóstico socioeconômico. In *La Investigación en Pastos dentro del Contexto Científico e Socioeconômico de los Paises*, pp. 217–246. David, Panama: Red Internacional de Evaluación de Pastos Tropicales.

Denevan, W. M., H. M. Treacy, J. B. Alcorn, C. Padoch, J. Denslow, and S. Flores Paitan. 1984. Indigenous agroforestry in the Peruvian Amazon: Bora Indian management of swidden fallows. *Interciencia* 9:346–357.

Estrada, R. D., C. Sere, and H. Luzuriaga. 1987. *Caracterización de Sistemas de Producción en la Selva Baja de la Provincia del Napo (Ecuador).* Cali, Colombia: Centro Internacional de Agricultura Tropical (CIAT).

González, A. and J. S. Ortíz de Villalba. 1977. *Biografía de una Colonización: Kms. 7–80 Lago Agrio a Coca.* Quito, Ecuador: CICAME.

Grubb, P. J., J. R. Lloyd, T. D. Pennington, and T. C. Whitmore. 1963. A comparison of montane and lowland rain forest in Ecuador. I. The forest structure, physiognomy, and floristics. *Journal of Ecology* 61:567–601.

Hecht, S. B. 1982. Agroforestry in the Amazon Basin: Practice, theory, and limits of a promising land use. In S. B. Hecht, ed., *Amazonia: Agriculture and Land Use Research*, pp. 331–371. Cali, Colombia: Centro Internacional de Agricultura Tropical (CIAT).

Hiraoka, M. and S. Yamamoto. 1980. Agricultural development in the Upper Amazon of Ecuador. *Geographic Review* 70:423–445.

Hudelson, J. E. 1987. *La Cultura Quichua de Transición: Su Expansión e Desarollo en el Alto Amazonas.* Quito, Ecuador: Museu Antropológico del Banco Central e Ediciones ABYA-YALA.

Irvine, D. 1987. Resource management by the Runa Indians of the Ecuadorian Amazon. Ph.D. Thesis. Stanford: Stanford University.

Nair, P. K. R. 1985. Classification of agroforestry systems. *Agroforestry Systems* 3:97–128.

Padoch, C., J. Chota Inuma, W. De Jong, and J. Unruh. 1985. Amazonian agroforestry: A market-oriented system in Peru. *Agroforestry Systems* 3:47–58.

Peck, R. B. 1983. Traditional forestation strategies of local farmers in the tropics. In K. F. Wiersum, ed., *Strategies and Designs for Afforestation, Reforestation, and Tree Planting*, pp. 205–216. Wageningen: Pudoc.

Posey, D. A. 1983. Indigenous ecological knowledge and development of the Amazon. In E. F. Moran, ed., *The Dilemma of Amazonian Development*, pp. 225–258. Boulder, CO: Westview Press.

Uquillas, G. 1984. Colonization and spontaneous settlement in the Ecuadorian Amazon. In M. Schmink and C. H. Wood, eds., *Frontier Expansion in Amazonia*, pp. 261–284. Gainesville: University of Florida Press.

4
LANDSCAPE RECOVERY

4. Landscape Recovery.—The so-called *paricá* tree (*Schizolobium amazonicum* Hub. ex Ducke) is a fast-growing timber species that flourishes on deforested sites. This species holds promise for reforestation of degraded landscapes in Amazonia.

12

Secondary Forests as a Land-Use Resource in Frontier Zones of Amazonia

■

JEAN C. L. DUBOIS

ABSTRACT

Secondary forests are an increasingly common phenomenon in recently set-tled areas of Amazonia. Although these forests are frequently perceived as indicators of land abandonment following shifting cultivation or pasture degradation, they are in fact used and managed within a wide variety of rural communities. This chapter characterizes various types of secondary forest use and management in the South American humid tropics. Examples show how these communities introduce or promote useful perennial species within secondary forests, which become increasingly manipulated as traditional systems of swidden agriculture become progressively sedentary. Other examples illustrate the utilization of secondary forests that naturally possess high concentrations of economic species; such forests can be readily managed and incorporated into agroforestry systems. This chapter illustrates the significant role of South American inhabitants in the process of landscape recovery and suggests that intensified use of secondary forests in already settled areas can reduce land-use pressures on the frontier.

Most small-scale farmers in the humid tropics practice a form of cultivation characterized by a relatively short period of agricultural production followed by a prolonged fallow period. Under this system, a plot of high forest (either primary or secondary) is cut and burned, and the farmer utilizes the soil enriched by the large quantity of fire-generated ash to establish annual or short-cycle crops. After two or three years, loss of soil fertility and infestation by weeds and pests often leads to abandonment of the site, which is subsequently covered by a young secondary forest composed almost exclusively of pioneer species (see Uhl et al., this volume). Forest regeneration on sites formerly cleared for short-term cultivation is generally rapid. In areas of low demographic pressure, restoration of soil fertility and reduction of weeds and pests are assured by a long fallow period (typically a minimum of twelve years). The farmer continues agricultural activities by successively cutting down other plots of primary or old secondary forest. This sequence, whether repetitive or not, is characteristic of so-called "shifting cultivation" or "swidden agriculture" (figure 12.1).

Various types of shifting cultivation exist, depending on cultural and socioeconomic factors. For example, sedentary cultures frequently develop more intensive and complex forms of swidden agriculture than do nomadic cultures. Likewise, the lengths of cultivation and fallow cycles vary according to demographic pressures, and the combinations of crops planted often depend on the availability of markets.

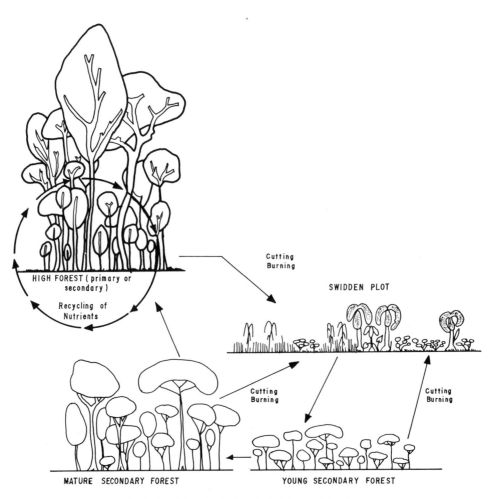

FIGURE 12.1. Model of traditional shifting cultivation sequence.

When comparing traditional systems of swidden agriculture practiced by Indian communities in the American tropics, one can observe a general land-use trend: as communities become progressively sedentary, manipulation or management of forest fallows becomes increasingly evident (Treacy 1982; Posey 1986; Raintree and Warner 1986; Dubois 1987).

In a parallel vein, there also exist secondary forests in the humid American tropics that contain high concentrations of economic species, and these forests are frequently utilized by native populations. The form of utilization varies from mere gathering of forest products to intensive management involving the incorporation of the forest into agroforestry systems.

The first trend begins with agriculture, which is progressively extended into the fallow period. In contrast, the second trend begins with the forest, which is progressively manipulated by agricultural practices. Both trends culminate with the development of agroforestry systems that present a wide variety of forms and opportunities for rural inhabitants.

In an attempt to illustrate this variety, I shall summarize a number of documented cases involving use and management of secondary forests in various locations of the American tropics, with special emphasis on Amazonia.

Agriculture and Management of Secondary Forests

Subsistence Systems

Indian communities exhibiting a wide degree of cultural evolution inhabit the middle reaches of the Putumayo River in Peru and the Caquetá River in Colombia. The most nomadic of these groups are the Matse, which settle at a given site for extremely short periods (under four years). The forest fallows that arise after shifting cultivation are invariably spontaneous, with little or no evidence of manipulation. Cultivation of fruit trees among the Matse is limited to species that produce in the first or second year, such as papaya (*Carica papaya* L.) and precocious varieties of peach palm (*Bactris gasipaes* H. B. K.); these varieties are unknown among more sedentary tribes of the region (Gasche 1980).

The Secoya, a tribe from the same region, change village sites less frequently than do the Matse. In their swidden plots, the Secoya plant peach palm (*Bactris gasipaes*), "ingá" (*Inga* spp.), and other fruit trees that produce after three years. These trees continue producing in the fallow, and the Indians return periodically to hunt and gather fruits from their forest plantations (Casanova 1975, 1980; Gasche 1975; Hödl and Gasche 1981). This clearly represents a case of fallow management.

Among various tribes, trees planted in regenerating forest fallow give usufruct rights, which permit long-term exploitation of plantations in forests that are frequently considered by outsiders to be abandoned. The Witoto and Bora Indians of Amazonia, which are more sedentary than the groups previously described, plant in their swidden plots fruit trees that require several years to produce, such as "umarí" (*Poraqueiba* sp.) and avocado (*Persea americana* Mill.) (Gasche 1980;

numerous other Indian and campesino groups throughout the humid tropics carry out similar practices. In general, the small swidden plots are separated by extensive areas of forest, which serves to decrease the dissemination of pests and diseases between plots, and also to increase the rate of forest regeneration after the more intensive cultivation of short-term crops ceases.

Subsistence and Market Systems

Treacy (1982) described a sequential agroforestry system utilized by the Bora Indians in the Peruvian Amazon. Some swidden plots may be occupied almost entirely by short-cycle crops with only scattered representation of relatively short-lived fruit trees (*Musa* spp., *Carica papaya*, *Bixa orellana* L., etc.). Other plots are enriched with longer-lived fruit trees (*Bactris gasipaes*, *Pourouma cecropiaefolia* Mart., *Poraqueiba* sp., *Inga* spp., *Chrysophyllum cainito* L., etc.), which are allowed to grow mixed with pioneer forest species after the last harvest of short-cycle crops has been gathered. From time to time, the Bora carry out selective weeding on fallowed sites, which favors the regeneration or growth of valuable timber species such as mahogany (*Swietenia macrophylla* King) and the Spanish cedar or "cedro vermelho" (*Cedrela odorata* L.). The Bora frequently visit these enriched fallows to obtain forest products for local consumption (e.g., fruits and game) as well as market goods (e.g., excess fruit production and timber). In sum, the Bora manage and utilize forest fallows for both subsistence and market products.

The mestizo community of Tanshiyacu, also located in the Peruvian Amazon, practices a form of agroforestry designed exclusively for production of market items that are sold in the city of Iquitos 35 km away. Under this system, forest fallows are managed and utilized over long periods (25–50 years). Long-lived fruit trees are planted together with short-cycle crops and are maintained during the fallow period, generating secondary forests comprised almost exclusively of economic species, most of which have multiple uses (Padoch et al. 1985). The most economically important species that are utilized in this system include "umari" (*Poraqueiba sericea* Tul.), Brazil nut (*Bertholletia excelsa* H.B.), "caimito" (*Chrysophyllum cainito*), cashew (*Anacardium occidentale* L.), peach palm (*Bactris gasipaes*), and "açaí" (*Euterpe precatoria* Mart.). Products harvested (fruits and palm hearts) and hunted (meat and skins) are sold in Iquitos, in addition to charcoal obtained from burning sites cleared for agriculture.

Management of Secondary Forests Dominated by Economic Species

Babaçu

In widespread areas of the humid tropics, secondary forests that naturally regenerate on previously cleared sites often contain surprisingly high concentrations of economically important tree species. In some cases, these forests represent virtually pure stands of a single species, which can have a strategic role in local economies. One of the most dramatic examples of such dominance involves the so-called "babaçu" palm (*Orbignya phalerata* Mart.). This species and others of the same genus range from Brazil to Mexico. In Brazil, natural stands of babaçu cover a total area of approximately 200,000 km², half of which lies in the state of Maranhão, on well-drained, upland soils of moderate fertility and excellent structure. Such sites are prime targets for shifting cultivation. The felling of primary forests for agriculture has resulted in the formation of the extensive stands of babaçu that blanket the landscape today (Anderson and Anderson 1983; Anderson and May 1985).

Babaçu is utilized in two traditional agroforestry systems that are widely practiced and exert important socioeconomic roles in the region (May et al. 1985a). The first—a silvopastoral system—occurs in planted pastures that typically contain densities of 50 to 120 adult palms per hectare. In this system babaçu provides shade for the cattle and organic material for the soil. The second—an agrosilvicultural system—occurs in areas subjected to swidden agriculture. At moderate densities (approximately 50 adult palms per hectare), babaçu apparently does not reduce the productivity of short-cycle crops. The palm provides numerous subsistence products for shifting cultivators during the fallow period, and its biomass represents an important source of fuel and nutrients when the forest is subsequently cleared again for agriculture.

The fruits of babaçu have multiple roles in both market and subsistence economies (May et al. 1985b). The fruit kernels are utilized by local industries for production of vegetable oil, soap, and margarine. The vegetable oil industry based on babaçu kernels is currently the largest in the world entirely based on a wild species. After oil extraction, industries use the pressed kernels to make feedcake for domesticated animals (principally milk cows) and as a nitrogen- and phosphorous-rich fertilizer. Industries and rural households alike also utilize the fruit residues that remain after kernel extraction to make charcoal; these residues represent the most important domestic source of cooking fuel in regions where babaçu forests abound.

Spanish Cedar

On sand bars and river terraces along the Atrato River in the Chocó region of Colombia's Pacific coast, extensive secondary forests are dominated by naturally regenerating populations of Spanish cedar (*Cedrela odorata*), which form relatively open stands associated with an understory composed of high grasses. As is the case throughout its natural range, the Spanish cedar in this region is attacked by the shoot borer, *Hypsipyla grandella*. But possibly due to its rapid growth on the relatively fertile soils characteristic of these sites, the trees appear to overcome the attacks and develop well-formed trunks. In newly regenerating stands of cedar, small-scale farmers have established an agrosilvicultural system in which plantations of rice, maize, sugarcane, and banana are established; the natural regeneration and growth of cedar within these plantation are actually enhanced through periodic weedings of less desirable competitors. This land use is managed for commercial purposes and covers approximately 3000 ha of alluvial soils in the middle reaches of the Atrato River (Leguizamo 1983). The system is similar to agrosilvicultural systems utilized in West Africa for production of bananas for export (Dubois 1979).

Floodplain Forests

In the estuary of the Amazon River, a land area of approximately 25,000 km^2 is subjected to periodic flooding and deposition of alluvial soils (Calzavara 1972). These soils are generally covered by floodplain forests that are readily acessible, contain a high concentration of economic species (Anderson, this volume), and have historically served as the region's principal source of forest products. In recent decades, forest exploitation in the Amazon estuary has concentrated on extraction of timber (especially from *Virola surinamensis* (Rol.) Warb., *Carapa guianensis* Aubl., *Hura crepitans* L., *Cedrela odorata*, etc.) and palm heart (furnished by the "açaí" palm, *Euterpe oleracea* Mart.). Because of this intensive exploitation—not only in recent decades but during millennia of continuous human occupation—the floodplain forests of the Amazon estuary have been profoundly altered and are almost exclusively secondary in nature.

The riverine populations in the estuary carry out various management practices in the floodplain forests. In areas where there are high concentrations of the açaí palm and accessible markets for sale of its fruits—which are used to produce a beverage that serves as a staple in the regional diet—the river dwellers manage the floodplain forests to favor this species. Management practices include the selective thinning of forest competitors and pruning of açaí clumps for palm heart extraction; these practices cause a significant increase in the production of fruits per stem (Anderson and Jardim 1989). In areas more distant from markets, similar management practices are utilized to favor semi-wild populations of cacao (*Theobroma cacao* L.).

In addition to açaí and cacao, the river dwellers utilize the floodplain forests as a source of game, timber, edible fruits, medicinals, latex, fibers, oilseeds, firewood, fertilizer, ornamental plants, honey, etc. (Anderson et al. 1985). This dependence on the forest for a wide variety of market and subsistence products often makes agriculture a less attractive activity in the estuary, despite the relatively high fertility of its soils.

A similar situation occurs in the Chocó region of Colombia, where the native floodplain forests are extremely rich in timber species. Land-use activities such as timber extraction and swidden agriculture for rice cultivation favor the regeneration of the "naidí" palm (*Euterpe cuatrecasana* Dugand), which forms high-density stands that are also utilized for palm-heart extraction and harvesting of fruits for production of a locally consumed beverage (Dubois 1987).

Discussion

A number of previously described case studies present forms of shifting cultivation that differs from the conventional view, in which agricultural activities are believed to be confined to a short period following forest clearing. In fact, many indigenous and campesino communities enrich their agricultural plots and forest fallows with perennial species of known utility (Treacy 1982; Dove 1983; Posey 1986). Through remarkably simple management practices, successional vegetation becomes a site for economic production as well as for landscape rehabilitation. The dynamic process by which agricultural plots are transformed into enriched fallows is illustrated in figure 12.2.

Other case studies described above show how various types of secondary forests, which arise spontaneously after removal of the original vegetation, contain high concentrations of economic species. These forests are frequently utilized by local populations for a wide variety of economic products and provide additional life-supporting functions (Hecht, Anderson, and May 1988). Due to their relative lack of complexity, such forests can be managed by simple modifications in structure and composition.

Among those species currently utilized in management of secondary forests in the humid tropics of the Americas, the following are especially noteworthy: 1) perennial fruit trees, such as *Bactris gasipaes, Orbignya phalerata, Euterpe* spp., *Astrocaryum* spp., *Bertholletia excelsa, Caryocar* spp., *Platonia insignis* Mart., *Pourouma cecropiaefolia* Mart., *Theobroma* spp., etc.; 2) semiperennial food plants that reproduce vegetatively, such as *Xanthoma* spp., *Dioscorea* spp., *Maranta arundinacea* Billb. ex Beurl., *Musa* spp., etc.; 3) an extraordinary variety of medicinal plants; 4) various fiber-producing plants; 5) hallucinogens and/or stimulants, such as *Banisteria caapi* Spruce ex Griseb., *Datura* spp., etc.; and 6) natural dyes, such as *Genipa americana* L.

Agricultural plots and young successional fallows are also prime sites for attracting game (Gross 1975; Beckerman 1979). Numerous species of animals are more abundant in secondary than in primary forests, and this is especially the case in secondary forests that are enriched with fruit trees (Posey 1986).

According to observations in a wide variety of traditional indigenous and campesino communities, as agriculture becomes progressively sedentary, forest fallows are increasingly utilized and manipulated. In contrast, in recently settled communities successional vegetation is rarely utilized or managed to promote economic return and/or site restoration. Such neglect appears to be associated with expansion of cattle pastures, increased land concentration, and a general breakdown of shifting cultivation (Hecht, Anderson, and May 1988).

There are, however, exceptions to this rule. For example, in the Brazilian state of Rondônia, fallows are frequently dominated by *Schizolobium amazonicum* Hub. ex Ducke ("paricá grande," "bandara"), a giant leguminous tree of exceptionally fast growth and high commercial value as a source of timber. These characteristics attracted the attention of a number of settlers, who have adopted the following production sequence: 1) establishment of an agricultural plot with short-cycle crops; 2) "abandonment" of the plot to fallow, which is maintained during 4–7 years; 3) selective cutting of the fallow, maintaining naturally regenerating trees of *S. amazonicum*; 4) controlled burn; and 5) establishment of understory plantations of cacau or coffee. Other tree species could be promoted or introduced in this sequence, including sources of food (e.g., *Bactris gasipaes*), timber (e.g., *Cordia alliodora* (R. et P.) Oken and *C. goeldiana* Hub.), or soil nitrogen (*Inga*

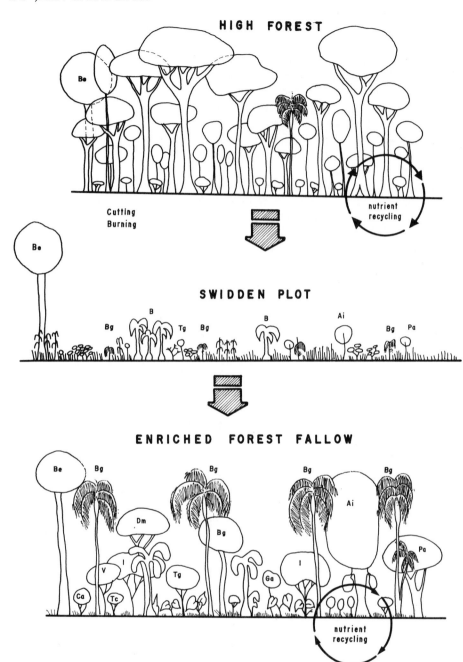

FIGURE 12.2. Sequence that leads to the formation of an enriched secondary forest. Be = *Bertholletia excelsa* Humb. et Bonpl.; Dm = *Didymopanax morototoni* (Aubl.) Decne. et Planch.; Ai = *Artocarpus integrifolia* L. f.; Pa = *Persea americana* Will.; Bg = *Bactris gasipaes* H. B. K.; V = *Vismia* sp.; Tg = *Theobroma grandiflorum* (Willd. ex Sprung.) Schum.; Ga = *Genipa americana* L.; I = *Inga* sp.; Ca = *Coffea arabica* L.; Tc = *Theobroma cacao* L.; and B = *Musa* sp.

spp.). In accordance with their light tolerance, these species could be introduced (or promoted) in the agricultural plot or during the subsequent fallow.

Figure 12.3 compares the conventional sequence of swidden agriculture practiced in recently settled areas with a sequence involving the introduction of *Cordia alliodora* ("freijó comum"), which is planted in the agricultural plot and develops into a emergent stand with a plantation of coffee in the understory. Should production decline, the coffee can be substituted by planted pasture for beef production.

Implications for Regional Development

A special effort should be made to implement the management of secondary forests in zones of rapid frontier expansion, such as occur over increasingly widespread areas of the Amazon Basin. Most of the settlers in these zones come from outside of Amazonia and, for this reason, are unfamiliar with the forms of land use that are most appropriate for the region (Brienza, Kitamura, and Dubois 1983). Putting the use and management of secondary forests into practice in these zones will require the following steps: 1) detailed studies of the techniques of secondary forest utilization and management already practiced in the region; 2) development of specific models for using and managing secondary forests, in consultation with small-scale producers; 3) establishment and management of demonstration plots with the active participation of rural communities; and 4) technical assistance focusing on the use and management of secondary forests.

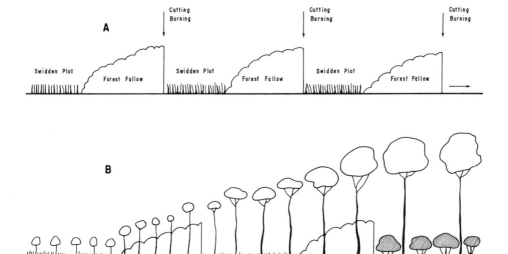

FIGURE 12.3. A: Traditional shifting cultivation sequence. B: Shifting cultivation sequence leading to a fallow enriched with *Cordia alliodora* (unshaded crowns) and, subsequently, a perennial crop plantation (shaded crowns).

In addition to these efforts, others should be carried out to assure a more intensive use of the land. One of the most promising techniques is the cultivation of short-cycle crops in corridors, known as "alley cropping" or "hedgerow intercropping" (Ssekabembe 1985; Burger and Carvalho 1986; Yamoah, Agboola, and Mulongoy 1986; Zimmerman 1986). In this system, the short-cycle crops are cultivated in relatively narrow corridors (2–4 m, or rarely up to 6 m in width), which are separated by densely planted strips of perennial species subjected to periodic pruning to reduce shade (e.g., *Leucaena leucocephala* (Lam.) de Wit, *Inga* spp., *Gliricida sepium* H.B.K., *Flemingia* spp., etc.). These species are excellent producers of organic material, and many are capable of fixing atmospheric nitrogen. Periodic pruning and litter production in these plantations permit the maintenance of high levels of organic material in the soil. Under this system, cultivation of short-cycle crops can continue for a longer period than under typical systems of swidden agriculture: 6 years is considered to be a reasonable maximum. When cultivation of short-cycle crops ceases, the perennial species are maintained and become incorporated into the natural fallow, growing together with native pioneer species. This incorporation of "regenerative" species contributes toward a more rapid recovery of soil nutrients during the fallow period.

Other innovative techniques that could contribute to the management of secondary forests include: 1) utilization of organic fertilizers generated outside of agricultural plots, such as animal dung; 2) diversification of perennial crops; and 3) integration of production on the farm level, through recycling of crop residues and increased utilization of animals in cropping systems.

In attempting to improve conditions for small-scale producers in zones of frontier expansion in Amazonia, mechanisms for generating income need to be based on production systems that are low in cost. In this sense, using and managing secondary forests can provide economic opportunities that are both ecologically rational and within the reach of most rural inhabitants.

REFERENCES

Anderson, A. B. and E. S. Anderson. 1983. People and the palm forest: Biology and utilization of babassu forests in Maranhão, Brazil. Final Report to USDA Forest Service, Consortium for the Study of Man's Relationship with the Global Environment, Washington, DC.

Anderson, A. B. and P. H. May. 1985. A palmeira de muitas vidas. *Ciência Hoje* 4(20):58–64.

Anderson, A. B., A. Gély, J. Strudwick, G. L. Sobel, and M. G. C. Pinto. 1985. Um sistema agroflorestal na várzea do estuário amazônico (Ilha das Onças, Município de Barcarena, Pará). *Acta Amazonica* (Suplemento) 15(1–2):195–224.

Anderson, A. B. and M. A. G. Jardim. 1989. Costs and benefits of floodplain forest management by rural inhabitants in the Amazon estuary: A case study of açaí palm production. In J. Browder, ed., *Fragile Lands of Latin America: Strategies for Sustainable Development.* Boulder, CO: Westview.

Beckerman, S. 1979. The abundance of protein in Amazonia: A reply to Gross. *American Anthropologist* 81:533–560.

Brienza, Jr., S., P. C. Kitamura, and J. C. L. Dubois. 1983. *Consideracões Biológicas e Econômicas sobre um Sistema de Produção Silvo-Agrícola Rotativo na Região do*

Tapajós. Boletim de Pesquisa No. 50. Belém: Centro de Pesquisa Agropecuária do Trópico Umido (EMBRAPA-CPATU).

Burger, D. and B. E. Carvalho. 1986. A produção de adubos orgânicos no sistema "cultivo em faixas". *EMBRAPA/CPATU Documentos* No. 40:223–243.

Calzavara, B. B. G. 1972. *As Possibilidades do Açaizeiro no Estuário Amazônico*. Faculdade de Ciências Agrárias do Pará, Belém, Boletim No. 5.

Casanova, J. 1975. El Sistema de cultivo Secoya. In *Cultures sur Brûlis et Evolution du Milieu Forestier en Amazonie du Nord-Quest*, pp. 129–141. Geneva: Société Suisse d'Ethnologie.

Casanova, J. 1980. Estudios sobre el cultivo de corte y queima en la Amazonia Peruana. In *Consulta Subregional sobre las Actividades de Corte y Quema en el Ecosistema Bosque Tropical*, pp. 21–36. Lima: Comité Nacional del Programa MAB (UNESCO).

Dove, M. R. 1983. Theories of swidden agriculture and the political economy of ignorance. *Agroforestry Systems* 1(2):85–99.

Dubois, J. C. L. 1979. Informaciones sobre sistemas agroforestales en uso en el Mayombe y Bajo Congo (Zaire). In *Taller Sistemas Agroforestales*, pp. 87–94. Turrialba, Costa Rica: CATIE.

Dubois, J. C. L. 1987. Impacto de los sistemas agroforestales en el desarrolo integral de las comunidades rurales del trópico americano. In *Reunión Nacional de Silvicultura Tropical: Impacto de la Investigación Silvicultural en el Desarrollo Económico Forestal Colombiano*. Bogotá: CONIF (mimeo).

Gasche, J. 1975. Le système cultural Witoto. In *Cultures sur Brûlis et Evolution du Milieu Forestier en Amazonie du Nord-Quest*, pp. 111–128. Geneva: Société Suisse d'Ethnologie.

Gasche, J. 1980. El estudio comparativo de los sistemas de cultivo nativos y su impacto sobre el bosque amazónico. In *Consulta Subregional sobre las Actividades de Corte y Quema en el Ecosistema Bosque Tropical*, pp. 61–74. Lima: Comite Nacional del Programa MAB (UNESCO).

Gross, D. R. 1975. Protein capture and cultural development in the Amazon Basin. *American Anthropologist* 77:526–540.

Hecht, S., A. B. Anderson, and P. H. May. 1988. The subsidy from nature: Shifting cultivation, successional palm forests, and rural development. *Human Organization* 47(1):25–35.

Hödl, W. and J. Gasche. 1981. Die Secoya Indianen und deren Landbaumethoden (Rio Yubineto, Peru). *Sitzungberichte der Gesellschaft Naturforschender Freunde zu Berlin* 20(21):73–96.

Leguizamo, B. A. 1983. Associaciones agroforestales con base en cedro en el Medio Atrato (Choco, Colombia). Bogota: CONIF (mimeo).

May, P. H., A. B. Anderson, J. M. F. Frazão, and M. J. Balick. 1985a. Babassu palm in agroforestry systems in Brazil's Mid-North region. *Agroforestry Systems* 3(3):275–295.

May, P. H., A. B. Anderson, M. J. Balick, and J. M. F. Frazão. 1985b. Subsistence benefits from the babassu palm (*Orbignya martiana*). *Economic Botany* 39(2):113–129.

Padoch, C., J. Chota Inuma, W. de Jong, and J. Unruh. 1985. Amazonian agroforestry: A market system in Peru. *Agroforestry Systems* 3(1):47–58.

Posey, D. A. 1986. Manejo da floresta secundária, campos e cerrados (Kayapó). In B. G. Ribeiro, ed., *Etnobiologia: Suma Ethnógica Brasileira*, vol. 1, pp. 173–188. Rio de Janeiro: Editora Vozes.

Raintree, J. B. and K. Warner. 1986. Agroforestry pathways for the intensification of shifting cultivation. *Agroforestry Systems* 4(1):39–54.

Ssekabembe, C. K. 1985. Perspectives on hedgegrow intercropping. *Agroforestry Systems* 3(4):339–356.

Treacy, J. 1982. Bora indian agroforestry: An alternative to deforestation. *Cultural Survival* 6(2):15–16.

Yamoah, C. F., A. A. Agboola, and K. Mulongoy. 1986. Decomposition, nitrogen release and weed control by prunings of selected alley-cropping shrubs. *Agroforestry Systems* 4(3):239–254.

Zimmermann, T. 1986. Agroforestry: A last hope for conservation in Haiti? *Agroforestry Systems* 4(3):255–268.

13

The Search for Sustainability in Amazonian Pastures

■

EMANUEL ADILSON SERRÃO
JOSE M. TOLEDO

ABSTRACT

In the past three decades, cattle ranching has become a major source of deforestation in the Amazon Basin, largely as a consequence of government incentives that have proved to be both ecologically and socioeconomically dubious. It is currently estimated that at least ten million hectares of forest have been converted to highly unstable pastures, of which about 50 percent are now in advanced stages of degradation. In this essay, we emphasize the need to reduce the rate of forest clearing for cattle ranching by increasing the longevity of still-productive pastures and by reclaiming those pastures that have been severely degraded. This paper 1) examines nutrient cycling in pasture ecosystems as the basis for sustainability; 2) describes the causes of biotic instability in pastures during their first and subsequent cycles; 3) outlines present and potential technologies for increasing pasture stability and for reclaiming degraded sites; 4) analyzes the potential of low-cost technology based on newly adapted germplasm of grasses and legumes for open pastures and agrosilvopastoral systems; and 5) suggests research priorities for intensifying land management and increasing pasture sustainability.

Ranching has historically served as an effective means of occupying frontier areas throughout the world. In the Amazon Basin, cattle ranching has assumed an especially prominent role in the past three decades and is currently one of the major contributors to regional deforestation. The spread of this land use has been largely fueled by socioeconomic or geopolitical pressures operating in the different countries of the region.

The area of tropical forests converted to pastures in the Amazon Basin is currently estimated at approximately ten million hectares. Of this total, approximately seven million hectares lie in Brazil (Serrão and Conto 1987), 1.2 million hectares in Colombia (Ramirez and Seré 1987), 500,000 hectares in Peru (Schaus 1987), and 1.1 million hectares in the remaining countries of the Basin (Costales et al. 1987). Amazon pastures currently support fewer than ten million head of cattle. Most cattle raising is oriented toward meat production on large holdings, especially in the Brazilian Amazon, where many ranches are highly subsidized by the government (SUDAM 1983; Serrão and Conto 1987). In contrast, in the Amazon regions of Colombia (Ramirez and Seré 1987) and Peru (Riesco et al. 1982), cattle raising is generally oriented toward both meat and milk production, which occurs on considerably smaller holdings that receive relatively few government subsidies.

The rapid spread of cattle pastures, especially as it is occurring in Brazil, has aroused considerable concern due to the generally low productivity of these systems, as well as their negative ecological and socioeconomic consequences. Conservationists frequently regard pastures as the principal cause of environmental degradation in Amazonia. At the other extreme, promoters of development view planted pastures as a rational form of land use that makes optimal use of the scarce capital and labor resources available in the region. The latter group would argue that, given sufficient resources, even small-scale producers convert areas utilized for subsistence agriculture into pastures for livestock production, which is considered a status symbol in the region.

The most reasonable position regarding Amazonian pastures lies between these two extremes. On the one hand, with the traditional land-use practices generally utilized by ranchers, pastures can indeed become an environmental threat due to their high instability, which is especially pronounced under the ecological conditions characteristic of the region—such as acidic, nutrient-poor soils and high pest pressures. Especially in the Brazilian Amazon, land speculation also contributes to instability by promoting conversion of forest to pastures merely as a means of occupying immense areas at relatively low cost. The productivity of such "speculative" pastures is generally low, as is interest in their long-term management. Largely due to the instability of this land use, pastures continue to be established in new areas of forest, with negative ecological and socioeconomic consequences.

On the other hand, however, pastures have the potential for long-term maintenance of soil fertility and livestock production. This potential can be attained through the use of currently available technology based on adapted forage germplasm, which can be used both for establishment of new pastures and rehabilitation of degraded sites. Implementation of such technology would remove one of the principal motives for continued conversion of forest to pasture in Amazonia: the chronically low productivity of pastures already established in forested areas.

After describing the process and principal causes of pasture degradation in Amazonia, this paper presents a number of technical solutions aimed at increasing the productivity of both functional and degraded pastures, thereby decreasing the pressure that this form of land use currently exerts on the Amazon forest.

Nutrient Cycling: The Basis for Stability

The stability of pasture systems ultimately depends on the quantity of nutrients at a given site and the efficiency of their recycling. These aspects are especially crucial on the acidic, nutrient-poor Oxisols and Ultisols that predominate on upland sites throughout the Amazon Basin (Cochrane and Sanchez 1982; Cochrane et al. 1985).

After the forest is felled and burned, the soil undergoes dramatic increases in potassium, calcium, magnesium, available phosphorous, and pH, as well as reduction in aluminum saturation (Falesi 1976; Serrão et al. 1979; Hecht 1982; Buschbacher 1984; Teixeira 1987). The temporarily high soil fertility is extremely propitious for pasture establishment.

According to Toledo and Serrão (1982), pastures that are composed of a mix of adapted grasses and legumes (figure 13.1) and subjected to proper management can be maintained indefinitely, even though the quantities of nutrients recycled in these systems are considerably less than those in an intact forest. Like the forest, pasture systems store nutrients in both the living and dead biomass and in the soil (Toledo and Serrão 1982; Buschbacher 1984; Spain and Salinas 1985). Rain carries atmospheric dust and nitrogen, and promotes the incorporation of nutrients in the soil. At the same time, the community of pasture plants absorbs nutrients from litter and soil, and nutrients are subsequently transferred to grazing animals. From the latter, people remove part of the nutrients in the form of meat and milk, and the rest returns to the soil in the form of feces and urine. Within the pasture, dead plants and plant parts decompose and are incorporated as organic material into the soil, thereby increasing the quantity of nutrients available for living plants. Pastures containing legumes presumably undergo fixation of atmospheric nitrogen and, as in an intact forest, denitrification. Also like the forest, loss of nutrients in pastures occurs through chemical fixation, leaching, and surface erosion; in well-managed pastures with a dense and constant coverage of the soil, the latter is probably minimal. In newly established pastures, the slow decomposition of unburned residues can persist for several years, providing a constant input of nutrients that counterbalances these losses (Buschbacher 1984).

Results of various studies (Silva 1978; Falesi, Baena, and Dutra 1980; Sanchez and Salinas 1981; Navas 1982) indicate that a good soil coverage with pasture can be considerably more efficient than many short-cycle crops in reducing erosion and maintaining the physical and chemical properties of soils, especially on topographically steep sites. Export of nutrients in such a pasture is more or less limited to production of meat and milk, which are chiefly composed of gaseous elements that exist in the air, such as carbon, hydrogen, oxygen, and nitrogen, and a small quantity of elements from the soil (Buschbacher 1984; Spain and Salinas 1985; Teixeira 1987).

Maintaining the stability of this system requires management practices such as strictly enforced herd rotation and pest control measures to minimize pasture

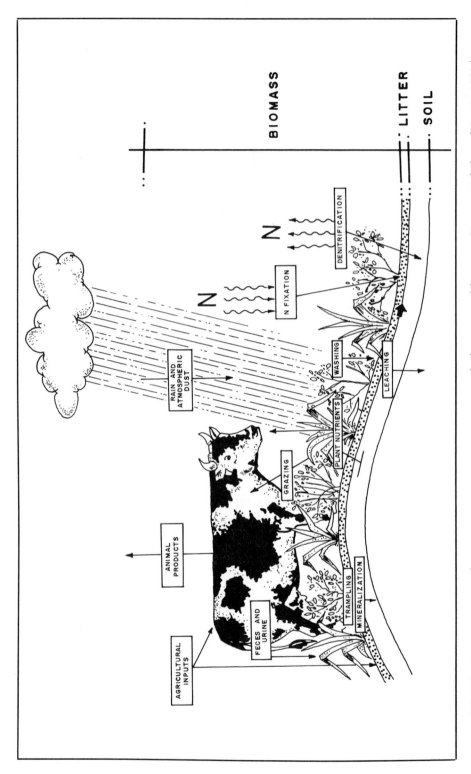

FIGURE 13.1. Nutrient cycling in a pasture ecosystem comprised of grasses and legumes. (Source: Toledo and Serrão 1982.)

degradation. In addition, although losses of nutrients through export are small in well-managed pastures, it is nonetheless necessary to make up for these losses through periodic application of soil fertilizers as well as mineral supplements for the herd (Toledo and Serrão 1982; Buschbacher 1984; Teixeira 1987).

Greater details concerning the storage and cycling of nutrients in regional pastures can be found in the recent studies of Buschbacher (1984, 1987) and Teixeira (1987), probably the only attempts to date to quantify nutrient cycling in Amazonian pastures.

Pasture Degradation: Processes and Causes

Only a small proportion of the pastures established during the past three decades in Amazonia conforms to the above description of stability. Pasture degradation has been the rule throughout the region. Of the approximately ten million hectares of pastures established during this period, at least 50 percent are in an advanced state of degradation, and the growth of the region's herds continues to exert pressure for increased expansion of pastures into formerly forested areas.

The Process

Changes in productivity over time in planted pastures in the Amazon Basin follow a general pattern described by Toledo and Ara (1977), Alvim (1978), Serrão et al. (1979), Dias Filho and Serrão (1982), Toledo and Serrão (1982), and Serrão (1988) and summarized in figure 13.2. This pattern is especially prevalent in pastures that 1) are established immediately after cutting and burning of mature forest; 2) are composed of planted grasses that have relatively high nutrient demands (e.g., *Panicum maximum* Jacq., *Hyparrhenia rufa* (C. G. Nees) Stapf., *Axonopus compressus* (Sw.) Beauv., *A. micay* H. Garcia-Barriga; and 3) do not contain planted legumes. During the first four to six years after establishment, productivity of the pasture is generally good. After this period, however, there is a gradual decline in the productivity of planted grasses, associated with an increased presence of weeds.

In figure 13.2, "A" indicates the point when the weed community begins to undermine the stability of the pasture; "B" when it is still economically viable to recuperate the pasture; "C" when the weed community has attained complete dominance and productivity of the planted pasture has declined to insignificant levels; and "D" when the weed community has attained complete dominance and the pasture is totally degraded. Table 13.1 summarizes the characteristics of these various stages of pasture productivity.

The process of degradation described above occurs in most of the pastures established in the Amazon region to date and is especially pronounced when the pasture consists of grasses that exhibit a clumped habit, low competitiveness, and high climatic and soil specificity. Pastures composed of less demanding and more aggressive grasses with a decumbent habit, such as *Brachiaria humidicola* (Rendle) Schweickt. and *B. decumbens* Stapf., tend to persist for greater periods of time in the phases of high and intermediate productivity as long as they are not dam-

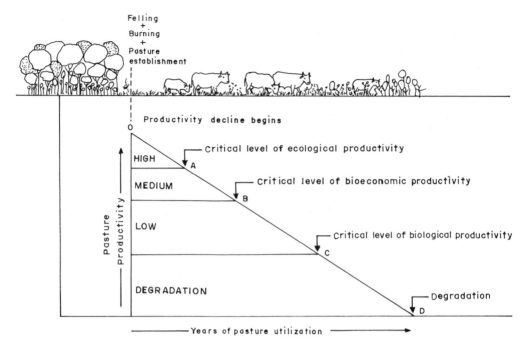

FIGURE 13.2. Changes in pasture productivity over time in first-cycle pastures managed with traditional technology in forested areas of the Amazon Basin. (Adapted from Toledo and Ara 1977; Serrão et al. 1979; Dias Filho and Serrão 1983; Toledo and Serrão 1984.)

aged by insect pests such as the pasture spittlebug. Although rare, examples do exist of pioneer pastures composed of *Panicum maximum* or other relatively demanding grasses that have maintained high or intermediate productivity for over fifteen years without addition of fertilizers.

As a pasture declines, the site is invaded by a weed community. Upon abandonment of the pasture, this community undergoes a process of ecological succession that can lead to reestablishment of closed forest. The rate of this process appears to be extremely variable and depends on the intensity of pasture use (Buschbacher et al. 1987a, b, 1988; Uhl et al. 1988; Nepstad, Uhl, and Serrão, this volume). In the most humid regions of the Amazon Basin (i.e., the Amazonian portions of Colombia, Ecuador, and Peru), where more intensive pasture systems occur in relatively small holdings, ranchers generally control weeds manually and/or chemically to extend the life of their pastures. As planted pasture species decline, native species often assume greater importance as sources of forage. Examples include the grasses *Paspalum conjugatum* Sw., *P. notatum* Flugge, and *Axonopus compressus,* and the herbaceous legumes *Calopogonium mucunoides* Desv., *Desmodium incanum* (Sw.) DC., *D. adcendens* (Sw.) DC., and *D. triflorum* (L.) DC. This native community, referred to as "torourco" in Peru and "grama" or "criadero" in Colombia, represents a relatively stable disclimax with a carrying capacity varying from 0.5 to 0.8 animal units per hectare (Toledo and Serrão 1987). In less humid regions, such as in the Brazilian Amazon, overgrazing as well as

TABLE 13.1. Characteristics of the Different Stages of Productivity in
Amazonian Pastures.

Stage of Productivity	Critical Level of Each Stage[a]	Relative Biomass of Weeds in the Pasture (%)	Potential Carrying Capacity (A.U.)[b]	Average Duration After Pasture Establishment (Years)
High	A	5–10	1.0–1.5	3–5
Medium	B	15–25	0.5–1.0	4–7
Low	C	30–60	0.3–0.5	7–10
Degradation	D	>80	<0.3	7–15

SOURCE: Serrão and Homma (1982), Toledo and Serrão (1982), Serrão (1988).

[a]See figure 13.2.

[b]Animal Unit = 450 kg of live weight.

biotic and edaphic factors cause further degradation, leading to communities of extremely low productivity dominated by relatively unpalatable species such as *Imperata brasiliensis* Trin., *Pteridium* spp., and *Homolepsis aturensis* (H. B. K.) Chase (Toledo 1987).

Causes of Degradation

The stability of pastures established on previously forested sites in Amazonia is strongly influenced by the soil, climate, flora, and human activities. The role of each of these factors in the degradation of Amazonian pastures is examined in the following sections.

Soil. Because Amazonian pastures are generally established on acidic and infertile soils (Oxisols and Ultisols), edaphic factors assume an extremely important role in limiting the stability of these systems.

As discussed previously, clearing and burning forests for pasture establishment produce substantial increases in soil fertility. But these increases are ephemeral, especially in poorly managed pastures planted with grasses that are highly demanding and provide sparse coverage of soil, such as commercial cultivars of *Panicum maximum, Hyparrhenia rufa, Pennisetum purpureum* Schum., and *Axonopus* spp. When pastures are well managed, however, it is possible to maintain more or less satisfactory levels of pH, Ca, Mg, K, and Al during periods of over twenty years (Falesi 1976; Serrão et al. 1979; Falesi et al. 1980; Teixeira 1987).

Figure 13.3 summarizes research findings concerning the dynamics of soil fertility in Amazonian pastures (Falesi 1976; Toledo and Serrão 1982; Serrão 1988). When management and biotic factors are not limiting, the decline in productivity of first-cycle pastures is directly related to the decline in soil fertility. In general, phosphorous has been found to be decisively limiting in these systems (Serrão et al. 1971, 1979; Toledo and Ara 1977; Rolim et al. 1980; Goncalves 1981; Italiano

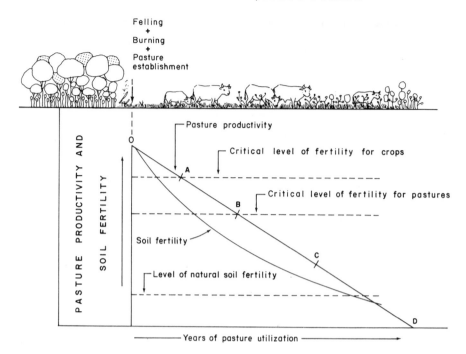

FIGURE 13.3. Relationship between pasture productivity and soil fertility (determined primarily by phosphorus availability) in first-cycle pastures managed with traditional technology in forested areas of the Amazon Basin. (Source: Serrão 1988, adapted from Alvim 1978; Serrão et al. 1979; Dias Filho and Serrão 1982.)

et al. 1982; Dias Filho and Serrão 1983), probably followed by nitrogen in more humid areas of Amazonia (Toledo and Ara 1977). In general, other elements have not been shown to be limiting in Amazonian pastures (Serrão et al. 1979; Empresa Brasileira de Pesquisa Agropecuaria 1980).

Climate. In years when the dry season is especially pronounced (such as 1987 in the Brazilian Amazon), lack of rainfall can dramatically reduce the growth of pastures as well as their capacity to compete with the weed community, which generally has deeper roots and, consequently, greater tolerance of water stress (Nepstad et al. 1989).

The generally high humidity that predominates in forested areas of the Amazon Basin favors the proliferation of pests and diseases, which can undermine the productivity and stability of pastures in the region. Among diseases, the fungi *Fusarium roseum* (Serrão et al. 1979) and *Tilletia airesii* (Freire et al. 1979) are especially important, lowering seed production in *Panicum maximum* and thus reducing the productive life of pastures comprised of this species. Other fungi affect forage production in a number of commercial legumes: examples include *Colletotrichum* sp., which attacks *Stylosanthes* spp. and reduces seed production in *Pueraria phaseoloides* (Roxb.) Benth.; and *Rhizoctonia solani*, which causes serious damage to the principal forage species of *Centrosema*, an important genus in the region (Dias Filho and Serrão 1983; CIAT 1987; Serrão, Moreno, and Veiga 1987).

The pasture spittlebug—known regionally as "cigarinha-das-pastagens," "salivazo," and "mion" and represented by *Deois incompleta* in Brazil (Silva and Magalhaes 1980) and *Zulia colombiana* in Colombia (Calderon 1983)—is undoubtedly the principal factor undermining the stability of pastures composed of *Brachiaria* spp. (principally *B. decumbens* and *B. humidicola*), which are widely used in the region due to their adaptability to soils of high acidity and low fertility. Other insects—such as the "cucarron" (*Eutheola* sp.), which attacks the roots of native grasses in Colombia, causing serious damage (Ramirez and Seré 1987), as well as the "cochonilla" (*Antonina graminis*), the grass caterpillar (*Mocis latipes*), the military caterpillar (*Spodoptera frugiperda*), and the leaf cutter ant (*Atta sextans sextans, A. cephalotes,* and *Acromirmex* sp.)—can also contribute decisively toward degradation of regional pastures (Silva and Magalhães 1980; Calderon 1983; Ramirez and Seré 1987).

Management. Appropriate grazing management, as well as minimal amounts of fertilization for pasture maintenance, are essential to maximize nutrient cycling and persistence of forage grasses and legumes. However, short-term financial interests often preclude the long-term investment in management that is necessary to maintain the productive life of regional pastures. For example, fire—a potentially important management tool—is generally used indiscriminately, thus contributing to pasture degradation. Other common examples of mismanagement include overstocking and insufficient livestock rotation in pastures. Both practices lead to rapid degradation through excessive reduction of forage biomass, soil compaction, and consequent dominance of weeds.

Weeds. Weeds probably represent the greatest obstacle to maintaining the stability of regional pastures. Ranchers in the Amazon Basin probably spend several million dollars each year combating weeds. As shown in figure 13.2 and table 13.1, the productivity of forages is inversely proportional to the presence of weeds in the pasture.

Rather than a cause *per se* of degradation, however, weeds should be viewed as a consequence of the lack of adaptability, vigor, and competitiveness of the forage species commonly used, as well as the general lack of appropriate management practices (such as controlled grazing and application of fertilizers). In regional pastures, the abundance or total dominance of weeds appears to be at least partially related to their almost exclusively native origin, which confers greater adaptiveness to regional conditions than exhibited by planted forage species—the majority of which are exotic (Hecht 1979; Buschbacher, Uhl, and Serrão 1987a; Uhl, Buschbacher, and Serrão 1988; Nepstad et al. 1989).

If the principal causal agents of degradation in regional pastures were solved or minimized, weed infestation would probably be reduced significantly. But regardless of how pastures are managed in the future, weeds will continue to be a persistent component of these systems (Buschbacher 1984).

Forage Germplasm. The lack of forages adapted to the region's climatic, edaphic, and biotic conditions is evident. In our opinion, this is the principal cause of pasture degradation in Amazonia. The most glaring examples of the paucity of commercial cultivars of grasses include *Panicum maximum* (highly demanding in relation to physical and chemical conditions in the soil, seeds susceptible to fungal attack, insufficiently aggressive, difficult to manage); *Hyparrhenia rufa* (insufficiently aggressive, susceptible to losses in palatability, highly demanding in relation to soil conditions); and *Brachiaria decumbens, B. humidicola,* and *B. ruziziensis* Gem. et Evrard. (susceptible to insect attack). In legumes, examples include *Centrosema pubescens* Benth. and *Stylosanthes guianensis* (Aubl.) Sw. (susceptible to fungal attack) and *Pueraria phaseoloides* (excessively aggressive, susceptible to losses in palatability during the rainy season, difficult to manage). With the exception of commercial cultivars such as *B. decumbens, B. humidicola,* and *P. phaseoloides,* all others currently used in the region were introduced by the seed industry without previous evaluation of their adaptability.

Although it should not be regarded as a panacea, new germplasm adapted to regional conditions should be the cornerstone in any strategy to enhance sustainability in regional pastures.

Noninclusion of Legumes. The vast majority of pastures established in the region are composed exclusively of grasses. In very few cases, especially in the Brazilian Amazon, the legumes *Peuraria phaseoloides* and *Centrosema pubescens* have been included in pastures, generally during the first cycle. The results have been less than satisfactory. On the one hand, *P. phaseoloides* tends to dominate the association due to its high aggressiveness and low palatability during the rainy season. On the other, commercial cultivars of *Stylosanthes guianensis* (principally) and *C. pubescens* do not persist in pastures, due to their susceptibility to fungal attack (Dias Filho and Serrão 1983, Serrão, Moreno, and Veiga 1987).

These experiences have led producers to establish pastures without inclusion of legumes, thus foregoing the benefit of nitrogen fixation that these plants provide (figure 13.1). As a result, even grasses such as *Brachiaria decumbens* and *B. humidicola,* which are adapted to infertile soils, may show clear signs of nitrogen deficiency within just a few months after planting; this deficiency can subsequently decrease competitiveness with weeds and thus reduce the productive life of the pasture (Toledo and Serrão 1987). Although the application of nitrogen fertilizers is biologically efficient, it is economically inviable. Given this fact, and considering the key role that nitrogen often plays as a limiting nutrient, the selection of legumes and grasses adapted for compatible and stable mixtures is a high priority in the search for sustainability in Amazonian pastures.

Institutions. Regional governmental institutions have thus far had a limited role in improving the low productivity and longevity characteristic of pastures in the Amazon Basin. One of the most glaring examples of institutional limitations involves the program of fiscal incentives provided for expansion of ranches in the Brazilian Amazon, which generally had little or no technical or scientific basis and suffered from inadequate monitoring. The lack of greater aggressiveness, interaction, and complementarity of regional research and extension agencies in generating and transferring technology is another factor that has contributed to the generally poor state of pastures in the region.

The Search for Stability

Expansion versus Intensification

Despite the generally negative experiences to date, as well as the numerous ecological and socioeconomic arguments against substitution of Amazon rain forest with pasture (Shane 1980; Fearnside 1980, this volume; Hecht 1982a, 1983; Kitamura, Dias Filho, and Serrão 1982; Buschbacher 1986, 1987; and Sioli 1987, among others), this form of land use is now an important part of the Amazon landscape. Moreover, it will probably remain so in the future, due to socioeconomic and geopolitical forces operating in the various countries of the region. The results of research conducted over the past fifteen years—as well as the experience of a number of ranchers in the region—indicate that, with the introduction of relatively simple technologies, pastures established on formerly forested sites can maintain satisfactory levels of productivity with minimal ecological risks. The most sensible course of action is thus to reduce the expansion of new pastures and intensify the utilization of those already established. Intensification should involve increasing the longevity of still-productive sites and recuperating those sites that have been severely degraded.

According to Serrão and Homma (1982), the short-term benefits that could be derived by more intensive use of already established pastures—rather than continued expansion of this form of land use—are ecological (reduced pressure on new areas of forest), microeconomic (lower costs to recuperate existing pastures than to establish new pastures), macroeconomic (increased production of 10,000 tons per year of meat produced in each 100,000 ha of reclaimed pastures, generating at least U.S. $12,000,000 per year), and social (increased labor opportunities, improved conditions for laborers, higher regional production of food, and reduction of land conflicts). These considerations apply not only to Brazil but to other countries of the Amazon Basin (Ramirez and Seré 1987; Schaus 1987).

Available Technology

As the vast majority of Amazonian pastures are still in their first cycle and as others will inevitably be established using currently available technology, figure 13.4 recommends specific management practices to prolong the life of the pasture or promote recuperation when degraded. These recommendations are based on research carried out in the region or on the direct experience of ranchers, principally in the Brazilian Amazon (Empresa Brasileira de Assistencia Técnica e Extensão Rural 1979; Serrão et al. 1979; Serrão and Homma 1982; Dias Filho and Serrão 1983; Serrão 1988).

The initial preparation of the site—cutting and burning the forest and planting forages—are decisive factors in the establishment and subsequent utilization

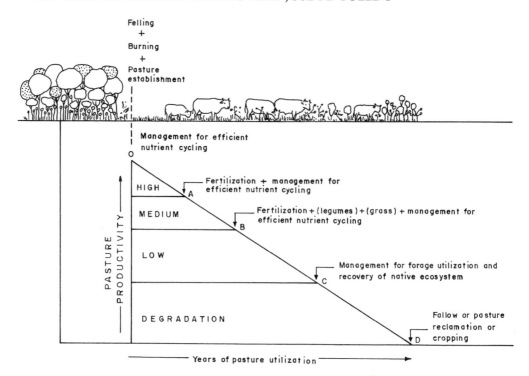

FIGURE 13.4. Management techniques aimed at maintenance of stability in first-cycle pastures and recovery of degraded sites in the Amazon. (Adapted from Serrão et al. 1979; Dias Filho and Serrão 1982; Serrão 1988.)

of pastures. Inadequate establishment inevitably results in pastures of low productivity and short-term use.

Once a vegetational cover composed predominantly of pasture forages is established, management practices (such as control of grazing, burning, and weed infestation; application of fertilizers; introduction of legumes; etc.) should be carried out in the stages of high and medium productivity to prolong the useful life of the pasture. Management practices carried out during these stages (between points "0" and "B" in figure 13.4) produce maximum biological as well as economic results. Observations in some of the few ranches in the Brazilian Amazon that have applied fertilizers in pastures indicate that productivity can be maintained at medium to high levels by applying 20–30 kg of phosphorous per ha (in a mixture of soluble and partially acidulated phosphates), every three to five years. The effect of these applications is greatest on soils containing 20–30 percent clay in the B horizon and a well-developed layer of litter at the surface.

After the productivity of the pasture declines to low levels and the pasture community is dominated by weeds (between points "B" and "C" in figure 13.4), the interventions listed above become economically inviable. Controlled burning of pastures during this stage can provide dramatic short-term effects, such as elimination of weeds and an increase in pasture productivity. But these effects are ephemeral, because the repeated destruction of biomass by fire leads to reduced nutrient cycling and, ultimately, enhanced opportunities for weed invasions. As discussed previously, burning in the more humid regions of western Amazonia tends to give origin to derived native pastures ("criaderos" or "torourcos").

As the productivity of pasture forages declines even further (between points "C" and "D" in figure 13.4), the best policy is to minimize interventions and allow succession to regenerate a native forest cover, even if this requires decades or even centuries to accomplish (Buschbacher, Uhl, and Serrão 1987a, 1987b, 1988; Uhl, Buschbacher, and Serrão 1988). It may even be possible to continue grazing on these sites, but at levels compatible with the low availability of planted and native forage species (Hecht 1979).

On sites with negligible forage productivity (point "D" in figure 13.4), ranchers have essentially two options depending on the aggressiveness of the existing weed community: 1) abandon the site and leave it in fallow for an indeterminate period, or 2) reestablish new pasture systems.

The recovery of native ecosystems after abandonment of degraded pastures depends on the intensity with which these sites were utilized (Buschbacher, Uhl, and Serrão 1987a, 1987b, 1988; Uhl, Buschbacher, and Serrão 1988; Nepstad, Uhl, and Serrão 1989). This issue is extremely relevant in the Brazilian Amazon, where the relatively large size of ranches permits the practice of fallowing; in other countries of the Amazon Basin, the smaller average size of holdings makes this practice less viable. Hence, whereas natural regeneration can provide an important means of recuperating degraded pastures in Brazil, in the other Amazonian countries it is less likely to do so.

Application of more intensive techniques to reclaim degraded pastures is becoming increasingly common, especially in the Brazilian Amazon. The methods employed usually involve practices associated with more intensive land uses, such as mechanization and application of fertilizers and pesticides. The grasses *Brachiaria humidicola* and, on a smaller scale, *Panicum maximum* cultivar "Colonião" are the forages most commonly used in pasture recuperation. Recently, other grasses such as *B. brizantha* (Hochst.) Stapf. cultivar "Marandu" and *Andropogon gayanus* Kunth. cultivar "Planaltina" have been found to be promising and are being increasingly used for pasture recuperation. In the past ten years, approximately 10 percent (600 to 700 thousand hectares) of the pastures formerly established in the Brazilian Amazon have been recovered. Intensification of land use is likely to make forest regeneration even more difficult after the site is finally abandoned (Buschbacher, Uhl, and Serrão 1987a, 1987b, 1988; Uhl, Buschbacher, and Serrão 1988). But the short-term recovery of degraded landscapes nonetheless serves to reduce pressures for clearing new areas of primary forest in Amazonia.

In the other Amazonian countries, especially Colombia and Peru, recovery of pastures has been carried out on an extremely small scale, due to the propensity of derived pastures composed of less palatable species to become established on sites subjected to intensive use. However, the continued spread of derived pastures and the growing need to increase pasture productivity make recovery of these ecosystems imperative. Recuperation of degraded pastures is thus likely to increase in these countries as well (Ramirez and Seré 1987; Salinas 1987; Schaus 1987).

Due to its high costs, pasture recuperation must result in highly productive systems to be economically viable. Research indicates that intercropping of food crops such as corn and rice with forages in the initial stages of pasture reclamation is a viable means of increasing economic returns (Veiga et al. 1985; Veiga 1987). Seeding of food crops and forages, as well as application of fertilizers, can be carried out in a single operation with the appropriate machinery. In some cases, forages (especially *Brachiaria humidicola*, because of its high tolerance of acidic, infertile soils) can be planted without fertilization or intercropping, following mechanical preparation of the site or simply by burning the degraded pasture. As a rule, however, such "shortcuts" actually prolong establishment and may ultimately reduce the productive life of the recuperated pasture.

This technology is commercially available and has been increasingly applied in the Brazilian Amazon during the past decade, primarily in response to the deterioration of regional pastures and for lack of better land-use options. From a purely technical perspective, these practices are effective in recuperating pasture ecosystems. Yet they are expensive due to their reliance on machinery, fertilizers, and pesticides; without generous government subsidies, application of these practices is economically as well as socially questionable (Fearnside 1980; Kitamura et al. 1982; Hecht 1983; Buschbacher 1986). In other Amazonian countries where capital is more scarce, this type of technology has little change of being adopted.

Alternative Technology

An alternative to the above approach is a technology that requires lower inputs and is based on grass and legume forages adapted to regional conditions and more productive than those currently in use. This new technology could be used in conventional pastures, agrosilvopastoral systems, or for recuperation of degraded sites.

Compared to the technology currently in use, this alternative technology is far more difficult to develop and thus represents an enormous challenge to institutions involved in improving regional pastures. However, the ecological and economic benefits of this technology are potentially high, as it could lead to significant increases in pasture productivity and sustainability, while reducing current pressures on forest ecosystems in Amazonia (Toledo and Serrão 1987).

Research Strategies. To promote development of low-cost options for improving pastures in the Amazon region, the International Network for Evaluation of Tropical Pastures (RIEPT) was recently established, under the coordination of the International Center for Tropical Agriculture (CIAT) and in collaboration with various research institutions in Brazil, Colombia, Ecuador, and Peru. The principal strategy of this network involves selection of new germplasm of grasses and legumes that are 1) adapted to nutrient-poor soils (Oxisols and Ultisols); 2) resistant to the principal pests and diseases in pasture ecosystems; 3) rapidly established; 4) persistent (i.e., with high production of seeds, stolons, rhizomes, etc.); and 5) in the case of legumes, efficient in nitrogen fixation and compatible with aggressive grasses.

The principal basis for developing this strategy are the existing germplasm collections within the region's most important genera of grasses such as *Brachiaria* (CIAT 1987), *Panicum* (Savidan, Jank, and Penteado 1985), and *Andropogon* (CIAT 1987), and of legumes such as *Centrosema* (CIAT 1987; Serrão, Moreno, and Veiga 1987), *Pueraria, Desmodium,* and *Stylosanthes* (CIAT 1987). In addition, further collections exist of other genera of grasses (e.g., *Paspalum* and *Axonopus*) and legumes (e.g., *Arachis, Leucaena,* and *Calopogonium*) with promising potential for the region.

In addition to this basic strategy, RIEPT promotes the application of new technologies, through 1) development of techniques for reclaiming degraded pastures (i.e., pest control, improvement of soil physical and chemical conditions, etc.), with special emphasis on sites in an advanced state of degradation; and 2) comparative testing and promotion of new technological options by all institutions involved in the network.

Promising Germplasm. In the past five years of germplasm evaluation, a number of species have revealed exceptional promise for use in regional pastures with minimal inputs. Among grasses, the species are *Brachiaria brizantha* cultivar "Marandu", *B. dictyoneura* Stapf. cultivar "Llanero" (CIAT 6133), *Andropogon gayanus* cultivar "Planaltina" (CIAT 621), and *Panicum maximum* cultivar "Tobiatā." Among legumes, the most promising species include *Centrosema pubescens* (CIAT 438), *C. acutifolium* Benth. (CIAT 5277), *C. macrocarpum* Benth. (CIAT 5713), *Stylosanthes guianensis* (CIAT 184 and 136), *Desmodium ovalifolium* Wall. (CIAT 350 and 13089), and *Arachis pintoi* Benth. (CIAT 17434).

This material, which is currently in an advanced state of evaluation, represents a new generation of germplasm adapted to the edaphic and biotic conditions of degraded pastures in the Amazon Basin. Experimental pastures composed of compatible combinations of grasses and legumes from this new generation have produced net annual gains of up to 500 kg of animal liveweight per hectare, with only minimal management inputs (CIAT 1987; Costales et al. 1987; Schaus 1987). When commercially available, these new technological options should permit substitution of currently degraded landscapes with recuperated pastures that are both ecologically and economically sustainable.

Agrosilvopastoral Systems. Today there is increased recognition of the need to recuperate degraded pasture sites with land-use systems that are more biologically stable and socioeconomically viable than pastures composed solely of grasses and legumes. As a result, research efforts are currently underway to develop agrosilvopastoral systems that combine forages and perennial tree crops, as well as annual crops for short-term returns.

In the Amazon region, research on these systems has just begun (Bishop 1982; Hecht 1982). Nevertheless, they have enormous potential, especially in the recuperation of degraded sites. A number of agroindustrial tree crops such as rubber (*Hevea* spp.), African oil palm (*Elaeis guineensis* Jacq.), and Brazil nut (*Bertholletia excelsa* H.B.) are being increasingly used in association with both planted and native pastures in the region. The same applies to forest trees such as *Pinus caribea* Morelet and *Gmelina arborea* Roxb.

Examples of agropastoral systems utilized in the region include associations of rubber and African oil palm with *Peuraria phaseoloides*; and Brazil nut with *Brachiaria humidicola* (cultivated), *Panicum maximum* (spontaneous), and other forages. Examples of silvopastoral systems include *Pinus caribea* and *Gmelina arborea* with *B. humidicola, P. maximum,* and other forages.

To promote development of agrosilvopastoral systems in Amazonia, there is a pressing need to seek a wider variety of components that can be integrated into these systems. Specifically, research should aim to select: 1) grass and legume forages that are tolerant of shading; 2) tree crops that are tolerant of acidic and infertile soils; 3) tree crops that can fix nitrogen; and 4) forages, annual crops, and trees that are compatible both among themselves and with grazing animals.

Future Research and Policies

The use of extensive areas of Amazon rain forest for ranching is a reality, and it is too late to dream of preserving the entire region. Great damage has already been done, and it is imperative now to avoid further damage and minimize that which has occurred. The intensification of land use with pasture-based cattle production systems, integrated with crops and trees, will play an important ecological and socioeconomic role in the reclamation of degraded pastures in the region.

Among the principal causes of instabilty in planted pastures in the Amazon Basin, lack of adapted germplasm is probably the most significant, and the main priority of applied research should be to correct this problem by developing adapted cultivars of grasses and legumes. Additional efforts in applied research should focus on 1) techniques of forage establishment; 2) pasture management practices; 3) application of fertilizers; 4) weed control; and 5) design of agrosilvopastoral systems. The priority of each of these areas is highly dependent on the pasture's stage of development (figure 13.2).

In terms of basic research, priorities include studies on 1) the ecology of the weed community in regional pastures; 2) the biology of the pasture spittlebug and other economically important pests; 3) the cycling of phosphorous in pasture ecosystems; and 4) the microbiology of soil organisms in pastures, with special emphasis on *Rhizobium* and mycorrhizae.

In addition to defining specific lines of research, there is an urgent need to integrate research efforts on both national and regional levels, so that transfer of technology can proceed more smoothly.

The search for sustainability in Amazonian pastures ultimately requires a change in current land-use policies, which generally encourage immediate exploitation of the rain forest. Instead of destruction, policies must be developed that promote preservation, restoration, and sound utilization of regional ecosystems. In the Brazilian Amazon, for example, government incentives for pastures should be redirected toward recovering the ecosystems that these incentives helped to degrade, instead of promoting the continued expansion of ranching.

Researchers from diverse fields, extension agents, policymakers, and producers must recognize that to be sound, development of the Amazon must be sustainable. The first step toward developing sustainable forms of land use is for the people involved or concerned with regional development to communicate objectively rather than merely generate controversy. With cooperation of people from diverse fields, it should be possible to move toward the goal of developing intensive pasture systems that require minimum areas of Amazon forest for maximum production, in a manner that is both ecologically and socioeconomically sustainable.

REFERENCES

Alvim, P. T. 1978. A expansão de fronteira agrícola no Brasil. In *Seminário Nacional de Política Agrícola.* Brasília.

Bishop, J. P. 1982. Agroforestry systems for the humid tropic east of the Andes. In S. B. Hecht, ed., *Amazonia: Agriculture, and Land Uses Research,* pp. 403–413. Cali, Colombia: Centro Internacional de Agricultura Tropical (CIAT).

Buschbacher, R. J. 1984. Changes in productivity and nutrient cycling following conversion of Amazon rainforest to pasture. Ph.D. dissertation. Athens: Institute of Ecology, University of Georgia.

Buschbacher, R. J. 1986. Tropical deforestation and pasture development. *Bioscience* 36(1):22–28.

Buschbacher, R. J. 1987. Government-sponsored pastures in Venezuela near the Brazilian border. In C. F. Jordan, ed., *Amazonian Rain Forests: Ecosystem Disturbance and Recovery,* pp. 46–57. Ecological Studies, 60, New York: Springer-Verlag.

Buschbacher, R. J., C. Uhl, and E. A. S. Serrão. 1987a. Forest development following pasture use in the north of Pará, Brasil. In *Anais do lo Simpósio do Trópico Umido,* vol. 6. 1984. Belém: Centro de Pesquisa Agropecuária do Trópico Umido (EMBRAPA-CPATU) (in press).

Buschbacher, R. J., C. Uhl, and E. A. S. Serrão. 1987b. Large-scale development in Eastern Amazonia: Pasture management and environmental effects near Paragominas, Pará. In C. F. Jordan, ed., *Amazonian Rain Forests: Ecosystem Disturbance and Recovery,* pp. 90–99. Ecological Studies, 60. New York: Springer-Verlag.

Buschbacher, R. J., C. Uhl, and E. A. S. Serrão. 1988. Abandoned pastures in Eastern Amazonia: II: Nutrient stocks in the soil and vegetation. *Journal of Ecology,* 76:682–699.

Calderón, M. 1983. Insect pests of tropical forage plants in South America. In J. A. Smith and V. W. Hays, eds., *Proceedings of the XIV International Grassland Congress,* pp. 778–780. Lexington.

CIAT. 1987. *Informe Anual del Programa de Pastos Tropicales.* Documento de Trabajo No. 24. Cali, Colombia: Centro Internacional de Agricultura Tropical (CIAT).

Cochrane, T. T. and P. A. Sanchez. 1982. Land resources, soil and their management in the Amazon region: A state of knowledge report. In S. B. Hecht, ed., *Amazonia: Agriculture and Land Use Research,* pp. 135–210. Cali, Colombia: Centro Internacional de Agricultura Tropical (CIAT).

Cochrane, T. T., P. A. Serrão, L. G. Azevedo, J. A. Porras, and C. L. Garver. 1985. *Land in Tropical America,* 3 vol. Cali, Colombia: Centro Internacional de Agricultura Tropical (CIAT).

Costales, J., H. D. Caballero, M. Hurtado, and R. Gonzalez. 1987. La Amazonia Equatoriana: Investigación en pasturas y diagnóstico socio-económico. In *La Investigación en Pastos dentro del Contexto Científico e Socioeconômico de los Paises,* pp. 217–246. David, Panamá: Red Internacional de Evaluación de Pastos Tropicales.

Dias Filho, M. B. and E. A. S. Serrão. 1982. *Recuperacão, Melhoramento e Manejo de Pas-*

tagens na Região de Paragominas, Pará. Documentos No. 5. Belém: Centro de Pesquisa Agropecuária do Trópico Umido (EMBRAPA-CPATU).

Dias Filho, M. B. and E. A. S. Serrão. 1983. *Principais Doenças Associadas às Gramíneas e Leguminosas em Ecossistema de Floresta na Amazônia Oriental Brasileria.* Comunicado No. 37. Belém: Centro de Pesquisa do Trópico Umido (EMBRAPA-CPATU).

Dias Filho, M. B. and E. A. S. Serrão. 1987. *Limitações de Fertilidade do Solo na Recuperação de Pastagem Degradada de Capim Colonião (Panicum maximum* Jacq.) *em Paragominas, na Amazônia Oriental.* Boletim de Pesquisa No. 87. Belém: Centro de Pesquisa do Trópico Umido (EMBRAPA-CPATU).

Empresa Brasileira de Assistência Técnica e Extensâo Rural. 1979. *Manual Técnico de Pecuária de Corte (Bovinos e Bubalinos). Pará, Amapá, Roraima.* Brasília, DF. 188 p.

Empresa Brasileira de Pesquisa Agropecuária. 1980. *Projeto Melhoramento de Pastagem da Amazônia (PROPASTO).* Relatório Técnico 1976/79. Belém: Centro de Pesquisa Agropecuária do Trópico Umido (EMBRAPA-CPATU).

Falesi, I. C. 1976. *Ecossistema de Pastagem Cultivada na Amazônia Brasileira.* Boletim Técnico No. 1. Belém: Centro de Pesquisa Agropecuária do Trópico Umido (EMBRAPA-CPATU).

Falesi, I. C., A. R. C. Baena, and S. Dutra. 1980. *Consequência da Exploracão Agropecuária sobre as Condicões Físicas e Químicas dos Solos das Microrregiões do Nordeste Paraense.* Boletim de Pesquisa no. 14. Belém: Centro de Pesquisa Agropecuária do Trópico Umido (EMBRAPA-CPATU).

Fearnside, P. M. 1980. The effects of cattle pasture on soil fertility in the Brazilian Amazon: Consequences for beef production sustainability. *Tropical Ecology* 21(1):125–137.

Freire, F. C. O., E. A. S. Serrão, and F. C. Albuquerque. 1979. Cárie do sino, uma séria doença da panícula de capim Colonião. *Fitopatologia Brasileira* 4(1):111.

Gonçalves, C. A. 1981. *Fontes de Fósforo na Producão de Capim Colonião (Panicum maximum* Jacq.) *em Porto Velho, Rondonio.* Comunicado Técnico No. 31. Porto Velho: Unidade de Execução de Pesquisa de Ambito Estadual (EMBRAPA-UEPAE).

Hecht, S. B. 1979. Leguminosas espontáneas en praderas amazonicas cultivadas e su potencial forrajero. In P. A. Sanchez and L. E. Tergas, eds., *Producción de Pastos en Suelos Acidos de los Trópicos,* pp. 71–78. Colombia: Centro Internacional de Agricultura Tropical (CIAT).

Hecht, S. B. 1982a. Cattle ranching development in the eastern Amazon: Evaluation of a development strategy. Ph.D. dissertation. Berkeley: University of California.

Hecht, S. B. 1982b. Agroforestry in the Amazon Basin: Practice, theory and limits of a promising land use. In S. B. Hecht, ed., *Amazonia: Agriculture and Land Use Research,* pp. 331–371. Cali, Colombia: Centro Internacional de Agricultura Tropical (CIAT).

Hecht, S. B. 1983. Cattle ranching in the eastern Amazon: Environmental and social implications. In E. F. Moran, ed., *The Dilemma of Amazonian Development,* pp. 155–188. Boulder: Westview Press.

Italiano, E. C., E. Moraes, and A. C. Santo. 1982. *Fertilicão de Pastagem de Capim Colonião em Degradacão.* Comunicado Técnico No. 31. Manaus: Unidade de Execuçâo de Pesquisa de Ambito Estadual (EMBRAPA-UEPAE).

Kitamura, P. C., M. B. Dias Filho, and E. A. S. Serrão. 1982. *Análise Econômica de Algumas Alternativas de Manejo das Pastagens Cultivadas, Paragominas, Pa.* Boletim de Pesquisa No. 41. Belém: Centro de Pesquisa Agropecuária do Trópico Umido (EMBRAPA-CPATU).

Navas, J. A. 1982. Considerations on the Colombian Amazon region. In S. B. Hecht, ed., *Amazonia: Agriculture and Land Use Research,* pp. 41–83. Cali, Colombia: Centro Internacional de Agricultura Tropical (CIAT).

Nepstad, D., F. H. Bormann, C. Uhl, R. Reynolds, O. Watrin, C. Pereira and E. A. S. Serrão. 1989. Deep roots and nutrients of an Amazon forest and abandoned pasture. Unpublished manuscript.

Ramirez, A. and C. Seré. 1987. *Caracteristicas del Sistema de Producción de Ganado de Doble Propósito y de la Adopción y Uso del Brachiaria decumbens en el Caquetá.* Informe Interno. Cali, Colombia: Centro Internacional de Agricultura Tropical (CIAT).

Riesco, A., M. de la Torre, C. Reyes, G. Meini, H. Huamán, and M. Garcia. 1982. *Analisis Exploratório de los Sistemas de Fundo de Pequeños Productores en la Amazonia.* Región Pucallpa. Puccallpa, Colombia: IVITA/UNMSN/CIID.

Rolim, F. A., P. M. Paolicchi, A. C. Costa, and H. M. Saito. 1980. *Resultados de Pesquisas Agrostológicas Desenvolvidas na Região de Paragominas—Pará e Barra do Garça— Mato Grosso.* Belém: Superintendência para o Desenvolvimento da Amazônia (SUDAM).

Salinas, J. G. 1987. *Recuperación con Pasturas de Areas Degradadas: Avances en la Investigación.* Documento de Trabajo: Proyecto Cooperativo de Investigacion et Pasturas Tropicales. Pucallpa, Peru: Centro Internacional de Agricultura Tropical (CIAT).

Sanchez, P. A. and J. G. Salinas. 1981. Low-input technology for managing oxisols and ultisols in tropical America. *Advances in Agronomy* 34:279–405.

Savidan, J. H., L. Jank, and M. I. O. Penteado. 1985. *Introducão, Avaliacão e Melhoramento de Plantas Forrageiras Tropicais no Brasil: Novas Propostas de Modus Operanti.* Documentos No. 24. Campo Grande: Centro Nacional de Pesquisa de Gado de Corte (EMBRAPA-CNPGC).

Schaus, R. A. 1987. El rol de la investigación en pasturas en la Amazonia peruana. In *La Investigación en Pastos dentro del Contexto Científico e Socioeconómico de los Paises,* pp. 463–498. David, Panamá: Red Internacional de Evaluación de Pastos Tropicales.

Serrão, E. A. S. 1988. Pasturas mejoradas en áreas de bosque húmedo brasileño: Conocimientos actuales. In O. P. Sierra, ed., *Segunda Conferencia Nacional de Producción y Utilización de Pastos y Forrajes,* pp. 43–85. Palmira, Colombia: AZZOVALLE.

Serrão, E. A. S. and A. J. Conto. 1987. Aspectos bio-sócio-econômicos relacionados às pastagens do trópico úmido amazônico brasileiro. In *La Investigación en Pastos dentro del Contexto Científico e Socioeconômico de los Paises,* pp. 91–145. David, Panamá: Red Internacional de Evaluación de Pastos Tropicales.

Serrão, E. A. S., E. S. Cruz, M. S. Simão Neto, G. F. Souza, J. B. Bastos, and M. C. F. Guimarâes. 1971. Resposta de treŝ gramíneas (*Brachiaria decumbens* Stapf, *Brachiaria ruziziensis* Germain et Everard e *Pennisetum purpureum* Schum.) a elementos fertilizantes em latosol amarelo textura média. *Série: Fertilidade de Solos* 1(2):1–38. Belém: Instituto de Pesquisias Agropecuárias do Norte (IPEAN).

Serrão, E. A. S., I. C. Falesi, J. B. Veiga, and J. F. Teixeira Neto. 1979. Productivity of cultivated pastures in low fertility soils of the Amazon of Brazil. In P. A. Sanchez and L. E. Tergas, eds., *Pasture Production in Acid Soils of the Tropics,* pp. 195–225. Cali, Colombia: Centro Internacional de Agricultura Tropical (CIAT).

Serrão, E. A. S. and A. K. O. Homma. 1982. *Recuperação e Melhoramento de Pastagens Cultivadas em Área de Floresta Amazônica.* Documentos No. 17. Belém: Centro de Pesquisa Agropecuária do Trópico Umido (EMBRAPA-CPATU).

Serrão, E. A. S., M. A. Moreno, and J. B. Veiga. 1987. Regional experience with *Centrosema:* Brasil—humid tropics. Paper presented in the Workshop on *Centrosema:* Biology, Agronomy and Utilization. CIAT, Cali, Colombia (in press).

Shane, D. R. 1980. *Hoofprints in the Forest: An Inquiry into the Beef Cattle Industry in the Tropical Forest Areas of Latin America.* Washington, DC: Office of Environmental Affairs, Department of State.

Silva, A. B. and B. P. Magalhães. 1980. *Insectos Nocivos às Pastagens no Estado do Pará.* Boletim de Pesquisa No. 8. Belém: Centro de Pesquisa Agropecuária do Trópico Umido (EMBRAPA-CPATU).

Silva, L. F. 1978. *Influência do Manejo de um Ecossistema nas Propriedades Edáficas dos Oxissolos de Tabuleiro.* Mimeograph. Itabuna, Brazil: Centro de Pesquisa do Cacau (CEPLAC).

Sioli, H. 1987. A ecologia paisagística da Amazônia e as perspectivas de uma utilização racional dos recursos. In *Anais do 1° Simpósio do Trópico Umido,* vol. 6. Documentos No. 36. Centro de Pesquisa Agropecuária do Trópico Umido (EMBRAPA-CPATU) (in press).

Spain, J. M. and J. G. Salinas. 1985. A reciclagem de nutrientes nas pastagens tropicais. In P. Cabala-Rosand, ed., *Reciclagem de Nutrientes e Agricultura de Baixos Insumos,* pp. 259–299. Ilhéus, Brazil: CEPLAC/SBCS.

SUDAM. 1983. *Controle Estatístico dos Incentivos Fiscais Administrados pela SUDAM.* Belém: Superintendência para o Desenvolvimento da Amazônia (SUDAM).

Teixeira, L. B. 1987. Dinâmica do ecossistema de pastagem cultivada em área de floresta na Amazônia Central. Tese de doutorado. Manaus: Instituto Nacional de Pesquisas da Amazônia (INPA)/Fundação Universidade do Amazonas (FUA).

Toledo, J. M. 1987. Pasturas en trópico húmedo: Perspectiva global. In *Anais do 1° Simpósio do Trópico Umido,* Vol. 5. Documentos No. 36. Belém: Centro de Pesquisa Agropecuária do Trópico Umido (EMBRAPA-CPATU) (in press).

Toledo, J. M. and M. Ara. 1977. *Manejo de Suelos para Pastura en la Selva Amazónica.* Lima, Perú: FAO/SIDA.

Toledo, J. M. and E. A. S. Serrão. 1982. Pasture and animal production in Amazonia. In S. B. Hecht, ed., *Amazonia: Agriculture and Land Use Research,* pp. 281–309. Cali, Colombia: Centro Internacional de Agricultura Tropical (CIAT).

Toledo, J. M. and E. A. S. Serrão. 1987. Pasture after humid tropical forest clearing in the Amazon. Paper presented at the International Symposium on Grassland in Forest Area, Harbin, R. P. China (in press).

Uhl, C., R. J. Buschbacher, and E. A. S. Serrão. 1988. Abandoned pastures in eastern Amazonia. I: Patterns of plant succession. *Journal of Ecology,* 76:663–681.

Veiga, J. B. 1987. Associação de culturas de subsistência com forrageiras na renovação de pastagens degradadas em áreas de floresta. In *Anais do 1° Simpósio do Trópico Umido.* Documentos No. 36. Belém: Centro de Pesquisa Agropecuária do Trópico Umido (EMBRAPA-CPATU) (in press).

Veiga, J. B., E. A. S. Serrão, L. C. T. Marques, A. P. Camarâo, L. G. Pereira Neto, L. C. G. S. Seixas, M. Calderón, and J. L. Covre. 1985. *Pesquisas Agropecuárias em Paragominas, PA—1984.* Comunicado Técnico No. 55. Belém: Centro de Pesquisa Agropecuária do Trópico Umido (EMBRAPA-CPATU).

14

Surmounting Barriers to Forest Regeneration in Abandoned, Highly Degraded Pastures: A Case Study from Paragominas, Pará, Brazil

■

DANIEL NEPSTAD

CHRISTOPHER UHL

E. ADILSON SERRÃO

ABSTRACT

We studied the barriers to tree establishment in a highly degraded, abandoned Amazon pasture with the goal of learning how to reforest such sites. Tree seedling establishment in our pasture study site was limited by a lack of seed dispersal, seed predation, seedling predation, and seasonal drought. Bats and birds dispersed small-seeded, pioneer tree species to our study site, but these seeds were frequently killed by leaf-cutter ants and small rodents; or if they germinated, they were eliminated by seedling predators or by their inability to withstand drought. By contrast, many large-seeded tree species had a much higher probability of avoiding predation and withstanding drought, but dispersal of such species to pasture clearings is unlikely.

Humans could help to coax degraded Amazon pastures back to forest. We illustrate how studies of the biological limitations to natural regeneration in degraded pastures can provide a basis for the development of low-cost reforestation strategies.

While forest reestablishment is relatively rapid following some forms of deforestation such as swidden agriculture, forest recovery on abandoned pastures with histories of heavy use may take centuries (Uhl, Buschbacher, and Serrão 1988).

Fortunately, these successionally arrested ecosystems of weedy grasses and herbs are currently rare. But the processes of landscape degradation that are occurring in regions of widespread pasture establishment, such as near the town of Paragominas in the Brazilian state of Pará (figure 14.1), suggest that these non-forest ecosystems will become more common in the future.

Humans can counteract the negative ecological impacts of replacing forest with nonforest ecosystems by accelerating forest regrowth where it is suppressed. In this paper, we first discuss the numerous obstacles to tree establishment in one abandoned pasture. We then employ these results to develop a strategy for promoting forest reestablishment on degraded lands and discuss how such a strategy might be implemented.

The Study System

Since 1984, we have been studying the factors that restrict forest reestablishment in an abandoned pasture with a history of heavy use near Paragominas, Pará. Our work has focused on the early stages of tree establishment because of the near absence of forest tree seedlings in the pasture. We have experimentally measured the potential importance of seed dispersal, seed predation, seedling predation, and seasonal drought in limiting tree seedling establishment. By working with an eco-logically, physiologically, and morphologically diverse group of tree species, we have identified the seed and seedling characteristics associated with successful plant establishment.

The study site is located on Fazenda Vitória (Victória Ranch, 2°59′, 47°31′W, figure 14.1), 7 km northwest of Paragominas. Mean annual rainfall is 1750 mm; monthly precipitation for July through November averages <100 mm. The soil is an Oxisol (Haplustox) with ca. 80 percent kaolinite and 20 percent gibbsite. Con-centrations of available soil macronutrients, percent organic matter, and pH are all higher in this nineteen-year-old pasture than in the nearby forest. There is a wide (300 m) zone of low, second-growth forest between the mature forest and abandoned pasture. Plant canopies are 30 to 50 m in the mature forest, 3 to 10 m in the second-growth forest, and 1 to 3 m in the abandoned pasture. We have found 171 tree species with diameter at breast height ≥20 cm in a 5-ha forest study plot. Sixty-six vascular plant species occur in the abandoned pasture where grasses (e.g., *Paspalum paniculatum* L.) and shrubs (e.g., *Rolandra argentea* Rottb.) dominate the canopy.

The pasture was formed in 1969 with *Panicum maximum* Jacq. and stocked at high densities of cattle during the 1970s. It was never bulldozed or fertilized but was frequently weeded (cleared with machetes), herbicided once, and burned several times. We completely excluded cattle in 1984.

Mechanisms of Tree Establishment in Abandoned Pastures

There are several pathways by which trees can establish in abandoned pastures (figure 14.2). Tree roots that persist in the soil following forest clearing can give

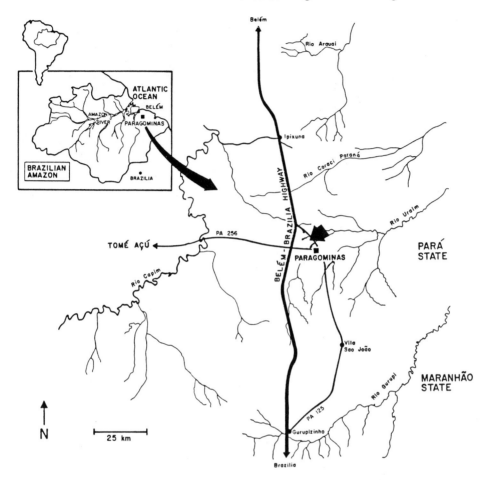

FIGURE 14.1. Location of the study site in eastern Amazonia.

rise to new stems by sprouting. In addition, seeds dispersed to the pasture from nearby forest and seeds persisting in the soil from the forest seed bank contribute to the pool of juvenile trees if they succeed in germinating. However, in our study pasture, which had a long history of intensive use, there is little potential for tree establishment from relict root systems or seed-bank seeds. We have observed no forest tree stems in 40 permanent plots (1 × 2 m) during 30 months of observation and no forest tree species germinated from 100 50-cm^2 soil samples taken from the pasture. We conclude that forest reestablishment in the abandoned pasture ecosystem does not depend on seedling production from relict seeds or roots; rather, it depends on seeds dispersed from the forest.

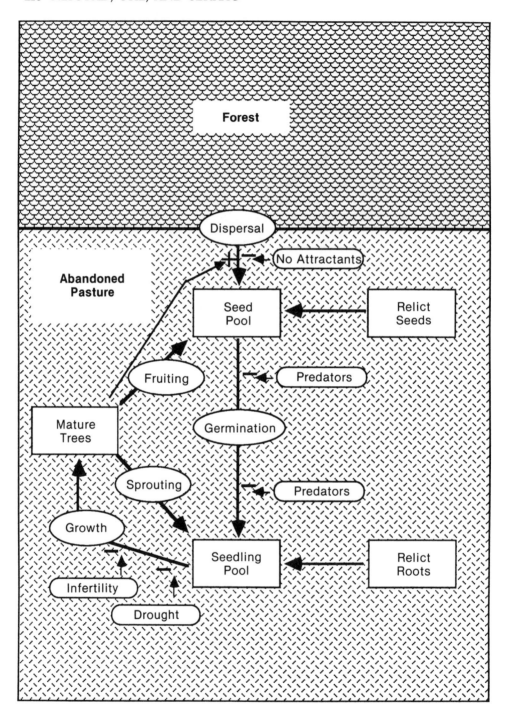

FIGURE 14.2. Mechanisms of tree establishment in an abandoned, grass-dominated pasture, Paragominas, Brazil. Note that in the absence of relict seeds and roots, seedling establishment is dependent on seed dispersal from the forest.

Barriers to Tree Establishment in Abandoned Pastures

Seed Supply

Tree establishment in the abandoned pasture is limited to those forest species with seeds that are transported into the grassland via animals or wind. At Fazenda Vitória, seed-carrying birds and bats are the main animal vectors for seed movement between the forest and the abandoned pasture. Although deer have been observed venturing into the abandoned pasture, we know of no other seed-eating, ground-dwelling animal that might carry seeds into the grassland. Wind probably carries very few tree seeds into the pasture since only 11 percent of the forest tree species are wind-dispersed and the forest is not upwind from the pasture.

We have designed our studies of tree seed availability in the pasture around three questions: 1) What bird and bat species might be carrying forest tree seeds into the abandoned pasture? 2) What group of forest seed species are they carrying? and 3) What are the pasture microhabitats into which forest seeds are transported? We have addressed these questions through a combination of mist-netting studies, field observations of bird movement and feeding patterns, and seed trapping.

There are relatively few fruit-eating bird and bat species that occur in both the mature forest and the abandoned pasture. As expected, bird species richness is related to vegetation complexity with 102 species observed in the mature forest, 90 in the second-growth forest, and 38 in the open pasture. The three habitats had 13 species in common with eight of these species known to be seed vectors. Of the 25 species occurring in both pasture and second-growth forest, seven are seed vectors; of the 39 species common to both second-growth and mature forest, 24 are known to carry seeds. We captured fewer species of bats than birds but found higher overlap of bats between habitats. For example, of the 15 bat species netted in mature forest, eight occurred in abandoned pasture and all of these are known to feed on fruits.

The secondary forest is a far more important source of tree seeds for the abandoned pasture than is the mature forest. Most of the tree seeds recovered from feces of birds and bats captured in the pasture belong to genera of small-seeded (<0.1 g) secondary forest species, such as *Banara, Cecropia, Rollinia, Solanum,* and *Vismia.* Seed dispersal, therefore, acts as an effective filter to many tree species (i.e., those with large seeds) that could potentially colonize the pasture.

Seeds transported into the pasture are not spread evenly over space but are concentrated beneath feeding and perching spots. By combining results from visual censuses and seed trapping studies, we have found that the majority of fruit-eating birds that venture into the pasture are attracted by shrub-like lianas and trees such as *Cordia multispicata* Cham. and *Solanum crinitum* Lam., respectively. These pasture species produce fruit throughout most of the year and are particularly attractive to fruit-eating birds during the early dry season, when fruit production in the secondary forest is low. For example, from July, 1987 through January, 1988, 3.9 tree seeds m^{-2} day^{-1} (representing 18 tree species) fell on cloth tarps placed beneath *Solanum crinitum* compared to 0.01 tree seeds m^{-2} day^{-1} (and one tree species) that fell on tarps placed in the grass vegetation.

Seed Survival

Seeds are concentrated packets of food and many animals depend on them for survival. The probability that tree seeds deposited in abandoned pastures survive to germinate is therefore largely a function of the attractiveness of these seeds to the animal community. We examined the fate of seeds transported to the abandoned pasture by observing seeds of 12 species placed on the pasture ground surface. The results were striking. Of the 160 to 240 seeds placed per species, all seeds were removed within 24 hours for one tree species (*Laetia procera* Eichl.), and more than 80 percent of the seeds were removed within 50 days for eight out of eleven species. By the end of the 200-day observation period, seedlings had been produced by only two of the eleven species, *Cordia goeldiana* Hub. and *Radlkoferella macrocarpa* (Hub.) Aubl.; seeds could still be found only for large-seeded, thick-shelled species, *Maximiliana maripa* (Corr. de Serr.) Drude and *Endopleura uchi* (Hub.) Cuatr.

Seed attractiveness to pasture animals depends on the size of the seed because the propagule's weight influences the type of animal that can handle it. Very small seeds (<0.01 g) are removed rapidly by small ants (e.g., *Pheidole* and *Solenopsis* sp.) but can also be removed by the leaf-cutter ant, *Atta sexdens*, and pasture rodents (principally *Akodon lasiurus* and *Oryzomys microtus*). Seeds up to 0.2 g can be handled only by *A. sexdens* and rodents, and larger seeds are vulnerable only to rodents (if *A. sexdens* cannot cut them into pieces). Seed weight alone explained 75 percent of the variation in seed removal rates for the eleven seed species placed in the pasture.

Seed attractiveness also depends on the substances present on the seed surface. Seeds that are oily (e.g., *Laetia procera*) or covered with pulp are removed more rapidly than seeds with "dry" seed coats such as the wind-dispersed species *Sclerolobium paraensis* Hub. The substances that attract birds and bats to fruits may also attract seed predators to seeds. Moreover, the attractiveness of seeds declines over time as substances on the seed surface are washed away by rain or consumed by microorganisms.

Seed survival in the pasture is partially a function of the strength of the tissue that surrounds the seed. *A. sexdens* and rodents cut or eat large seeds that are not hard-shelled (e.g., *Dipteryx odorata* Willd.). Seeds protected by thick, hard mesocarps (e.g., *Maximiliana maripa*) or seed coats (e.g., *Radlkoferella macrocarpa*) can pesist for long periods on the soil surface. But even large, tough-coated seeds can become vulnerable to seed predators at the time of germination. Seeds of *Hymenaea courbaril* L., for example, are consumed by rodents shortly after they begin to imbibe water and crack their seed coats.

What is the fate of seeds removed by animals? Most of the seeds carried into the nests of *A. sexdens* and *Solenopsis* sp. are probably stored in caches more than 15 cm below the soil surface and are unlikely to survive if they germinate (C. Yohn, unpublished data). We do not know if any seeds transported by rodents survive to germinate; many thin-shelled seeds are presumably consumed quickly.

The animals in degraded pastures may therefore act as a second filter on the type of tree species that can establish. Large, tough-coated seeds are the most likely to survive in the abandoned pasture although they, too, become vulnerable during germination. Small seeds with oil or pulp on their surfaces and fleshy seeds with soft seed coats stand little chance of surviving to germinate.

Seedling Survival and Growth

If seeds are transported to the pasture, escape seed predators and germinate, they must survive and grow before tree establishment is complete. We discuss here the role of seedling predation and seasonal drought in limiting the survival and growth of tree seedlings in the abandoned pasture.

Seedling Predation. Rodents and ants exert a considerable influence on the types of plants that can grow to maturity in abandoned pastures. We determined animal seedling preferences by comparing damage to seedlings of seven species planted together in soil-filled basins. Twenty basins, each with one seedling per species, were buried to ground-level in the study pasture and in treefall gaps in the nearby mature forest. After 16 days, 30 to 80 percent of the seedlings of each tree species had been defoliated in the pasture site while no grass (one species) or shrub (two species) seedlings had been attacked. *A. sexdens* was the principal predator as judged by the cuts left on the seedling stems (figure 14.3); a few seedlings had

FIGURE 14.3. The cutter ant, *Atta sexdens*, harvesting the leaves and stem apex of a *Radlkoferella macrocarpa* seedling. The latex slows the rate of cutting but does not prevent the ants from completely defoliating seedlings. (Photograph by Eduardo Garcia Rosas.)

been chewed by rodents. No seedlings were defoliated in the forest gaps over the 16-day observation period. We propose that herbivory rates, like seed removal rates, are greater in the pasture because of high populations of the cutter ant, *A. sexdens*, and rodents, *Akodon lasiurus* and *Oryzomys microtus* (none of which are present in the forest).

Seed size appears to influence the ability of seedlings to withstand clipping. Small-seeded species, such as *Bagassa guianensis* Aubl. and *Didymopanax morototoni* Decne. et Planch., produce tiny seedlings that die if clipped within the first few months following germination. By contrast, the large-seeded *Radlkoferella macrocarpa* can survive clipping by *A. sexdens* shortly after germination because of the carbohydrates and nutrients stored in its cotyledons and because of its capacity to sprout from dormant buds near the base of the stem. Since small seedlings appear to be more vulnerable to clipping by *A. sexdens* or rodents than large seedlings, large-seeded species have a higher probability of surmounting the barrier to survival imposed by seedling predators.

Seasonal Drought. It is widely accepted that most tree species of tropical moist forests require treefall gaps to attain reproductive maturity because of low levels of resources (e.g., light) encountered by seedlings in closed forest (Denslow 1987). Large gaps tend to have higher levels of light and soil moisture near the ground surface than small gaps and are therefore colonized by tree species that grow rapidly but require high resource levels. Within this paradigm, abandoned pastures might be considered as very large openings in the forest and should have high levels of resources near the ground. Unlike treefall gaps, however, these grasslands support dense vegetation that reduces the availability of light, soil moisture, and perhaps nutrients near the ground surface. Tree establishment in abandoned pastures is restricted to those species that can acquire sufficient resources as seedlings to survive and grow. In this section, we discuss the potential role of soil moisture availability in limiting tree seedling survival in abandoned pasture.

During the five-month dry season, soil moisture is sometimes in short supply in the abandoned pasture. For example, water potential (the best measure of soil moisture availability to the plant) in the upper 15 cm of soil is below -1.5 MPa, or the permanent wilting point, for several weeks each year in the abandoned pasture but rarely drops below -1.0 MPa in closed forest.

Differences in soil moisture availability between the abandoned pasture and the closed forest are probably caused by differences in the root systems of these ecosystems. Although root mass is three times greater in the forest than in the pasture, root length in the upper 50 cm of soil is four times higher in the pasture. Since water uptake at low soil moisture availability is primarily a function of root length per unit soil volume (Caldwell and Richards 1986), the grass-dominated ecosystem can reduce soil moisture availability near the soil surface more rapidly than the forest ecosystem. The forest ecosystem is also able to tap deeper soil moisture supplies than the pasture. Roots in the forest extend to at least 12 m depth while those in the grassland taper off at 7 m.

The effect of low soil moisture availability on plant survival and growth depends on the plant's ability to tolerate and avoid drought. The best measure of drought tolerance in plants is the turgor loss point, defined as the leaf water potential at which leaf turgor is lost. Drought-tolerant plants maintain leaf turgor even at low leaf water potentials (i.e., with large internal water deficits) and can therefore continue turgor-dependent processes such as carbon dioxide uptake (necessary for photosynthesis) and cell expansion (necessary for growth) despite low soil moisture availability (Turner and Jones 1980).

What types of seedlings are able to tolerate drought in the abandoned pasture? We compared the drought tolerance of a variety of tree seedlings that we planted in the pasture by measuring their turgor loss point using pressure-volume curves (Cheung, Tyree, and Dainty 1975). The turgor loss point of 10 tree species ranged from −1.1 (*Solanum crinitum*) to −3.0 MPa (*Orbignya phalerata* Mart.) and appeared to vary depending on the ecological class of the tree species. Light-demanding plants with the potential for fast growth (e.g., *S. crinitum, Cecropia obtusa* Trec., and *Jacaranda copaia* (Aubl.) D. Don) exhibited very low drought tolerance while shade-tolerant, slow-growing species (e.g., *O. phalerata* and *Radlkoferella macrocarpa*) exhibited very high drought tolerance. Studies of seedling drought tolerance on Barro Colorado Island, Panama, have also revealed that shade-tolerant species of the forest understory are more drought-tolerant than light-demanding species that colonize treefall gaps (Robichaux et al. 1984).

Of the tree species that we planted in the pasture, those that were drought-tolerant also tended to avoid drought by rooting deeply. We excavated a sample of one-year-old seedlings of seven tree species and found that roots of most species were restricted to the upper 15 cm of soil while drought-tolerant palms, *Maximiliana maripa* and *Orbignya phalerata*, and two-year-old seedlings of *Radlkoferella macrocarpa* had rooted from 80 to 200 cm depth. The ability to avoid drought by rapidly developing a deep root system and thereby tapping deep soil moisture reserves may depend on the amount of carbohydrate and nutrient reserves contained in the seed. Large-seeded species, such as *M. maripa, O. phalerata*, and *R. macrocarpa*, are not as dependent on photosynthesis shortly after germination as are small-seeded species and can produce tap roots even before the shoots emerge. *M. maripa* and *O. phalerata* for example, have a "cryptogeal" mode of germination (*sensu* Jackson 1974), in which the germinating seed produces embryonic tissue that penetrates into soil; shoots and roots arise from meristems at the tip of these subterranean tissues, 10 to 30 cm below-ground.

Seedling drought tolerance and drought avoidance are associated with high rates of survival in the abandoned pasture. More than 90 percent of the seedlings of *M. maripa, O. phalerata*, and *R. macrocarpa* that established in the pasture during the wet season were still alive at the end of the dry season. In contrast, survival of seedlings with low drought tolerance and avoidance capacity was less than 10 percent for most species during the dry period, including seedling populations protected from *Atta sexdens*.

Although some tree seedlings can survive in the abandoned pasture, they grow very slowly (i.e., generally less than 10 cm per year). Since height growth did not appear to increase when the foliage of the pasture vegetation was pushed back (thereby increasing light intensity), we hypothesize that growth is limited in the pasture by belowground constraints. We tested the relative importance of soil fertility, soil strength, and root competition in a field experiment with seedlings of a forest tree, *Schizolobium amazonicum* Hub. ex Ducke. Competition with roots of pasture vegetation had the greatest effect on height growth of this species, suggesting that the vegetation of abandoned pastures restricts tree seedling growth by sequestering scarce soil resources.

Although large treefall gaps in forests can be considered environments of high resource availability for seedlings, abandoned, grass-dominated pastures are characterized by low resource levels near the ground. We have illustrated that low soil moisture availability during the dry season is limiting to the survival of some tree species and that the species most vulnerable to drought stress are small-seeded and light-demanding. In short, the species that are most likely to be deposited in the pasture are the least likely to survive.

The Role of Grasses

Directly or indirectly, grasses present barriers to tree seedlings at every step of establishment in abandoned pastures with histories of intensive use. Seed dispersal into grass-dominated vegetation is low because grasses do not attract birds and bats that eat fleshy fruits of forest trees. Grasses provide food and shelter for large populations of rodents that consume tree seeds and seedlings and create suitable living conditions for *A. sexdens* as well. The dense root systems of grasses produce severe soil moisture deficits during the dry season and compete for available soil nutrients. Finally, grasses favor fire so that tree seedlings that do surmount the numerous obstacles to establishment are periodically burned.

Seedling Establishment Nuclei in Abandoned Pastures

Abandoned pastures contain patches of woody vegetation that appear to be more amenable for tree seedling establishment. For example, a 6 m individual of *Stryphnodendron pulcherrimum* Hochr. has become a nucleus of natural forest regeneration at our research site through seedling establishment from other woody species and by way of new stems produced from root sprouts. We encountered several tree species and 150 new stems (root sprouts) of *S. pulcherrimum* within a 40-m radius of the original tree. Similarly, we have found seedlings of forest tree species within clumps of the liana, *Cordia multispicata* (I. Vieira, unpublished data). Tree seedling establishment is far greater within these patches of woody vegetation because they attract seed-carrying birds and/or bats and, perhaps, because some of the many impediments to seedling survival and growth are less severe there.

Synopsis

Because of its history of heavy use, the abandoned pasture seed bank has few forest species and there are few living tree root systems remaining from the forest. Therefore, establishment of forest trees depends on seed transported to the pasture from the forest. Bird and bat movement into the abandoned pasture is probably limited by the small number of plant species that produce fleshy fruits as well as the low stature of the pasture vegetation (i.e., there is a lack of food and perches in the pasture). Seed and seedling predation are particularly high in the pasture, largely because of the influence of *A. sexdens* and pasture rodents, which appear to prefer tree species over grassland herbs and shrubs. The dense root systems of grasses control belowground resources, outcompeting those tree seedlings that are unable to tolerate and avoid drought.

Tree seed size emerges as the best single predictor of colonization success in derived grasslands, as we illustrate in figure 14.4. Supposing that 1,000,000 seeds of a large-seeded tree species (e.g., *Radlkoferella macrocarpa*, 7.0 g) and a small-seeded tree species (e.g., *Bagassa guianensis*, 0.004 g) are broadcast into an abandoned, grass-dominated pasture, our field studies indicate that 40,000 *R. macrocarpa* seedlings will establish compared to <10 seedlings of *B. guianensis*. Whereas larger seeds have a greater probability of surviving at every stage of establishment, only smaller seeds have vectors by which to be dispersed into the pasture.

A Low-Capital, High-Information Strategy for Accelerating Forest Regrowth in Highly Degraded, Abandoned Pastures

There are many obvious ways in which people can intervene to facilitate tree establishment in abandoned, grass-dominated pastures. For example, we can plant nursery-grown seedlings of *Eucalyptus* into sites prepared by scraping away the pasture vegetation with bulldozers, tilling the soil and applying chemical fertil-

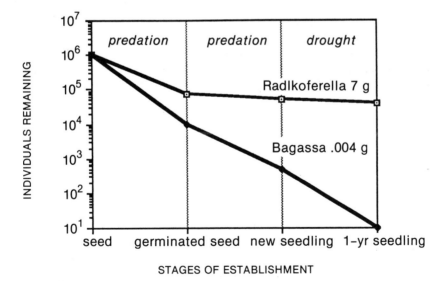

FIGURE 14.4. The predicted fate of 1,000,000 seeds of *Radlkoferella macrocarpa* and *Bagassa guianensis* placed in an abandoned, grass-dominated pasture from calculations based on field experiments. Note that the large-seeded species is strongly affected only by seed predation while the small-seeded species is strongly affected at every establishment stage.

izer. This procedure has been successfully used to establish tree plantations in Amazonia, but it has a serious drawback: It is very expensive.

An alternative strategy for encouraging forest regrowth in abandoned, grass-dominated pastures employs information from our studies in Paragominas. We sketch here a high-information, low-capital strategy for reforesting these ecosystems.

Site Preparation

Abandoned, grass-dominated pastures are inhospitable environments for young tree seedlings. The tree species that naturally invade abandoned pastures do so when the pasture vegetation is disturbed by fire or bulldozing. In a field experiment, for example, we found that establishment of *Solanum crinitum*, a common pasture shrub, occurred only after cutting and burning the pasture vegetation. Thus, the first step in reforesting an abandoned pasture should be in setting the ecosystem ablaze.

Although a single fire prepares the site for the introduction of tree propagules and seedlings, additional fires are undesirable since they may kill the young trees that are established. Site preparation must therefore include installation of fire-breaks. At our Paragominas study site, we make fire-breaks by cutting 10-m swaths of pasture vegetation around the study area, piling the cut vegetation in the middle of the swaths and burning the material. Fire breaks are an integral part of the reestablishment of dry forest in grass-dominated vegetation of Santa Rosa, Costa Rica (Janzen 1986).

Atta sexdens is a major impediment to tree establishment at our Paragominas study site and is an important seed and seedling predator in abandoned lands throughout tropical America. This insect must be given careful consideration in site preparation. If colony density is high, fungicidal baits (e.g., Mirex) can be placed to poison the fungal gardens of the colonies. Entrances to the colonies are easily spotted immediately following a burn. This poison has unknown long-term effects and should be used sparingly. Cheap alternatives to poison are urgently needed.

Species Selection

Several criteria should be used in selecting tree species for introduction into the prepared site. For direct seeding, species should have hard-coated, large (>5 g) seeds so as to have a high probability of escaping seed predators. Large seed size is probably also associated with the capacity to recover from defoliation and with rapid root penetration following germination. The species should be drought-tolerant, that is, it should have a low turgor loss point to improve survival during the dry season. The first species we plant in the prepared site must also be tolerant of full sun. We are currently screening more than 30 Amazon tree species for these traits.

We must plant trees that serve as establishment nuclei for forest species. Trees that produce abundant fruit for long periods each year can increase seed input into the pasture by attracting avifauna from nearby primary and secondary forest. Tree species should be included that attract large dispersal agents, such as agoutis, to encourage transport of large seeds into the abandoned pasture. Rapidly-growing trees can lure birds into the pasture by providing high perches. *Sclerolobium paraense* grew 2 m in 18 months in weeded (but not fertilized) plots at our research site and is a good candidate for reforestation efforts.

The incentive to plant trees in abandoned pastures is increased greatly if the trees are economically important. *Orbignya phalerata* ("babaçu") is in many ways an ideal candidate for use in abandoned pastures because 1) its large seeds contain high-quality oil and the fruit husks can be used to make charcoal; 2) its seeds are protected by a thick, hard shell and are invulnerable to many seed predators; 3) it produces deep roots rapidly; and 4) it is drought tolerant. The disadvantages of *O. phalerata* are that 1) it matures very slowly, taking several years to form a stem and at least 14 years to produce fruit (Anderson and Anderson 1983); and 2) it can form dense stands that are not easily invaded by other tree species.

Techniques for Establishing Trees

A mixture of tree species can best be achieved in a reforestation effort by fine-tuning the planting techniques to each species. Some types of trees, such as *O. phalerata*, require only fruit dispersal to establish and can presumably be started by flinging the fruits into the pasture vegetation. Seeds or seedlings that are vulnerable to predation by *A. sexdens* may have to be planted as stem or root cuttings, or as seedlings. All species probably benefit from practices that reduce competition for belowground resources. By burning the pasture vegetation as part of the site preparation, root competition should be dramatically reduced and ash should supply a pulse of nutrients to the soil. This effect is temporary, however. Long-term reduction of root competition for tree seedlings may best be achieved by planting the seedlings in holes filled with loose soil so that roots can rapidly penetrate below the zone of highly concentrated grass roots near the soil surface. Animals may provide a less labor-intensive means of reducing competition with grasses. In Santa Rosa, Costa Rica, cattle and horses fed with tree seeds are introduced to sites where trees are desired. The animals consume grass, thereby reducing competition, and disperse the seeds in nutrient- and moisture-rich microenvironments (Janzen 1986).

Another method for reducing root competition with tree seedlings is emerging from our studies of liana and tree patches. Seedling survival and growth may be enhanced considerably by simply planting within clumps of *Cordia multispicata* and other patch-forming woody species where root competition should be considerably lower than beneath grasses. Moreover, we are just beginning to explore ant nests and other microhabitats as appropriate seedling establishment sites.

Seedling establishment nuclei provide us with a model for initiating forest regeneration in abandoned pastures. They illustrate that reforestation projects will be most efficient if they initiate the formation of forest islands by establishing trees that attract dispersal agents, reduce competition from grasses, and create favorable microclimatic conditions for tree seedling establishment beneath their canopies. Forest is eventually formed by the coalescence of forest islands.

Strategies for accelerating forest regrowth should be designed to minimize the required inputs of capital and human labor and maximize the contribution of natural processes. We believe that abandoned, grass-dominated pastures can be reforested cheaply if we learn how to catalyze forest regeneration processes. The initial goal of reforestatation strategies should be the establishment of trees that attract a diversity of seed-carrying animals. As tree cover develops, more seed carriers will move between the forest and the pasture; grasses will eventually be shaded out, perhaps reducing populations of *A. sexdens* and rodents. Dry season soil moisture deficits and competition for soil nutrients should decrease as the dense root systems of the grassland ecosystem are replaced by those of the new forest. As tree cover is established, the flammability of the ecosystem will decline as well.

Implementation of the Reforestation Strategy

Who will reforest abandoned pastures? The answer to this question depends on the economic and cultural future of the Paragominas region. If ranchers continue to be the predominant managers of the Paragominas landscape, then they must be encouraged to facilitate forest regeneration on abandoned lands by establishing trees. While it is unlikely that many ranchers would show interest in planting trees in abandoned pastures, they might be encouraged to plant trees in active pastures if it can be demonstrated that such an undertaking is profitable because of the forage and shade provided by pasture trees. Inexpensive tree establishment techniques, based on knowledge of the barriers to tree establishment such as we have presented in this chapter, would increase the profitability of incorporating trees into cattle production systems. Once abandoned, tree-based cattle production systems should revert to forest much more rapidly than abandoned, grass-dominated pastures.

But the future of the ranching industry in the Paragominas region is uncertain. Government financial incentives for cattle production have been severely reduced and the rapid increases in land value that are needed to make ranching profitable in this region (Hecht, Norgaard, and Possio 1988) have tapered off. As the lumber that is presently being used to finance pasture reformation is depleted, cattle production will decline and more pastures will be abandoned. Only dramatic improvements in the sustainability (i.e., profitability) of cattle production through innovations described in Serrão and Toledo (this volume) might counteract this trend.

The new generation of land managers in the Paragominas landscape will hopefully be composed of innovative agriculturalists who implant a diversity of tree-based production systems on abandoned pastures. Through our studies at Fazenda Vitória, we believe that such a scenario is possible because the major limitation to tree growth in severely degraded pastures is not low soil fertility but, rather, a suite of biological factors that can be surmounted with creative—and potentially inexpensive—techniques. To the extent that agriculturalists incorporate trees into existing and future land uses, they contribute toward landscape restoration in Amazonia.

ACKNOWLEDGMENTS

The staff of EMBRAPA/CPATU, Belém, Brazil, provided invaluable support and assistance for this work. In addition, C. Pereira and O. Watrin assisted in the field and laboratory, respectively. The studies reported here were funded by grants from the National Geographic Society and the National Science Foundation.

REFERENCES

Anderson, A. B. and E. S. Anderson. 1983. People and the palm forest. Biology and utilization of babassu forests in Maranhão, Brazil. Final report to USDA Forest Service.

Caldwell, M. M. and J. H. Richards. 1986. Competing root systems: Morphology and models of absorption. In T. J. Givnish, ed., *On the Economy of Plant Form and Function*, pp. 251–273. Cambridge: Cambridge University Press.

Cheung, Y. N. S., M. T. Tyree, and J. Dainty. 1975. Water relations parameters on single leaves obtained in a pressure bomb and some ecological interpretations. *Canadian Journal of Botany* 53:1342–1346.

Denslow, J. S. 1987. Tropical rainforest gaps and tree species diversity. *Annual Review of Ecology and Systematics* 18:431–451.

Hecht, S. B., R. B. Norgaard, and G. Possio. 1988. The economics of cattle ranching in eastern Amazonia. *Interciencia* 13(5):233–240.

Jackson, G. 1974. Cryptogeal germination and other seedling adaptations to the burning of vegetation in savanna regions: The origin of the pyrophytic habit. *New Phytologist* 73:771–780.

Janzen, D. H. 1986. *Guanacaste National Park: Tropical Ecological and Cultural Restoration.* San José, Costa Rica: Editorial Universidad Estatal a Distancia.

Robichaux, R. H., P. W. Rundel, L. Stemmermann, J. E. Canfield, S. R. Morse, and W. E. Friedman. 1984. Tissue water deficits and plant growth in wet tropical environments. In E. Medina, H. A. Mooney and C. Vazques-Yanes, eds., *Physiological Ecology of Plants of the Wet Tropics*, pp. 99–112. Boston: Dr. W. Junk.

Turner, N. C. and M. M. Jones. 1980. Turgor maintenance by osmotic adjustment: A review and evaluation. In N. C. Turner and P. J. Kramer, eds., *Adaptation of Plants to Water and High Temperature Stress*, pp. 87–103. New York: Wiley.

Uhl, C. R., Buschbacher, and E. A. S. Serrão. 1988. Abandoned pastures in eastern Amazonia. I. Patterns of plant succession. *Journal of Ecology* 73:663–681.

5
IMPLICATIONS FOR REGIONAL DEVELOPMENT

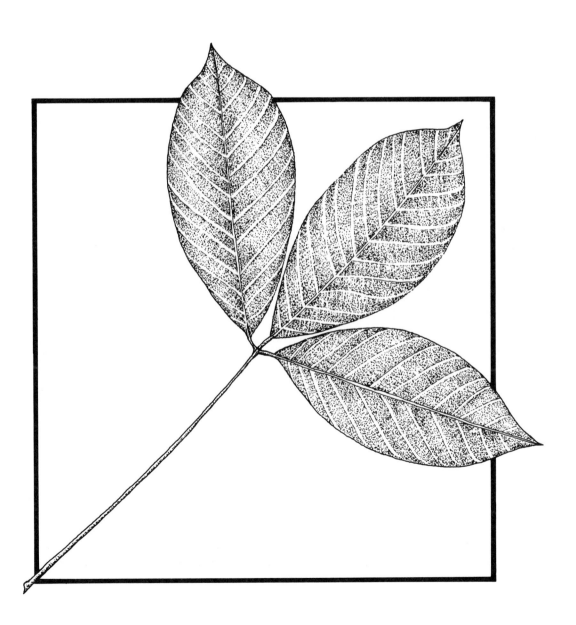

5. Implications for Regional Development.—The rubber tree (*Hevea brasiliensis* (Willd. ex A. Juss.) M. Arg.) is symbolic of the recent movement for establishment of extractive reserves in Amazonia. Hundreds of thousands of extractivists depend on wild rubber trees as their primary source of cash income. Such ecologically sustainable forms of livelihood hold potential for combining conservation and use of the Amazon rain forest.

15

Predominant Land Uses in Brazilian Amazonia

■

PHILIP M. FEARNSIDE

ABSTRACT

The land uses that now predominate in Brazilian Amazonia are unlikely to produce sustainable yields, and they also tend to close off potentially sustainable alternative uses. Cattle pastures—either functional or abandoned—now occupy most deforested land. Rather than beef production, the principal motive for planting pasture is often its low cost and high effectiveness as a means of securing speculative land claims. Pasture and cattle yields are low and, after use for about a decade, the planted grasses are outcompeted by secondary forest species or inedible grasses. Depletion of available phosphorus in the soil is a major cause of yield decline; Brazil's relatively modest phosphorus deposits, virtually all of which are outside of Amazonia, make fertilizer use unfeasible for the vast areas now rapidly being converted to pasture. Converting a substantial portion of Amazonia to pasture would have potential climatic effects. Areas that can be planted in annual and perennial crops are restrained by world markets, as well as by soil quality and Brazil's limited stocks of the inputs needed for intensive agriculture.

Recent research on land-use alternatives could be a first step toward changing predominant forms of land use in Brazilian Amazonia. Policies are urgently needed to slow deforestation, to discourage unsustainable uses, and to make sustainable alternatives profitable.

An ecological analysis of the predominant land uses in Amazonia indicates the urgent need to redirect the processes that are rapidly transforming the region's forests into unsustainable forms of development. Land uses should be promoted that are not only agriculturally sustainable but also economically and socially feasible. The landscape should be viewed as a patchwork of areas designed to fulfill distinct social and ecological functions, and where different economic and environmental criteria apply. In addition to agroecosystems, the landscape must contain substantial reserves of natural ecosystems, including those inhabited by indigenous peoples.

In practice, however, proposed development projects in Amazonia are rarely formulated on the basis of technical information concerning potential sustainability, environmental impacts, or even economic profitability. Instead, projects are often motivated by political factors (Fearnside 1984a, 1986a) and carried forward even in the face of technical evidence indicating their almost certain failure (Fearnside 1986b). For example, the prospects for sustainability, the long-term economic return to society, and the environmental and social impacts of cattle pasture all compare poorly with other land-use options (Fearnside 1983a). Yet it is precisely this most undesirable land use that dominates the occupied landscapes of Amazonia today.

Pasture Conversion

Causes

The dominant types of development vary greatly among different parts of the Amazon region (figure 15.1). The most widespread is cattle ranching, which has taken over the majority of the cleared land in areas like Mato Grosso and southern Pará. Satellite imagery indicates these areas are centers of deforestation (Tardin et al. 1980; Fearnside 1986c).

Ranching dominates the region not because it produces beef, but rather because of the attraction of fiscal incentives and especially because it is the cheapest way to secure land claims for speculative purposes (Mahar 1979; Fearnside 1979a, 1983b, 1987a; Hecht 1985). Incentives have allowed companies and individual investors from southern Brazil to apply a portion of the income tax owed on profits made elsewhere in the country to ranching schemes in Amazonia. Generous financing terms provide loans at rates below those of Brazilian inflation, thus creating a powerful motive to initiate the schemes even if beef production is negligible.

The Superintendency for Development of the Amazon (SUDAM), the agency responsible for the largest incentives program, altered its policies in 1979 to grant "new" incentives only to projects outside of Amazonia's "dense forest" area. Three major loopholes allow continued clearing with incentives: (1) the substantial areas of forest still being felled in "old" projects already approved for the subsidies (Hecht 1985); (2) the wide zone classified as "transition forest" where clearing is preferentially directed at dense forest interdigitated with "cerrado" (scrubland) vegetation (Dicks 1982); and (3) a very restrictive definition of what constitutes "dense forest" (Fearnside 1985a). Brazil's economic crisis in the 1980s has meant that less government money has been available than previously for cash contributions

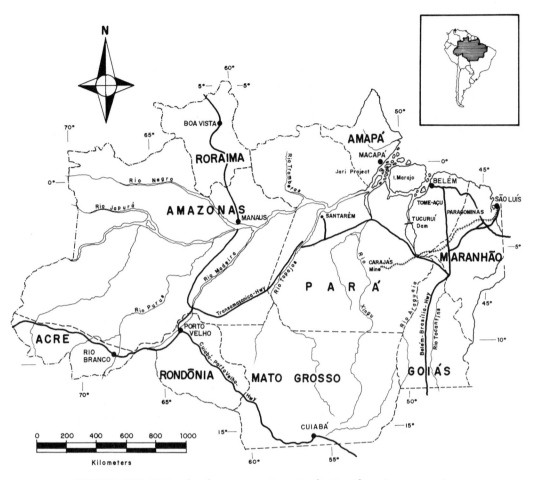

FIGURE 15.1. Major development projects in the Brazilian Amazon region.

to the ranching schemes, although subsidies continue through tax revenues the government forgoes under the fiscal incentives program.

Important as incentives are, pasture expands rapidly even in the absence of these windfalls. A LANDSAT satellite survey of 445,843 has cleared along the Belém-Brasília Highway indicated that 45.4 percent of this deforestation was done without incentives even in this highly subsidized ranching area (Tardin et al. 1978:19; see Fearnside 1979a). Land speculation provides ample motive for replacing forest with pasture even when little or no beef is produced. The value of Amazonian ranchland has consistently risen at rates exceeding inflation (Mahar 1979; Hecht 1985), motivating speculators to plant pasture so that the land will not be taken by squatters or by other ranchers. In the vast areas without legal documentation, pasture has the powerful additional attraction of being considered an improvement ("benfeitoria") that qualifies the rancher for title to the land.

Effects

Pasture has pernicious effects on Amazonian society. Ranching drives small farmers off the land, either by violence (Valverde and Dias 1967; Martins 1980; Schmink 1982) or by tempting smallholders to sell their plots to more wealthy newcomers (Fearnside 1984b; Coy 1987). Land tenure distribution becomes highly skewed toward large holdings with absentee owners. Only a minimal amount of employment is generated after the initial clearing phase is over. The beef produced is often exported from the area, bringing little benefit to local residents. The low productivity of pastures fuels inflation, since money is invested without a corresponding return of products to the marketplace; this creates a vicious cycle leading to greater speculative motive for pasture expansion (Fearnside 1987a).

The most worrisome characteristic of pasture conversion is that there is no immediate limit to its continuation. Unlike annual and especially perennial crops, market limits for the system's products are unlikely to halt its expansion: The demand for beef is tremendous and would be even greater if more meat were available. Nor does labor availability restrain pasture as it does other crops, because of low labor demands of the extensive systems used in Amazonia (Fearnside 1980a, 1986a). Pasture's dominance among land-use choices allows a small human population to exert maximum impact on regional forest ecosystems (Fearnside 1983b).

Soil Fertility. Pasture is not sustainable in the region without heavy and antieconomic inputs. Pasture grasses grow progressively more slowly following the first two or three years of use. Measurements of dry weight production over a full annual cycle in Ouro Preto do Oeste (Rondônia) indicate that a twelve-year-old pasture produces at about half the rate of a three-year-old pasture (Fearnside, unpublished data). Yields decline due to invasion by inedible weeds, soil compaction, and decreasing levels of available phosphorus in the soil (Fearnside 1979b, 1980b; Hecht 1981, 1983). Over the long term, erosion can be expected to further exhaust soil fertility: Measurements under various land uses at Ouro Preto do Oeste (Rondônia) and near Manaus (Amazonas) indicate that soil erosion rates in grazed pasture are much greater than in intact forest (Fearnside, unpublished data).

The necessity of phosphate fertilizers dampens the prospects for maintaining pasture over large areas of Amazonia. In the early 1970s, when the fiscal incentives program for Amazonian pastures was rapidly expanding, the agency that is now the Brazilian Enterprise for Agriculture and Cattle Ranching Research (EMBRAPA) maintained that pasture improved the soil (Falesi 1974, 1976). Unfortunately, available phosphorus declines sharply from the peak caused by ash from initial burning of the forest; after 10 years, levels of this critical element are at least as low as those under virgin forest and far below the amounts required by pasture grasses (Fearnside 1980b; Hecht 1981, 1983). In 1977 EMBRAPA changed its position that pasture improves the soil, recommending instead that productivity be maintained through annual applications of 50 kg/ha of phosphorus, equivalent to about 300 kg/ha of superphospate (Serrão and Falesi 1977; Serrão et al. 1979).

The much greater productivity of pasture when fertilized with phosphate is obvious (Koster, Khan, and Bosshart 1977). The problems are the cost of supplying phosphate and the absolute limits to mineable stocks of phosphate. Almost all of Brazil's phosphates are in the state of Minas Gerais, a site very distant from most of Amazonia. Brazil as a whole is not blessed with a particularly large stock of phosphate—the United States, for example, has deposits about 20 times larger (de Lima 1976). On a global scale, most phosphates are located in Africa (Sheldon 1982). Continuation of post–World War II trends in phosphate use would exhaust the world's stocks by the middle of the next century (Smith et al. 1972; United States, Council of Environmental Quality and Department of State 1980). Although simple extrapolation of these trends is questionable because of limits to continued human population increase at past rates (Wells 1976), Brazil would be wise to ponder carefully whether its remaining stocks of this limited resource should be allocated to Amazonian pastures.

Pests and Weeds. Large expanses of pasture can be expected to be subject to disease and insect outbreaks in the same way as other large monocultures. Switching the grass varieties planted can counter such problems to some extent, but the cost and frequency of such changes are likely to increase.

Brachiaria decumbens Stapf. ("braquiária"), a pasture grass formerly common on the Belém-Brasília Highway, was devastated in the early 1970s by outbreaks of the pasture spittlebug, known as "cigarrinha" (*Deois incompleta* Ceropidae). Guinea grass or "colonião" (*Panicum maximum* Jacq.) subsequently became a favorite in the area, and its performance was described by EMBRAPA as "magnificent" (Falesi 1974). Yield declines later became apparent with depletion of available phosphorus and increased invasion of weeds. Weed invasion in planted pastures of *Panicum maximum* is facilitated by the bunchy growth habit of this species, which leaves bare spaces between the tussocks of grass, and by poor germination of seeds produced by grass in the field. By the 1980s, the spittlebug had adapted to *Panicum maximum* as well, but not yet at the devastating levels reached in *Brachiaria decumbens*. Despite its disadvantages, *Panicum maximum* remains the most common pasture grass in Brazilian Amazonia today.

In the late 1970s, EMBRAPA began recommending creeping signal grass or "braquiária da Amazônia" (*Brachiaria humidicola* (Rendle) Schweickt.). This species was at first tolerant of spittlebug attack, but the insects have become increasingly well adapted to feeding on this species. EMBRAPA now recommends *Andropogon guianensis* Kunth pasture grass. The continual changing of species and fertilizer recommendations does not alter the basic characteristics of pasture that ultimately undermine its sustainability.

Climate. Conversion of a substantial fraction of Amazonia to pasture would have severe impacts on regional and global climate. Global warming from the "greenhouse effect" caused by increasing CO_2 in the atmosphere would have its greatest effect in temperate and arctic latitudes rather than in Amazonia itself. Were all of the five million square kilometers of Brazilian Amazonia converted from its original vegetation to cattle pasture, 50 billion metric tons (50 gigatons) of carbon would be released (Fearnside 1985b, 1986d, 1987b). Were the conversion to pasture to take place over a span of 50 years—which is conservative considering the pace of conversion in the past two decades (Fearnside 1982, 1986c; Fearnside and Salati 1985)—carbon would be released at a rate of one gigaton per year over the coming decades. Since global release of carbon from all sources has been taking place at the rate of about five gigatons per year (Bolin et al. 1979), the release from conversion to pasture in the Brazilian portion of Amazonia alone could contribute on the order of one fifth of the total to this serious global problem. Potential consequences include a redistribution of rainfall patterns around the world, with the result that many of the earth's present agriculture breadbaskets would become drier, and a rise in mean sea level by up to five meters, thereby flooding both a portion of Amazonia and many centers of human population.

A second climatic consequence of massive conversion to pasture would be a decrease in rainfall in Amazonia and in neighboring regions. Various lines of evidence indicate that half of the rainfall in Amazonia is derived from water that recycles through the forest as evapotranspiration, rather than from water vapor in clouds originating over the Atlantic Ocean (Molion 1975; Villa Nova, Salati, and Matusi 1976; Marques et al. 1977; Salati, Marques, and Molion 1978). Only by seeing the Amazon River at flood season can one fully appreciate the immense volume of water involved: What one sees in the river is the same volume that is returning unseen to the atmosphere through the leaves of the forest. That the leaves of the forest are constantly giving off water is evident to anyone who has tied a plastic bag over a handful of leaves: in only a few minutes the inside of the bag is covered with water droplets condensed from evapotranspiration. Summing over the several hundred billion trees in Amazonia, a vast amount of water is returned to the atmosphere. Since evapotranspiration is proportional to leaf area, the water recycled through forest is much greater than that recycled through pasture, especially in the dry season when the pasture is dry while the forest remains evergreen. This difference is accentuated by the much higher runoff under pasture. Increases in runoff by one order of magnitude have been measured near Manaus (Amazonas), Altamira (Pará), and Ouro Preto do Oeste (Rondônia) (Fearnside, unpublished data). Soil under pasture quickly becomes highly compacted, inhibiting infiltration of rainwater into the soil (Schubart, Junk, and Petrere 1976; Dantas 1979). Rain falling on the compacted soil runs off quickly, becoming unavailable for later release to the atmosphere through transpiration.

The potential damage of lowered rainfall for the remaining natural ecosystems is indicated by the seasonal and spatial variations in water vapor found by Salati, Marques, and Molion (1978) and Salati et al. (1979). The relative contribution of recycled water to rainfall is greatest in the dry season, and increases as one moves farther away from the Atlantic Ocean. This means that in the western states of Rondônia and Acre, where rapid deforestation is taking place, the proportion of rainfall derived from forest could be much higher than the roughly 50 percent average for Amazonia as a whole. The greater dependence in the dry season means that conversion to pasture may cause this period to become longer and more severe, a change that could wreak havoc on the forest even if the annual precipitation total were to remain unchanged. Many rain forest trees are already at their limits of tolerance for drought stress (Nepstad, Uhl, and Serrão, this volume). In patches of forest isolated by cattle pasture near Manaus, the trees on the edges of forest patches die at a much greater rate than do those in continuous forest (Lovejoy et al. (1984). Since many of these trees die "on their feet" rather than being toppled by wind, the dry condition in the air or soil near the reserve edges is a likely explanation for the mortality. Precipitation in Amazonia is characterized by tremendous variability from one year to the next, even in the absence of massive deforestation (Fearnside 1984c). Were the forest's contribution to dry season rainfall to decrease, the result would probably be a very severe drought once in every 20 to 50 years that would kill many trees of susceptible species. Since Amazonian forest trees live upwards of 200 years, the probability would be much higher that they would encounter an intolerably dry year sometime during their lifespan. The result would be replacement of the tropical moist forest with more drought-tolerant forms of scrubby, open vegetation resembling the "cerrado" of central Brazil (Fearnside 1979c). Such a change could set in motion a positive feedback process leading to less dense forests that transpire less, increasing the severity of droughts, thereby causing even more tree mortality and forest thinning (Fearnside 1985c).

If a substantial portion of the region were converted to pasture, the severe droughts provoked by deforestation could threaten the remaining tracts of forest. In Amazonia at present, burning is almost entirely restricted to areas where trees have been felled and allowed to dry before being set ablaze. The fire stops burning when it reaches the clearing edge rather than continuing into unfelled forest. This fortuitous situation, however, could change. In forested areas that have been disturbed by logging along the Belém-Brasília Highway, fires from neighboring pastures have already been observed to continue substantial distances into standing forest (Uhl and Buschbacher 1985). During 1982–1983 (an unusually dry year because of the El Niño phenomenon), approximately 45,000 km^2 of tropical forest on the island of Borneo burned when fires escaped from shifting cultivators' fields (Malingreau, Stephens, and Fellows 1985). At least 8,000 km^2 of the 35,000 km^2 burned in the Indonesian province of East Kalimantan was primary forest, while 12,000 km^2 was selectively logged forest (Malingreau, Stephens, and Fellows 1985). Devastation would be catastrophic should fires such as this occur in Amazonia during one of the droughts aggravated by deforestation.

Other Regional Land Uses

Pioneer Agriculture

Indigenous peoples have been supporting themselves for millennia through shifting cultivation and exploitation of animal and plant resources in natural habitats. These systems are vanishing as Luso-Brazilians continue to take lands away from indigenous groups, in addition to the decreases in tribal populations caused by violent conflicts, infectious diseases, and acculturation. The idea that there exist "lands without men" waiting to be occupied in Amazonia is a myth: all of the region's land can be considered already occupied, if not by Luso-Brazilians, then by indigenous peoples.

Colonization by small farmers is concentrated in certain parts of the region, with modes of organization that vary from place to place. Colonists were installed in government projects on the Transamazon Highway in the state of Pará and in colonization areas in Rondônia (Fearnside 1986b; Moran 1981; Smith 1982). In the Grande Carajás Program area, various government projects settled farmers at an accelerated pace in an attempt to reduce land conflicts (Fearnside 1986e). In northern Mato Grosso, colonization is organized by private enterprises that sell parcels of land to farmers and provide them with roads and other infrastructure. Spontaneous settlement is important in areas receiving intense influxes of migrants, such as Rondônia, Acre, and southern Pará. These are all centers of intense deforestation.

The pioneer agriculture practiced by settlers is usually based on annual crops such as rice. These crops are planted for one or two years before the field is either allowed to revert to secondary forest or converted to cattle pasture. Unlike indigenous peoples, pioneer farmers do not have the cultural tradition of leaving their previously cultivated fields in secondary forest for a sufficient time to restore soil quality. The fallow periods used are usually too short to make the system sustainable as a form of shifting cultivation (Fearnside 1984b). Soil degradation through erosion occurs during the cropping phase (Fearnside 1980c). A variety of problems associated with soil fertility, insects, vertebrate pests, weeds, weather, transportation and marketing make returns to the farmers highly uncertain (Smith 1978; Fearnside 1986a). Prolonged use in shifting cultivation-like agriculture can lead to soil degradation and replacement of the area by unproductive secondary forests, as has occurred in the Zona Bragantina in Pará (Egler 1961; Ackermann 1966; Penteado 1967; Sioli 1973).

Under shifting cultivation, fallow plots are usually dominated by woody secondary forest species such as *Cecropia* and *Vismia*. This may not always remain the case. In southeast Asia, for example, fallow plots with an area of more than about 100 m² are usually dominated by grasses such as the very aggressive *Imperata cylindrica* L. (Richards 1964). In the Gran Pajonal of Peru, the less-aggressive neotropical relative *Imperata brasiliensis* Trin. dominates fallows for an extended period (Scott 1978). On heavily degraded sites in Amazonia, succession could come to resemble more closely that of southeast Asia. Diversion to a grass dysclimax would both diminish the regeneration of site quality for agriculture and increase the climatic and other impacts of deforestation.

Pioneer farmers have been overshadowed by large ranchers and speculators in many parts of Brazilian Amazonia. Even in pioneer areas, cattle pasture soon becomes the predominant land use (Fearnside 1983b; Leite and Furley 1985; Léna 1986; Coy 1987). The relative importance of pioneer farmers could increase greatly if the Brazilian government's agrarian reform program goes forward on a large scale. Agrarian reform usually implies redistributing large landholdings, but owners of these properties understandably exert strong pressure to have the program redirected to a distribution of public lands. Since virtually all of Brazil's public land is located in Amazonia, such a redefinition of "agrarian reform" would equate the term with what in past decades has been known as "colonization." Brazil has an estimated ten million landless rural families; since the Legal Amazon has an area of five million square kilometers, a complete distribution of the region including forest and indigenous reserves, parks, and privately owned land would yield only one half square kilometer, or 50 ha, per family. This is half the size of lots distributed in colonization schemes of the 1970s and is equal to the size of lots distributed in recent projects in Rondônia—all of which have severe agricultural problems. Agrarian reform must be addressed in the regions where the population is now located, rather than in Amazonia (Fearnside 1985d).

Logging

Logging has been rapidly increasing in areas of Amazonia relatively accessible to Brazilian markets and ports. Southern and eastern Pará, northern Mato Grosso, and Rondônia are presently experiencing an unprecedented explosion in the number of sawmills. This exploitation has been taking place without any attempts to manage the forests for sustainable production of timber.

Although the area now influenced by logging is unknown, the most valuable species are sought from all accessible forest in the region. In areas nearer markets, the list of species exploited lengthens. The rapid spread of highways has opened up vast new lands to logging, including those on the previously inaccessible borders of Brazil and Peru. Logging is one of the principal forms of disturbance in indigenous reserves in Rondônia and Acre.

Timber exploitation has so far been limited by competition from logging in southeast Asia, where tropical forests are characterized by a higher density of commercially valuable trees. Southeast Asian forests are dominated by a single plant family (Dipterocarpaceae), making it possible to group the vast number of individual tree species into only six categories for the purposes of sawing and marketing. In addition, most Asian woods are light in color, making them more valuable in Europe and North America where consumers are accustomed to light woods such as oak and maple. Amazonia's generally dark-colored, hard-to-saw, and extremely heterogeneous timber has therefore been spared the pressure of large multinational timber corporations. The approaching end to commercially significant stocks of tropical timber in Asia can be expected to change this situation radically.

Wood removal for charcoal is a new addition to major land uses in Amazonia. The Grande Carajás Program offers incentives to charcoal production for use in pig-iron mills; the first began operation on January 8, 1988. So far incentives have been granted for eleven industries planned to function with charcoal: seven for pig-iron, two for iron alloy, and two for cement. At least twenty pig-iron mills are planned. Although official statements often mention silvicultural plantations as a future wood source for charcoal, the native forest appears to be the most likely source. At least in theory, firms are required to obtain the wood used for charcoal from sustainable sources after a given period. At present, their principal source is wood from lands being clearcut for pasture. As this source becomes exhausted in the area of the mills, the charcoal suppliers are supposed to mount "forestry management" schemes. Experiments are underway at Buriticupu (Maranhão) to measure growth after wood removal at a variety of intensities, including clearcutting (Jesus 1984; Jesus, Menandro, and Thibau 1984; Thibau 1985). It is possible that charcoal suppliers will clearcut native forest and then allow the areas to regenerate in secondary forest as a form of "forestry management." Such an interpretation of what constitutes "forestry management" would allow firms to avoid the onus of investing in more costly systems. If, after free wood from native forest has been exhausted it then is suddenly discovered that the "forestry management" plans are uneconomic or unproductive, the firms could scrap or move their equipment, and simply take their profits and leave.

Extraction of Forest Products

Extraction of forest products such as rubber and Brazil nuts has supported human populations in the Amazonian interior since long before the present massive migration to the region. These systems can produce indefinitely, so long as the products are extracted with the minimal precautions already known to rubber tappers and Brazil nut gatherers in the region. At present the principal problems impeding maintenance of the systems are: low economic return in comparison with short-term profits derived from deforestation (especially profits from real estate speculation), and the inability of the extractivists to secure their claims to the land in the face of appropriation by ranchers or squatters.

The present trend has been for more and more extractive areas to be appropriated by ranchers, speculators, squatters, and colonization programs. This process is sometimes concentrated in the most productive areas because of the bureaucratic advantage conferred by existing documentation of the claims of rubber and Brazil nut "barons" (Bunker 1980). The shrinking of extractive areas may not continue unopposed: Rubber gatherers have organized themselves to press for legal recognition of "extractive reserves" (Schwartzman and Allegretti 1987; Allegretti, this volume). These areas would be defended against invasion and would be shared by traditional extractivists. Possible improvements include enrichment of the forest with trees producing marketable products and expanding the range of products exploited.

A key factor in making the extractive reserve scheme viable is the price of rubber. Rubber in Brazil is heavily subsidized by government pricing policies. Because *Microcyclus* fungus does not exist in southeast Asia, plantation rubber is inherently cheaper to produce there than it is in Amazonia. World rubber markets have been depressed in the 1980s to the point where many productive plantations in Indonesia and Malaysia have been cut to replant with other crops. Brazil imports two thirds of its rubber; the remaining third is produced within the country and bought at a price that, although low from the point of view of rubber tappers, is far above that of international commodity markets. The difference represents a subsidy that is being paid by Brazilian consumers when buying products made of rubber. A subsidy of this kind can be conceded so long as the amount of rubber produced in Brazil remains relatively small. The same subsidy goes to the owners of rubber plantations that are now expanding in the Northeast and Center-South regions of the country.

The great advantage of the extractive reserve system is that it maintains the forest's environmental functions and genetic resources. It also serves an important social function for the traditional extractivists that have so far been the victims of expulsion and economic marginalization. If designed to abut Amerindian reserves, extractive reserves could play an additional role in buffering these against invasion. These factors—which would be labeled by economists as "externalities," implying that they are peripheral benefits—are in this case the principal product while the rubber produced is a mere windfall. Means of assigning values to the long-term and nonmonetary benefits of extractive reserves are urgently needed, as a basis for determining policies in relation to this land use.

Silviculture

Silviculture has been implanted in the Jari Project, where yields have been lower than those expected by the project's designers, as well as by planners who have suggested it as an appropriate model for larger initiatives in other parts of the region. Based on the yields at Jari, it can be calculated that plantations of *Eucalyptus* in the Grande Carajás Program would have to total almost ten times the planted area at Jari in order to supply charcoal to the 20 pig-iron plants, plus associated industries, planned for the area (Fearnside 1988a). Biological problems associated with the scale of the plantations, such as pests and diseases, would be likely in these vast stands of *Eucalyptus* (Fearnside and Rankin 1982a).

Perennial Crops

Despite government research, financing, and extension programs, plantations of cacao, coffee, rubber, black pepper, oil palm, and other perennial crops occupy only a very small fraction of the region. Official interest in these crops is high because of their perceived potential for sustained production, and because they produce goods for export for foreign exchange. Perennial crops that cover the soil, such as cacao and rubber, offer better prospects of avoiding soil erosion and other forms of degradation in already deforested areas. However, expansion of these crops on a large scale is improbable because of losses caused by fungal diseases and the limited capacity of world markets to absorb the increased production (Fearnside 1984d, 1985d).

Plant diseases are a major limitation of perennial crops. The much longer life cycle of trees relative to disease-causing fungi means that pathogens can evolve means of overcoming disease resistance faster than plant breeders can obtain new varieties (Janzen 1973). When attacked, the cost of replacing treecrops with new species or varieties is greater than for annuals. Diseases in perennial crops include the South American Leaf Blight or SALB (*Microcyclus ulei* (P. Henn.) v. Aix) in rubber, witches' broom (*Crinipellis perniciosa* (Stahel) Singer) in cacao, and Margarita disease (*Fusarium solani* f. *piperi* (Mart.) App. & Wr.) in black pepper. Establishment of a perennial crop on a new continent often provides effective but temporary protection against disease. This protection is absent for crops native to Amazonia such as rubber and cacao, but it has been effective in recent arrivals like black pepper and oil palm. The honeymoon period for black pepper ended, however, when *Fusarium* arrived in Brazil in 1960 and spread rapidly through widely scattered pepper growing areas in the 1970s (Fearnside 1980d). Oil palm plantations near Belém began experiencing an outbreak of shoot rot disease in 1987, but this has not yet reached the larger plantation in Tefé (Amazonas) (J. Dubois, pers. comm. 1987).

Floodplain Settlement

The "várzea" (whitewater floodplain), which covers approximately 2 percent of the Amazon Basin, is occupied in large measure by small holders raising subsistence crops and fiber crops such as jute (*Corchorus* spp.) and malva (*Malva rotundifolia* L.). Mechanized cultivation of irrigated rice is presently limited to the Jari Project plantations (see Fearnside and Rankin 1980, 1982b, 1985). In areas such as Marajó Island and in the Jari Project, water buffalo raising is increasing. This activity, which generates income for absentee investors more readily than does the small-scale agriculture it frequently replaces, is being encouraged through government programs in the state of Amazonas.

The principal advantage of the floodplain is its annual renewal of soil fertility by the deposition of silt during the high water period. Its principal disadvantage is the necessity of vacating extensive areas during the high-water period, and the uncertainty of the height and duration of each phase of the river cycle. Increased deforestation will increase this risk by provoking higher and more irregular floods, although the lower river levels at low water will expose more land. Despite these limitations, the floodplain has far greater potential than the unflooded uplands for cultivation of short-cycle crops.

Experimental Systems

Although experimental systems are not to be confused with predominant land uses, it is important to consider whether any of the systems now under development are likely to expand to a significant extent in the region. One must be careful not to allow extended discussion of experimental or "model" systems to obscure the fact that degraded pasture is the predominant land use (see exchange of views between Revelle 1987 and Fearnside 1987c). The existence of systems with "promising prospects" in no way substitutes for effecting structural changes to discourage the rush to convert forest to unsustainable cattle pasture.

Various experiments have been undertaken to develop sustainable systems of production in Amazonia. Fertilized pasture has been tested in Brazil and in Peru (Koster, Kahn, and Bosshart 1977; Serrão and Falesi 1977; Serrão et al. 1979). Although production on a per-area basis is much higher than in pasture without treatment, the amount of labor necessary to maintain the pasture free of weeds is uneconomic and the high cost and limited availability of fertilizers would prevent the system's application on the vast scale that would be needed to treat the areas of degraded pasture in the region (Fearnside 1979b, 1980a, 1985d). More recent experimental approaches to pasture recuperation are still under analysis (see Nepstad, Uhl, and Serrão, this volume; Serrão and Toledo, this volume), but none has been shown to be economically viable.

A system to make sustainable the continuous cultivation of annual crops is under testing at Yurimaguas, Peru (Sánchez et al. 1982; Nicholaides et al. 1983, 1984, 1985). Despite the enthusiasm for the results expressed in publications of the research group responsible for the trials, serious doubts exist regarding the economic viability of the system, its applicability in many areas of the region, and its suitability for use with the shifting cultivators who are identified as the system's intended beneficiaries. The system requires heavy applications of fertilizers, the doses of which are constantly adjusted for each field according to results from analysis of soil samples. The infrastructure that would be necessary to analyze these samples and communicate the results would greatly impede widespread use of the system. Even with the subsidized inputs in the experimental program at Yurimaguas, the system has not proved economically attractive (Fearnside 1987d).

Other systems under testing include different forms of agroforestry (reviewed by Hecht 1982). These systems frequently mimic the natural succession by substituting secondary forests that occupy the fields during the fallow period with plantations of economically valuable trees. A number of interplanting combinations have been devised to make the best use of the light and nutrients. These include intercropping with nitrogen-fixing legumes and alley cropping, in which rows of annual crops alternate with rows of deep-rooted perennial shrubs that minimize the losses of nutrients to leaching (Dickinson 1972; Kass 1978; Fearnside 1988b). Other regional systems utilize diversified plantings of fruit trees and other arboreal species (Alcorn, this volume; Subler and Uhl, this volume). Agroforestry systems appear to be especially suited land-use alternatives for areas that have already been deforested in Amazonia. For areas still covered with primary forest, however, land uses that maintain this cover would be preferable.

Research on the management of Amazonian forest for sustained production is still in its infancy. Systems under testing include the removal of different percentages of the basal area of the forest, leaving the smaller trees for subsequent harvests after they have grown to the requisite minimum size (Carvalho 1980, 1984, 1985; de Graaf and Poels, this volume). Other systems include the poisoning of low-value trees in order to accelerate the growth of the remaining commercialy valuable species (e.g., Jonkers and Schmidt 1984; Sarrailh and Schmitt 1984), removal of vines or other undesirable components, and enrichment of the forest through planting seeds or seedlings of commercial species. One system for producing charcoal removes the smaller trees to permit recolonization by fast-growing species (Jesus, Menandro, and Thibau 1984; Thibau 1985); the most extreme treatments, however, are clearcutting or nearly clearcutting of the forest. The sustainability of this latter practice is far from proven (Fearnside 1989). Finally, a system under testing in Peru for hardwood timber production involves cutting the forest in strips to permit recolonization by native species coming from strips that are left in forest (Hartshorn, this volume).

Alternative Policies

So far no system has been developed that is attractive for the bulk of lowland Amazonia under present economic conditions. Accelerated research, along with increased preservation, are necessary to guarantee future implementation of forest management when economic conditions provide greater value to products that the forest can produce sustainably. Policy changes are required both within and outside the region (Sawyer, this volume).

The first questions that need to be addressed when delineating plans for regional development are: "for whom?" and "for how long?" is this development to serve. Although not usually the case, I suggest that "for whom" should refer to the residents of the region and to their descendants, and "for how long" should mean for an indefinite period. Even though Amazonia is geographically immense, it is not capable of solving the problems of other regions, such as lack of effective land reform, which is the cause of much of the current wave of migration to Amazonia. Such problems can be solved only in the areas where they originate.

Deforestation can be slowed by implementing major policy changes including: (1) halting road building in Amazonia; (2) ending subsidies to the region from country-wide price standardization for petroleum products, electricity, and other items; (3) abolishing all direct and indirect subsidies for pasture and other non-sustainable land uses; (4) levying heavy taxes on speculative profits from land sales; (5) ceasing to recognize pasture establishment as a basis for legitimizing land claims; (6) carrying out agrarian reform by redistribution of large private landholdings; (7) slowing population growth; and (8) creating urban employment opportunities in the regions from which migrants are now being forced to leave for Amazonia.

Without these changes, the chance will be lost to break the chain of events that inexorably leads to predominant land uses that are unsustainable, unproductive, and economically and socially undesirable.

ACKNOWLEDGMENTS

I thank Summer Wilson, Anthony Anderson, and three anonymous reviewers for comments on the manuscript.

REFERENCES

Ackermann, F. L. 1966. *A Depredação dos Solos da Região Bragantina e na Amazônia.* Belém: Universidade Federal do Pará.

Bolin, B., E. T. Degens, P. Duvigneaud, and S. Kempe. 1979. The global biogeochemical carbon cycle. In B. Bolin, E. T. Degens, S. Kempe, and P. Ketner, eds., *The Global Carbon Cycle,* pp. 1–56. Scientific Committee on Problems of the Environment (SCOPE) Report No. 13. New York: Wiley.

Bunker, S. G. 1980. Forces of destruction in Amazônia. *Environment* 22(7):14–43.

Carvalho, J. O. P. de. 1980. Inventário diagnóstico da regeneração natural da vegetação em área da Floresta Nacional do Tapajós. Empresa Brasileira de Pesquisa Agropecuária (EMBRAPA)-Centro de Pesquisa Agropecuária do Trópico Úmido (CPATU) *Boletim de Pesquisa* No. 2. Belém: EMBRAPA-CPATU.

Carvalho, J. O. P. de. 1984. Manejo de regeneração natural de espécies florestais. Empresa Brasileira de Pesquisa Agropecuária (EMBRAPA)-Centro de Pesquisa Agropecuária do Trópico Úmido (CPATU) *Documentos* No. 34. Belém: EMBRAPA-CPATU.

Carvalho, J. O. P. de. 1985. Resultados de pesquisa da EMBRAPA/IBDF-PNPF sobre manejo de floresta no trópico úmido brasileiro. Paper presented at the 1° Seminário Internacional sobre Manejo em Florestas Tropicais, Serra dos Carajás & São Luis, 28 January–1 February 1985. (Manuscript.)

Coy, M. 1987. Rondônia: Frente pioneira e Programa POLONOROESTE. O processo de diferenciação sócio-econômica na periferia e os limites do planejamento público. In G. Kohlhepp and A. Schrader, eds., *Homem e Natureza na Amazônia*, pp. 253–270. Tübinger Geographische Studien 95 (Tübinger Beiträge zur Geographischen Lateinamerika-Forschung 3). Tübingen, F. R. Germany: Geographisches Institut, Universität Tübingen.

Dantas, M. 1979. Pastagens da Amazonia Central: Ecologia e fauna de solo. *Acta Amazonica* 9(2) suplemento: 1–54.

Dickinson, J. C. III. 1972. Alternatives to monoculture in the humid tropics of Latin America. *Professional Geographer* 24(3):215–222.

Dicks, S. E. 1982. *The Use of LANDSAT Imagery for Monitoring Forest Cover Alteration in Xinguara, Brazil*. Master's thesis. Gainsville: University of Florida.

Egler, E. G. 1961. A Zona Bragantina do Estado do Pará. *Revista Brasileira de Geografia* 23(3):527–555.

Falesi, I. C. 1974. O solo na Amazônia e sua relação com a definição de sistemas de produção agrícola. In Empresa Brasileira de Pesquisas Agropecuárias (EMBRAPA). *Reunião do Grupo Interdisciplinar de Trabalho sobre Diretrizes de Pesquisa Agrícola para a Amazônia (Trópico Úmido), Brasília, Maio 6–10, 1974*, vol. 1, pp. 2.1–2.11. Brasília: EMBRAPA.

Falesi, I. C. 1976. *Ecossistema de Pastagem Cultivada na Amazônia Brasileira*. Boletim Técnico No. 1. Belém: Centro de Pesquisa Agropecuária do Trópico Úmido (CPATU).

Fearnside, P. M. 1979a. The development of the Amazon rain forest: Priority problems for the formulation of guidelines. *Interciencia* 4(6):338–343.

Fearnside, P. M. 1979b. Cattle yield prediction for the Transamazon Highway of Brazil. *Interciencia* 4(4):220–225.

Fearnside, P. M. 1979c. O processo de desertificação e os riscos de sua ocorrencia no Brasil. *Acta Amazonica* 9(2):393–400.

Fearnside, P. M. 1980a. The effects of cattle pastures on soil fertility in the Brazilian Amazon: Consequences for beef production sustainability. *Tropical Ecology* 21(1):125–137.

Fearnside, P. M. 1980b. Land use allocation of the Transamazon Highway colonists of Brazil and its relation to human carrying capacity. In F. Barbira-Scazzocchio, ed., *Land, People and Planning in Contemporary Amazonia*, pp. 114–138. Cambridge University Centre of Latin American Studies Occasional Paper No. 3. Cambridge: Cambridge University.

Fearnside, P. M. 1980c. The prediction of soil erosion losses under various land uses in the Transamazon Highway Colonization Area of Brazil. In J. I. Furtado, ed., *Tropical Ecology and Development: Proceedings of the 5th International Symposium of Tropical Ecology, 16–21 April 1979, Kuala Lumpur, Malaysia*, pp. 1287–1295. Kuala Lumpur, Malaysia: International Society for Tropical Ecology-ISTE.

Fearnside, P. M. 1980d. Black pepper yield prediction for the Transamazon Highway of Brazil. *Turrialba* 30(1):35–42.

Fearnside, P. M. 1982. Deforestation in the Brazilian Amazon: How fast is it occurring? *Interciencia* 7(2):82–88.

Fearnside, P. M. 1983a. Development alternatives in the Brazilian Amazon: An ecological evaluation. *Interciencia* 8(2):65–78.

Fearnside, P. M. 1983b. Land use trends in the Brazilian Amazon Region as factors in accelerating deforestation. *Environmental Conservation* 10(2):141–148.

Fearnside, P. M. 1984a. Brazil's Amazon settlement schemes: Conflicting objectives and human carrying capacity. *Habitat International* 8(1):45–61.

Feaernside, P. M. 1984b. Land clearing behaviour in small farmer settlement schemes in the Brazilian Amazon and its relation to human carrying capacity. In A. C. Chadwick and S. L. Sutton, eds., *Tropical Rain Forest: The Leeds Symposium*, pp. 255–271. Leeds, U. K.: Leeds Philosophical and Literary Society.

Fearnside, P. M. 1984c. Simulation of meteorological parameters for estimating human carrying capacity in Brazil's Transamazon Highway colonization area. *Tropical Ecology* 25(1):134–142.

Fearnside, P. M. 1984d. A floresta vai acabar? *Ciência Hoje* 2(10):42–52.

Fearnside, P. M. 1985a. Deforestation and decision-making in the development of Brazilian Amazonia. *Interciencia* 10(5):243–247.

Fearnside, P. M. 1985b. Brazil's Amazon forest and the global carbon problem. *Interciencia* 10(4):179–186.

Fearnside, P. M. 1985c. Environmental change and deforestation in the Brazilian Amazon. In J. Hemming, ed., *Change in the Amazon Basin: Man's Impact on Forests and Rivers*, pp. 70–89. Manchester, U. K.: Manchester University Press.

Fearnside, P. M. 1985d. Agriculture in Amazonia. In G. T. Prance and T. E. Lovejoy, eds., *Key Environments: Amazonia*, pp. 393–418. Oxford, U. K.: Pergamon Press.

Fearnside, P. M. 1986a. *Human Carrying Capacity of the Brazilian Rainforest*. New York: Columbia University Press.

Fearnside, P. M. 1986b. Settlement in Rondônia and the token role of science and technology in Brazil's Amazonian development planning. *Interciencia* 11(5):229–236.

Fearnside, P. M. 1986c. Spatial concentration of deforestation in the Brazilian Amazon. *Ambio* 15(2):72–79.

Fearnside, P. M. 1986d. Brazil's Amazon forest and the global carbon problem: Reply to Lugo and Brown. *Interciencia* 11(2):58–64.

Fearnside, P. M. 1986e. Agricultural plans for Brazil's Grande Carajás Program: Lost opportunity for sustainable development? *World Development* 14(3):385–409.

Fearnside, P. M. 1987a. Causes of deforestation in the Brazilian Amazon. In R. F. Dickinson, ed., *The Geophysiology of Amazonia: Vegetation and Climate Interactions*, pp. 37–53. New York: Wiley.

Fearnside, P. M. 1987b. Summary of progress in quantifying the potential contribution of Amazonian deforestation to the global carbon problem. In D. Athie, T. E. Lovejoy, and P. de M. Oyens, eds., *Proceedings of the Workshop on Biogeochemistry of Tropical Rain Forests: Problems for Research*, pp. 75–82. Piracicaba, São Paulo: Universidade de São Paulo, Centro de Energia Nuclear na Agricultura (CENA).

Fearnside, P. M. 1987c. Reply to comments. In R. F. Dickinson, ed., *The Geophysiology of Amazonia: Vegetation and Climate Interactions*, pp. 57–61. New York: Wiley.

Fearnside, P. M. 1987d. Rethinking continuous cultivation in Amazonia. *BioScience* 37(3):209–214.

Fearnside, P. M. 1988a. Jari at age 19: Lessons for Brazil's silvicultural plans at Carajás. *Interciencia* 13(1):12–24.

Fearnside, P. M. 1988b. Prospects for sustainable agricultural development in tropical forests. In *ISI Atlas of Science: Animal and Plant Sciences*. Philadelphia, Pennsylvania: Institute for Scientific Information (ISI) (in press).

Fearnside, P. M. 1989. Forest management in Amazonia: The need for new criteria in evaluating economic development options. *Forest Ecology and Management* (in press).

Fearnside, P. M. and J. M. Rankin. 1980. Jari and development in the Brazilian Amazon. *Interciencia* 5(3):146–156.

Fearnside, P. M. and J. M. Rankin. 1982a. Jari and Carajás: The uncertain future of large silvicultural plantations in the Amazon. *Interciencia* 7(6): 326–328.

Fearnside, P. M. and J. M. Rankin. 1982b. The new Jari: Risks and prospects of a major Amazonian development. *Interciencia* 7(6):329–339.

Fearnside, P. M. and J. M. Rankin. 1985. Jari revisited: Changes and the outlook for sustainability in Amazonia's largest silvicultural estate. *Interciencia* 10(3):121–129.

Fearnside, P. M. and E. Salati. 1985. Explosive deforestation in Rondônia, Brazil. *Environmental Conservation* 12(4):355–356.

Hecht, S. B. 1981. Deforestation in the Amazon basin: Magnitude, dynamics and soil resource effects. *Studies in Third World Societies* 13:61–108.

Hecht, S. B. 1982. Agroforestry in the Amazon basin: Practice, theory and limits of a promising land use. In S. B. Hecht, ed., *Amazonia: Agriculture and Land Use Research*, pp. 331–371. Cali, Colombia: Centro Internacional de Agricultura Tropical (CIAT).

Hecht, S. B. 1983. Cattle ranching in the eastern Amazon: Environmental and social implications. In E. F. Moran, ed., *The Dilemma of Amazonian Development*, pp. 155–188. Boulder, CO: Westview Press.

Hecht, S. B. 1985. Environment, development and politics: Capital accumulation and the livestock sector in eastern Amazonia. *World Development* 13(6):663–684.

Janzen, D. H. 1973. Tropical agroecosystems: Habitats misunderstood by the temperate zones, mismanaged by the tropics. *Science* 182:1212–1219.

Jesus, R. M. de. 1984. Manejo e utilização florestal. Linhares, Espírito Santo: Florestas Rio Doce, S. A. (Manuscript.)

Jesus, R. M. de, M. S. Menandro, and C. E. Thibau. 1984. Manejo florestal em Buriticupu. Linhares, Espirito Santo: Florestas Rio Doce, S. A. (Manuscript.)

Jonkers, W. B. J. and P. Schmidt. 1984. Ecology and timber production in tropical rainforest in Suriname. *Interciencia* 9(5):290–297.

Kass, D. C. L. 1978. Polyculture cropping systems: Review and analysis. Cornell International Agriculture Bulletin 32. Ithaca, New York: Cornell University.

Koster, H. W., E. J. A. Khan, and R. P. Bosshart. 1977. *Programa e Resultados Preliminares dos Estudos de Pastagens na Região de Paragominas, Pará, e nordeste de Mato Grosso junho 1975-dezembro 1976.* Belém: Superintendência do Desenvolvimento da Amazônia (SUDAM), Convênio SUDAM/Instituto de Pesquisas IRI.

Leite, L. L. and P. A. Furley. 1985. Land development in the Brazilian Amazon with particular reference to Rondônia and the Ouro Preto colonisation project. In J. Hemming, ed., *Change in the Amazon Basin: The Frontier after a Decade of Colonisation*, pp. 119–139. Manchester, U.K.: Manchester University Press.

Léna, P. 1986. Aspects de la frontière Amazonienne. *Cahiers des Sciences Humaines* 22(3–4):319–343.

Lima, J. M. G. de. 1976. *Perfil Analítico dos Fertilizantes Fosfatados.* Ministério das Minas e Energia, Departamento Nacional de Produção Mineral (DNPM) Boletim No. 39. Brasília: DNPM.

Lovejoy, T. E., J. M. Rankin, R. O. Bierregaard, Jr., K. S. Brown, Jr., L. H. Emmons, and M. E. Van der Voort. 1984. Ecosystem decay of Amazon forest remnants. In M. H. Nitecki, ed., *Extinctions*, pp. 295–325. Chicago: University of Chicago Press.

Mahar, D. J. 1979. *Frontier Development Policy in Brazil: A Study of Amazonia.* New York: Praeger.

Malingreau, J. P., G. Stephens, and L. Fellows. 1985. Remote sensing of forest fires: Kalimantan and North Borneo in 1982–83. *Ambio* 14(6):314–321.

Marques, J., J. M. dos Santos, N. A. Villa Nova, and E. Salati. 1977. Precipitable water and water vapor flux between Belém and Manaus. *Acta Amazonica* 7(3):355–362.

Martins, J. de S. 1980. Fighting for land: Indians and *posseiros* in Legal Amazonia. In F. Barbira-Scazzocchio, ed., *Land, People and Planning in Contemporary Amazonia*, pp. 95–105. Cambridge University Centre of Latin American Studies Occasional Paper No. 3. Cambridge, U.K.: Cambridge University.

Molion, L. C. B. 1975. A Climatonomic Study of the Energy and Moisture Fluxes of the

Amazonas Basin with Considerations of Deforestation Effects. Ph.D. dissertation, University of Wisconsin at Madison. Ann Arbor, MI: University Microfilms International.

Moran, E. F. 1981. *Developing the Amazon.* Bloomington: Indiana University Press.

Nicholaides, J. J., III, D. E. Bandy, P. A. Sánchez, J. R. Benites, J. H. Villachica, A. J. Coutu, and C. Valverde S. 1985. Agricultural alternatives for the Amazon Basin. *BioScience* 35(5):279–285.

Nicholaides, J. J., III, D. E. Bandy, P. A. Sánchez, J. H. Villachica, A. J. Coutu, and C. Valverde S. 1984. Continuous cropping potential in the Upper Amazon Basin. In M. Schmink and C. S. Wood, eds., *Frontier Expansion in Amazonia*, pp. 337–365. Gainsville: University Presses of Florida.

Nicholaides, J. J., III, P. A. Sánchez, D. E. Bandy, J. H. Villachica, A. J. Coutu and C. Valverde S. 1983. Crop production systems in the Amazon Basin. In E. F. Moran, ed., *The Dilemma of Amazonian Development*, pp. 101–153. Boulder, CO: Westview Press.

Penteado, A. R. 1967. *Problemas de Colonização e de Uso da Terra na Região Bragantina do Estado do Pará.* Belém: Universidade Federal do Pará.

Revelle, R. 1987. Comments on "Causes of deforestation in the Brazilian Amazon." In R. E. Dickinson, ed., *The Geophysiology of Amazonia: Vegetation and Climate Interactions*, pp. 54–57. New York: Wiley.

Richards, P. W. 1964. *The Tropical Rain Forest*, 2nd ed. Cambridge: Cambridge University Press.

Salati, E., A. Dall'Olio, E. Matusi and J. R. Gat. 1979. Recycling of water in the Brazilian Amazon Basin: An isotopic study. *Water Resources Research* 15:1250–1258.

Salati, E., J. Marques, and L. C. B. Molion. 1978. Origem e distribuição das chuvas na Amazônia. *Interciencia* 3(4):200–206.

Sánchez, P. A., D. E. Bandy, J. H. Villachica, and J. J. Nicholaides III. 1982. Amazon Basin soils: Management for continuous crop production. *Science* 216:821–827.

Sarrailh, J. M. and L. Schmitt. 1984. État des recherches menées en Guyane Française sur la transformation et l'amelioration des peuplements forestiers naturels. Paper presented at the IUFRO symposium on "Impacts de l'homme sûr la forêt," Strasbourg, 16–17 September 1984. (Manuscript.)

Schmink, M. 1982. Land conflicts in Amazonia. *American Ethnologist* 9(2):341–357.

Schubart, H. O. R., W. J. Junk, and M. Petrere, Jr. 1976. Sumário de ecologia Amazônica. *Ciência e Cultura* 28(5):507–509.

Schwartzman, S. and M. H. Allegretti. 1987. Extractive production in the Amazon and the rubber tappers' movement. Washington, DC: Environmental Defense Fund. (Mimeo.)

Scott, G. A. J. 1978. *Grassland Development in the Gran Pajonal of Eastern Peru: A Study of Soil-Vegetation Nutrient Systems.* Hawaii Monographs in Geography, No. 1. Honolulu: University of Hawaii at Manoa, Department of Geography.

Serrão E. A. S. and I. C. Falesi. 1977. *Pastagens do Trópico Úmido Brasileiro.* Belém: Empresa Brasileira de Pesquisa Agropecuária—Centro de Pesquisa Agropecuária do Trópico Úmido (EMBRAPA-CPATU).

Serrão, E. A. S., I. C. Falesi, J. B. Viega, and J. F. Teixeira Neto. 1979. Productivity of cultivated pastures on low fertility soils in the Amazon of Brazil. In P. A. Sánchez and L. E. Tergas, eds., *Pasture Production in Acid Soils of the Tropics: Proceedings of a Seminar held at CIAT, Cali, Colombia 17–21 April 1978*, pp. 195–225. CIAT Series 03 EG-05. Cali, Colombia: Centro Internacional de Agricultura Tropical (CIAT).

Sheldon, R. P. 1982. Phosphate rock. *Scientific American* 246(6):31–37.

Sioli, H. 1973. Recent human activities in the Brazilian Amazon Region and their ecological effects. In B. J. Meggers, E. S. Ayensu, and W. D. Duckworth, eds., *Tropical Forest Ecosystems in Africa and South America: A Comparative Review*, pp. 321–334. Washington, DC: Smithsonian Institution Press.

Smith, F., D. Fairbanks, R. Atlas, C. C. Delwiche, D. Gordon, W. Hazen, D. Hitchcock, D. Pramer, J. Skujins, and M. Stuiver. 1972. Cycles of elements. In *Man in the Living Environment*, pp. 41–89. Madison: University of Wisconsin Press.

Smith, N. J. H. 1978. Agricultural productivity along Brazil's Transamazon Highway. *Agro-Ecosystems* 4:415–432.

Smith, N. J. H. 1982. *Rainforest Corridors: The Transamazon Colonization Scheme.* Berkeley, California: University of California Press.

Tardin, A. T., A. P. dos Santos, E. M. I. Moraes Novo, and F. L. Toledo. 1978. Projetos agropecuários da Amazônia: Desmatamento e fiscalização—relatório. *A Amazônia Brasileira em Foco* 12:7–45.

Tardin, A. T., D. C. L. Lee, R. J. R. Santos, O. R. de Assis, M. P. dos Santos Barbosa, M. de Lourdes Moreira, M. T. Pereira, D. Silva, and C. P. dos Santos Filho. 1980. *Subprojeto Desmatamento, Convênio IBDF/CNPq-INPE 1979.* Instituto Nacional de Pesquisas Espaciais (INPE) Relatório No. INPE-1649-RPE/103. São José dos Campos, São Paulo: INPE.

Thibau, C. E. 1985. Forest management and exploitation in Forest Reserve of Buriticupu. Paper presented at the *Ist International Seminar on Management in Tropical Forests,* Serra dos Carajás and São Luis. 28 January–1 February 1985. (Manuscript.)

Uhl, C. and R. Buschbacher. 1985. A disturbing synergism between cattle-ranch burning practices and selective tree harvesting in the eastern Amazon. *Biotropica* 17(4):265–268.

United States, Council on Environmental Quality and Department of State. 1980. *The Global 2000 Report to the President.* New York: Pergamon Press. 3 vols.

Valverde, O. and C. V. Dias. 1967. *A Rodovia Belém-Brasília: Estudo de Geografia Regional.* Rio de Janeiro: Instituto Brasileiro de Geografia e Estatística (IBGE).

Villa Nova, N. A., E. Salati, and E. Matusi. 1976. Estimativa da evapotranspiração na Bacia Amazônica. *Acta Amazônica* 6(2):215–228.

Wells, F. J. 1976. *The Long-Run Availability of Phosphorus: A Case Study in Mineral Resource Analysis.* Baltimore: Johns Hopkins University Press.

16

Extractive Reserves: An Alternative for Reconciling Development and Environmental Conservation in Amazonia

■

MARY HELENA ALLEGRETTI

ABSTRACT

Scientists are often excluded from the political decisions that determine development policies in Amazonia. One way they can assume a more active role is to conduct research in response to tangible social needs within the region. The need to reconcile regional development with conservation has recently been recognized by a large, indigenous population of rubber tappers in the Brazilian state of Acre, who depend on the rain forest for their livelihood. Destruction of rain forest and expulsion of rubber tappers by regional development projects sparked a social movement which led to the formation of the National Council of Rubber Tappers. Currently supported by a broad coalition of indigenous and environmental groups, as well as by policymakers and government officials in and out of Brazil, this organization calls for the establishment of so-called "extractive reserves"—public lands designated for the specific purpose of sustainable use of forest products such as rubber, Brazil nut, and palm heart by the resident population. Scientists can have a potentially crucial role in designing these reserves and seeking alternative forms of resource management that will promote social wellbeing while preserving the environment.

The rapid increase in deforestation during the past decades in Amazonia indicates a significant transition in the exploitation of natural resources. In the past, and especially during the rubber boom of the late nineteenth and early twentieth centuries, the region's principal sources of wealth were represented by specific plant products that could be obtained without destroying the forest as a whole. In contrast, today the Amazon rain forest is being dismembered into separate parts, each of which has become a source of economic value: the minerals in the soil, valuable hardwoods, and even the forest biomass. Exploiting these resources requires or ultimately leads to deforestation, and the Amazon rain forest, once a source of wealth, has become a mere impediment to economic development.

These considerations make it apparent that implementing rational alternatives to deforestation in Amazonia requires that rain forests be perceived as having greater value when intact than when destroyed. Although recent research supports this observation (e.g., Gradwohl and Greenberg 1988), it has clearly not influenced regional development policies, which continue to treat the forest as an impediment to development and provide numerous incentives for its destruction.

A shift in current policies toward a form of regional development that integrates rather than precludes environmental conservation will require activities on two distinct yet complimentary fronts: 1) demonstration by the scientific community of the economic value of the rain forest in its intact state and of the technologies available for its profitable and sustainable exploitation; and 2) social pressure by groups interested in the maintenance and rational use of the rain forest.

There are numerous obstacles on both of these fronts. Scientists rarely influence politicians and the power to shape policies is largely out of their control. Furthermore, the relatively few existing studies relevant to land-use alternatives in Amazonia are often overly specific and unrelated to the larger socioeconomic and political contexts of the region.

Among the groups interested in the maintenance and rational use of the Amazon rain forest are regional populations that extract forest products, such as rubber tappers ("seringueiros"), Brazil nut gatherers ("castanheiros"), and riverside dwellers ("ribeirinhos"), as well as Indian groups. These populations depend on the rain forest for their survival and have a direct stake in its conservation. However, they currently have little demographic, economic, or political significance: They live in highly dispersed and isolated communities, are materially impoverished and subsist at the margins of the market economy, and are politically disorganized. Furthermore, even today a significant proportion of these populations live in conditions of virtual slavery under a regional form of debt peonage ("aviamento").

A social movement originating among rubber tappers in the western portions of the Brazilian Amazon is beginning to change this situation. Threatened by increasing deforestation, organized in rural labor unions, and supported by legislation that assures homesteading rights, rubber tappers in the state of Acre started a movement at the end of the 1970s aimed at resisting two common effects of rural development in the Amazon: wholesale expulsion of resident populations and widespread conversion of rain forest to pastures.

An alliance between the members of this movement and scientists involved in studies of the rubber tappers led to a unique proposal for protection of rain forest areas. The proposal calls for the creation of so-called extractive reserves, which would provide legal rights to lands historically occupied by social groups that utilize forest products in an ecologically sustainable fashion.

The involvement of scientists from Brazil and abroad is transforming the concept of extractive reserves into a widely recognized development alternative and an increasing source of pressure on regional policymakers. This transformation reveals that scientists can influence development policies by conducting research in response to the needs of social groups. Extractive reserves may become a prime site for such research.

This essay will examine how the creation of extractive reserves represents an alternative to deforestation in Amazonia. Three themes will be developed in detail: 1) the historical context and the current forms of resource exploitation practiced by the rubber tappers; 2) the proposal for creation of extractive reserves and its meaning in the context of regional development; and 3) the lines of research required for establishing extractive reserves and the role that scientists can potentially assume in defining alternatives to regional development in the Amazon.

Historical and Social Aspects of Rubber Tapping

Contemporary rubber tappers are descendants of migrants from the Brazilian Northeast who migrated to Amazonia in the late nineteenth and early twentieth centuries, when the latter region was the world's exclusive producer of rubber. Despite numerous financial crises, rubber tapping continues in the region today. A brief review of the history of this activity will provide a basis for understanding the current movement to establish extractive reserves in Amazonia.

Origins

The commercial exploitation of Amazonian rubber began on a large scale in response to increased demand by the industrialized nations in the mid-nineteenth century. The expansion of rubber commerce resulted in a rapid process of occupation that extended from the mouth of the Amazon River to the headwaters of tributaries bordering Peru and Bolivia, within the present-day state of Acre.

The collection and processing of rubber were carried out by poor laborers recruited from the Brazilian Northeast, who were inserted from the start in a highly regressive system of debt peonage. In this system, market goods were supplied at inflated prices by credit, in exchange for rubber (Wagley 1977; Santos 1980).

The migration of Northeasterners to Amazonia occurred in two waves: the first, at the end of the nineteenth and beginning of the twentieth centuries, was the largest and brought approximately 500,000 people to the region. The second, which was smaller in scale, occurred during the Second World War as a result of commercial agreements between Brazil and the United States to guarantee supply of strategic goods.

The Amazonian rubber monopoly was broken as soon as plantations established by the British in Southeast Asia began production. Amazonia's highest annual rubber production (42,000 tons) occurred in the early twentieth century, followed by an abrupt decline and progressive substitution by cultivated and synthetic sources (Pinto 1984; Santos 1980). Up until the Second World War, the population of Amazonia steadily declined and the share of rubber in the region's market economy was surpassed by other forest products such as timber and animal skins. Following a brief surge in world prices, the postwar collapse almost resulted in the definitive elimination of rubber production in the region. This did not occur because of protective policies adopted by the Brazilian government, which guaranteed purchase of all production at artifically high prices, despite the lack of competitiveness in relation to rubber obtained from Asiatic plantations. These policies have had a crucial role in sustaining the regional structure of rubber production (Pinto 1984). Recent policies promoting introduction of new technologies have resulted in increased productivity, although the internal market price remains three times greater than that of imported rubber (SUDHEVEA 1985).

The continued maintenance of policies that subsidize uncompetitive production of rubber from wild trees in the Amazon cannot be justified on purely economic grounds. These policies originally arose in response to political pressure by economic groups linked with the commercialization and industrial transformation of rubber which, in the absence of subsidies, would not be able to operate at international price levels. Furthermore, rubber represents a strategic commodity, and maintenance of internal sources was considered prudent. Finally, Brazil's current debt burden has compelled maximum reduction of imports by subsidizing the domestic production. The current trend is toward increased domestic production through incentives for plantation establishment outside of Amazonia, which should ultimately meet internal demand at a reduced cost.

In 1980, the regional population involved in rubber tapping was estimated at 68,000 families, distributed in the following states and territories: Amazonas (32,300), Acre (23,200), Pará (8,300), and the remainder (4,200) in Rondônia, Amapá, and Roraima (FIBGE 1982). Assuming a mean of five people per family, approximately 340,000 people are directly dependent on tapping native rubber trees for their livelihood.

Modes of Production

Two major systems of rubber production predominate today in Amazonia. The more traditional system is concentrated in areas relatively distant from commercial centers and functions according to patterns established at the outset of the rubber boom. To obtain usufruct rights, rubber tappers are required to pay rent to the patron, or "seringalista." Economic relations between rubber tappers and the patron are governed by debt peonage, in which the landowner provides industrialized goods that are paid for in kind at the end of the rubber harvest. There is no monetary circulation and in most cases the value of the rubber production is insufficient to pay off debts, leading to a permanent indebtedness.

The second production system is referred to in the region as "autonomous" because it does not involve subordination to a patron, which means that rubber tappers can freely commercialize their production. This autonomous mode of production is gradually undermining the traditional production system and is currently concentrated in more accessible areas, where debt peonage has encountered greater difficulties in reproducing.

Autonomous rubber tappers consider themselves "freed" and refer to their counterparts in the traditional system as "captive." The transformation from "captive" to "freed" occurred intensively during the 1970s and was associated with the consolidation of a more diversified local economy, based on a combination of rubber extraction with other forest-based activities such as shifting cultivation, hunting, fishing, and harvesting of various forest products.

Under the autonomous system, a family's or group of families' landholding ("colocação") produces a mix of both subsistence and market goods (Almeida 1988). This mix generally consists of one or two regionally commercialized products such as rubber (*Hevea brasiliensis* (Willd. ex A. Juss.) M. Arg.) and Brazil nut (*Bertholletia excelsa* H. B.), combined with other forest products of more restricted occurrence such as "copaiba" (*Copaifera langsdorfii* Desf.), a medicinal resin, and "sorva" (*Couma utilis* M. Arg.), another type of latex. Together with extraction of forest products, families practice shifting cultivation, which generally includes traditional crops such as manioc; crops that can substitute industrialized goods, such as tobacco and sugarcane; and both native and exotic fruit trees. The economic activities of the autonomous rubber tapper also include gathering of native plants (such as fruits and palm hearts of the "açaí" palm (*Euterpe precatoria* Mart.), medicinal plants, etc.), fishing, and hunting.

The greater diversification of economic activities under the autonomous system assures a better quality of life, because these activities are aimed at meeting the actual needs of the family unit and not merely the payment of accumulated debts. Rubber tapping and gathering of Brazil nuts are carried out during alternate periods of the year and, by selling these products, families can obtain industrial goods that are essential for production or domestic consumption. Additional activities such as agriculture, gathering, hunting, and fishing are all aimed at domestic consumption and are carried out according to the availability of labor within the family unit.

These observations acquire greater significance when compared with the patterns of commercial production and subsistence that are predominant under the traditional or debt-peonage system (Allegretti 1979). Here the overriding objective is rubber production, and subsistence activities are clearly subordinate. Agriculture is only permitted when it does not interfere with rubber tapping, and can only occur when families possess sufficient laborers to carry out both activities simultaneously. All consumer needs are attended through credit to the patron, who also determines the prices paid for forest products. In addition, the rubber tappers must obtain a margin to cover the rent charged by the patron for the right to exploit the rubber stand.

Previous studies have described production and social organization under both systems at specific locales (Allegretti 1979; Almeida 1988). However, there is currently no information concerning the relative sizes of the traditional and autonomous systems, either in terms of area or of laborers involved. This lack of information reflects a general neglect of marginal economic groups by public entities in Amazonia. At least in the case of rubber tappers, this situation is likely to change in the near future.

Land Conflicts

The autonomous system of rubber production, which is based on a diversity of economic activities, has never obtained secure property rights. Brazilian legislation assures such rights for homesteaders who constantly utilize an area for a period in excess of one year without conflicting claims by other parties. Yet the homesteading rights guaranteed by this legislation have thus far not produced legal land titles for rubber tappers. At present, autonomous rubber stands are by definition areas in which landowners are absent. In some cases, although they possess legal property titles, the patrons have abandoned these areas; in others, the position of patron is exercised even in the absence of legal titles.

Recognition of rubber tappers' homesteading rights under existing Brazilian law did not come easily. It resulted from numerous conflicts that erupted during the 1970s in rubber stands located in various areas of Amazonia subject to frontier expansion. In most cases, the stands were acquired by business groups from southern Brazil intent on converting them to pastures. In addition to destroying the rain forest, such conversion also meant expulsion of the rubber tappers and their families, since cattle ranching absorbs relatively little labor.

Initially the cases of expulsion predominated, and there was little organized resistance on the part of the rubber tappers. Gradually, however, the situation began to change. Through the work of the National Confederation of Agriculture (CONTAG) and the Catholic Church's grassroots community organizations, the rubber tappers became aware of their rights under Brazilian legislation, and resistance to expulsion increased. As a result, resolution of land conflicts began to take on a new form, which could vary from compensation for property improvements to appropriation of contested land and redistribution to rubber tappers in individual lots.

The most important outcome of these conflicts occurred in western Amazonia in the late 1970s, when autonomous rubber tappers in the Acre River Valley began using a peculiar form of nonviolent resistance to defend their lands. This resistance (referred to locally as "empate") took the form of impeding forest clearing operations associated with development projects. The conflict over rights to traditionally occupied lands, a frequent phenomenon in frontier areas of Brazil, gradually took on a new dimension, as rubber tappers realized that deforestation eliminates the very resource base on which their livelihoods depend.

Each year, rubber tappers in Acre act to impede deforestation at the outset of the dry season (May–June), when clearing operations begin. These actions are not always successful. In fact, leaders of the movement have been murdered, such as the rubber tapper Wilson Pinheiro, former president of the Rural Workers Union of Brasileia, who was shot near the Bolivian frontier in 1979.[1]

Despite these setbacks, resistance to deforestation has produced significant results, such as the appropriation of contested lands for redistribution to rubber tappers in individual lots. Yet many such lots are subsequently sold or abandoned, and their owners end up migrating to cities.

The reason for this abandonment is that traditional forms of subsistance were eliminated in the individual lots. The main problem involves the size of the lots.

The holding of an autonomous rubber tapper is traditionally 300 to 500 hectares, whereas individual lots are typically 60 to 100 hectares. Unable to exploit the rain forest as in an autonomous rubber stand, the rubber tappers sell or abandon their lots and migrate to cities.

To search for solutions to these conflicts and problems, a national meeting of Amazonian rubber tappers was organized in August of 1985, with the support of the University of Brasilia, the Ministry of Culture, and nongovernment organizations. For the first time in the history of rubber production in Brazil, numerous representatives (approximately 130) of rubber tappers from various areas of Amazonia met in Brasilia. As a result of this meeting, a representative entity, the National Council of Rubber Tappers, was established. In addition, the meeting called for the creation of extractive reserves, in which property rights would be designated according to traditional patterns of land use rather than imported models of occupation. The concept of extractive reserves is examined in the following section.

The Concept of Extractive Reserves

In many respects, the concept of extractive reserves represents a radical departure from the way in which regional development has been carried out thus far in Amazonia. In contrast to colonization projects, extractive reserves already contain people and do not require relocating settlers who are unfamiliar with local conditions. Because a knowledgeable population is already present, development within extractive reserves will require the active participation of local residents. Ongoing discussions between communities of rubber tappers and scientists have led to the consensus that extractive reserves should not be established merely to preserve traditional economic activities, but rather to permit these activities to evolve. New forms of resource use can be generated by the interplay between scientists and local residents, but always within the overriding prerogatives of conservation. Finally, the legal recognition of property rights proposed for extractive reserves follows traditional patterns of land-use space and social organization.

In summary, the concept of extractive reserves reflects an ongoing dialogue between a traditional social group expressing its needs and scientists seeking the technical means of transforming these needs into reality. Various aspects of extractive reserves are examined in greater detail below.

Patterns of Land-Use Space

A family's or group of families' landholding ("colocação") forms the basic land production unit within a rubber stand. This landholding is defined by the combination of rubber trees in production or at rest, which are called rubber trails ("estradas de seringa"); agricultural plot(s); areas utilized for hunting, fishing, and gathering; the site or sites designated for housing and processing of rubber; and the stream(s) or river(s) that invariably flow through the landholding. Each landholding is generally recognized and respected by all residents in a given area. Yet divisions between holdings are subtle. For example, the rubber trees along the trail of a given holding may lie within an area recognized as pertaining to another holding. Likewise, if a Brazil nut tree is on the boundary of a holding, the nuts that fall to one side belong to one household, and those that fall to the other side to the other household (Schwartzman 1989). In the rubber tappers' world, it is the natural resources of the land and not the land *per se* that confers value and determines the boundaries of each holding. As a result, holdings do not conform to conventional geographic shapes. Yet such subtleties rarely result in internal conflict between the residents of a rubber stand.

The size of landholdings varies considerably. A holding typically contains three rubber trails, which are worked sequentially (one path per day) during the harvest period ("fabrico"), which occurs during the dry season (May to October in Acre). Each trail contains an average of 120 rubber trees, which are dispersed in approximately 100 to 150 hectares of rain forest. As a result of this low density, land production units are necessarily large, and neighboring households are typically separated by a one-hour walk. A given holding may be occupied by more than one household, depending on the size of the area and its concentration of resources.

Defining the legal status of land rights in rubber stands consequently requires special care. The subtlety of the boundaries between production units contrasts sharply with those of more conventional landholdings. Likewise, designating a production unit as priviate property, such as occurs in conventional colonization projects, will not necessarily assure the long-term conservation of the area: Private owners are free to use the land as they wish and can sell it to third parties.

An alternative approch was proposed by the National Council of Rubber Tappers, based on studies carried out by the Institute of Amazon Studies, a nongovernmental organization involved in articulating the rubber tappers' movement. This proposal calls for the delimitation of a perimeter around the entire group of landholdings within a given rubber stand, without issuing specific deeds for individual family units. This arrangement avoids potentially disruptive privatization and preserves the current form of land division that predominates in the rubber stand. Further details on the proposed legal status of land in extractive reserves are provided in the following section.

Economic Viability

The concept of extractive reserves in large part originated from the crucial role of a rain forest resource—rubber—in the lives of hundreds of thousands of rural inhabitants in Amazonia. But this role is likely to change in the future, especially because the long-term prospects of wild rubber in the Brazilian economy are not bright. Rather than crystalizing current patterns of resource exploitation, the establishment of extractive reserves should be accompanied by policies aimed at altering current income levels derived from rubber and promoting exploitation of other rain forest products.

The apparent lack of competitiveness of rubber tapping from wild Amazonian stands is based on detailed comparisons with Asiatic plantations (SUDHEVEA

1985). Yet such comparisons are questionable due to the lack of reliable data on regional production costs. These costs are extremely difficult to quantify and many are currently borne by the rubber tappers.

Ever since the end of the rubber boom, the patrons have coped with the economic crisis by transferring many of their production costs to the rubber tappers. For example, the maintenance of rubber trails and processing equipment, which was once carried out by paid employees, is currently carried out by rubber tappers. Likewise, a significant portion of the rubber tappers' reproduction costs is currently borne by the rain forest through the range of subsistence activities described above. In traditional rubber stands, the only costs borne by the patron are related to transport within the community (which are generally carried out by donkeys or small boats) and to market centers outside (generally on rafts or small boats). Yet in areas of traditional production, even these costs are frequently transferred to the rubber tappers.

In autonomous areas, rubber commerce is generally carried out by small-scale intermediaries or even, in some cases, by the producers, thus further reducing production costs. Additional reduction could be achieved by organizing cooperatives for sale of rubber and purchase of industrialized goods.

A final factor involves the technology utilized in native rubber stands. Although technologies currently exist to increase productivity and product quality (primarily in the form of small-scale processing plants), such innovations have not received governmental incentives. A report from the Brazilian Ministry of Industry and Commerce, which sets national rubber policies through a subordinate entity (SUDHEVEA), states that introduction of existing technologies could increase production of native rubber stands by at least 40 percent (MIC 1986).

In summary, the policies that sustain rubber production in Brazil can be changed to strengthen the position of autonomous rubber tappers. Such a move is justified by the fact that native stands still account for 80 percent of the national production (MIC 1986). Until rubber plantations are established on a large scale in other areas of Brazil, policies aimed at increasing production from native stands can be justified for a number of reasons: Brazil is not self-sufficient in rubber, internal demand continues to grow, importation requires expenditures in hard currencies, and many of the native stands occur in frontier areas that are crucial for national security.

To be economically successful, extractive reserves will require small-scale processing plants and cooperatives for rubber production and sale. In addition, other forest products will need to be systematically exploited. Finally, alternative national and international markets must be found for direct sale of a wider variety of goods that can be produced within the reserves.

Legal and Institutional Aspects

As discussed previously, the existing land legislation in Brazil fails to take into account the unique forms of social and economic organization that characterize rubber extraction areas. The most incompatible aspects, which are generally adopted by settlement projects, involve the size of individual lots and the privatization of property.

To guarantee the continuity of their livelihood patterns while permitting these patterns to adapt to changing circumstances, the National Council of Rubber Tappers has proposed an alternative that contains familiar elements blended in a unique way. From indigenous reserves, they borrowed the idea of an area guaranteed by the state, in which native peoples can practice traditional cultural and economic activities. From extraction, they realized the need for recognizing a highly specific economic activity that distinguishes them from other rural laborers such as colonists.

The very terms associated with extractive reserves take on unique meanings. In conventional use, "extractive," derived from "extraction," implies a destructive form of resource use (see Anderson, this volume), while "reserve" carries the connotation of an area off limits for human use. Within the concept of the rubber tappers, however, "extractive" refers to a specific economic activity that depends on the long-term maintenance of rain forest areas, and "reserve" denotes an area under protection by the State.

To provide an institutional and judicial basis for this concept, a working group was established within the now-extinct National Institute of Colonization and Agrarian Reform (INCRA), with the participation of the National Council of Rubber Tappers and the Institute of Amazon Studies. Following the recommendations of this group, INCRA issued Decree 627 on July 30, 1987, which established guidelines for settlement of extractive areas as a specific mode of agrarian reform in the Amazon region.

In relation to property, the decree utilized the judicial concept of land-use concessions, by which the State assumes ownership of the reserves and cedes them for exclusive use by practitioners of traditional extractive activities during a minimum period of 30 years, in accordance with specific regulations governing land use. This form of concession seeks to avoid the subdivision of land into private units that normally occurs in colonization projects. The decree also establishes a mechanism used in indigenous reserves, by which the State acts as mediator between inhabitants of a reserve and outside economic interests, a crucial measure in areas of conflict.

Institutionally, the reserves will be administered by a group elected by the local inhabitants; this group can either assume the form of an association or a cooperative, according to local conditions. Statutes involving the judicial, economic, social, and environmental aspects of the reserve will govern the internal functioning of each reserve. After delimiting the perimeter and granting the concession, socioeconomic and environmental projects will be designed to improve living conditions and establish rational resource management practices.

Another form of legalizing extractive areas is being developed by the government of the state of Rondônia. Here such areas are defined as State Forests designated exclusively for extractive purposes, following existing environmental legislation.

There is a key difference between State Forests as defined by existing environmental legislation and extractive reserves as defined by the INCRA decree.

The former classifies extractive areas as conservation units and seeks to adapt them to existing legislation, whereas the latter defines these areas as unique entities and makes specific provisions for their legal status. The National Council of Rubber Tappers continues to use the latter term as it more clearly expresses the dual concepts of economic production and environmental protection.

The legal basis for extractive reserves could be further promoted by classifying this entity as a special conservation unit requiring specific legislation. A definition that could be adopted synthesizes the principal characteristics discussed previously: "Extractive Reserves or Extractive Forests are areas of public domain, occupied by social groups that depend on forest products for their survival and that carry out, under land-use concession, sustained use of natural resources, according to a pre-established management plan" (SEMA 1988).

Conclusions

The greatest single impediment to the establishment of extractive reserves in Amazonia is the current devaluation of rain forest products. In today's economy, most people perceive the rain forest in its intact state as possessing less value than when it is destroyed. Recognition that when sustainably managed, the rain forest can in fact generate greater wealth and social wellbeing, constitutes the first crucial step toward making conservation an economically viable proposition in Amazonia.

The economic benefits that could be derived by establishing extractive reserves are far greater than the possible increases in production of rubber and other forest resources. The viability of this development model can be viewed from two perspectives: its immediate socioeconomic and ecological impacts; and its potential contribution to scientific knowledge, which in turn could orient future development in the region.

Extractive reserves are likely to exert the following impacts on regional development in Amazonia:

Impacts on Regional Development

1. *Minimization of migration.* Establishment of extractive reserves could minimize regional migration to urban centers by offering new opportunities for employment and improving the general quality of life for the rural population.

2. *Likelihood of success.* The chances for success of extractive reserves are likely to be far greater than programs designed from the top down by governmental agencies. This is especially the case in areas currently contemplated for establishment of extractive reserves: grassroots organizations have sprung up in these areas with virtually no governmental support.

3. *Low reproduction costs.* The reproduction costs of populations that live in the rain forest are likely to be considerably lower than those of populations in urban centers, due to the former's intimate independence on natural subsidies that are provided free of cost.

4. *Low protection costs.* Extractive reserves probably represent one of the most economically viable forms of environmental protection, as they contain a residential population with an intimate knowledge of the rain forest and with a direct stake in its preservation.

Lines of Research

The first extractive reserves have recently been established in Acre; others are under study in Rondônia and Amapá. Establishment of these areas offers a unique opportunity for initiating basic and applied research programs involving the interactions between traditional social groups and their environment, and specifically their use and management of natural resources. Some of the most promising lines of research are as follows:

1. A holistic analysis of the economic value of the rain forest, considering its entire potential for sustainable exploitation for food, raw materials, medicinal plants, energy, etc.

2. Investigation of the most efficient ways to intensify use of natural resources so as to increase carrying capacity without undermining long-term productivity.

3. Analysis of channels for marketing unconventional as well as traditional forest products that could minimize reliance on intermediaries.

All of these research lines will require intensive interaction with traditional inhabitants, who are most intimately familiar with the natural resource base. Beginning with traditional patterns of resource use, technological modifications should be introduced to increase economic opportunities without sacrificing environmental quality.

In summary, extractive reserves could represent dynamic laboratories for investigating both traditional and innovative forms of human interaction with the Amazonian environment. In such a setting, the distinction between "pure" and "applied" research loses its meaning, as does any illusion that science is a politically neutral activity. Although scientific methods can and should be purged of human biases, the choice of what to study is ultimately a political one. The gulf between scientific research and reality in Amazonia today will be bridged only when scientists realize the political nature of their choice.

ENDNOTE

1. The level of violence associated with the rubber tappers' movement has been steadily escalating. In the region of Xapuri in the state of Acre, three rubber tappers were as-

sasinated in 1988, including Francisco ("Chico") Mendes Filho, president of the Rural Workers' Union of Xapuri and recipient of the Global 500 Prize of the United Nations for his crucial role in the rubber tappers' movement.

REFERENCES

Allegretti, M. H. 1979. Os seringueiros: Estudo de caso de um seringal nativo do Acre. M. A. thesis. Brasília: Universidade de Brasília.

Almeida, M. W. M. de. 1988. As colocações como forma social, sistema tecnológico e unidade de recursos naturais. Paper presented at the Seminar, "O Desenvolvimento da Amazônia e a Questão Ambiental." Rio Branco, Acre, Brazil.

FIBGE. 1982. *Censo Demográfico de 1980: Acre, Amazonas, Pará, Roraima, Amapá, Rondônia.* Rio de Janeiro: Fundação Instituto Brasileiro de Geografia e Estatística.

Gradwohl, J. and R. Greenberg. 1988. *Saving Tropical Forests.* London: Earthscan Publications Ltd.

MIC. 1986. *Relatório da Comissão Criada pela Portaria 12/86 para Sugerir Alternativas de Política para a Cultura da Seringueira.* Brasília: Ministério da Indústria e do Comércio.

MIRAD. 1987. Projeto de Assentamento Extrativista. Brasília: Ministério da Reforma e do Desenvolvimento Agrário.

Pinto, N. P. A. 1984. *Política da Borracha no Brasil: A Falência da Borracha Vegetal.* São Paulo: Editora Vozes.

Santos, R. 1980. *Historia Economica da Amazonia (1800–1920).* São Paulo: Editora T. A. Queiroz.

Schwartzman, S. 1989. Extractive reserves: The rubber tappers' strategy for sustainable use of the Amazon rain forest. In J. Browder, ed., *Fragile Lands of Latin America: The Research for Sustainable Uses.* Boulder, CO: Westview Press.

SEMA. 1988. *Plano Nacional de Meio Ambiente.* Brasília: Secretaria Especial de Meio Ambiente.

Wagley, C. 1977. *Uma Comunidade Amazônica: Estudo do Homem nos Trópicos.* São Paulo: Companhia Editora Nacional.

17

The Future of Deforestation in Amazonia: A Socioeconomic and Political Analysis

■

DONALD SAWYER

ABSTRACT

Analysis of the socioeconomic and political forces that determine deforestation provides grounds for guarded optimism regarding its future pace and the adoption of technical alternatives in Brazilian Amazonia. Both capital and labor have been induced to move to Amazonia by a particular model of development and by offical incentives that resulted more in speculation and instability than in productive settlement. The precariousness of settlement generates constant new pressures for further frontier expansion. This process could be slowed by cutting official incentives, relieving pressures that generate frontier migration, consolidating existing frontier settlement, and using less predatory forms of new settlement. Since deforestation depends to such a large extent on artificial stimuli, slowing it is more politically feasible than may be apparent.

The foregoing essays in this book present a wide variety of technical alternatives to deforestation in Amazonia. It may seem that, given the means now at hand, the problem can be readily solved. Questions loom, however, as to what extent the alternatives are economically, socially, and politically feasible.

The prevailing point of view is that deforestation is inevitable, increasingly rapid, a necessary cost of development, and merely a question of time, measured in decades or even years (e.g., Fearnside 1984). Based on a socioeconomic and political analysis of the broader context, this paper offers a more optimistic view. The focus is on Brazil, although many of the arguments probably apply to the other Amazonian countries as well. The basic point is that environmental problems in Amazonia reflect essentially social problems and that their solutions must also be social.

If deforestation has profound social causes, there is no easy technological solution or "fix," nor can nature be preserved by decree. Appropriate technology and effective enforcement of protective measures are, of course, important and necessary elements in slowing deforestation, but they are not sufficient. In order for protection to be achieved, it is necessary to understand why firms and individuals stay put or move into the forest, why they use or do not use certain technologies, and why they destroy nature or leave it be.

This essay approaches the question from a structural and historical perspective. Firms and individuals are not seen as destroying Amazonian rain forest because of lack of law enforcement, information, technology, ecological consciousness, or goodwill. Rather, it is argued, both capital and labor have been induced to move to the frontier and to behave as they do by government policies and, on a deeper level, by Brazil's economic and social system. Policies followed by the Brazilian government have worked in such a way as to concentrate land ownership and income, excluding the poor majority from the benefits of economic growth, which are channeled to social classes or groups who are already most favored (Furtado 1972). The specific mode of capitalist development in Brazil is based on political domination that is labor-repressive (Velho 1973). Such unequal development involves profound social conflicts.

If destruction of the Amazon rain forest has such deep social roots, one might conclude that it will only cease when the structure is radically changed. In this paper, I take an alternative view and focus on the prospects for preservation of the Amazon environment with only limited change in the existing socioeconomic and political structure.[1] The basic point is that if certain reforms are undertaken in such a way that society has more control over the State, destruction of the forest can to a large extent be avoided. Thus, characterizing the problem of deforestation as "social"[2] instead of "natural" does not mean that it is inevitable, but rather that it can be slowed, given political will.

The analysis deals with social origins of Amazon settlement, its environmental consequences, suggested new policy guidelines, political feasibility, and strategies to be followed.

The Social Origins of Amazon Settlement

This section focuses on the determinants of the migration of capital and labor to the Amazon frontier in recent years. The deep structural determinants are difficult to modify, even in a democratic regime, but the proximate determinants are more subject to change, especially when they do not conflict with overall economic growth.

In contrast to historical patterns, in which commercial and argicultural capital dominated the Amazonian economy, the business interests involved in recent frontier expansion in Amazonia are based in industry and finance, mostly within Brazil. Like entrepreneurs anywhere, they are motivated by possibilities for profits. What needs clarification is why they began to move so suddenly, starting in the late 1960s, and how they make their profits (or failed to make as much profit as they expected).

As a first approximation, frontier profits can be divided into two types, productive and speculative. Productive profits come from the output of new farms and ranches and from exploitation of natural resources, especially minerals and wood. The basic cause of expansion of the "resource frontier" into Amazonia was the cumulative and constant process of economic and demographic growth and depletion of natural resources in more settled and developed regions. Because of horizontal expansion, with low productivity of land and labor and limited sustainability, land and forests had been largely depleted in the rest of Brazil by the late 1960s, while they remained abundant on the Amazon frontier.

This gradual process, however, does not explain the rush of capital to Amazonia after the mid-1960s, which was due to strong stimuli provided directly and indirectly by the State after the military coup in 1964. The main indirect stimulus was the building of roads and other transportation and telecommunications infrastructure. In addition to providing profits for construction firms, the opening of a vast network of roads, undertaken for basically national security reasons, sparked a real estate boom that provided spectacular opportunities for land speculation. At the same time, the enterprises that established projects in the region took advantage of direct official stimuli in the form of generous tax and credit incentives for groups that provided political support for the new regime. Few government incentives actually reached their supposed destination (Mahar 1979; Hecht 1982; Gasques and Yokomizo 1986).

The rush of migrants to Amazonia is sometimes exaggerated. The numbers were large for the region but not for Brazil. Net interregional migration in the 1970–1980 decade was less than one million, compared to about 20 million net rural-urban migrants in Brazil (Martine 1987). Still, while they did less damage than ranchers, pioneer farmers were responsible for a significant part of deforestation (Mahar 1988).

As in the case of big business, the frontier settlers also responded to both long-term structural trends and policy incentives of the new regime. The cumulative and constant structural trends were rapid population growth in the postwar period and highly skewed distribution of income and property, which generated centrifugal forces pushing people outward from the center to the periphery. The principal political factors attracting migrants were ambitious land settlement projects along the Transamazon Highway, as part of the National Integration Programs, and in Rondônia, in the western Amazon (Sawyer 1984).

The migrants sought land dor other means (placer mining, small business, etc.) to gain sustenance in the present and security for the future. They wanted to be their own bosses. Their search for autonomy, which ran contrary to the overall tendency of formation of a propertyless working class in Brazil, was contemplated and partially attended by official plans. Frontier migration served as an escape valve, at least symbolically, relieving pressures for land reform and other profound changes in the Northeast, Southeast, and South of Brazil (cf. Velho 1973).

This summary analysis points to the conclusion that the recent transfer of capital and population to the Amazon region was to a great extent induced by a particular model of development and particular policies. Its genesis was, to be sure, capitalist development in Brazil. Nonetheless, frontier expansion was due to policies and programs that had more to do with military or private interests than with the capitalist system as a whole or with the majority of the population, within the region or elsewhere. The move to the frontier was hardly essential or necessary for capitalist development, which could have followed a more distributive route without providing special favors to specific business groups. Incentives and colonization could even have been contrary to overall development efforts because of their unfruitful allocation of public funds.

Environmental Consequences of Frontier Expansion

As in the case of origins, the effects of frontier expansion on the rain forest environment can be examined in terms of the two principal participants, firms and migrants.

The business interests involved in frontier expansion in Amazonia established new latifundia (large landed estates), many of which covered tens of thousands of hectares and some of which reached hundreds of thousands of hectares. These properties differ from old latifundia in settled parts of Brazil not only in their larger size, but also in their function. Large estates in the rest of Brazil are basically for two types: 1) traditional latifundia—unproductive properties found most frequently in the Northeast that are maintained by rural oligarchies for purposes of power and prestige and that respond poorly to economic incentives (Barraclough 1973); 2) modern latifundia—landholdings generally located in the Southeast that modernized their production methods through adoption of new technology and large-scale production in response to urbanization, industrialization, and government policies during the 1970s (Muller 1982).

In Amazonian latifundia established by big businesses in the 1960s and 1970s, land plays an economic role, but not primarily for production. Not only is there no "hamburger" connection," as in Central America, but Amazon beef production is also inadequate for the region's own consumption needs (Browder 1988). The land itself is a commodity and a reserve of value in a highly inflationary economy (Hecht, Norgaard, and Possio 1988). The purported use of the land is cattle ranching. In retrospect, it can be seen that ranching served more as a pretext than for production. In order to justify their claims to land, which were often of dubious legality, ranchers cut down vast expanses of forest. While such conversion produces pasture initially rich in nutrients, the undertaking soon succumbs to loss of soil fertility, weed invasions, pests, and overgrazing (Hecht 1982; Buschbacher 1986; Serrão and Toledo, this volume; Nepstad, Uhl, and Serrão, this volume). The final result is at best degraded pasture, if not scrubby secondary growth or even sandy and eroded "deserts." Ranching resulted in forms of occupation at the same time precarious and predatory.

Modern extractive activities in Amazonia, targeted at wood and minerals, also received official incentives, in hopes that they would generate foreign exchange needed to pay Brazil's looming foreign debt. These extractive activities are different from ranching in that they are more directly involved in production and less in speculation, although there is also a strong dose of speculation in mining rights. Mineral extraction is currently more important to industrialized countries than plant extraction. In the case of iron and aluminum ore, primary processing requires local production of vast quantities of energy, which in Amazonia comes primarily from charcoal and hydroelectric plants. These energy sources have externalities that the consuming countries do not want in their own territories, and Brazil has responded by producing charcoal from the forests near Carajás and electricity from the reservoir of Tucuruí. The environmental onus for Amazonia, by fire or water, is enormous.

On a much smaller scale, the migrants who were able to establish farms on land left aside by the modern latifundia or in official settlement projects have also contributed to deforestation (Schmink 1987). Because of the lack of capital and credit, insecurity about land tenure, unfavorable terms of trade, uncertainty about prices, high transportation costs, exploitation by middlemen, and the effects of tropical disease, among other problems, they are reluctant to incorporate permanent crops or make the land improvements needed for more stable settlement (Sawyer 1979). For small-scale farmers the only real alternative is shifting agriculture, with constant clearing of new forest areas. Like the big companies, the activities of small-scale farmers can also result in environmental degradation. What is important to recognize here is that their settlement is predatory because it is precarious.

The precariousness and instability of frontier settlement due to artificial stimuli, based primarily on speculative rather than productive interests, generate constant new pressures for further frontier expansion, acting in a "carcinogenic" way on the rest of the Amazonian organism. There is a negative feedback process: Precariousness generates degradation, which provokes further expansion, in a vicious cycle.

New Guidelines

The foregoing summary analysis of the social character of deforestation in Amazonia suggests that there is a degree of reversibility or at least of compatibility between frontier expansion and environmental preservation. It is unnecessary to posit an all-or-nothing choice between development and preservation of the Amazon. It is more realistic and useful to seek ways of redirecting existing policies to promote compatibility. Suggested guidelines for such reorientation provide for positive and negative incentives within the region and in the rest of Brazil.

Cutting Official Incentives. The first general guideline would be to cut official incentives that favor precarious and predatory use of land. To some extent, the economic crisis of the 1980s and disappointing results of previous incentives have already led to cuts, by default. Conscious policy decisions, however, would be desirable. As a rule, new penetration roads, such as the Transacreana in Acre, should not be built or paved. New settlement projects, even if they are labelled "agrarian reform," should not be undertaken in remote areas. Tax incentives and subsidized credit should not be provided for ranching and timber activities, especially the former. Incentives need not be totally eliminated, but they should be provided in such a way as to reinforce activities that are economically feasible and ecologically sustainable, without attracting opportunists who are more interested in the incentives themselves than in production and who cannot survive without them.

Relieving Centrifugal Pressures. Pressure on the Amazon environment would be less intense if thee were better living conditions in the Northeast, Southeast, and South of Brazil. If there were agrarian reform, urban reform, health and welfare reform, and other changes leading to better distribution of means of production and the benefits of development, urban and rural workers and small farmers would be more secure and would not have to seek sustenance in the rain forest.

Consolidation of Existing Settlement. Population and development in Amazonia would be more compatible with each other and with the environment if existing settlements were more solid and stable. The key concept is consolidation. Obviously, this does not mean consolidation as it usually occurs in Brazil, with expulsion of the disadvantaged, but would have to involve retention. This could be done through installation of infrastructure, paving and maintaining already existing roads, strengthening of the urban network, and use of traditional and new perennial crops. Paradoxically, it would involve greater substitution of forest by agriculture in the areas already partially occupied. Such additional deforestation where agriculture is more sustainable because of proximity to infrastructure, services, and markets means less deforestation on the distant frontier, where agriculture is less sustainable.

Less Predatory Forms of New Settlement. In addition to conventional forms of farming and ranching, which necessarily involve destruction of the forest, there are alternative forms of land use that permit conservation of the forest, many of which are described in this text. Unfortunately, other than a few perennial crops, these alternatives have not been incorporated into official development plans in Brazil.

Political Feasibility

Environmental laws in Brazil are advanced in concept but are poorly enforced. The fact that they date from the authoritarian periods of the Vargas dictatorship (1937–1945) and the military regime (1964–1985) raises a question about the compatibility between environmental protection and democracy (Sawyer 1987). Can governments in less developed countries reconcile popular support and protection of natural resources? Put more directly: Can people worry about nature when they are poor and hungry?

In the case of Amazonia, the answer is certainly "yes." Existing settlement patterns based on ranching and colonization produce very little and do not solve the problems of poverty or hunger, for migrants or for other Brazilians. Slowing present devastation would not imply deprivation for anyone.

The artificial and perverse character of frontier expansion in Amazonia means that, at least in principle, change is possible. Since the process is not an inexorable and necessary feature of capitalist development, preserving the rain forest is not unrealistic, romantic, utopian, or impossible. Of course, it will not be easy, but the attempt to slow down the process that degrades both people and their environment is not a quixotic undertaking.

There are signs that protection of the environment is not rowing entirely against the current. Despite the rate and scale of frontier expansion to date, there is some evidence of deceleration. There are reasons to believe that spatial reconcentration of agriculture in already settled areas and debilitation of the distant frontier can be expected as a logical outcome of economic and ecological processes (Sawyer 1984, 1986; see also Buschbacher 1986). Modern agriculture, which increases the productivity of land, requires a degree of infrastructure and market integration that is only available in relatively accessible areas. On the frontier, transport costs increase with distance and the humid tropical environment multiplies needs for modern inputs and technology. The "Green Revolution" thus favors more developed areas and generally avoids the "Green Hell."

Something similar may be occurring on a global scale. Technical progress and attempts at self-sufficiency make the developed countries less dependent on natural resources in the Third World, especially those of plant and animal origin. At new levels of technological development, in which biotechnology finds wide application, developed countries will have an increased stake in the sustained utilization and preservation of tropical rain forests, thus assuring that the rich gene pool characteristic of these ecosystems will not be destroyed.

In addition to economic debilitation, there may also be demographic involution of the frontier. New generations of Brazilians seem to be less willing than their parents and grandparents to seek out a living in the backwoods. This is especially true once it becomes clear that the dream of having their own land, the moving force behind migration, is more illusion than reality. Many recent frontier areas are losing population, which moves to new frontiers, to cities within Amazonia, or to other regions (Sawyer and Pinheiro 1984; Torres 1987).

To the extent that the various economic and demographic centripetal forces gain strength in relation to centrifugal forces, environmental protection in Amazonia becomes more feasible. There is also an ecological reaction. Although trees are defenseless against axes, chainsaws, and bulldozers, the rain forest ecosystem fights back. The high temperature and humidity that favor growth of crops also favor proliferation of weeds, pests, and diseases (Serrão and Toledo, this volume). Farms that use temperate-zone technology with large areas of monocultures are most vulnerable. Settlers in the midst of the forest are themselves subject to nature's counterattacks in the form of malaria and other diseases (Sawyer and Sawyer 1987). Investors and migrants are becoming increasingly aware of these diverse environmental risks and their costs.

What Should Be Done?

If defense of the Amazon rain forest is not a lost cause, as it may seem at first sight, the question is what can be done in practical terms. What political strategy should be followed? What role can scientists, regional inhabitants and public opinion play, in the region and elsewhere?

First of all, it is important to learn from history and attempt to skip some of its stages. Ecological consciousness appeared first in the developed countries, when it was too late to preserve what had already been lost. In Brazil, ecological consciousness needs to be stimulated before similar levels of development—and environmental destruction—are reached, both in Amazonia and the rest of the country. Because the mass media are relatively well developed in Brazil, the task is less difficult than it might otherwise be.

Scientists can seek theoretical and technical foundations for policy initiatives. At the theoretical level, existing approaches to the environment certainly need to be rethought in the Brazilian and Amazonian context (Hecht 1985). As this book shows, there has been considerable progress in discovery of technical alternatives, but many details remain to be worked out in the fields of natural forest management, agroforestry, and recovery of degraded lands. One of the great gaps has to do with the economic feasibility of these alternatives in different settings. Another area that needs clarification is the quantity and type of labor that these alternatives absorb, that is, their demographic impact. In addition, technical knowledge must be translated into terms that can be understood by the people who can adopt it directly or adapt it to their needs. As many of the preceding papers in this volume have demonstrated (Gómez-Pompa and Klaus; Anderson; Alcorn; Subler; Dubois), the rural inhabitants of Amazonia already possess considerable practical knowledge from which land-use research could benefit greatly.

This call for scientific research and for reconciliation between development and conservation does not rule out radicalism. Popular mobilizaton depends not only on science, but also on emotion. Power structures usually only respond to concrete pressures, even if they are not very "rational." The technical approach should complement, but not substitute for, a political approach.

It is necessary to identify and mobilize all the social and political forces capable of contributing to these goals. The allies and enemies are not clearly defined. As a peripheral region, with even less political leverage in a democratic regime based on popular elections, Amazonia has little power. On the other hand, the distance from the center of power may leave more room for maneuvering. The federal government, state-owned companies like the Companhia Vale do Rio Doce, and the international development banks, located in places like Brasília and Washington, have enormous power. The ecological movement is also strongest farthest away from Amazonia, in Southeastern Brazil and especially in the United States and Europe. This spatial correlation between power and environmentalism should be exploited but not perpetuated.

One of the problems of placing external pressure on external agencies is that environmentalists farthest from Amazonia—with notable exceptions, especially among scientists—know least about the region. It is important to educate the activists. They should understand, for example, that if international lending agencies simply pull out, massive invasions of Indian and forest reserves could occur. Investing less in areas already partially occupied will tend to favor further deforestation within these areas as well as on new frontiers.

Although advantage should be taken of environmental consciousness outside Amazonia, efforts should also be made to stimulate awareness and movements within the region. There are signs that a new mentality is emerging, especially among those who have lived there longest, like the rubber tappers (Allegretti, this volume). One can hope it will also develop among migrants and their children, who may no longer see the rain forest as a strange and threatening obstacle to be removed, but as "home."

Ecological movements will probably be successful only to the extent that they coincide with social movements. In Amazonia, social process in partially occupied areas, as in the rest of the country, alleviates pressures on the rain forest. If until now social conflicts in Brazil hve provoked destruction of the forest, it may be that in the future the new directions of these conflicts will favor its preservation.

ACKNOWLEDGMENTS

An earlier version of this paper was presented in the Seminar "O Desenvolvimento da Amazônia e a Questão Ambiental," organized by the Secretaria de Desenvolvimento Urbano e Meio Ambiente and the Instituto de Estudos Amazônicos, Rio Branco, Acre, Brazil, February 5–7, 1987. Helpful comments were provided by Anthony Anderson, Peter May, Wim Groeneveld, Leticia Santos, Roberto Santos, Roberto Luis Monte-Mór, and members of the Grupo de Estudos Amazônicos at the Federal University of Minas Gerais. None are responsible for its daring generalizations or its deficient details.

ENDNOTES

1. While it has parallels with the "political ecology" approach used by Schmink and Wood (1986), the present analysis does not presume that economic and environmental goals are necessarily at odds.

2. For simplicity, "social" is used here to mean social, economic, and political, as opposed to "natural" or "technical."

REFERENCES

Barraclough, S. 1973. *Agrarian Structure in Latin America: A Resumé of the CIDA Land Tenure Studies of Argentina, Brazil, Chile, Colombia, Ecuador, Guatemala, Peru.* Lexington, MA: Lexington Books.

Browder, J. O. 1988. The social costs of rain forest destruction: A critique and economic analysis of the "Hamburger Debate." *Interciencia* 13(3):115–120.

Buschbacher, R. J. 1986. Tropical deforestation and pasture development. *Bioscience* 14(3):161–187.

Fearnside, P. 1984. A floresta pode acabar? *Ciência Hoje* 2(10):42–52.

Furtado, C. 1972. *Análise do "Modelo" Brasileiro.* Rio de Janeiro: Civilização Brasileira.

Gasques, J. G. and C. Yokomizo. 1986. Resultados de 20 anos de incentivos fiscais na agropecuária da Amazônia. In *Anais do XIV Encontro Nacional de Economia*. São Paulo: Associação Nacional de Centros de Pós-Graduação em Economia, pp. 47–84.

Hecht, S. 1982. Cattle Ranching in the Brazilian Amazon: Evaluation of a Development Strategy. Ph.D. dissertation, Berkeley: University of California.

Hecht, S. 1985. Environment, development and politics: Capital accumulation and the livestock sector in eastern Amazonia. *World Development* 13(6):663–684.

Hecht, S. B., R. B. Norgaard, and G. Possio. 1988. The economics of cattle ranching in eastern Amazonia. *Interciencia* 13(5):233–240.

Mahar, D. 1979. *Frontier Development Policy in Brazil: A Study of Amazonia*. New York: Praeger.

Mahar, D. 1988. *Government Policies and Deforestation in Brazil's Amazon Region*. The World Bank Environment Department Working Paper No. 7, Washington, DC.

Martine, G. 1987. Migração e absorção populacional no trópico úmido. Paper presented at the *Seminário CEPAL/IPEA sobre Tecnologias para os Assentamentos Humanos no Trópico Umido*, Manaus, Brazil.

Muller, G. 1982. Agricultura e industrialização do campo no Brasil. *Revista de Economia Política* 2(2):47–77.

Sawyer, D. R. 1979. Peasants and Capitalism on an Amazon Frontier. Ph.D. Thesis. Cambridge, MA: Harvard University.

Sawyer, D. R. 1984. Frontier expansion and retraction in Brazil. In M. Schmink and C. Wood, eds., *Frontier expansion in Amazônia*, pp. 180–203. Gainesville: University of Florida Press.

Sawyer, D. R. 1986. A fronteira inacabada: Industrialização da agricultura brasileira e debilitação da Fronteira Amazônica. In C. Mora B. and C. E. Aramburú, eds., *Desarrollo Amazônico: Una Perspectiva Latinoamericana*, pp. 319–354. Lima: CIPA-INANDEP.

Sawyer, D. R. 1987. População, desenvolvimento e meio-ambiente na Amazônia Brasileira: O Papel das Politicas Publicas. Paper presented at the *Seminário Internacional, América Latina: Población, Recursos y Médio Ambiente*, PROLAP, Quito, Ecuador.

Sawyer, D. R. and S. M. G. Pinheiro. 1984. A dinâmica demográfica das regiões de fronteira. In *Anais do Quarto Encontro Nacional de Estudos Populacionais*, vol. 4, pp. 2017–2047. São Paulo: Associação Brasileira de Estudos Populacionais.

Sawyer, D. R. and D. O. Sawyer, eds. 1987. *Malaria on the Amazon Frontier: Economic and Social Aspects of Transmission and Control*. Belo Horizonte: CEDEPLAR.

Schmink, M. 1987. The rationality of tropical forest destruction. In J. C. Figueiroa Colón, F. H. Wadsworth, and S. Branham, eds., *Management of the Forests of Tropical America: Prospects and Technologies*, pp. 11–30. Rio Piedras, Puerto Rico: Institute of Tropical Forestry, Southern Forest Experiment Station, U.S.D.A. Forest Service.

Schmink, M. and C. Wood. 1986. The political ecology of Amazonia. In P. D. Little and M. M. Horowitz, eds., *Lands at Risk in the Third World*, pp. 175–191. Boulder, CO: Westview.

Torres, H. G. 1987. Desistência e substituição de colonos em projetos de colonização de Rondônia: Um estudo de caso. Paper presented at the *Encontro Regional Amazônia, Programa de Intercâmbio de Pesquisa Social em Agricultura*, Rio Branco, Acre, Brazil.

Velho, O. G. 1973. Modes of Capitalist Development, Peasantry and the Moving Frontier. Ph.D. dissertation. Manchester, England: University of Manchester.

INDEX